ANCIENT SCEPTICISM

This volume offers a comprehensive survey of the main periods, schools, and individual proponents of scepticism in the ancient Greek and Roman world. The contributors examine the major developments chronologically and historically, ranging from the early antecedents of scepticism to the Pyrrhonist tradition. They address the central philosophical and interpretive problems surrounding the sceptics' ideas on subjects including belief, action, and ethics. Finally, they explore the effects which these forms of scepticism had beyond the ancient period, and the ways in which ancient scepticism differs from scepticism as it has been understood since Descartes. The volume will serve as an accessible and wide-ranging introduction to the subject for non-specialists, while also offering considerable depth and detail for more advanced readers.

RICHARD BETT is Professor of Philosophy and Classics at Johns Hopkins University. His previous publications include *Pyrrho, his Antecedents and his Legacy* (2000), and translations of Sextus Empiricus' *Against the Ethicists* (1997, with commentary) and *Against the Logicians* (2005).

The Cambridge Companion to

ANCIENT
SCEPTICISM

Edited by

Richard Bett

Johns Hopkins University

CAMBRIDGE UNIVERSITY PRESS
Cambridge, New York, Melbourne, Madrid, Cape Town, Singapore,
São Paulo, Delhi, Dubai, Tokyo

Cambridge University Press
The Edinburgh Building, Cambridge CB2 8RU, UK

Published in the United States of America by
Cambridge University Press, New York

www.cambridge.org
Information on this title: www.cambridge.org/9780521874762

First published 2010

Printed in the United Kingdom at the University Press, Cambridge

A catalogue record for this publication is available from the British Library

Library of Congress Cataloguing in Publication data
The Cambridge companion to ancient scepticism / [edited by] Richard Bett.
    p.   cm. – (Cambridge companions to philosophy)
ISBN 978-0-521-87476-2 (hardback)
    1. Skeptics (Greek philosophy)   2. Skepticism – Rome.   I. Bett, Richard
Arnot Home.
B525.C36   2010
186–dc22

                                                            2009036361
ISBN 978-0-521-87476-2 Hardback
ISBN 978-0-521-69754-5 Paperback

CONTENTS

CONTRIBUTORS

JAMES ALLEN is Professor of Philosophy at the University of Pittsburgh. He is the author of *Inference from Signs: Ancient Debates about the Nature of Evidence* (2001) and a range of articles about aspects of Stoicism, Epicureanism, ancient scepticism, ancient medicine, and Aristotelian logic, among other things. He is currently working on a book about the Aristotelian disciplines of argument (logic, rhetoric, and dialectic).

RICHARD BETT is Professor of Philosophy and Classics at Johns Hopkins University. His scholarly work has focused particularly on the ancient sceptics. He is the author of *Pyrrho, his Antecedents and his Legacy* (Oxford, 2000), and has translated Sextus Empiricus' *Against the Ethicists* (Oxford, 1997, with introduction and commentary) and *Against the Logicians* (Cambridge, 2005, with introduction and notes). He is currently working on a translation of Sextus Empiricus' *Against the Physicists* for Cambridge University Press. He has also published articles on Plato, Socrates, the Sophists, the Stoics, and Nietzsche.

LUCIANO FLORIDI is Professor of Philosophy at the University of Hertfordshire, where he holds the Research Chair in Philosophy of Information, and Fellow of St Cross College, University of Oxford. He works on scepticism, the philosophy of information and information ethics. He is President of the International Association for Computing and Philosophy and Gauss Professor of the Academy of Sciences in Göttingen. His forthcoming book is *The Philosophy of Information* (OUP).

R. J. HANKINSON is Professor of Philosophy and Classics at the University of Texas at Austin. He has published numerous articles on many aspects of ancient philosophy and science; his books include *The Sceptics* (1995), *Cause and Explanation in the Ancient Greek World* (1998), and *Galen on Antecedent Causes* (1998).

MI-KYOUNG LEE is Associate Professor of Philosophy at the University of Colorado at Boulder. She is the author of *Epistemology after Protagoras: Responses to Relativism in Plato, Aristotle and Democritus* (Oxford, 2005), which is an investigation into some of the sources of ancient Greek scepticism.

CARLOS LÉVY is Professor of Philosophy and Latin Literature at the University of Paris-Sorbonne. He specializes in Hellenistic and Roman philosophy, and is founder of the Centre d'études sur la philosophie hellénistique et romaine at the University of Paris XII. Among his publications are *Cicero Academicus* (Rome, 1992); *Philon d'Alexandrie et le langage de la philosophie* (Paris, 1998); *Les philosophies hellénistiques* (Paris, 1997); *Les scepticismes* (Paris, 2008).

PIERRE PELLEGRIN is Directeur de Recherche at the Centre National de la Recherche Scientifique in Paris. He directs the Centre d'Histoire des Sciences et des Philosophies arabes et médiévales. His fields of research are mainly Aristotle, with publications both on biology and politics, and ancient scepticism. Among his principal publications are *Aristotle's Classification of Animals* and (edited, with Mary Louise Gill) *A Companion to Ancient Philosophy*.

CASEY PERIN is Associate Professor of Philosophy at the University of Massachusetts, Amherst. He is the author of *The Demands of Reason: An Essay on Pyrrhonian Scepticism* (forthcoming from Oxford University Press) and articles on Aristotle, Stoicism, Academic Scepticism, and Descartes.

EMIDIO SPINELLI teaches History of Ancient Philosophy at the University of Rome "La Sapienza," where he was educated. Besides many articles on different topics in ancient philosophy (Presocratics, Atomists, Socrates/minor Socratics, Plato, Stoics, Epicureans, literary and philosophical papyri), his main publications on ancient scepticism include *Sesto Empirico. Contro gli etici* (Naples, 1995); *Sesto Empirico. Contro gli astrologi* (Naples, 2000); *Questioni scettiche. Letture introduttive al pirronismo antico* (Rome, 2005). He is also co-editor (with M. De Caro) of *Scetticismo. Una vicenda filosofica* (Rome, 2007).

GISELA STRIKER is Walter C. Klein Professor of Philosophy and of the Classics at Harvard University, where she teaches ancient philosophy in both the philosophy and the classics departments. She has published papers and monographs on Hellenistic philosophy, Aristotle, and Plato.

SVAVAR HRAFN SVAVARSSON is Associate Professor of Philosophy at the University of Iceland. He has published articles on ancient epistemology.

HARALD THORSRUD is Assistant Professor of Philosophy at Agnes Scott College. He has written articles on Cicero and Sextus Empiricus and is the author of *Ancient Scepticism* (Acumen Publishing, 2009).

KATJA MARIA VOGT teaches Philosophy at Columbia University. She specializes in ancient philosophy and ethics, and has published *Law, Reason, and the Cosmic City: Political Philosophy in the Early Stoa* (Oxford, 2008), *Skepsis und Lebenspraxis: Das pyrrhonische Leben ohne Meinungen* (Freiburg, 1998), as well as a number of articles on Plato, Stoic and sceptic philosophy, Kantian ethics, and friendship. Currently, she is working on scepticism, and on various versions of the guise of the good account of action.

MICHAEL WILLIAMS is Krieger-Eisenhower Professor at the Johns Hopkins University and a Fellow of the American Academy of Arts and Sciences. He is the author of *Groundless Belief, Unnatural Doubts,* and *Problems of Knowledge.* His is currently working on *Curious Researches: Essays on the Significance of Philosophical Scepticism.*

PAUL WOODRUFF is Darrell K. Royal Professor in Ethics and American Society at the University of Texas at Austin, where he teaches philosophy and classics. He has published on Plato, the sophists, and ancient Pyrrhonism. He has also brought out a number of translations from the Greek of Plato, Sophocles, and Thucydides. His books include *Reverence: Renewing a Forgotten Virtue* (2001), *First Democracy: The Challenge of an Ancient Idea* (2005), and *The Necessity of Theater* (2008).

ABBREVIATIONS

Acad.	*Cicero, Academica*
Fin.	*Cicero, De Finibus*
DC	Decleva Caizzi, *Pirrone: Testimonianze* ([10] in Bibliography)
DK	Diels-Kranz, *Fragmente der Vorsokratiker*
DL	Diogenes Laertius, *Lives of the Philosophers*
IG	Inwood and Gerson, *Hellenistic Philosophy: Introductory Readings* (2nd edn.)
LS	Long and Sedley, *The Hellenistic Philosophers* ([24] in Bibliography)
Col.	Plutarch, *Adversus Colotem (Against Colotes)*
M	Sextus Empiricus, *Adversus Mathematicos*
PH	Sextus Empiricus, *Outlines of Pyrrhonism*
SVF	*Stoicorum Veterum Fragmenta*
TLG	*Thesaurus Linguae Graecae*

Other abbreviations for ancient texts are given in the Index Locorum.

Introduction

I ANCIENT VERSUS MODERN SCEPTICISM

This volume focuses on scepticism as it was understood and practised in the ancient Greek and subsequently the ancient Greco-Roman world. The title of the volume is therefore less than ideal. "Ancient" should not in general be used as a shorthand for "ancient Greek" or "ancient Roman," as if the rest of the world did not exist. And there is a particular reason for unease in this case, seeing that a plausible case can be made for regarding some figures and movements in ancient Indian philosophy as sceptical. For this reason I originally proposed "Ancient Greek Scepticism" as the title. But it was correctly pointed out that some important figures to be discussed – most obviously Cicero – were definitely not Greek, and that it is by no means certain even that Sextus Empiricus, the one Pyrrhonist sceptic of whom we have substantial surviving writings, was Greek. My second proposal, "Greco-Roman Scepticism," was in turn subject to quite reasonable criticism on grounds of its unfamiliarity. So with some reluctance I had to agree that "Ancient Scepticism" was the best title available.

The sceptical philosophers and traditions to be discussed are, then, firmly located in the history of Western philosophy. And it is of course also true that scepticism has been a topic of central importance in modern Western philosophy at least since Descartes, and continues to excite widespread interest today. But "scepticism" means rather different things in the two periods.

Nowadays, scepticism is largely understood as a position in epistemology, consisting in a denial of the possibility of knowledge – or, on more stringent versions, even reasonable belief – in some domain.

There are positions referred to as moral scepticism that are not epistemological in character; most famously, John Mackie referred to the claim with which he began his book *Ethics: Inventing Right and Wrong*,[1] "There are no objective values," as a form of scepticism. But this is something of an anomaly, and in general when one speaks of scepticism in philosophy, it is understood that an epistemological thesis is meant. Scepticism in the ancient period was not like this; it was not restricted to epistemology – or, for that matter, to any one area of philosophy – and, just as important, it was not a thesis. Scepticism, rather, was a certain kind of intellectual *posture* – specifically, a posture of suspension of judgement. And there was in principle no restriction on the subject matter to which this suspension of judgement could be applied. Sextus Empiricus, for example, covers the main topics in all of the three standardly recognized areas of philosophy, logic (which included what we call epistemology, but also what we call logic), physics, and ethics, and also the specialized sciences grammar, rhetoric, geometry, arithmetic, astrology, and music. Broadly speaking, the procedure throughout is to induce suspension of judgement about the truth of the various competing theories or views on the topic in question. Since what is generally at issue is the adequacy of the reasons in favor of any given theory, epistemological questions, such as that of the justifiability of beliefs, are at least in the background most of the time, and often in the foreground. But except when epistemology actually is the area under discussion, the primary focus is not on, say, the general question what it takes for a belief to be justified, or to amount to knowledge; rather, it is on the process of subverting the reader's confidence in some particular theory on some particular (frequently non-epistemological) topic, leading to suspension of judgement about its correctness.

There is also, regardless of the topic under discussion at any given time, a broadly *ethical* aspect – that is, a practical aspect – to scepticism in the ancient period. Scepticism was something not just to be talked about, but to be lived. Nowadays, it is rare for philosophers to identify themselves as sceptics; scepticism is typically regarded as a *threat* to be warded off, not as an outlook to be embraced. And even aside from that point, scepticism is typically regarded as an issue of purely theoretical import; the question whether one could or should "live" one's scepticism does not even arise. This is true even of Mackie's moral scepticism, which one might think would make a practical difference; while he understands his scepticism to indicate that morality has to be made rather than discovered, he regards this purely as an insight concerning how to *conceive* of the activity of deciding what one ought to do, not as something that might actually affect what one decided. But ancient scepticism was something to be put into practice; a sceptic was someone who suspended judgement, and this attitude of suspension of judgement was something one held on to not merely when engaged in theoretical discussion, but also when engaged in the activities of everyday life. This is why the sceptics were regularly faced with what was called the *apraxia* or "inactivity" objection, that is, the objection that it is impossible actually to put into practice a policy of across-the-board suspension of judgement; the point is that the sceptics claimed to do precisely that. One sceptical tradition, the Pyrrhonist tradition, even claimed profound practical benefits from the sceptical life; the sceptic achieves *ataraxia*, "freedom from worry" – a goal that others are assumed to be seeking as well, but to be thwarted in achieving because of their failure to suspend judgement.

II THE MAIN CHARACTERS

I have already referred to the Pyrrhonists. They are the ones who, at least in the later stages, actually called themselves *skeptikoi*, "inquirers." As Sextus explains in the opening sentences of his best-known work *Outlines of Pyrrhonism* (standardly abbreviated to *PH*, the initials of the Greek title in transliteration), this is to distinguish them from people who think they have discovered the truth, and also from people who have come to the definite conclusion that the truth is undiscoverable; the sceptic, as he presents it, is the one who has not closed off any options, but is still looking. It is an interesting question how this "inquiry" is to be connected with the procedure already mentioned, that of inducing suspension of judgement, with *ataraxia* as the result. But in Sextus' official introductory characterization of scepticism (*PH* 1.8), it is the process of inducing suspension of judgement (together with the further effect of *ataraxia*) that is emphasized, not "inquiry" in any normal sense of the term. And it is by virtue of the centrality of suspension of judgement in Sextus' account of scepticism that the term is commonly applied not just to the Pyrrhonists, but also to the members of the Academy, the school founded by Plato, for a considerable period of its history. The Academic sceptics did not use this term of themselves, but they too engaged in forms of argument the intended effect of which was suspension of judgement.

In a little more detail, but still in bare outline, the history of scepticism in the ancient Greek and Greco-Roman world is as follows. The figure usually recognized as the first sceptic is Pyrrho of Elis (c.360–270 BCE). The evidence on Pyrrho is scarce and difficult to interpret; so it is a matter of considerable debate to what extent Pyrrho actually did anticipate the sceptical outlook adopted by those who later called themselves Pyrrhonists. But since he was claimed, on whatever basis, as an inspiration or founding father by these later thinkers, it is natural to accord him a place in the sceptical canon. It is also likely that Pyrrho himself drew inspiration from earlier thinkers – Greek thinkers and perhaps also, if one is to believe a tantalizing and undeveloped remark in Diogenes Laertius (9.61), Indian thinkers whom he encountered on his travels with Alexander's expedition. But at least in the case of the Greek tradition, while we may well see elements in the philosophies of the earlier period that seem to anticipate the thought of Pyrrho, or of other later sceptics, these are best regarded precisely as sceptical *elements*, rather than as adding up to a full-fledged sceptical philosophy, as that term was later understood.

The adoption of Pyrrho as a figurehead did not happen for some time. He had a few immediate followers, and an enthusiastic publicist in his follower Timon of Phlius, who wrote numerous books of which only fragments survive, but was then apparently forgotten for some two centuries. In the interim came the sceptical phase of the Academy. The first Academic to take the school in a sceptical direction was Arcesilaus of Pitane (316/5–241/0 BCE). It has been suggested that Pyrrho was in some way an influence on Arcesilaus, and this is possible (though neither he nor anyone else in the Academy is known to have acknowledged it). But Arcesilaus did claim to have learned from Socrates (Cicero, *Acad.* 1.45); and certainly Socrates' argumentative practice in many of Plato's dialogues could well have served as a model for someone in the business of constructing sets of opposing arguments, with a view to suspension of judgement. In any case, this became the characteristic philosophical activity of the Academics for roughly two centuries; the other important sceptical Academic was Carneades of Cyrene (214–129/8 BCE).

By the early first century BCE, however, the scepticism of the Academy seems to have gone soft. The last head of the Academy with any claim to be called sceptical was Philo of Larissa (159/8–84/3 BCE). But instead of maintaining a rigorous suspension of judgement, Philo clearly allows the holding of views; the only requirement is that one hold them tentatively, recognizing that certainty is not to be had and that these views may at some point need to be replaced with others. Philo's Academic contemporary Antiochus abandoned scepticism altogether, setting up a rival Academy which he claimed to represent the genuine Academic philosophy, the philosophy of Plato, on which, he claimed, both Aristotle and the Stoics agreed in all essentials. After these two the Academy ceased to exist as an organized school, although a few later thinkers, notably Favorinus of Arles (c.85–165 CE), claimed to be continuing the spirit of Academic scepticism. But out of the ruins of the Academy, so to speak, came a new sceptical movement setting itself against the Academy and identifying itself with Pyrrho.

The leader of this new movement was Aenesidemus of Cnossos (dates uncertain, but apparently active in the early first century BCE). It looks as if he was himself at first a member of the Academy; but he is reported as denouncing the Academics, and especially those of his own day, for being much too willing to make definite assertions about how things are. Claiming instead to do philosophy along the lines of Pyrrho (though it is not clear at what level of specificity he meant this), Aenesidemus boasted of eschewing definite assertions. The interpretation of this, too, is a matter of considerable dispute – as with Pyrrho himself, we are dependent on very incomplete and not always reliable evidence – but it seems clear that Aenesidemus takes himself to be making a renewed commitment to some form of suspension of judgement, which he detects in the thought of Pyrrho, but finds missing in the thought of at least the Academics who were his rough contemporaries, Philo and Antiochus. It is also clear that for Aenesidemus, following Pyrrho, scepticism has the benefit of bringing *ataraxia*; this had never been a component of Academic scepticism.

The Pyrrhonist tradition initiated by Aenesidemus is what eventually leads to the voluminous surviving writings of Sextus Empiricus (probably second century CE). (I use the terms "tradition" or "movement" because there is no good reason to believe that Pyrrhonism was ever a formal "school," in the sense that the term is used of the Stoics or Epicureans.) We know the names of a few other Pyrrhonists, but to us they are really no more than names. Just as there is serious dispute about the philosophy of Aenesidemus, there is also dispute about whether or how Pyrrhonism developed in the significant time between Aenesidemus and Sextus. The interpretation of Sextus' own philosophy is itself by no means free from controversy. But in his case, uniquely among the sceptics of the ancient Greek and Greco-Roman periods, we can read what he has to say for ourselves. Diogenes Laertius (9.116) names one pupil of Sextus, Saturninus, but he too is no more than a name to us. And at that point, as far as we can tell, an active, continuous Pyrrhonist movement comes to an end. Sextus' writings did not apparently excite much interest in late antiquity – still less so in the medieval period. But the Renaissance saw a revival of interest in them, together with the Academic writings of Cicero (who studied as a youth with Philo and Antiochus). And this renewed interest had much to do with the resurgence of scepticism as an issue in early modern philosophy – despite the notable differences, alluded to earlier, between scepticism as understood since Descartes and scepticism in the ancient period.

The surviving writings of Sextus Empiricus have a peculiar nomenclature; given his importance in this volume, some clarification of this is worthwhile at the outset.[2] His best-known work, as already noted, is *Outlines of Pyrrhonism* (*PH*), in three books: the first is a general account of Pyrrhonism, while the second and third address the three standard areas of philosophy, logic, physics, and ethics (logic in book 2, physics and ethics in book 3). Covering roughly the same ground as *PH* 2 and 3, but at much greater length, are two books *Against the Logicians*, two books *Against the Physicists*, and one book *Against the Ethicists*. At least, these are the titles generally given to these books today. But it is clear that these five books all belong to a single, large-scale work; and Sextus himself appears to refer to this work in several places by the title *Skeptika Humpomnêmata*, *Sceptical Treatises*. It is also clear that this work in its original form was even larger than the portion we now have. The first sentence of *Against the Logicians* refers back to a just-completed general treatment of scepticism – in other words, to something corresponding to *PH* 1. This was long thought to be a reference back to *PH*. But this cannot be right, since *PH* as a whole is not a general treatment of scepticism; the reference must therefore be to a lost book or books.[3] There are indications (subtle, but relatively cogent) that this lost general treatment actually consisted of *five* books.[4] If so, unless these were very short books, *Sceptical Treatises* was a work of truly gigantic proportions.

Whatever its size, *Sceptical Treatises* is not the title by which this work is generally known today; and the confusion caused by the loss of the general book or books may have been part of the reason for this. In addition to the works so far mentioned, there is a third work that survives complete in six books. This is the work that scrutinizes the six specialized sciences mentioned earlier, and it is called (probably by Sextus himself) *Pros Mathêmatikous* (or *Adversus Mathematicos* in its Latin rendering), *Against the Professors* (standardly abbreviated to *M*). Despite the fact that the closing of the sixth and final book makes quite clear that it marks the conclusion of the entire work, at some point the five surviving books of *Sceptical Treatises* came to be viewed as a continuation of this work; as a result, *Against the Logicians* came to be referred to as *M* 7–8, *Against the Physicists* as *M* 9–10, and *Against the Ethicists* as *M* 11. This is thoroughly misleading, but the convention is deeply entrenched. I have myself been criticized for perpetuating it,[5] but to expect a wholesale change at this point is not realistic.

III ABOUT THIS BOOK

The bare-bones sketch in the previous section may have raised many questions. The essays in this volume fill out the story, and in the course of doing so, offer avenues for answering these questions. We begin with six essays detailing the origins and development of the two sceptical traditions. Mi-Kyoung Lee examines possible antecedents to scepticism in the period prior to Pyrrho. Svavar Svavarsson analyzes the evidence relating to Pyrrho himself and his immediate followers, especially Timon. Harald Thorsrud discusses the two leading Academic sceptics, Arcesilaus and Carneades. Carlos Lévy traces the later history, demise, and aftermath of the Academic sceptical tradition. R. J. Hankinson deals with the rise of the later Pyrrhonist tradition in the person of Aenesidemus. And Pierre Pellegrin focuses on the thought of Sextus Empiricus, who for us represents the culmination of the Pyrrhonist tradition, and indeed of Greek or Greco-Roman scepticism as a whole.

Next come seven essays on somewhat more specific topics, many of which have been major bones of contention in recent scholarship. The first three of these address issues concerning what might be called the practice or the implementation of scepticism. Casey Perin considers what kinds of belief, if any, are open to a sceptic. Katja Vogt investigates whether, or how, a sceptic can allow for choice and action of a recognizably human kind. And I look at the ways in which scepticism might or might not be compatible with an ethical outlook. All three of these essays at least touch on both the Academics and the Pyrrhonists, but the Pyrrhonists, and especially Sextus Empiricus, get the majority of the attention, if only because of the state of our evidence. The next essay, by Gisela Striker, takes up directly a theme that is at least partly in view in the three just mentioned, and in a few others as well: the comparison between the Academic and Pyrrhonist varieties of scepticism. The following three essays address topics specific to the Pyrrhonist tradition: the various sets of Modes, or standardized forms of sceptical argumentation, devised by members of the Pyrrhonist tradition (Paul Woodruff); the links between Pyrrhonism and the medical theory of the time (James Allen); and Sextus' treatment of the specialized sciences (as opposed to philosophical topics) in *Against the Professors* (Emidio Spinelli).

The volume ends with two essays about the response to these sceptical traditions beyond antiquity. Luciano Floridi surveys how far they were even noticed, and if so, how they were regarded in the thousand years or more between the end of antiquity and the Renaissance and early modern periods, ending with Descartes. Finally, in a more purely philosophical spirit, Michael Williams compares and contrasts scepticism as understood in Descartes and scepticism in the ancient period – especially Pyrrhonist scepticism, but also Academic scepticism, at least as represented by Cicero. It would, of course, have been possible to continue the story beyond Descartes. Numerous other modern philosophers either have interesting (if sometimes misguided) views about the ancient sceptics, or else admit of interesting comparisons between their own philosophies and one or another variety of ancient scepticism; Hume and Nietzsche are prominent representatives of both categories. But this volume is primarily about the ancient period, and one has to stop somewhere.

As this brief overview has no doubt suggested, there is some overlap in the topics and figures considered in the various essays. This is deliberate; it seemed desirable to have a variety of perspectives on the same material. Sometimes two essays, although addressing some common topic in the context of their own different main themes, will agree in their conclusions; at other times they will disagree. These points of correspondence are sometimes marked by explicit cross-references among the essays; cross-references also occur in places where one essay just mentions or deals very briefly with some issue addressed at greater length in another essay. The cross-references are, however, selective; given the degree of interconnection among the questions considered in the volume, it would have been easy for them to become tedious and overdone.

More generally, I have sought out a group of authors who, besides being acknowledged experts, could be expected to offer a variety of opinions about the subject. (One consideration here, though by no means the only one, is that a variety of nationalities is represented.) As in most vigorous scholarly fields, there is much disagreement even about central matters of interpretation, and the present volume reflects this. The result is a little disconcerting at times for the editor, whose own previously expressed opinions on some of these matters come in for considerable criticism in several of the essays to follow. Still, this is as it should be; the purpose of the volume is to introduce the sceptics themselves, but also to give a representative impression of the range of ways they are understood in current scholarship. One might say that this is especially suitable to the subject of ancient scepticism, centered as it is around suspension of judgement among opposing alternatives. But scepticism is, of course, by no means alone in being a subject of scholarly contention. And I do not mean to suggest that the volume's goal is to induce suspension of judgement in the reader about alternative possible interpretations. What is intended is rather that the reader get some sense of the existence of such alternatives.

The thinkers and topics considered in this volume have been a flourishing field of study for some decades. But this was not always so, at least in the English-speaking world. It was not until around the late 1970s that Hellenistic philosophy in general, and the Greek sceptical traditions in particular, came to receive serious and widespread philosophical scrutiny. Since then a great deal has been written, and a good proportion of this scholarly activity is represented in the bibliography (with a certain bias, given the likely readership of this volume, towards work written in English). But there has not, until now, been an accessible volume of essays designed to give a comprehensive picture of the field as it stands today. I hope that this volume succeeds in filling that gap.

NOTES

1   Mackie [434].
2   This is further discussed by Pierre Pellegrin, Chapter 6 "Sextus Empiricus."
3   This was first argued in Janáček [33].
4   See Blomqvist [37].
5   In Machuca [43].

I Origins and Development

1 Antecedents in early Greek philosophy

I INTRODUCTION

Scepticism was first formulated and endorsed by two different schools or groups, the Academics in the third century BC and the Pyrrhonist sceptics in the first century BC. It is, properly speaking, a product of the Hellenistic period. However, it is sometimes assumed that earlier philosophy was marked by a naïve complacency about whether knowledge is really possible. According to this view, philosophers in the classical period may have asked what knowledge is, but not whether knowledge is even possible at all.

This is mistaken for two reasons. First, earlier thinkers anticipated many of the arguments employed by Hellenistic sceptics. "Sceptical" arguments were in the air from the period of the Presocratics on, although not in the form of a well-defined position, but in the form of certain loosely related ideas and arguments. And they did not go unnoticed; the potentially destructive force of these "sceptical" arguments was appreciated by philosophers like Plato, Aristotle, and Democritus. Their formulation of the problems confronting the possibility of knowledge, together with their responses and attempts at defusing those problems, would inspire and anticipate many of the debates between sceptics and their opponents in the Hellenistic period.

II SCEPTICAL ARGUMENTS IN THE EARLY AND CLASSICAL GREEK PERIOD

Philosophers in the early and classical Greek period worried that knowledge might be impossible for two reasons. The first has to do with the nature of things; things might be such, in and of themselves, that having secure or real knowledge of them might be impossible. I will call these reasons "metaphysical," for they start with an independent characterization of how things are, and then lead to the conclusion that we may not be able to say how things are ((c) below). The second kind of reason has to do with possible limits on our abilities to think, to gather experiences and evidence, and to reason. I will call these reasons "epistemological," for they start with difficulties about our cognitive abilities and then draw conclusions about whether it is possible for us to have or acquire knowledge ((a),(b) below).

Of course, a number of these arguments appear in the service not of scepticism but of relativism, roughly, the position that nothing is anything in itself, but is just as it seems to one. Relativism incorporates a number of proto-sceptical ideas, such as an attack on the distinction between expert knowledge and mere opinion, the idea that disagreement is all-pervasive and intractable, and the idea that nothing is anything in itself, or in any sense definitely one way as opposed to another. I will discuss some of these features of relativism in (b), and compare relativism and Hellenistic scepticism in (d).

(a) Difficulties in determining how things really are

Consider the following argument: we distinguish between how things really are and how they appear to us. But unfortunately we cannot know how things really are; we are only able to say how things appear to us. Knowledge is a special achievement requiring irrefutable proof, say, which is more difficult to acquire than mere belief. Therefore, knowledge is impossible.

The premises of this argument are implicitly endorsed by various Presocratic philosophers. Many of them aspire to determine the true nature of things (e.g. the Milesians), and seem to make a distinction between reality and appearance; this is often accompanied by an exhortation to actively reason and inquire into how things are, instead of passively accepting received opinion or convention (Xenophanes, Parmenides). Sometimes this takes the form of a scornful rejection of other people's limited opinions, and an assertion that only the thinker himself has discovered the truth (e.g. Heraclitus). But some thinkers consider the possibility that it might not be possible to know how really things are – because it is too difficult or impossible to provide proof (unnamed people referred to by Aristotle in *Posterior Analytics* 1.3), or because the evidence is beyond human capability to acquire (e.g. we can't see atoms (Democritus) or get direct evidence of what God is like (Xenophanes)), or because there is something wrong with the process by which we arrive at our beliefs (e.g. bias and prejudice, wishful thinking, anthropocentrism, etc.). That is, there may be a problem in arriving at knowledge if (i) the bar to knowledge is so high that no one can reach it; or (ii) even if it has not been set particularly high, we may be handicapped in various ways from meeting it, at least as far as we can tell from our track record so far. Once one has posited a sharp distinction between appearance and reality, it does not take much to realize that the quest for knowledge which goes beyond appearances might end in failure. Let us take a closer look at some examples.

(i) Socrates in Plato's dialogues emphasizes that to know anything about anything (e.g. whether virtue can be taught), one must first of all be able to give an account of what the thing (e.g. virtue) is. And this is not simply a matter of having linguistic competence concerning the term, say, or being able to point to examples of it; one must be able to give a general account of it, one which explains why things are like this. This turns out to be extremely difficult; we see Socrates' inter- locutors repeatedly failing to be able to do it. Socrates in the *Apology* says that he thinks that the Delphic oracle pronounced him to be the wisest of all men because he alone realizes that he doesn't have knowledge. For later philosophers, especially the Academic sceptics, the Socrates of the aporetic dialogues comes to represent a properly humble attitude about one's attainment of certain knowledge.

Although, in works like the *Republic*, Plato seems to think that he can provide answers to at least some of the questions his teacher was asking, he also considers the idea that attaining knowledge might be impossible. The *Meno* investigates the sophistical puzzle about whether inquiry into X is possible, if as Socrates maintains, one does not know at all what X is (80d-e); according to this argument, one cannot search either for what one knows or for what one does not know, since in the first case there is no need to search, and in the second case, one does not know what to look for and would not recognize it if one found it. This paradox presents a problem about whether learning and teaching are possible. Plato attempted to solve the paradox with a demonstration of successful inquiry into geometry (*Meno* 81a-86c), together with the doctrine that all learning is recollection. But the paradox continued to generate interest and responses; see, for example, Aristotle's discussion in *Posterior Analytics* 1.1 and 2.19, as well as Sextus Empiricus' arguments against the possibility of learning and teaching (*M* 1.9–38, 11.216–57, especially 237–8, with parallel passages in *PH* 3.252–73). Aristotle entertains a related challenge to the possibility of knowledge in *Posterior Analytics* 1.2-3, where he discusses someone who demands a proof for the premises used in a proof, and in turn a proof for the premises in those proofs, and so on. The problem seems to come from the generally accepted principle that all knowledge depends upon justification. Both Plato's *Meno* argument and the argument about knowledge and justification in Aristotle's *Posterior Analytics* raise important and troubling problems for the very possibility of knowledge, and they were taken up by Hellenistic philosophers, both those concerned to defend the possibility of knowledge, such as the Stoics and the Epicureans on the role of perceptions and conceptions as starting points for knowledge, and by those concerned to attack it, such as the Academics and the Pyrrhonist philosophers, who reformulated the problems first raised by Plato and Aristotle.

(ii) Even if one's requirements for knowledge are not particularly demanding, one might still take a dim view of our ability to meet them. Xenophanes thus points out that our representations of the gods bear a suspiciously close resemblance to our own appearances and features (DK 21B14, B15): the suggestion is, perhaps, that when we attempt to achieve knowledge about things which cannot be directly observed, we simply begin with what is familiar and tweak it. Thus, we construct little more than a fiction based on our limited perspectives and experience. One might then conclude that no matter how hard we try, we cannot get beyond our limited perspective – we cannot know what the gods are really like. As Xenophanes says:

And the clear truth no man has seen nor will anyone know concerning the gods and about all the things of which I speak; for even if he should actually manage to say what was indeed the case, nevertheless he himself does not know it; but belief [*dokos*] is found over all. (Sextus Empiricus, *M* 7.49 = DK 21B34)

In passages like these, Xenophanes seems to cast doubt on the possibility of knowledge about things beyond the reach of direct observation.

Democritus comes even closer to concluding that knowledge is impossible because of limitations to our epistemic powers. In many places in his writings he seems to reject any possibility of knowledge whatsoever (M 7.135). But Sextus Empiricus emphasizes that, in these passages, Democritus is in fact specifically attacking the senses, though he thinks this has the consequence of removing all knowledge (M 7.137). What was the basis for Democritus' attack on the senses? Theophrastus tells us that Democritus had an extensive theory of the senses and sensible qualities, according to which what the senses perceive is not atoms in themselves, but the *effect* of aggregates of atoms on the sense-organs (*De Sensibus* 60–1, 63–4).[1] Thus, for example, when I smell and see a cup of coffee in front of me, what I perceive is not the atoms of the cup of coffee, but rather the effect produced by the atoms coming from the cup of coffee on my nasal passages, mouth, and eyes. As far as the senses go, "We in reality have no reliable understanding, but one which changes in accordance with the state of the body and of the things which penetrate and collide with us" [= DK 68B9]. If the senses are the "yardstick" for reality, then "By this yardstick man must know that he is cut off from reality" [= DK 68B6]. Democritus thinks that "this argument too shows that in reality we know nothing about anything, but each person's opinion is something which flows in [or 'is a reshaping']" [= DK 68B7]. For what the senses tell us is not how things really are, only how we have been affected at any given time by the atoms which flow into our sense organs.

Democritus attacks the senses as a source of knowledge, therefore, because what they detect are not, as we would say, objective qualities of objects but their relational properties – properties they only possess relative to perceivers, such as appearing red or sweet or loud. The real nature of things lies in their material constitution, i.e. atoms and void. But one can only find out the truth about these by means of reason, since atoms and void cannot be seen or touched. Hence, the senses cannot grasp the true nature of things.

One might then go on to reject the testimony of the senses entirely. But Democritus does not. Instead, he famously has the senses reply to the attack by means of a self-refutation argument, as Galen reports:

Who does not know that the greatest confusion of any reasoning lies in its conflict with what is evident? If someone cannot even make a start except from something evident, how can he be relied on when he attacks his very starting-point? Democritus was aware of this; when he was attacking the appearances with the words "By convention colour, by convention sweet, by convention bitter, but in reality atoms and void" he made the senses reply to thought as follows: "Wretched mind, you get your evidence from us, and yet you overthrow us? The overthrow is a fall for you" [= B125]. (Galen, *On Medical Experience* (Walzer [326]), p. 114 = 179c Taylor [27], trans. Frede and Taylor)

Even if the senses are limited in what they can tell us, rejecting them entirely is not an option, because reason itself depends on the evidence of the senses. That is, reason is not a cognitive faculty entirely independent from the reports of the senses. Reasoning begins with what the senses tell us about the world, and then proceeds, by means of inference to the best explanation, to theories about how things really are.

In sum, Democritus argues as follows:

(1)   All knowledge is based on perception; without the senses, knowledge is impossible.
(2)   Perception should be rejected because it only tells us about the subjective properties of things, not their intrinsic objective properties.
(3)   Therefore, knowledge is impossible.

But since he thinks that knowledge *is* possible (Sextus Empiricus, *M* 7.139 = DK 68B11), he rejects (2), by insisting upon the evidentiary value of perception: even if it doesn't tell one how things really are, still it does provide us with the starting points for further inquiry without which knowledge would be impossible.

Much depends, of course, on supposing that Democritus intends to reject (2), thereby avoiding the sceptical implications of this argument. If, however, one thought that Democritus recommends both premises (1) and (2) above, then the conclusion, that knowledge is impossible, seems inevitable. According to this reading, Democritus is committed to the thesis that the senses' testimony is worthless, and since he is also committed to the thesis that no knowledge is possible without the senses, it follows for him that knowledge is impossible.[2] This presents a darker epistemic outlook, one which proved to be of considerable use to the sceptics in developing their critiques of positive theories of knowledge (even though Sextus does not count Democritus as a sceptic, *PH* 1.213–14). For whether or not Democritus himself endorsed the premises of the argument above, he offers an argumentative strategy to any would-be sceptic against all forms of empiricism. Since premise (1), the thesis that all knowledge depends on perception, was pretty much taken for granted in the Hellenistic period, this meant that Hellenistic philosophers developing theories of knowledge had to contend with various forms of Democritus' objection used by the Academic and Pyrrhonist sceptics against them.

Even if Democritus himself did not accept the sceptical implications of his argument, at least one of Democritus' followers, Metrodorus of Chios, apparently did, when he said at the beginning of his book *On Nature* "None of us knows anything, not even this, whether we know or we do not know; nor do we know what to not know or to know are, nor on the whole, whether anything is or is not" (Cicero, *Acad.* 2.73 = DK 70B1; see also Sextus, *M* 7.48, 87–8; Eusebius, *Praep. evang.* 14.19.9).[3] Unfortunately we do not have enough context for this remark in Metrodorus; one reason for caution is the fact that he seems otherwise to have held solidly to the tenets of atomism (DK 70A3), and all of the other fragments and testimony for Metrodorus seem to be robustly dogmatic pronouncements about the nature of reality. Even so, this opening line from Metrodorus' book shows, first, that sceptical ideas were in the air, very likely prompted by Democritus' books on knowledge and the senses. Secondly, Metrodorus' sceptical ideas – whatever form they took exactly – show a certain refinement and sophistication, indicating awareness of the problem of inconsistency and containing careful qualification of the thesis that "no one knows anything" by adding "not even this."

(b) Variability and conflicting appearances

Let us now take a look at a special kind of epistemological worry concerning knowledge. Consider the following argument: things appear both F and not-F (e.g. the wine appears sweet to some and not to others, capital punishment appears just to some and not to others). But there is no good basis for deciding that one appearance is correct rather than another. For any possible method of deciding either begs the question, or is open to objection. For example, should one decide by majority vote? Should we say that things are as they appear to most people? Surely it is possible that everyone besides a few might be ill, deranged, or somehow unreliable in judgement. Similar arguments could be made against any other method of deciding in favor of one judgement rather than another. This argument–pattern is epistemological; it starts from the supposed fact that perceptions and opinions on any matter vary widely, and ends with the conclusion that there is no non-biased non-arbitrary method for adjudicating these disputes.

The two principal moves in the argument – examples of conflicting appearances together with an undecidability argument – would later become the principal stock-in-trade of the Pyrrhonist sceptics. They are enshrined in the so-called Ten Modes of Aenesidemus, the collection of argument-types attributed to Aenesidemus, and found in Diogenes Laertius' and Sextus Empiricus' reports of Pyrrhonist scepticism. There, the argument ends with the result that one cannot make up one's mind, that one must or cannot help but suspend judgement. This frame of mind is compared to one's attitude towards the question of whether the number of stars is odd or even. But in the classical period, the argument does not end with scepticism and suspension of judgement. It is rather an argument-pattern used (at least in the extant texts of the fifth and early fourth centuries BC) to support Protagorean relativism.

Both Plato and Aristotle attribute to Protagoras the use of conflicting appearances to argue for the thesis that things are for each as they appear to each (Plato, *Theaetetus* 152b10) or that "all appearances are true" (*Metaphyiscs* 4.5, 1009a8). "Now doesn't it sometimes happen that when the same wind is blowing, one of us feels cold and the other not? Or that one of us feels rather cold and the other very cold? ... Well then, in that case are we going to say that the wind itself, by itself, is cold or not cold? Or shall we listen to Protagoras, and say it is cold for the one who feels cold, and for the other, not cold?" (*Theaetetus* 152b). Protagoras' answer is, evidently, that we should say that the wind is cold if it seems so to one, and hot if it seems so to one; that is, the wind is not anything, hot or cold, in itself. As Aristotle puts it, "Which, then, of these impressions are true and which are false is not obvious; for the one set is no more true than the other, but both are alike" (*Metaphysics* 4.5, 1009b9–11). We are supposed to draw this conclusion from cases of perceptual conflict between two individual perceivers, conflict between the perceptions

of different species of animals, and even conflict between the perceptions for a single individual (*Theaetetus* 154a3–8; cf. Aristotle,
Metaphysics 4.5, 1009b2–12, 1010b3–9). The examples of conflicting
appearances in Plato and Aristotle's discussions of Protagorean relativism are probably among the original sources for the first mode of
Aenesidemus (variations in appearances between humans and other
animals, see Sextus Empiricus, *PH* 1.40–78), the second (variations
in appearances between humans, *PH* 1.79–90), the third (variations in
appearances between senses, *PH* 1.91–99), the fourth (variations in
appearances owing to circumstances, *PH* 1.100–17) and the fifth
mode (variations in appearances owing to positions, distances, and
locations, *PH* 1.118–23).[4]

In the *Theaetetus*, Plato presents the undecidability argument
separately as a response to a potential objection to Protagoras' claim
that things are for each as they appear to each (158b8-e4). The objection is that the beliefs of the madman or the dreamer are obviously
false; surely these are not "true for them" (157e1–158b8). But
Socrates tells us that, far from refuting Protagoras' claim, these are
the very sorts of examples which Protagoreans embrace. For they
argue that since each party to a dispute has equal conviction about
how things really are, there is no more reason to think that things are
as they appear for the waking person than that they are as they appear
for the dreamer. For example, we are awake and asleep for equal
periods of time, and while asleep we are convinced of the truth of
our dream-thoughts whereas while we are awake we are equally
convinced of our waking thoughts. Of course, in the case of disease
and madmen, the times may not be equal – but then "Are we going to
fix the limits of truth by the clock?" (158d11–12). Plato's version of
this argument (which is perhaps the earliest extant statement of the
undecidability argument, but which he seems to expect to be familiar
to his readers (158b)) makes it clear that the argument is meant to
undermine any attempt to insist that some appearances are obviously
false. It does so by placing the burden of argument on the opponent to
show that there is some non-arbitrary way of deciding which ones are
true and which ones are false. We are left to infer that any attempt to
mark off some appearances as false would inspire a similar response:
one could only do this legitimately by establishing the existence of
some kind of norm or standard by which to decide this question.
Aristotle makes this explicit in his version of the argument: any

attempt to establish a principle for deciding can be met "by asking, who is the judge of the healthy man, and in general who is likely to judge rightly on each class of questions" (*Metaphysics* 4.6, 1011a3–6). This type of argument fits what we know of Protagoras' *Truth*, which seems to have been in part an attack on those who try to put themselves forward as authorities; Protagoras demonstrates in his *Truth* the methods one can use to undermine any claims to authority and expertise.[5]

Thus, even though the conflicting appearances and undecidability argument were used in the classical period in the service of relativism, not scepticism, they still raise problems for the possibility of knowledge, especially expert knowledge. For they undermine one's confidence that we can tell for any given question which answer is true and which is false, on the assumption that the true answer must be true to the exclusion of the other (which would be the assumption of anyone aspiring to expert knowledge). In general, these arguments attempt to shift the burden of argument onto one who wishes to maintain that knowledge and false thinking are possible.

(c) Contradictionism, flux, and indeterminacy

Consider now the following argument-pattern. We distinguish between how things really are and how they appear; as usual, knowledge is only of the former. But if we assume that something is really F only when it is F invariably and without qualification, that is, only when it is not in any way or to any degree not-F, we open the door to the possibility that nothing is really F: perhaps everything is both F and not-F (let us call this "contradictionism"), or everything is always changing from F to not-F ("flux"), or nothing is any more F ("*ou mallon*") or is determinately F to any greater extent than it is not-F.[6] If then all of nature is fundamentally indeterminate, and nothing that exists has a definite nature, then it will be impossible to say how things are, since any attempt to do so will vainly try to pin things down as being one way rather than another.

This argument for the impossibility of knowledge is based on metaphysical claims about how things are. It has its roots in early Greek speculative metaphysics. Contradictionism and flux are associated with Heraclitus when he says, for example, that "the road up and the road down are one and the same" (DK 22B60) or that "we step and do not step into the same rivers, we are and we are not" (DK 22B49a; see also 22B10, 22B61). Now Heraclitus himself does not draw the conclusion that things are unknowable; indeed, in many fragments, he speaks of wisdom and understanding as available to anyone who listens to his account of the truth (e.g. DK 22B114, 22B1, 22B2, 22B35). But Heraclitus' pithy and memorable sayings lend themselves to different interpretations. Thus, in the *Theaetetus*, Plato has Socrates attribute contradictionism and flux to him – and to most of his predecessors besides Parmenides (152de). Socrates goes on to argue that this ultimately implies that knowledge is impossible. Roughly, he shows that the "Heraclitean" doctrine implies that *anything* which is F will also be not-F (181d–183b). This in turn shows that the theory cannot support Protagoras' doctrine or Theaetetus' definition of knowledge according to which knowledge is perception, because it turns out that if it makes someone's perception that x is F true, it also makes it false, since it tells us that F-ness itself is changing and that perceiving is also not-perceiving. Indeed, it seems to make language impossible (183b). A proponent of extreme contradictionism and flux is effectively rendered speechless, since there is nothing that one can truthfully say about anything. Socrates' conclusion is that if flux and contradictionism are true, then language, thought, and knowledge are impossible. Of course, although Plato intends this to be a refutation of extreme flux and contradictionism, it might in fact be something that a die-hard contradictionist or flux theorist is willing to embrace.

Aristotle too thinks that the theses of contradictionism and flux lead people to conclude that knowledge is impossible, or at least convince them to give up looking for it. For the thesis that everything is in flux seems to imply that nothing is assertible, as follows:

And again, because they see all this world of nature is in movement, and that about that which changes no true statement can be made, they say that of course, regarding that which everywhere in every respect is changing, nothing can truly be affirmed. It was this belief that blossomed into the most extreme of the views above mentioned, that of the professed Heracliteans, such as was held by Cratylus, who finally did not think it right to say anything but only moved his finger, and criticized Heraclitus for saying that it is impossible to step twice into the same river; for *he* thought one could not do it even once. (*Metaphysics* 4.5, 1010a7–15[7])

The idea of flux, taken to an extreme, leads Cratylus to the conclusion that "nothing can be affirmed of anything":

And at the same time our discussion with him is evidently about nothing at all; for he says nothing. For he says neither "yes" nor "no," but both "yes" and "no"; and again he denies both of these and says "neither yes nor no"; for otherwise there would already be something definite. (*Metaphysics* 4.4, 1008a31–4)

This then leads people to give up searching for knowledge, according to Aristotle:

And it is in this direction that the consequences are most difficult. For if those who have seen most of such truth as is possible for us (and these are those who seek and love it most) – if these have such opinions and express these views about the truth, is it not natural that beginners in philosophy should lose heart? For to seek the truth would be to follow flying game. (*Metaphysics* 4.5, 1009b33–1010a1)

The "most difficult consequence" of such views is that one may be led to conclude that the search for truth is futile. Here we have one of the clearest reports in pre-Hellenistic philosophy of the sceptical predicament, of the idea that though one may search for truth, it may not be possible to find it.

Aristotle offers the following diagnosis for the predicament:

The reason why these thinkers held this opinion [namely, that knowledge is impossible] is that while they were inquiring into the truth of that which is, they thought "that which is" was identical with the sensible world; in this, however, there is largely present the nature of the indeterminate – of that which exists in the peculiar sense which we have explained [sc. being characterized by opposites]; and therefore, while they speak plausibly, they do not say what is true. (1010a1–5)

As Aristotle makes clear, the sceptical conclusion does not result from epistemological worries about our capacity to know and inquire. Rather, it results from the idea that the nature of reality is indeterminate, which makes it impossible to assert anything truly about anything. What reduces Cratylus to simply moving his finger is the notion that nothing can be said correctly about the world, and hence that it is better to say nothing at all.

Plato himself is associated with the position that things in the sensible realm are both F and not-F. In the *Republic* (475d–480a), he has Socrates argue for the existence of Forms as a condition for the possibility of knowledge precisely because, if the Forms did not exist, then since the sensible world is characterized by radical indeterminacy (where nothing has pure being but is "rolling around as intermediates between what is not and what purely is" (479d)) nothing can be known. For if none of the things in the sensible world are determinately F as opposed to not-F, they cannot tell us what it is to be F, as opposed to not-F. Thus, someone who does not acknowledge the existence of Forms can only have belief, not knowledge. By contrast, the Forms are what they are stably and determinately, and so they can be objects of knowledge.

Thus far, we have seen hints or explicit statements of contradictionism and flux in Heraclitus and in Plato. Plato and Aristotle, who are our main sources for these ideas, bring out explicitly the fact that these ideas are a threat to the possibility of knowledge. But there are also a number of thinkers from the fourth century BC, not mentioned by Plato or Aristotle, who may have endorsed some version of the indeterminacy argument for scepticism, including Anaxarchus of Abdera and, most famously, Pyrrho.[8]

Anaxarchus and Pyrrho were said by ancient doxographers to belong to "the school of Democritus"; this was probably based on little more than the fact that they came from the same area of Greece as Democritus and they seem to have been influenced by or connected with him in some way. According to some interpretations, Pyrrho espoused the indeterminacy of nature:[9]

[Timon] says that [Pyrrho] reveals that things are equally indifferent and unstable and indeterminate; for this reason neither our sensations nor our opinions tell the truth or lie. For this reason, then, we should not trust them, but should be without opinions and without inclinations and without wavering, saying about each single thing that it no more is than is not or both is and is not or neither is nor is not. (Aristocles in Eusebius 14.18.1–5 = LS 1F, trans. Bett [143], p. 16)

Pyrrho seems to begin with the thought that "things are equally indifferent and unstable and indeterminate," that is, with the thesis of indeterminacy and flux. We cannot specify why exactly he felt reality was indeterminate, but he does go on to conclude that nothing is assertible in such a way as to exclude the opposite or contradictory proposition, and that "neither our sensations nor our opinions tell the truth or lie" because nothing is one way any more than any other.[10]

We are told by Sextus that Anaxarchus, along with the Cynic Monimus, "likened existing things to stage-painting and took them to be similar to the things which strike us while asleep or insane" (M 7.88). Some have compared this to the sceptical arguments of Descartes' First Meditation, where we are confronted with the possibility that our experiences may be dream states, or states of a madman.[11] Others, however, argue that Anaxarchus is not talking about our experiences at all, but rather comparing *existing things* with stage-paintings and dreams.[12] He is not then saying that our perceptions and beliefs are like dreams in being unrepresentative and false, but rather that things in the world are, like *trompe l'oeil* decorations, not what they present themselves as being. This would not then be an epistemological argument, but rather the expression of the consequences of a certain metaphysical view.[13]

(d) Proto-sceptical arguments in the classical period

In sum, there can be found in early and classical Greek philosophy two types of considerations, epistemological and metaphysical, which lead to the conclusion that knowledge is difficult or impossible. But one should not suppose that any of these ideas constitutes full-blown scepticism, for two reasons. First, the position that knowledge is impossible is not a position that anyone explicitly adopts in the texts we have been considering. For example, Aristotle, who opposes such ideas, does not think that anyone would be happy to conclude that nothing can be known; indeed, he doesn't actually think of it as a philosophical position at all. If one has been led, by some course of reasoning, to the conclusion that it is impossible to have knowledge, or that the search for it is inevitably fruitless, then he thinks that gives one good reason to re-examine the assumptions that led one to this idea in the first place. That would change in the Hellenistic period.

Secondly, Hellenistic sceptical arguments lead to *epochê*, or suspension of judgement – including on the very question whether knowledge is possible – whereas these arguments end in various specific, positive conclusions, making them "dogmatic" in Hellenistic terms. Many of the arguments we have been looking at first appear in the service of relativism – the position Plato develops on Protagoras' behalf in the *Theaetetus*. The two positions are distinct, of course; the sceptic confines himself to suspending judgement about how things really are, whereas the relativist concludes that things are simply as they appear to each, and cheerfully maintains that we know lots of things, although of course we have to give up claims about how things are determinately and in themselves. However, these two positions are still related. First, relativism, like Pyrrhonian scepticism, starts from the idea that disagreement is all-pervasive, and argues that it is intractable. On both views, it is supposed that things appear F to some and not-F to others, and that there is no principled way to decide which are correct and which are mistaken.

Secondly, relativism amounts to a denial that there is any meaningful distinction to be made between how things appear and how things are. Things only have properties relative to thinkers and perceivers. By contrast, scepticism takes for granted the distinction itself, and then suspends judgement about how things are – not about there being any such thing as how things really are, but simply about how things really are. What these positions have in common is the dim prospects for rational inquiry; on both views, further inquiry into how things really are is futile and pointless.

Thirdly, relativism is often summarized by the slogan "everything is relative," meaning that nothing is F in itself, but is only F relative to someone to whom it appears F. This bears some resemblance to the position later adopted by the Pyrrhonists that one can only say how things appear to one, not how they are in themselves.[14] This, together with the fact that the Pyrrhonists happily took over the conflicting appearance arguments used by Protagoras, leads to some conflation of relativist and sceptical arguments in the later Pyrrhonist tradition.[15]

III ARGUMENTS AGAINST SCEPTICAL IDEAS IN THE CLASSICAL PERIOD

The sceptical ideas and arguments discussed in the previous section did not go unremarked in the classical period; indeed, we know of some of them only because they were criticized by philosophers who understood the threat they posed to the possibility of objective knowledge. Of course, these philosophers did not expressly recognize these ideas as constituting "scepticism," as that term was later used in the Hellenistic period. But their objections to these ideas were well-known to later self-proclaimed sceptics who recognized that they deserved a reply in turn. Plato's and Aristotle's arguments against these proto-sceptical ideas were thus an important impetus for the development of Hellenistic scepticism.

Five important objections to various ideas we have considered so far were formulated by Plato and Aristotle. First, Plato argues in the *Theaetetus* 169d3–171e9 that these positions are self-refuting and lead to problems of consistency.[16] This highlights, for the sceptics, the need to avoid inconsistency in general, and self-refutation in particular (though some sceptics, such as Sextus at *M* 8.480–1, may instead have embraced self-refutation as congenial to the sceptical stance). Secondly, Aristotle argues that there are numerous logical and metaphysical reasons for rejecting contradictionism (*Metaphysics* 4.5, 1009a30–38). I will not focus on these two arguments because they are less directly connected to Hellenistic scepticism. More significant are the following three objections they raise. (1) Plato and Aristotle argue that if contradictions are true together, then language and thought are impossible. (2) Aristotle raises numerous objections to the undecidability argument, most important of which is the so-called "inactivity" argument. (3) Aristotle defends the possibility of knowledge based on the nature of proof and demonstration. Let us now take a closer look at these three arguments.

(a) The inassertibility objection

At *Theaetetus* 181a–183b Plato explores the implications of extreme instability and contradictionism, and concludes that it will be impossible to assert of anything that it is anything, and that language will become impossible, except perhaps for the thoroughly non-committal expression *oud' houtôs*, roughly "not at all thus" (183b4). Aristotle makes the same point when he argues, in support of the principle of non-contradiction, that someone who embraces contradictionism – someone who really thinks that for every x, x is always both F and not-F – cannot be speaking, or thinking, anything at all:

If all are alike both right and wrong, one who believes this can neither speak nor say anything intelligible; for he says at the same time both "yes" and "no." And if he makes no judgement but thinks and does not think, indifferently, what difference will there be between him and the plants? (*Metaphysics* 4.4, 1008b7–12)

Someone who genuinely thinks that for all *p*, both *p* and not-*p* is not asserting anything, let alone expressing a belief.

Of course, as we noted earlier, one might refuse to see this as a refutation, and instead view it as the natural and inevitable result of one's inquiries into nature. Aristotle thinks Cratylus is ridiculous, but others might view his predicament more sympathetically. Indeed, later Greek sceptics regard as highly defensible the idea that one might have nothing positive to assert.

(b) The inactivity argument and other objections to the undecidability argument

Aristotle argues that no one really believes that things are equally F and not-F. "For why does a man walk to Megara and not stay at home thinking he ought to walk? Why does he not walk early some morning into a well or over a precipice, if one happens to be in his way? Why do we observe him guarding against this, evidently not thinking that falling in is alike good and not good? Evidently he judges one thing to be better and another worse" (*Metaphysics* 4.4, 1008b14–19). A person may claim that for all *p*, both *p* and not-*p*, but Aristotle thinks his actions show that he does think that something is the case, and not the contradictory as well.

Aristotle's objection is equally effective against any position that maintains that, for all *p*, there is no more reason to think that *p* is true than that not-*p* is true. Aristotle thinks we do not really put equal weight on conflicting appearances, that we are not unable to decide what color things are or what their magnitudes are, that we prefer judgements made up close over those made from far off, that we prefer judgements made by those who are awake over those made by dreamers. He says, referring to people in general, that "obviously they do not think these to be open questions" – meaning, that no one is really unable to decide which one is correct and which is not correct. Thus, one who is in Libya but imagines being in Athens one night does not thereupon immediately set out for the Odeum, because he does not put equal weight on every thought that occurs to him (*Metaphysics* 4.5, 1010b3–11).

The inactivity argument raises a problem for anyone who makes use of the undecidability argument, whether he be a contradictionist, Protagoras, or a would-be sceptic. Aristotle says, referring to Heraclitus, that just because someone says something doesn't mean that he really believes it (*Metaphysics* 4.3, 1005b25); the same could be said of anyone who says, for all p, that there is no more reason to believe p than not-p. This is the sort of objection that presumably gave rise to the apocryphal stories concerning Pyrrho, that he had to be prevented by his friends from walking into the paths of oncoming carts or walking off precipices – stories that simply make vivid Aristotle's objection to the undecidability argument. For it puts pressure on the would-be sceptic to explain how it is possible to live his scepticism.

The undecidability argument is also attacked by Plato and Aristotle by means of the "argument from the future." In the *Theaetetus* (177c–179c), Plato argues that the expert and the ignorant man are not equally correct in their predictions about whether a person will get well or not, contrary to Protagoras, who endorses the undecidability argument that there is no reason to prefer any one opinion over another. That is, they may be correct in their judgements about the present – Plato is willing to grant that to Protagoras, at least for the moment. But when it comes to judgements about what is good or useful, and what will prove to be so in the future, Socrates argues that not all opinions are equally authoritative. For example, if asked whether a certain drug will produce health in a certain kind of patient, a doctor is more likely to be correct than someone who is ignorant of medicine; an expert orator will be more authoritative than a novice about what is persuasive to an audience (179ab; see also Aristotle, *Metaphysics* 4.5, 1010b11–14). This argument works against Protagoras, as long as he admits that events confirm which prediction comes true, that of the expert vs. that of the layman. Because Plato and Aristotle's attacks on the undecidability argument and their defense of the idea of expert knowledge are so forceful, it is not surprising that Hellenistic sceptics were concerned to offer some kind of reply. Thus, there is a strand of argument in Sextus of challenging the notion of an expert and the correlative notions of teaching and learning in general (see *M* 1.9–38, *M* 11.216–57, and parallel passages in *PH* 3.252–73).

Finally, Aristotle draws upon his own theory of perception in order to argue that conflict between perceptions *can* be decided, because not all perceptions are equally authoritative (*Metaphysics* 4.5, 1010b1–9). First of all, though he thinks that perception of the proper objects of the senses (such as colors, smells, sounds) is always (or usually) true, this does not mean that all perceptual beliefs are true, since for Aristotle there is a difference between a perception and a judgement or belief based on that perception. Secondly, each sense is authoritative about its own proper objects (sight is authoritative about colors), and so there can be no real conflict between the senses. And one sense cannot conflict with itself, since perceptions will be of objects at a particular time and place. It never happens that a single sense-modality will make conflicting reports about the same thing at the same time. Thus, there is no reason to think that conflicting perceptions are all-pervasive and can never be resolved; in many cases, it will be quite obvious that one perception is correct and the other is mistaken. However, Aristotle doesn't take seriously enough the possibility that in other cases, disagreement may be irresolvable. The First and Second Pyrrhonist Modes collect examples of things which may appear one way (say, bitter and intolerable) to humans and another way (say, pleasant and drinkable) to animals or to a different set of humans – often disagreements reflecting genuine physiological differences in constitution – where there does not appear to be any non-arbitrary or meaningful way to settle the question. In such cases, disagreement may signal a difficulty about the property being disagreed about, such as sensible qualities and value properties, suggesting that these properties may be relational, not intrinsic properties of the things that bear them.

(c) Who should be the judge?

Aristotle's confidence that there is no disagreement or conflict between opinions that cannot be decided can seem blindly optimistic, or even "dogmatic" in the usual sense of the word. The proponent of the undecidability argument tries to make this apparent by insisting on a proof or further argument establishing who can determine which side is correct and which is incorrect.

In *Metaphysics* 4.6, Aristotle is fully aware that his opponent will make this move:

There are, both among those who have these convictions and among those who merely profess these views, some who raise a difficulty by asking, who is the judge of the healthy man, and in general who is likely to judge rightly on each class of questions. But such inquiries are like puzzling over the question whether we are now asleep or awake. And all such questions have the same meaning. These people demand that a reason shall be given for everything; for they seek a starting-point, and they seek to get this by demonstration, while it is obvious from their actions that they have no conviction. But their mistake is what we have stated it to be; they seek a reason for things for which no reason can be given; for the starting-point of demonstration is not a demonstration. (*Metaphysics* 4.6, 1011a3–13)

The argument from his opponent which Aristotle is summarizing is clearly intended to make difficulties for his earlier claim that no one is really puzzled about conflicting appearances, that we prefer the healthy person's judgements over that of the sick person, waking experiences over dreams. Aristotle says that such questions are part of a general class of questions asking "who is likely to judge rightly on each class of questions?" Such questions are meant to neutralize one's natural preference for the opinions of experts and authorities by raising doubts about whether we can tell who is an expert and who has the authority to judge. In general, if you say "we prefer the beliefs of X to those of Y," the would-be sceptic will undermine whatever grounds you have for preferring X to Y by asking either for some kind of proof that X *is* more authoritative than Y, or some infallible criterion by which you can determine who is right and who is wrong.

This type of objection attempts to block an appeal to ordinary notions of authority (e.g. one should ask a doctor) or ordinary means for deciding questions (e.g. one should go and look for oneself), and to demand that one produce some further principle for showing who or what has the authority to judge or to decide. The Pyrrhonist sceptics later incorporate these objections into the Five Agrippan Modes. Aristotle correctly sees that the issue is not simply about how you can tell whether you are awake or dreaming, or whether you can tell who is sick and who is healthy. The real issue is much bigger; it is, as T. Irwin puts it, "whether we are justified in believing p only if we can prove p by appeal to some further principle q that we are justified in believing independently of p."[17] If the sceptic can succeed in getting you to sign on to this conception of justification, the game is over for you, for any further principle q which you might produce will itself require further justification. And as Aristotle sees in *Posterior Analytics* 1.3, this leads to the specter of an infinite regress of justification, or a vicious circle.[18] The real issue is thus about what it is to ask for justification or for a demonstration, and when sufficient justification or demonstration has been given. For this reason, Aristotle says that what is needed is not the proof his opponent demands – the proof of who should be regarded as an authority and judge – but, rather, careful consideration of what requires proof and what does not.[19] Thus, his own treatment of demonstration in the *Posterior Analytics* begins with this question, and identifies a number of ways in which one could fail to understand what it is to ask for a demonstration, by demanding a proof for what should be regarded as the starting point. The details of his answer to these questions belong to another discussion. But we can see at least in outline Aristotle's response to the would-be sceptic: the very idea of demonstration or justification presupposes the idea of a starting point, something which does not itself require justification. If one recognizes this, and understands what method should be used to identify those starting points, one will see that one should reject the universal applicability of the undecidability argument and other strategies designed to get us to doubt whether we can ever say anything without justification. It is surely not an accident that the Five Modes of Agrippa attempt to continue the debate by taking over many of the proto-sceptical arguments Aristotle puts in the mouths of his unnamed opponents and responds to in the *Posterior Analytics*.[20]

IV CONCLUSION

Sceptical ideas and arguments were familiar to philosophers in the classical Greek period. But virtually no one during this period deliberately embraced the position that nothing can be known, or argued for suspension of judgement on all matters. And no one opposing these ideas thought that their starting point had to be the refutation of sceptical ideas. Epistemology during this period does not start, as it has for some philosophers in the modern period, with the problem of scepticism, for example, scepticism about the external world.

This would change in the Hellenistic period with two important developments. First, Epicurus introduced a theory of the criterion of truth, which formally endorsed the Democritean idea that all knowledge is based on perception. Epicurus couched this in terms of an innovative framework, that of an infallible criterion of truth which determines what is true by itself being true; this in turn would attract attention from detractors who tried to show that nothing can be a criterion of truth in this sense.[21] Secondly, the Academic and Pyrrhonist sceptics embraced scepticism as a viable position. The need to reply to the objections raised by Plato and Aristotle in the earlier period proved to be a stimulating challenge for these later philosophers – one that is partly responsible for the character and shape of scepticism in Hellenistic philosophy.

NOTES

1 See Taylor [27], Lee [134], pp. 181–250, esp. pp. 200–16.
2 Or one might conclude that one can only know how one has been affected, not what the causes of those affections are; so the Cyrenaics argue, arguably in agreement with Democritean worries about knowledge. For discussion, see Tsouna [139].
3 The text of the Metrodorus fragment is corrupt, and the precise form of the Greek is unclear; see Brunschwig [126].
4 For a comparison of Aristotle's treatment of these arguments with the Aenesideman modes, see Long [135].
5 For further discussion, see Lee [134], pp. 8–29. In the Hellenistic period, debates about knowledge were cast in terms of responses to the question, what is the criterion of truth?; sceptics would deny that any conclusive answer could be found (see Striker [119]).
6 This is not, of course, how the slogan *ou mallon* is used when it becomes a catchphrase of the Pyrrhonists; see Pierre Pellegrin, Chapter 6 "Sextus Empiricus" (especially n.19 and accompanying text).
7 Translations of passages from Aristotle's *Metaphysics* are by W. D. Ross, rev. J. Barnes, in *The Complete Works of Aristotle: The Revised Oxford Translation* (J. Barnes (ed.), Princeton: Princeton University Press, 1984), with occasional modifications.
8 Xeniades of Corinth may also have endorsed this argument. According to Sextus, he "said that everything was false, that every impression and opinion is false, and that everything which comes to be comes to be from what is not and everything which is destroyed is destroyed into what is not" (*M* 7.53, see also *PH* 2.76; cf. Brunschwig [127]).
9 See Bett [143], p. 117, for discussion and further references.
10 For further discussion (from a partially differing point of view), see Svavar Svavarsson, Chapter 2 "Pyrrho and Early Pyrrhonism."

11 See Hankinson [68], pp. 54–55, Burnyeat [129].

12 Bett [143], p. 162.

13 Another possibility is that Anaxarchus is expressing a detached attitude toward life rather than a kind of epistemological scepticism. The same can perhaps be said of the Cynic Monimus, to whom Sextus also attributes the "stage-painting" remark; Monimus may have been commenting on the vanity of things and of human life. This would certainly be consistent with the Cynics' repudiation of theoretical inquiry in philosophy (DL 6.103).

14 For contrasting views on the significance of relativity in Pyrrhonism, see R.J. Hankinson, Chapter 5 "Aenesidemus and the Rebirth of Pyrrhonism" and Paul Woodruff, Chapter 11 "The Pyrrhonian Modes."

15 Sextus Empiricus, PH 1.38–39, 135–40, 177, 3.232.

16 The details of the argument are controversial; see the classic paper Burnyeat [128], with some criticisms by Fine ([131], [132]) and Sedley's development of an improved Burnyeat-style interpretation (Sedley [136], pp. 57–62).

17 Irwin [133], p. 194.

18 See Barnes [55], p. 106, Barnes [124], Barnes [125], Barnes [270].

19 Metaphysics 4.4, 1006a5–11, where Aristotle presumably has in mind his discussion of proof at Posterior Analytics 1.2–3.

20 See further Paul Woodruff, Chapter 11 "The Pyrrhonian Modes."

21 For more on Epicurus, see Striker [118], Taylor [138].

2 Pyrrho and early Pyrrhonism

Pyrrho's (365/60–275/70 BC) name has carried great weight in the history of philosophy ever since it was attached to one of the two main branches of ancient scepticism.[1] Traditionally, Pyrrho's own philosophy has been interpreted as the early version of the more sophisticated philosophy recorded by Aenesidemus and preserved in the writings of Sextus Empiricus. This traditional view is not, however, unchallenged, and in recent years alternative interpretations have been offered that suggest a dogmatic Pyrrho, whose position would be incompatible with that of later Pyrrhonian sceptics, although having enough in common with it to serve as its distant historical source.

To what extent is the appropriation of Pyrrho by the later sceptics legitimate? It is important for an appraisal of Pyrrho's place in the history of scepticism to ascertain which insights, if any, were common to Pyrrho and the later Pyrrhonists. But the contours of Pyrrho's philosophy are blurred; the evidence is scant and subject to conflicting interpretations. Perhaps the situation was not a great deal better in the first century BC, when Aenesidemus introduced Pyrrhonism as radical scepticism, as opposed to the mitigated scepticism of the Academy, or in the late second century AD, when Sextus was at work. Their references to Pyrrho are cautious and hardly exegetical. Later accounts often emphasise his admirable state of mind, variously called indifference (*adiaphoria*), impassivity (*apatheia*), and tranquility (*ataraxia*). Sextus claims to call his scepticism "Pyrrhonian" "from the fact that Pyrrho appears to us to have attached himself to scepticism more vigorously and conspicuously than anyone before him" (*PH* 1.7).

I EVIDENCE FOR PYRRHO'S LIFE
AND PHILOSOPHY

Timon of Phlius (325/20–235/30 BC) is the most important source of our information concerning the philosophical views of Pyrrho.[2] His importance is such that it has proved tempting to regard him as the real author of the philosophical views commonly attributed to Pyrrho, in particular epistemological views. Most of the philosophical accounts of Pyrrho, wherever we find them, are attributed to Timon, including the most important one, recounted by the Peripatetic philosopher Aristocles of Messene, at work in the first century AD, in his *On Philosophy*, and preserved by Bishop Eusebius of Caesarea (ca. AD 260–339) in his *Preparation for the Gospel* (henceforth abbreviated to *Praep. evang.*). Timon took it upon himself to explicate and promulgate Pyrrho's views, and to distinguish them from those of other philosophers, partly by explaining his views and praising his way of life, partly by inveighing against other thinkers.[3] He was, so Sextus claims (*M* 1.53), Pyrrho's interpreter.

Timon wrote voluminously, both plays and poems, to judge from Diogenes Laertius, whose biography of Timon (9.109–16) follows that of Pyrrho (9.61–108).[4] Most of the extant lines come from the three books of his *Lampoons* (*Silloi*), and a few from the *Images* (*Indalmoi*).[5] While these are poetical pieces, the Aristocles passage itself may derive from the *Pytho*, a prose dialogue in which Pyrrho perhaps explains his views in answer to Timon's questions.[6] It is difficult to rule out Timon's authorship of the views traditionally attributed to Pyrrho, especially the epistemological ones.[7] It is unclear what inferences to draw if one were to accept the claim that Timon is in large measure expounding his own views under the influence of Pyrrho. Perhaps Pyrrho was an unsystematic moral sage.[8] It is no doubt impossible to know for sure what Pyrrho, as opposed to Timon, really said, since he wrote nothing, as Theodosius, a later explicator of scepticism, cautiously pointed out (DL 9.70). Nevertheless, while it is sensible to bear in mind the possibility of Timon's substantial contribution, in most testimonies a reference to Pyrrho is clearly intended, except in a group of fragments that purport to explain the role of "the apparent" in decision-making; we shall return to these at the end of this chapter. Thus, in the Aristocles passage, Timon claims to rehearse Pyrrho's stance. Diogenes reports, perhaps on the authority of Antigonus, that

Pyrrho "could both discourse at length and also sustain a cross-examination" (DL 9.64). Neither Aenesidemus nor Sextus promote Timon at Pyrrho's expense.

There is another major source for our knowledge of Pyrrho, more anecdotal in character. Diogenes Laertius, probably writing at the beginning of the third century AD, in his life of Pyrrho, refers to his main biographical authority as the afore-mentioned Antigonus of Carystus, a biographer who, to judge from the contents of his reports, seems to have been less interested in philosophy than in the perceived eccentricity of Pyrrho's lifestyle.[9] This perception may have been due to Pyrrho's views, or their absence; a person who believes nothing is liable to behave in an unconventional manner, even to be in mortal danger. Again, it may have owed its prevalence to Pyrrho's emphasis on indifference as the ideal state of mind. Indeed, he seems to have been most famous for this indifference. Later Pyrrhonists were understandably at pains to play down accounts of Pyrrho's difficulties in managing to get through the day (cf. DL 9.62). Antigonus was probably at work after the middle of the third century BC, some time after the death of Pyrrho, but within the life-span of Timon, to whom he may have owed at least some of his information (DL 9.111).

Even though Cicero probably wrote his books on Academic scepticism after the resurgence of Pyrrho in the writings of Aenesidemus, he betrays little knowledge of Pyrrho and none of Pyrrhonism.[10] The ignorance of such a learned man engaged in the history and explication of scepticism, if not feigned, may indicate the obscurity and perceived inconsequentiality of Pyrrho's views at the time, a mere curiosity, with little bearing on scepticism. Cicero's remarks pertain to the Pyrrho who postulated indifference as an ideal state of mind, with no reference to its epistemic source. This view may have resulted from Antigonus' biographical picture of Pyrrho. A reference to Pyrrho predating Cicero and postdating Antigonus and Timon is that of the encyclopaedic Stoic philosopher Posidonius, Cicero's rather older contemporary and teacher (DL 9.68). That reference is also to Pyrrho's admirable state of mind.

When push comes to shove, we are left with little to hold on to. The testimonies give us a Pyrrho who is flexible enough to emerge in the works of later scholars as sceptic or dogmatic, guru or epistemologist aware of his philosophical heritage, Timon's creation or authentic source of his student's exposition. He is a puzzle in the history of philosophy. Before we turn to the philosophical testimonies, consider those for his life, the source of Pyrrho as the icon of indifference.

II LIFE OF PYRRHO

After unsuccessfully practicing painting for a while in his native town of Elis on the Peloponnese, Pyrrho became "a student of Bryson, son of Stilpo" (DL 9.61); these may be names of Megarian philosophers. This alleged studentship has prompted scholars to place Pyrrho in a Megarian context. But the chronology puts the suggestion in doubt.[11]

It is Anaxarchus, a rough contemporary, to whom Pyrrho may have turned and with whom he travelled to India, in Alexander's entourage. Anaxarchus seems to have been interested in the ideal of indifference and came to admire Pyrrho as an example of one successfully indifferent. He is usually classified as a follower of Democritus, sometimes even called a sceptical atomist.[12] Pyrrho is said to have "mentioned Democritus most often" (DL 9.67), which reflects a perceived (and quite possibly a real) debt to a Democritean tradition; Democritus himself and his adherent Metrodorus of Chios (*fl.*ca. 350 AD) both express epistemological worries. In India, Pyrrho apparently met "naked wise men and magi" (DL 9.61). According to Ascanius of Abdera, it was his association with Anaxarchus, or his acquaintance with Eastern philosophy, if not both, that led him to avow "inapprehensibility (*akatalêpsia*) and suspension of judgement (*epochê*)" (DL 9.61). This explanation is a later projection of central Pyrrhonian concepts onto Pyrrho, and as such indicates the traditional view of Pyrrho as the first Pyrrhonist.[13]

The anecdotes about Pyrrho's life reflect two sides of the views Timon attributes to him. On the one hand, Pyrrho harbours such an active distrust of the senses – so the story goes – that he would have lost his life had his friends not constantly kept him out of harm's way (DL 9.62). He is nevertheless said to have fled from an advancing dog and exclaimed that it was difficult to shed one's humanity (9.66). Although he would have been helped by his friends, he is not portrayed as having returned the favor, for when Anaxarchus fell into a swamp he walked by, to his companion's praise (9.63). Not surprisingly, given the dangers, Pyrrho is said to have led a quiet and reclusive life, although he is also said to have undertaken long journeys with complete strangers (9.63). He lived close to ninety years, as did Timon. The sort of behaviour ascribed to Pyrrho makes little sense and does less to recommend his way of life to others, and it was precisely as a model for a way of life that the later Pyrrhonists would depict him. Hence, they paid little heed to such stories. The stories themselves, apart from being excellent material for anecdotes, may be viewed as making the point, which became standard in similar contexts (known as *apraxia*- or inactivity-arguments), that either one has beliefs on which one acts or else one is utterly inactive. We shall consider below what sort of basis, other than beliefs, Pyrrho – or Timon in his place – would or could claim for his actions.

On the other hand, there are stories that tell us about Pyrrho's indifference, impassivity, and tranquillity, and these are more numerous. The immediate reason why Pyrrho refused to help the fallen Anaxarchus (apart from not believing his eyes) was his complete indifference, and it is this trait that earned Anaxarchus' praise. He was indifferent as to what tasks he performed, even stooping to carrying meat and washing pigs, menial tasks beneath respectable citizens (DL 9.66). When speaking, it did not matter whether anyone was listening (9.64); when cauterized by a doctor, he did not flinch (9.67). Cicero mentions Pyrrho in the context of such superhuman indifference (*Acad.* 2.130 = DC 69A). One story relates that, when suffering a storm on board a ship, Pyrrho kept his calm and pointed in admiration to a pig that totally disregarded the weather and kept on eating: "in such tranquillity (*ataraxia*) should the wise man keep himself" (DL 9.68). Plutarch tells the same story (*On Moral Progress* 82F = DC 17B), except that the term used is "impassivity" (*apatheia*). The behavior characterized by this state of mind, while neither suicidal nor requiring the constant vigilance of his companions, is certainly unconventional, even flaunting social acceptability.

Timon insists that Pyrrho did indeed reach this state of mind, and he offers an explanation. He says that Pyrrho conquered what had overpowered all others, "affections (*pathê*), opinion, and pointless legislation" (*Praep. evang.* 14.18.19 = DC 58). Again, in a fragment from the *Lampoons*, Timon asks Pyrrho how he rid himself of the opinions of sophists and all persuasion (DL 9.65). The implication is that it is by ridding himself of opinions and affections that he achieves his impassivity and tranquillity. How would Pyrrho have answered Timon's question? Plutarch relates that "it must be acquired from reason and philosophy." A similar point is perhaps being made in Diogenes' biography, when Pyrrho, having given in to fear, says that "one should strive as much as possible against things, first by one's deeds, but if not thus, then by reason" (DL 9.66). We begin by looking for Pyrrho's reasoning in the Aristocles passage, the most detailed account of it that we possess, before returning to the claim that Pyrrho's philosophy led him to tranquillity.

III PYRRHO ACCORDING TO TIMON ACCORDING TO ARISTOCLES IN EUSEBIUS

This testimony (*Praep. evang.* 14.18.1–5 = DC 53), short as it is, contains troublesome phrases. Included within parentheses is the transliterated Greek of the most debatable ones, to which reference will be inevitable later on:

It is above all necessary to investigate our own knowledge; for if we by our nature know nothing, then there is no need to inquire into other matters. There have also been some among the ancients who made this pronouncement, against whom Aristotle has argued. Pyrrho of Elis was also a powerful advocate of such a position; but he himself has left nothing in writing, while his disciple Timon says that whoever wants to be happy should consider these three questions. First, how things are by their nature; second, in what way we should be disposed towards these things, and lastly, what will happen to those so disposed. He says that he [Pyrrho] declared that (1a) things are equally indifferentiable and unmeasurable and undecidable (*adiaphora kai astathmêta kai anepikrita*); (1b) because of this neither our perceptions nor opinions tell the truth or lie (*dia touto mête tas aisthêseis mête doxas alêtheuein ê pseudesthai*). (2a) Because of this, then, we must not trust them, (2b) but we must be without opinions and lean to neither side and remain unwavering (*adoxastous kai aklineis kai akradantous*), (2c) saying concerning each individual thing that it no more is than is not or both is and is not or neither is nor is not (*ou mallon estin ê ouk estin ê kai esti kai ouk estin ê oute estin oute ouk estin*). What happens to those so disposed, according to Timon, (3a) is first non-assertion, and then (3b) tranquility (*ataraxia*), while Aenesidemus says pleasure. These, then, are the main points of what they say.

According to Aristocles, Pyrrho was of the view that "we by our nature know nothing." Without pausing to reflect on the self-refutation to which such claims are liable, he goes on to imply that the basic question is how one becomes happy, which then is divided into three questions. We seem to get an epistemological and metaphysical argument for an ethical conclusion.

The first question is about the nature of things. We are told that our perceptions and opinions neither tell us the truth nor lie because (and this is presumably the answer to the question) things are indifferentiable, unmeasurable, and undecidable. If this is the correct interpretation of the text – it is far from certain that it is – the meaning seems to be that statements about things are neither true nor false since *we cannot differentiate between things, or measure them, or decide how they are*. It is not true, for example, that a wind is cold, when it may feel cold to one, nor is it false, and the *reason* for this state of affairs is our inability to decide how the wind is. Our perplexity tells us this much about the wind. This is not a sceptical claim that Sextus would have made, relying as it does on a view on the relation between decidability and reality. Sextus would merely suspend judgement in light of the failure to decide how things are. But on this reading Pyrrho nevertheless has one thing in common with Sextus (and all ancient sceptics): an emphasis on our inability to decide how things are.

The above reading suggests that Pyrrho is referring to our cognitive shortcomings, and one might argue that the adjectives of statement 1a are best understood thus, especially the adjective *anepikritos*, "undecidable."[14] Let us call such a reading of the adjectives *subjective*; it brings to the fore the theme common to Pyrrho and Sextus: an inability to decide how things are. But another reading is possible, according to which the adjectives refer to things as they are in themselves regardless of our cognitive capacities. On this reading they should be translated "indifferent and unstable and indeterminate."[15] Call this reading *objective*. Although it attributes an ontological view to Pyrrho that is far removed from the scepticism of Sextus, the context may demand this objective reading.

These are the two most common approaches to the Aristocles passage, and they depend on different interpretations of the three adjectives of statement 1a. A crucial difference between the approaches emerges at once. A subjective reading is better suited to account for the traditional view of Pyrrho as a bona fide Pyrrhonist, whose fundamental premise would be the claim that we cannot decide how things are. This claim is stronger than Sextus would allow, but nevertheless recognizably Pyrrhonian. According to an objective reading Pyrrho's fundamental premise is that things in themselves are indeterminate. This reading indicates that Pyrrho held as fundamental a dogmatic view, incompatible with Sextan scepticism. In the remainder of this section I shall describe the salient features of each reading, suggesting one that is qualifiedly subjective.[16] It is akin to the objective one in that it holds that Pyrrho's overall views are incompatible with Sextan scepticism. But it preserves the subjective reading's emphasis on unde-cidability, and thus places Pyrrho securely within the sceptical tradition.

The most compelling reason for adopting the objective reading is negative in that its proponents claim that a subjective reading makes no sense, at least if the text is allowed to stay unaltered; hence one should settle for the objective one. What is regarded as nonsensical is the inference from statement 1a to statement 1b. Postpone for a moment the question whether the inference in fact makes no sense. For at all events, the force of this charge has convinced many scholars that either the subjective reading should be dropped or the text emended. Some have followed the latter course.

In the text, the state of affairs indicated in statement 1a has con-sequences spelled out in statement 1b: "because of this (dia touto) neither our perceptions nor our opinions tell the truth or lie." Eduard Zeller changed *dia touto* to *dia to* ("because"), turning consequent into antecedent.[17] Thus, we cannot decide how a thing is by nature *since* our perceptions and opinions neither tell the truth nor lie. In this way Zeller could retain a subjective reading and the fundamental insight that we cannot decide how things are.

The subjective reading still faces problems, for the inference actually still seems to make little sense.[18] Pyrrho tells us that our perceptions and opinions neither tell the truth nor lie; they are neither true nor false. It seems unjustifiable to infer from this claim that things are undecidable, and thus cling to a subjective reading. In turn, it has been proposed that Pyrrho may mean that perceptions and opinions are neither *consistent* truth-tellers nor consistent liars. Accordingly, state-ment 1b may say that perceptions and opinions do not *always* tell the truth or lie, that they are not an infallible criterion.[19]

But this solution is open to serious challenges. It is odd to pair together perceptions and opinions as failing to be consistent truth-tellers or liars; in this context, thought or reason is better suited to accompany perception.[20] The subjectivist would also have to inter-pret the verb *alêtheuein* to mean "always and reliably tell the truth."[21] The negation would then latch on to the temporal operator "always," and likewise with the verb *pseudesthai*. Another puzzle would be: Why does Pyrrho say "neither tell the truth *nor lie*"? Unreliable perceptions and opinions are usually those that do not always tell the truth; "not always lying" is superfluous. However, the answer to that question may be, this subjective reading states that, according to Pyrrho, perceptions and opinions are fallible, and *hence* we cannot decide how things are by nature. If one rejects this reading as unsatisfactory, for the reasons stated above, the appeal of Zeller's emendation lessens.

Although this rejection does not spell the end of a subjective reading, its proponents, following the unemended text, are still faced with the task of explaining an inference that seems to make little sense: "we would be being told that the nature of things is undiscoverable, and that 'for this reason neither our perceptions nor our opinions tell the truth or lie.' But this makes no sense at all," as the most forceful critic of the subjective reading says.[22] Therefore, it is urged, we should reject the subjective reading of the unemended text.

There are different versions of the objective reading of the passage.[23] According to the most detailed of them, Pyrrho advances an "indeterminacy thesis": reality is in itself indeterminate and therefore no statement about it is true or false.[24] The main argument for this reading is that only on it can statement 1b make sense as an inference from statement 1a. For statement 1b clearly states, not (as a subjective reading would claim) that one cannot tell whether perceptions and opinions are true or false, but that they actually are neither true nor false.

Against this claim there is the general reason to retain a subjective reading. Whereas, on the objective reading, Pyrrho's basic concern is not with the impossibility of deciding how things are by nature, the subjective reading preserves as fundamental the sceptical insight that one cannot decide how things are by nature. Can one argue for a subjective reading by other means than by appeal to this general reason?

Assuming that the objective reading is correct in that statement 1b does not supply a reference to our inability to decide the truth of perceptions and opinions, a subjective reading would have to answer two questions: (i) What does statement 1b supply; (ii) What does supply a reference to our cognitive inability? Consider the first question: What does Pyrrho mean when he says that neither our perceptions nor opinions tell the truth or lie?

The words "tell the truth" render the Greek verb *alêtheuein*. The noun *alêtheia* can mean "truth," or "an account of reality," but also just "reality," "how things *really* are," even "how they are *by nature*," as opposed to "how they *appear* to be." On this conception, if one tells the truth, one gives a true account, an account of the *nature* of things. The occurrence of the verb *alêtheuein* in statement 1b is to be expected. Pyrrho is answering the first question asked, i.e. how things are by nature, and telling us that perceptions and opinions do not give an account of the nature of things for the reason given in statement 1a. On this understanding, if I say *truly* that "x is F," then x is *really* F. Pyrrho says that perceptions do not tell the truth. So, it is not true that "x is F," i.e. *x is not really F*. But this statement does *not* mean that perceptions lie, as one would have expected, for Pyrrho also says that perceptions do not lie. So, "not telling the truth" is not equivalent with "lying," and "not lying" is not equivalent with "telling the truth." There is a difference of scope. It turns out that it is not false that "x is F," either, which can only mean that *x is not really not-F*. According to statement 1b, then, when perceptions and opinions say "x is F," *x is not by nature F and x is not by nature not-F*. Now, if being F is part of a things's *nature* – as opposed to being some merely temporary or contingent feature of it – then the thing cannot, while remaining the same thing, become not-F; conversely, if it is *by nature* not-F, it cannot become F. Hence the statement "x is not by nature F and not by nature not-F" implies that, on the one hand, x is not F *to the exclusion of being not-F*, and, on the other, that x is not not-F *to the exclusion of being F*. X is not *exclusively* either F or not-F. But this leaves open the possibility of x having *both* characteristics – being both F and not-F – or again, having neither. And, as we shall see in the next section, in statement 2c Pyrrho appears to allow precisely these two possibilities.[25] The statement that our perceptions and opinions do not tell the truth or lie carries with it, then, a number of implications concerning how things are in reality or by nature. And it is this statement that is presented as a consequence of statement 1a, that things are equally indifferentiable, unmeasurable, and undecidable. But we have yet to see how the inference from the one to the other works.

The shortcomings of perceptions and opinions, and also the defectiveness of their objects, were well documented by the time of Pyrrho. We find the same idea, that x is not exclusively F or not-F, emphatically stated in Plato's *Republic* 478d–e; any object of opinion, Socrates says, "cannot correctly be called purely one or the other" (e2–3) (for example, purely large or small, beautiful or ugly) where "purely" (*eilikrines*) indicates precisely the exclusion of one quality by its opposite. Similarly, statement 1b tells us that x is not by nature F – that is, F to the exclusion of its being not-F – or *vice versa*. It is nonetheless possible that a thing could be both F and not-F, or neither F nor not-F. Pyrrho's statement does not exclude either possibility.

So much for the first question. Consider now the second question: What does supply a reference to our cognitive inabilities? If we adopt the subjective reading of statement 1a, the answer is clear. For, according to it, things are equally indifferentiable, unmeasurable, and undecidable; we have no means with which to differentiate, measure, and decide how things are. The subjective reading of statement 1a in effect consists of finding a reference to our lack of cognitive abilities in the statement. The interesting question is why Pyrrho would think that we were cognitively stunted in this way. Let us postpone that question for just a moment and consider what statements 1a and 1b tell us on this reading. Since statement 1b is supposed to follow from statement 1a, Pyrrho is evidently spelling out a connection between decidability and reality: if it is undecidable that x is F (or not-F), then x is not by nature F (or not-F). The first part of this conditional is found in statement 1a: it is undecidable that x is F (or not-F). And if one accepts the above reading of statement 1b, the second part of the conditional is found in statement 1b: x is not by nature F and not by nature not-F. Pyrrho relies on this condition, which we can term the decidability-of-nature condition.[26]

It remains to be seen whether sense can be made of this condition with regard to other testimonies for his views. But a general point is in order. It concerns what I take to be a view prevalent at least among Pyrrho's predecessors on this connection between reality and knowledge; we find it clearly stated both in Plato and Aristotle. In the *Republic*, Socrates states that "what is completely is completely knowable" (477a). Likewise, in the *Physics*, Aristotle says that first principles are knowable by nature and altogether (184a10–21). In both cases, what is primarily and fundamentally real is knowable; what is not knowable is not primarily and fundamentally real.[27] If this presumptuous realist conception was the norm among Greek philosophers, it is quite plausible that Pyrrho shared it. His rejection of the possibility of knowing that x is F (or not-F) would then have the implication that x would not really be F (or not-F). Statements 1a and 1b would simply spell out this view.

Why, then, would Pyrrho think that we had no means with which to judge perceptions and opinions? The fundamental point behind many ancient arguments that attempt to undermine our ability to reach conclusions about the nature of things through perception and opinion is the variability and conflict of appearances.[28] Noting this variability of perception and opinion is the practice of such different thinkers as Heraclitus, Democritus, Protagoras, and Plato, the last of whom held perception and opinion in little regard exactly for the reason of their variability and conflict.[29] It is because of the conflict of appearances that the decidability-of-nature condition cannot be met. The invariability of appearances is the only means that enables one to decide how things are by nature. It is because things do not invariably appear F (or not-F) that one cannot decide that they are F (or not-F), and therefore they are not by nature F (or not-F). Pyrrho has answered the first question, how things are by nature.

This reading attributes to Pyrrho an interest in the decidability of things, the possibility of knowing how things are by nature, or rather its impossibility, which he dogmatically asserts. Insofar as this assertion is dogmatic, Pyrrho's stance is different from the careful scepticism of Sextus. Nevertheless, it is much closer to Sextus' insight than the objective readings of the Aristocles passage, according to which Pyrrho's main concern was not with the decidability of things but rather with their ontological indeterminacy. But this reading is different from other subjective ones in that it accepts the inference from undecidability to a view about the nature of things, an inference that would perhaps have been shared by some other Greek philosophers.

Now Pyrrho turns to his other two questions, how we should be disposed towards things and what will happen to those so disposed.

IV OUR REACTION TO THE UNDECIDABILITY OF NATURE

Since perceptions and opinions are neither true nor false, Pyrrho infers that (2a) "we must not trust them." The stories of Pyrrho's life and declarations evidently refer to this distrust of perceptions and opinions. What this lack of trust tells us about how one should be disposed is spelled out in statement 2b, while it is not explained how one is to act (or be able to act) while preserving one's distrust; we have to look to other testimonies for a possible reply to that question. Statement 2b explains that "we should be without opinions and lean to neither side and remain unwavering."

The first term of statement 2b, "without opinions," came to play an important role in the writings of Sextus, usually in the form of the adverb "undogmatically" as opposed to "dogmatically" or "with opinion." Since the two following words of statement 2b (like several other terms of the passage) are not part of Hellenistic philosophical terminology, and Aristocles in general seems to be faithful to the use of words found in his sources,[30] we here find a terminological link between early and late Pyrrhonism, which indicates an exploitable similarity.

Pyrrho continues his explanation: one should lean to neither side and remain unwavering. What is meant by "lean to neither side"? Given statement 1b, that opinions and perceptions are neither true nor false, it would seem that Pyrrho had in mind that one should not say either "x is F" or "x is not-F". The third adjective, however, implies that one should not oscillate between saying "x is F" and "x is not-F." If this third characterization is to add anything to the second one, the intended advice seems to be that one should not say at one point "x is F" and at another "x is not-F."

It has been proposed that these three descriptions of the disposition one should adopt answer to the three epithets of statement 1a. Such correspondence seems too artful.[31] It is likelier that Pyrrho explains statement 2b with his account of what one should actually say "concerning each individual thing" in statement 2c. What one should say is this: "that it no more is than is not or both is and is not or neither is nor is not (*ou mallon estin ê ouk estin ê kai esti kai ouk estin ê oute estin oute ouk estin*)."

Here we encounter another much discussed passage, in which the Greek can be interpreted in different ways. The connective *ê* is ambiguous between the disjunctive "or" and the comparative "than." Accordingly, one can interpret the first *ê* as comparative, but the second and third as disjunctive. Then the statement means that each individual thing no more is than is not, or both is and is not, or neither is nor is not. This interpretation, adopted in the translation above, is consistent with the interpretation of statements 1a and 1b

above, and a fairly straightforward reading of the Greek. But according to another interpretation, all the cases of *ê* are comparative, and
the passage means: "a thing is no more than it is not, it is no more
than it both is and is not, it is no more than it neither is nor is not."
The argument in favor of this latter more complicated reading is that
it precludes all affirmation, while the first affirms something.[32] What
does the first reading have Pyrrho affirm, and why would that affirmation convict Pyrrho of inconsistency?

The phrase "x is no more F than not-F" means that x is not
exclusively F or not-F. This implies that x might be both F and not-
F (a stance associated with Protagoras and Heraclitus), and that it
might be neither F nor not-F (a stance associated with Democritus).[33]
If Pyrrho is allowing these two options as explanations of the "no
more" phrase, he neither contradicts what he has already said in
statements 1a and 1b, nor affirms anything that he has not already
implied. Pyrrho can allow that x may be both F and not-F or neither,
just so long as he does not affirm that it is exclusively F or not-F.[34]

In statement 3a, Pyrrho affirms that something happens to people
who are disposed in the way described in statements 2a–c. First,
people succumb to *aphasia*. This Greek term probably means "non-
assertion." Pyrrho will not affirm of anything that it is exclusively F
or not-F.[35] *Aphasia* as non-assertion in effect amounts to suspension
of judgement, *epochê*. As such, it again brings Pyrrho close to the
Pyrrhonism of Sextus. Nevertheless, there remains the crucial difference that Pyrrho's *aphasia* is not based on equipollence and undecidability *in the same way* as Sextan suspension of judgement is. For
Pyrrho, accepting undecidability leads to a thesis about how things
are by nature. Sextus just finds himself at a loss and suspends judgement. One term he uses to express this condition of suspension of
judgement is in fact the term used in the Aristocles passage, *aphasia*
(*PH* 1.192). Pyrrho's *aphasia* indicates that he will not say of x that it
is F or that it is not-F. This non-assertion is presented as a consequence of holding the view that x is not F or not-F. Pyrrho goes beyond
the limits of Sextus' scepticism; he denies both that x is F and that it is
not-F, and he allows that x may be both or neither. But Pyrrho refuses
to characterize things positively or negatively, as F or not-F. In that
sense, Pyrrho neither affirms nor denies anything, just like Sextus.
This may be what Timon has in mind in his explanation of the phrase
"no more" (which we encountered in the Aristocles passage) as

"determining nothing and not setting forth" (DL 9.76). In Pyrrho's case *aphasia* is prompted by the insight that one cannot choose between features of things because nothing has any particular feature by nature, to the exclusion of its opposite. We see how Pyrrho's outlook is close enough to Sextus' to have been exploitable by the tradition that called itself Pyrrhonist; both Pyrrho and Sextus end up suspending judgement, albeit for different reasons.

Once the attitude of *aphasia* has been acquired, one is tranquil (statement 3b). No space is given in the passage to explain this, as if no explanation were needed.

V OTHER TESTIMONIES FOR PYRRHO'S VIEWS ON THE NATURE OF THINGS

The Aristocles passage leaves us with three concerns. First, how do other testimonies for Pyrrho's philosophy align themselves with respect to the different readings of the Aristocles passage? To anticipate the answer: most other testimonies, if not all, seem compatible with both a subjective and an objective reading of the Aristocles passage. Secondly, do other testimonies indicate how Pyrrho would have explained the possibility of acting without opinions? Thirdly, do other testimonies allow us to gauge how Pyrrho conceived of the transition from non-assertion, based on the absence of opinions, to tranquillity? In order to address these concerns it is first necessary to turn to another philosophically substantial and again much debated testimony for Pyrrho's views.

The lines in question, a pair of elegiac couplets, preserved in Sextus (*M* 11.20 = DC 62), come from Timon's *Images*. They have most often been rendered in the following way (again we cannot avoid including some Greek within parentheses):

Come, I will speak a word of truth (*mython alêtheiês*), as it appears (*kataphainetai*) to me to be, who have a correct yardstick (*orthon echôn kanona*), that the nature of the divine and the good is forever, from which [or: is at any time that from which] life becomes most equable for man.[36]

According to this reading, and the variant within brackets, Pyrrho (or indeed Timon) actually has a positive view on the nature of the divine and the good, namely that there is such a thing and that it is the source of man's equable life. Such a reading is inconsistent with most if not all reasonable interpretations of Pyrrho's fundamental view, encountered in the Aristocles passage, according to which Pyrrho claims that the nature of things is undecidable (subjective reading) or indeterminate (objective reading).[37] The task at hand is to find a reading of the couplets that is consistent with Pyrrho's fundamental view (on any reading) and deflates the couplets' apparent claim about there being a nature of the divine and good. We would then be in a position to evaluate whether it adds anything substantial to other testimonies.

First, consider what appears to be a typically sceptical hedging remark, "as it appears to me to be." Although this translation of the verb *kataphainesthai* is possible, the most common meaning is "be evident."[38] If that latter meaning is intended, Pyrrho was not qualifying his statement in the manner of the later Pyrrhonists; the suspicion arises that we are reading Sextus into Pyrrho.[39] Secondly, the "correct yardstick" (*orthon kanona*) need not stand alone but rather with the phrase "of truth." In fact, this is what an epistemological yardstick often is, a yardstick of truth, and as such it is a commonplace in Greek and especially Hellenistic philosophy. The reason why "of truth" has not been attached to "yardstick" is that it is paradoxical to hedge one's remarks when one possesses the correct yardstick of truth. But if Pyrrho is not hedging his remarks, but rather explaining what is evident to him, then there is good reason to attach "of truth" to "yardstick." Finally, the word *mythos* can readily mean "fiction" or simply "myth," and it is not unlikely that at the time of Pyrrho and Timon such would have been its primary meaning.

If we accept these interpretative changes, the possibility of a different translation opens up:

Having a correct yardstick of truth, I will relate a fiction, as it evidently is to me, that the nature of the divine and the good is forever, from which life becomes most equable for man.

What would this reading entail? First, Pyrrho proposes to relate a fiction. It is evident to him that what he will relate is a fiction since he possesses the yardstick of truth; his truth is opposed to the fiction. Secondly, the sentence "as it evidently is to me" qualifies the fiction, but not the truth that Pyrrho possesses. Pyrrho will relate to us a fiction – as it evidently is to him who knows the truth. Thirdly, the dogmatic account that follows, in which Pyrrho refers to the nature of the divine and the good, is a fiction. The couplets now tell us that Pyrrho actually thought that it was a fiction that the nature of the divine and the good was forever (or at any time) the source of the most equable life for man. This reading would seem to secure consistency with other testimonies, both on an objective reading and on the subjective reading advanced above.

Consider now the first question asked at the outset of this section, concerning the alignment of other testimonies for Pyrrho's philosophy to the different readings of the Aristocles passage. When considering that passage, I claimed that the basic observation behind Pyrrho's views was that appearances conflict, and that he then claimed that this conflict was undecidable. But the Aristocles passage makes no mention of conflicting appearances. Nevertheless, Aristocles else-where does claim that Pyrrho argued from "opposites" (*Praep. evang.* 14.2.4 = DC 26A), or what he also terms "antilogies" (14.18.31 = DC 26B). Diogenes attributes to Aenesidemus the view that Pyrrho defined nothing dogmatically "because of antilogy" (DL 9.106 = DC 8). It seems reasonable to infer that Pyrrho is being depicted as making use of the conflict of appearances.[40]

Evidence, independent of the Aristocles passage, for the claim that Pyrrho held such conflict to be undecidable is slender. Nevertheless, Aristocles seems to subscribe to such a view, since, according to him, Pyrrho claimed that nothing is apprehensible; in general, Aristocles regards Pyrrho as worried about our incapacity to apprehend things.[41] It is possible that Aristocles was influenced by a later sceptical inter-pretation of Pyrrho, i.e. that of Aenesidemus. Hence, his evidence is far from conclusive. It is consistent both with a subjective and an objective interpretation of statement 1a. According to the subjective interpretation, the conflict of appearances is undecidable just because there is no means with which to decide the conflict.

The plot thickens when we start looking for independent testi-mony for Pyrrho's purported *inference*, by the decidability-of-nature assumption, from the claim that we cannot decide how things are by nature to the claim that things are no specific way by nature. There is none apart from the Aristocles passage.[42] If he makes this move, Pyrrho seems to reject the law of the excluded middle, insofar as the nature of things is concerned; he claims that things are not by nature F or not-F.[43] Nevertheless, according to Diogenes (9.61), Pyrrho did hold that things are no specific way, claiming that "nothing is good or bad, just or unjust, and equally in all cases that nothing is in truth, but that people do everything by law and custom, for each thing is no more this than that." Although this testimony does not rule out an objective reading, it is consistent with the subjective reading offered above, according to which, since we cannot decide how things are by nature, things are no specific way by nature.

VI REASONS FOR ACTING AND TRANQUILLITY

Finally, we have to address the role of appearances in Pyrrho's philosophy in order to answer the second question above, namely whether other testimonies offer insight into Pyrrho's answer to the question of how one can act without opinions. This question assumed great importance in the debates between Stoics and Academic sceptics, and received extensive comment from Sextus. It has always been considered a powerful weapon against a scepticism that does not insulate theoretical issues from ordinary life. At stake is the possibility of life without opinions.[44] Diogenes Laertius (9.105) supplies most of what we know about early Pyrrhonian answers:

Again, the dogmatists say that they [the sceptics] destroy life itself in that they throw out everything that life consists in. The others say that the dogmatists are wrong, for they [the sceptics] do not deny that one sees, but that they do not know how one sees. For we [the sceptics] accept the apparent, but not as being such [as it appears]. We also perceive that fire burns, but suspend judgment as to whether it has a flammable nature ... For when we say that a picture has projections, we are reporting the apparent. But whenever we say that it does not have projections, we are not saying what appears but something else. Therefore Timon says in the *Pytho* that he has not departed from the customary. And in the *Images* he says: "But the apparent prevails everywhere, wherever one might go." And in *On Perceptions* he says: "I do not affirm that honey is sweet, but agree that it appears so."

No mention is made of Pyrrho. It is Timon who claims not to have departed from the customary.[45] In the absence of a reference to Pyrrho, it may be that the emphasis on the apparent derives from Timon.[46] But it is also reasonable to assume that Timon takes himself to be offering a view in accordance with Pyrrho's stance. Perhaps "the apparent" is supposed to fill a philosophical gap left by Pyrrho, even answer allegations of the practical impossibility of adopting his philosophy, and as such to offer a criterion of action.[47] If that is the case, then Timon is far from deploring the rule of the apparent (for the passage above could be interpreted thus), but rather claiming it as the only guide to action. The apparent as a practical criterion did become associated with Pyrrhonism, as can be seen from various later sources: Aenesidemus, the anonymous commentator on Plato's *Theaetetus*, and not least Sextus himself.

No testimony directly associates Pyrrho with a view on a practical criterion. And as we already saw, Pyrrho claimed, again according to Diogenes (9.61), that "nothing is good or bad, just or unjust, and equally in all cases that nothing is in truth, but that people do everything *by law and custom*, for each thing is no more this than that." Does this comment express contempt for conventional behavior, or does it imply that even Pyrrho must follow law and custom? Since we have reason, on the basis of the biographical accounts, to suppose that his behavior was unconventional, the first option is the likelier.

There is evidently some tension between the accounts of Pyrrho's reported behavior and Timon's claim that the follower of Pyrrho does not transgress the customary and follows the apparent. The tension is the greater if "laws and customs" are themselves examples of the apparent, and part of a practical criterion.[48] It seems safest to infer that Pyrrho himself left it unclear what could guide one's actions, given an active distrust of perceptions and opinions. It fell to Timon to find a practical criterion, the apparent, and to insist that he did not transgress the customary.

We reach the third and last question: How does the absence of opinions lead to tranquility?[49] Pyrrho's unconventionality is closely linked with the attitude for which he was famous, and which featured prominently in the biographical accounts: his indifference, impassivity, and tranquility. At the end of the Aristocles passage, Timon claimed that tranquility followed from the disposition of non-assertion, which in turn is based on having realized that perceptions and opinions are neither true nor false. As already mentioned, Timon says that Pyrrho acquired this state of mind by conquering what had overpowered all others, "affections, opinion, and pointless legislation" (*Praep. evang.* 14.18.19 = DC 58). Again, in a fragment from the *Lampoons*, Timon asks Pyrrho how he rid himself "from servitude to the opinions and empty theorising of sophists, and loosened the shackles of every deception and persuasion" (DL 9.64).[50] His tranquility, Timon implies in another testimony, consists in being "uniformly free from movement, paying no heed to the whirls of sweet-voiced wisdom" (*M* 11.1 = DC 61C).

These passages imply that for Pyrrho it is the realization that perceptions and opinions are neither true nor false, and the consequent attitude characterized by non-assertion that brings about this state of mind, tranquility. If that is so, having opinions, especially about natural values, creates perturbations. We saw that, according to one testimony (*M* 11.20 = DC 62), Pyrrho thought that those who hold opinions falsely believe that there is a nature of the good and the divine, and think that they can achieve "the most equable life" by acquiring the natural good. This belief presumably precludes impassivity and tranquility. The passage may have been intended to explain the dogmatic error, to show where those who hold opinions go wrong, in order to explain how one can achieve the good life, namely through realizing that nothing is by nature good or bad. Sextus offers a similar explanation of the Pyrrhonist tranquility in *M* 11.68–95, although his argument must have been dialectical: nothing is good or bad by nature, and realizing this leads to tranquility, since one sheds the desire for the supposed goods.[51] This explanation is also in tune with Timon's remark that "desire is absolutely the first of all bad things" (Athenaeus 8.337A = DC 65).

NOTES

1   The testimonies for Pyrrho's life and thought are collected in DC; see also LS sections 1–3. The most comprehensive study of Pyrrho's philosophy is that of Bett [143]; see also von Fritz [163].

2   For the fragments of Timon, see Diels [21], DC, Lloyd-Jones and Parsons [23]; see also LS sections 1–3, Di Marco [11].

3   On Timon's philosophical style, see Long [158].

4   For a detailed discussion of Diogenes' account of Pyrrhonism, see Barnes [219].

5   On the *Silloi*, see Long [158], Di Marco [11], who includes biographical testimonies. On the *Indalmoi*, see Brunschwig [150].

6   Cf. Ferrari [155], DC, commentary on 53, Long [158], p. 71 n. 4, Bett [143], pp. 9–11.

7   For arguments for Timon's authorship see Frede [74], 806, Frede [65], p. 262, Brunschwig [149], who argues from a close reading of the Aristocles passage, Brunschwig [152], pp. 250–51, and Warren [121], pp. 97–99. Bett [143], pp. 8–13, 17–18, argues for viewing Timon mostly as a reporter of Pyrrho's views.

8   Cf. Long [158], p. 75, and Hadot [106], pp. 111–13.
9   On Antigonus, see Wilamowitz-Moellendorf [165], Long [158], p. 72, Bett
     [143], pp. 6–13.
10 Unless *Acad.* 2.32 refers to Aenesidemus.
11 See Stopper [82], 266–68, Bett [143], pp. 165–66.
12 Brunschwig [152], pp. 235–38 has played down the connection; for a more
     positive evaluation, see Warren [121], ch. 3. On possible philosophical
     links between Pyrrho and both Democritus and Anaxarchus, see also Mi-
     Kyoung Lee, Chapter 1 "Antecedents Early Greek Philosophy."
13 On possible Eastern influences, see Hadot [106], pp. 96–97, and Flintoff
     [157]. But Pyrrho's stance is comprehensible in Greek terms.
14 See Castagnoli [144], 447.
15 So Bett [143], p. 16.
16 For a more detailed account, see Svavarsson [162].
17 Zeller [123], p. 501. There are syntactical reasons for (Brennan [147], 432–
     33), and against (Bett [142], 141–44).
18 As pointed out by Bett [142], 167–69, [143], p. 27.
19 See Stopper [82], 292–93 n. 53 and Brennan [147], 430–33.
20 Cf. Stopper [82], 292 n. 53.
21 Cf. Brennan [147], 430–32, for, and Bett [143], pp. 60–62, against.
22 Bett [143], p. 22.
23 The following have an objective reading in common, although they differ
     in the details: DC, pp. 225–27, Ferrari [156], p. 363, Reale [159], pp. 315–
     31, LS 1F with commentary, Hankinson [68], pp. 59–62, Bett [142], 149–
     52, [143], pp. 18–29, Bailey [60], pp. 27–30, Chiesara [19], pp. 93–97,
     Warren [121], pp. 90–94. Ausland [140] takes the adjectives to refer to
     the moral indifference of things. Brunschwig [149], pp. 190–211, suggests
     that the adjectives refer to the perceptions and opinions. Long [135] favors
     a subjective reading without adopting Zeller's emendation. Stopper [82],
     Annas and Barnes [269], and Brennan [147], are the most recent examples
     of those adopting a subjective reading.
24 Bett [143].
25 See further Svavarsson [162], p. 274 n. 44. Thanks to Richard Bett for his
     generous comments on this issue.
26 See Svavarsson [162].
27 For another comparison of Plato and Pyrrho, see Bett [143], who suggests
     that Pyrrho might be seen as Plato without the Forms (p. 138).
28 Cf. Bett [143], p. 114 ff., and Svavarsson [162].
29 For the importance of the conflict of appearances for Plato's theory of
     Forms, see Svavarsson [137].
30 LS vol. II, commentary on 1F, Bett [142], 170–80, Chiesara [19], p. 86 ff.
31 Cf. Bett [142], 155 n. 50.

32 Most commentators lean towards the latter interpretation. Exceptions
    are LS 1F with commentary, Hankinson [68], pp. 63–64, Long [135]
    (revised version), pp. 68–69.

33 See P. DeLacy [130] and Bett [143], pp. 32–33 n. 36.

34 The Greek can readily be understood so as to allow for the last two
    disjunctions to be an explanation of the first. Such is Hankinson's sug-
    gestion [68], pp. 63–64, as well as that of Brunschwig [152], pp. 245–46; see
    further Svavarsson [162], 278–79.

35 Another less obvious possibility is "speechlessness"; see Brunschwig
    [151], pp. 297–320.

36 On this passage, see Burnyeat [153], Bett [141], [143], Svavarsson [161].

37 Burnyeat's reading [153] is that within brackets. It does not give us as
    blatantly inconsistent a Pyrrho as others.

38 See Ferrari [156], p. 359, DC, p. 256, and Bett [141], 315–20.

39 The lines are used by Sextus in a specific context; on how he may have
    understood them, see Svavarsson [161], 254–56.

40 Cf. Bett [143], pp. 114–23, Svavarsson [162].

41 See *Praep. evang.* 14.2.4 = DC 26A, 14.17.10 = DC 25B, and 14.18.6 = DC
    46. Aristocles' views are the same as those of the anonymous commen-
    tator on the *Theaetetus* (60.48–61.46 = DC 80, LS 71D). Cf. Brennan [147],
    427–29.

42 The same argument is apparent in Sextus (*M* 11.69–78), where it is
    surely used dialectically; see Svavarsson [162], 263–69. For its use in
    Aenesidemus, and as explaining his "Heracliteanism," see Schofield [232].

43 Aristotle accused his opponents, i.e. those who say "neither 'thus' nor
    'not thus', but 'both thus and not thus', and again 'neither thus nor not
    thus,'" of much the same in *Met.* IV.

44 See articles in Burnyeat and Frede [79].

45 On the meaning of the term "the customary" (*sunêtheia*), see Bett [143],
    pp. 89–90.

46 Suggested by Bett [143], p. 93. It should also be noted that Timon's
    contemporary, Arcesilaus, advanced "the apparent" alongside "the rea-
    sonable" (*to eulogon*) as the criterion, if Plutarch is to be believed; *Col.*
    1122E–F, cf. 1118A.

47 Cf. Bett [143], pp. 85–93.

48 As they became in Sextus; see *PH* 1.23–24.

49 For the status of *ataraxia* as happiness, see Striker [120] and Warren [121].

50 For other testimonies of a similar nature, see Bett [143], p. 71 ff.

51 For more on this argument (from a different perspective), see Richard
    Bett, Chapter 9 "Scepticism and Ethics."

3   Arcesilaus and Carneades

Arcesilaus initiated a sceptical phase in the Academy after taking over in c. 268 BCE. He was motivated in part by an innovative reading of Plato's dialogues. Where his predecessors found positive doctrines to be systematically developed, he found a dialectical method of arguing and the sceptical view that nothing can be known (*akatalêpsia, De Or.* 3.67, see DL 4.28, 4.32). He also advanced this conclusion in opposition to the ambitious system of the Stoics, claiming further that the appropriate response to the pervasive uncertainty generated by his method is the suspension of judgement (*epochê*).

Arcesilaus' dialectical method was practiced without significant modification in the Academy until Carneades, who became head sometime before 155 BCE.[1] Carneades both continued and strengthened Arcesilaus' method (*ND* 1.11, *Acad.* 2.16, see also *Acad.* 1.46, and Eusebius, *Praep. evang.* 14.7.15). Sextus marks the change by referring to Plato's Academy as Old, Arcesilaus' as Middle, and Carneades' as New (*PH* 1.220).

Since the main interpretative issues regarding both Arcesilaus and Carneades depend on the concepts of *akatalêpsia* and *epochê*, we must try to determine what they mean, how they are related, and what attitude the Academics take towards them – i.e. in what sense, if any, are these their sceptical doctrines?

I   ARCESILAUS

The view that Arcesilaus derived from Plato's dialogues might have taken one of two very different forms. He might have discovered some arguments that show knowledge is not possible. Or he might have been impressed by the fact that none of Socrates' interlocutors were able to justify their beliefs. In the latter case he will not have come away with a firm conclusion but rather the impression or suspicion that knowledge is not possible.[2]

The central move on the first account is to assemble arguments against the existence of transcendent Forms, as Plato does in the *Parmenides*. The argument then proceeds straightforwardly: if the only proper object of knowledge is what invariably is what it is (*Rep.* 477a, *Tim.* 51d–e), and if we have good reason to doubt the existence of transcendent Forms, we are left with the flux and uncertainty of this world.[3]

A similar line of thinking is evident in Arcesilaus' claim that the Presocratics were led to a confession of ignorance because of the obscurity of things, the limitations of our minds and senses, and the brevity of life (*Acad.* 1.44–45). There is no reason to suppose Arcesilaus thought there was a common sceptical argument endorsed by all of the Presocratics. The important point is that, for a variety of reasons, they maintained that appearances are not reliable guides to reality.[4]

These sceptical conclusions will only follow, however, if we accept the corresponding accounts of reality and our access to it. For example, Democritus' assertion that the senses are not only dim, but full of darkness (*Acad.* 2.73) presupposes the truth of his atomism: reality is not accessible to the senses. So it seems that Arcesilaus could not avail himself of the sceptical portion of the Presocratics' theorizing without biting off more than he would wish to chew.

Furthermore, the confident conclusion that knowledge is not possible is at odds with both his promotion of *epochê* and his thoroughgoing disavowal of knowledge.[5] If Arcesilaus had been able to prove that nothing can be known he should have been willing to affirm that he knew at least that much. However, he denies himself even this residual piece of knowledge (*Acad.* 1.45). So he must have regarded these proofs for the impossibility of knowledge as inconclusive.

Rather than discovering some decisive arguments in the dialogues, it is more likely that he discovered a dialectical method. In order to explain this method and how it motivates his confession of ignorance, we need to refer to Plato's Socrates.

In some of his dialogues, Plato highlights the therapeutic nature of Socrates' project. We see him rousing the Athenians from their sluggish dogmatism and helping to remove the obstruction of poorly founded conviction (e.g. *Ap.* 30e, *Tht.* 148e–151d). In pursuit of these ends, Socrates reveals that his interlocutors are committed to inconsistent views and thus that they are not knowledgeable. Insofar as his examination focuses on what his interlocutors believe, it is irrelevant whether he himself believes any of the propositions examined. The neutrality provided by this dialectical method becomes a key feature in Arcesilaus' appropriation of it.

Even if Socrates remains neutral regarding the views he elicits from his interlocutors, his method appears to commit him to (at least) two importantly substantive claims. First, he implicitly identifies knowledge with virtue, which he takes to be necessary if not also sufficient for a good life (see, e.g. *Ap.* 20c, 21b). And secondly, he supposes that if someone has this knowledge, he cannot be refuted. To know p is to know why p is true in such a way that no argument can undermine your grasp of that truth (see *Gorg.* 473b, *Meno* 85c). This assumption is evident in Socrates' efforts to determine whether his interlocutors can provide consistent accounts of the virtues.

The upshot is that as long as we lack this knowledge, the only thing worth doing is to earnestly pursue it, whether by looking for someone with irrefutable knowledge, as Socrates did, or by submitting our own views to Socratic examination. We must not rest content with even the most thoroughly defended position as long as it is possible that it might be refuted. As long as that possibility remains, we cannot be confident that we have the knowledge necessary for our flourishing. Hence, the unexamined life is not worth living.

And yet Socrates' examination is never complete. None of his interlocutors are able to defend themselves successfully. It is easy to imagine how this experience could produce the expectation not only that the next interlocutor will fail but that all interlocutors will fail. Insofar as Socrates is sincere and proficient in his refutations, it is likely that he would come to suspect that nothing can be known with certainty.

Arcesilaus seems to have modeled himself on just such an interpretation of Socrates.[6] He revived the Socratic practice of eliciting his interlocutors' views in order to argue against them (*Fin.* 2.2, *ND* 1.11, see also *Fat.* 4, *Acad.* 1.16). On the basis of their own commitments, he drew consequences that they themselves could not accept. He is also credited with counterbalancing his interlocutors' conviction by producing equally powerful arguments in opposition (DL 4.28, *Acad.* 1.45). All of this is consistent with the aporetic outcome of the Socratic dialogues. Socrates unintentionally promotes *epochê* insofar as he offers nothing to replace the views he has refuted; he leaves his interlocutors in a state of *aporia*, that is, puzzled and uncertain as to what they should now think (*Meno* 80a–b).

Like Socrates, Arcesilaus never wrote any philosophical works.[7] The best explanation of this is that he aimed at helping others remove the obstruction of poorly founded convictions. Discussion is more effective than writing in accomplishing this end since it allows one to fit his arguments to the occasion.[8] A therapeutic agenda also explains why Arcesilaus thought that particular suspensions of judgement are genuinely good (*PH* 1.233, see also Eusebius, *Praep. evang.* 14.4.15). Suspending judgement is good only insofar as it is preferable to persevering with inadequately justified beliefs. But it is only second-best to the ultimate good of irrefutable knowledge.[9]

On this view, Arcesilaus' arguments for *akatalêpsia* are part of his dialectical strategy. In arguing that knowledge is not possible he would not be advancing his own view, but rather leading his dogmatic interlocutors to admit that they themselves are unwittingly committed to it. Alternatively, he may be showing that the arguments for and against the possibility of knowledge are equally convincing. The result, in either case, is that his interlocutors no longer know what to believe, and so they suspend judgement.

Just as Socrates appears to be puzzled about the nature of knowledge by the end of the *Theaetetus*, it is likely that Arcesilaus suspended judgement himself regarding the possibility of knowledge. Even so, he must have developed the same expectation that Socrates had. The fact that he was so successful in undermining his interlocutors' convictions must have inspired the suspicion that knowledge is not possible. Whether or not this expectation amounts to a belief, the crucial point is that Arcesilaus would not have promoted it as the most rationally defensible position.

If this captures Arcesilaus' attitude towards *akatalêpsia*, we may also appeal to it in explaining the attribution of other beliefs to him. He may have initially accepted the claims that motivate Socrates' philosophical project but then later realized there are equally powerful considerations opposed to them. Even while suspending judgement as to what constitutes wisdom, it may have continued to seem that seeking the irrefutable truth is the only thing worth doing. One may continue to engage in some activity, even philosophical activity, despite having given up one's rational justification for it.

This interpretation is consistent with Arcesilaus' somewhat tenuous connection with Pyrrho. Sextus claims that Arcesilaus' scepticism is virtually identical to Pyrrhonism since they make no assertions about the reality of anything, nor do they prefer one thing to another as being more or less convincing – instead they suspend judgement about everything (*PH* 1.232). Numenius similarly reports that in all but name, Arcesilaus was a follower of Pyrrho, since he overthrew (i.e. refuted) all things, truth, falsehood, and even plausibility (Eusebius, *Praep. evang.* 14.6.5).

Further testimony to the connection comes from a contemporary Stoic, Aristo, who describes Arcesilaus as a philosophical chimera, composed of Plato in front, Diodorus (the dialectician) in the middle, and Pyrrho behind (DL 4.33, *PH* 1.234, Eusebius, *Praep. evang.* 14.5.13). Although the significance of this quip is contested, it is likely that Aristo objected to Arcesilaus' sceptical appropriation of Plato and Socrates. On the Stoic account, Socrates was thought to be either a sage or at least well on his way. The insult then would be that Arcesilaus had constructed a monstrous identity for himself by grafting the antithetical figures of Plato and Pyrrho together by means of the subtle dialectical practices of Diodorus (Sedley [71], p.15).

Despite his admiration for Pyrrho, there is no indication that Arcesilaus followed him in linking *epochê* to tranquillity. Had he done so he would have been hard pressed to claim the mantle of Socrates, for whom *aporia* is a spur to further inquiry, not a welcome state of calm as it is for Pyrrho.

II THE ACADEMIC ATTACK ON STOIC EPISTEMOLOGY

Before Arcesilaus' sceptical appropriation of Plato, Zeno of Citium had discovered quite a different Socrates, first in some books and later as a student in Polemo's Academy.[10] Arcesilaus witnessed the development of Zeno's Stoicism and probably saw this vigorous new school as a threat to his sceptical interpretation of Plato and Socrates.[11] In any case, the ambitious Stoic view became the main target of the sceptical Academics.

Zeno endorses the presuppositions underwriting Socrates' project: the notion that virtue is a kind of knowledge that is sufficient for happiness (*Fin.* 4.14, *Acad.* 1.42, DL 7.127–28, *Fin.* 4.47, *Acad.* 1.35–36), and the irrefutability of knowledge (DL 7.47, *Acad.* 1.41–42, 2.77). His all-important innovation is an empiricist account of how it is possible to acquire the irrefutable knowledge required for virtue and happiness (Frede [104]).

Between the knowledge of the sage and the ignorance of the fool is a cognitive state that he terms apprehension (*katalêpsis*, *Acad.* 1.42). Apprehension occurs when we assent to a certain kind of impression (*kataleptikê*). Unlike other impressions, a kataleptic one (i) arises from what is, and (ii) is stamped, impressed and molded just as it is (*Acad.* 2.77), not with respect to *every* property, but those that are capable of being grasped (*Acad.* 1.42). The transition from folly to wisdom is accomplished, in part, by learning to see the complex and mutually supportive interrelations among individual kataleptic impressions. The sage assents only to kataleptic impressions, so everything he believes, he knows to be true, and all of these truths are mutually supported and reinforced by everything else he believes. Without apprehension providing the raw material, such a remarkable achievement would not be possible. If no impressions were kataleptic, there would be nothing worthy of the sage's assent.

In Cicero's account, Arcesilaus opens his challenge by asking for clarification: What if a true impression were of the same sort as a false one? Zeno flatly rejects this possibility, further stipulating that (iii) the kataleptic impression is of such a kind as could not arise from what is not (*Acad.* 2.77, *M* 7.252). Arcesilaus agrees that this is a suitable addition and then goes on to develop the objection implicit in his initial question: for any true impression, we can imagine a false one that is indistinguishable from it.

Zeno's definition seems to set out the causal conditions an impression must meet to be kataleptic: it must be formed in the right way, stamped and impressed precisely in accordance with what it represents. And Arcesilaus' objection seems to be that we can never confidently verify that an impression has met these conditions. But if so, they are arguing at cross-purposes. If Arcesilaus takes "kataleptic" to mean "exhibiting some mark that certifies to the subject the truth of the impression," and Zeno takes it to mean "being formed in the appropriate way," then there is no real disagreement. (We may refer to these as internalist and externalist interpretations respectively insofar as the distinguishing features of kataleptic impressions are internal or external to the agent's awareness.)

Furthermore, it is plausible to claim that lots of impressions are as a matter of fact properly formed, and just as plausible to claim that we can never be entirely certain of that fact. We may be in possession of many true beliefs without being able to identify which they are. Something like this appears to have been the position adopted by Philo of Larissa at the end of the long debate between the Stoics and Academics (*PH* 1.235, see Hankinson [203], Brittain [195]).

But even if the debate was finally resolved in such a compromise position, it probably did not arise from a simple misunderstanding. If Zeno and later Stoics had been defending an externalist account, surely someone would have noticed that the Academic's internalist objections were missing the point. Yet Carneades and other Academics continued to press this sort of objection for many years. Also, because of the role that kataleptic impressions are supposed to play in the Stoic system, it must be possible to learn to differentiate them from non-kataleptic impressions. Otherwise, it is not clear how they could facilitate the transformation from folly to wisdom. The sage is irrefutable because he is aware of the reasons and evidence that justify the truth of what he assents to. On the other hand, if the Stoics did not move towards some sort of externalism, Arcesilaus' objection seems conclusive. Surely the Stoics would not have continued to defend a position that is so vulnerable to refutation. Charity requires that we find some genuine disagreement along with strong enough considerations on both sides to sustain it (Reed [116]).

Given this goal, we will examine the details of the Academic objections and Stoic replies. Arcesilaus' objection is meant to show that there is no distinct type of impression that satisfies all three of Zeno's conditions. In one version of the objection, we focus on vacuous impressions, the kind that arise from what is not, to make the point that they are indistinguishable from those that satisfy the first two conditions (*Acad.* 2.88–90, *M* 7.403–8). When one is dreaming, for example, his vacuous impressions may be just as vivid and convincing as impressions that (i) arise from what is, and (ii) are stamped and impressed precisely in accordance with what is. This is even more evident in cases of madness where one is moved to do things that should require a great deal of confidence. Hercules, for example, in a fit of madness, shot his own children, taking them to be his enemy's. The fact that these vacuous impressions no longer seem true after one wakes up, or recovers his sanity, is beside the point. At the time, they are as compelling as true impressions. And that indicates that at the time they are indistinguishable from true impressions.

In another version of the objection we may imagine that an impression satisfies the first two conditions in order to show that, contrary to (iii), it is still of such a kind as *could* arise from what is not. For example, even if an impression of my close friend arises from, and is stamped and impressed precisely in accordance with, that person, it remains a distinct possibility that the impression arose from someone else who bears a remarkable similarity to my friend. Cast in this way we can see the objection is not meant to be limited to impressions of people who actually have a twin, or of objects that are produced by the same process, e.g. grains of sand, eggs, or imprints in wax made by the same ring (*Acad.* 2.85–87). The objection points to the general, counterfactual possibility that the causal history of an impression could always have been different from what appears to be the case (Perin [187]). Consequently, there *are* no impressions of such a kind as could not have come about from some state of affairs other than what is represented.

The Stoic response to both types of objection relies on the principle of the identity of indiscernibles along with the notion that all distinct entities are at least in principle discernible (*Acad.* 2.57–58, 2.85–86, *M* 7.252). The Stoics insist that each existing thing has its own unique, individuating properties. No two things are identical in every respect. This applies to impressions as well. So all impressions formed in the abnormal conditions of dreaming or insanity differ in some way from allegedly indistinguishable impressions. Similarly, in normal conditions, impressions of any objects, no matter how similar, will differ in some ways.

The sage is always so attuned to his mental condition that he will be aware when he is in abnormal conditions and withhold his assent. But what will enable him in practice to eliminate the counterfactual possibility that even in optimal conditions the causal history of an impression could be different from what appears to be the case? The Stoics insist that when the agent has his rational and sensory organs in the proper state, and other relevant conditions are optimal, his impressions are formed in a craftsmanlike way (*M* 7.250–51). Differences between very similar objects will not be apparent to the untrained eye. The expert's impression, however, will precisely report the unique, individuating properties of the object. The process by which the craftsmanlike impression is formed ends with the agent's awareness of the unique, individuating properties. If we can make sense of such a process, the Stoics will have bridged the divide between internalism and externalism and provided a plausible response to Arcesilaus' objection.

Even so, as long as the Stoics acknowledge the internalist requirement that the agent be aware of something distinctive about kataleptic impressions, the counterfactual possibility remains problematic. In other words, it remains the case that two impressions might exhibit a higher degree of similarity than any actual human being is able to differentiate. The Stoic account succeeds in establishing that it is logically possible to develop our cognitive and sensory equipment to such an extent that only kataleptic impressions appear convincing. But in practice, the skill necessary to infallibly grasp an impression as kataleptic remains elusive (see *Acad.* 2.85).

In response to the Academic attack, the Stoics were forced to distinguish the requirements that an impression must meet to be kataleptic from the conditions that we must be in if we are to recognize them as such. It is precisely this separation of the conditions that make an impression true from the conditions that enable us to grasp that truth that sustains the sceptical attack. And it is precisely this separation that Zeno tried to resist in issuing his third condition. By stating that a kataleptic impression is such that it could not arise from what is not, Zeno insists that the causal conditions that produce kataleptic impressions include the conditions that enable us to grasp them as such, but without guaranteeing that we will do so – at best, kataleptic impressions can *practically* drag us to assent (*M* 7.257, see also *Acad.* 2.38).

As long as the Stoics retain the internalist requirement they are vulnerable to the Academic objection. If the causal history of an impression could always have been different from what appears to be the case, even those with the most highly developed skill of discernment may still err.

Arcesilaus' objection is clearly not meant to show that knowledge is not possible. All it can show is that there are no impressions that meet the Stoic definition of apprehension. But if his aim is to undermine the Stoics' confidence and lead them to suspend judgement, this is all the argument needs to show.

III ARCESILAUS' PRACTICAL CRITERION[12]

In addition to defending themselves by developing their epistemology, the Stoics also went on the attack. Suppose we were to suspend judgement about everything, as Arcesilaus urges. In that case, they claimed, we will be left in a state of inaction (*apraxia*), since action requires assent. According to the Stoics, human action involves three elements: impression, impulse, and assent. An impulse towards or away from an object is the necessary antecedent to any intentional action. And impulse itself cannot occur unless the agent assents to the evaluative proposition embodied in the relevant impression. An impression alone is not supposed to be enough to induce action. Not only do I need to receive the impression, say of a hot bath, I must also see that bath in a way that will lead to action. Only if I assent to it as, for example, something to be enjoyed, will I have an impulse to get into the bath.[13]

Arcesilaus' response is that impression and impulse can occur without assent (*Col.* 1122A–D). The result seems to be a crude stimulus-response model: we are moved automatically by impulsive impressions without any intervention or adjudication. In that case, Arcesilaus is vulnerable to the further objection that those who suspend judgement are not able to *decide* to do anything (*Col.* 1122E, Striker [190]). They may be able to navigate through the world, but their actions will be no different in kind from the actions of non-rational animals. If universal *epochê* involves the rejection of what is distinctively human, it will also preclude the possibility of a good human life.

This is the objection that Sextus has in mind when he remarks that it was necessary for Arcesilaus to offer some criterion of action to explain how one might attain happiness. According to Sextus:

Arcesilaus says that one who suspends judgement[14] about everything will regulate choice and avoidance and actions in general by "the reasonable" [*to eulogon*]; and that happiness is acquired through prudence, and prudence resides in right actions, and right action is whatever, once it has been done, has a reasonable justification; therefore one who attends to the reasonable will act rightly and be happy. (*M* 7.158, translation LS 69B)

It is difficult to understand why one would bother to provide a reasonable justification for the kind of action that Arcesilaus thinks is consistent with *epochê*. Typically, a justification for an action explains *why* we did something. But if my action is not the result of any judgement or decision, there appears to be very little to say about why I did it.

Perhaps a reasonable justification is simply a matter of saying that whatever I did seemed reasonable or appropriate given the situation: without assenting I was moved to act because of my desire and the way things seemed. In particular, I will not have reflected on my desire and endorsed it as worthwhile. In that case, the "justification" cannot show that I was right to act as I did. Consequently, it is also difficult to see how it could lead one to act rightly and be happy.

On the other hand, the very issue at stake might be whether right actions are right only insofar as they are justified, and more generally, whether happiness depends on having justified beliefs. Arcesilaus might be offering, in stark contrast to the Stoic view, an account of happiness that is relatively easy to attain and consistent with *epochê*. Perhaps we are mistaken to rest our conception of happiness on what we take to be distinctively human, and perhaps it is not such a rare and spectacular achievement after all.

Whether Arcesilaus himself endorses this account of action and happiness is controversial. If he does, we must explain how his endorsement is consistent with *epochê*. And if he does not, we must explain why he would respond to an objection with an account he does not approve of.

Taking up the latter option first, some have seen the account as part of a dialectical strategy (Couissin [179], Striker [190]). Arcesilaus remains uncommitted while leading his Stoic interlocutors to conclusions that they find unacceptable. In particular, he shows the Stoics what sort of life would be possible in the absence of kataleptic impressions, given their other commitments. For the Stoics, only the sage performs right actions because only he has firm, irrefutable knowledge enabling him to properly evaluate all the things he encounters. The rest of us are able to perform appropriate actions, which may not differ outwardly from the sage's actions, but will differ in the cognitive and dispositional states that give rise to it. The Stoics define these appropriate actions as those that have a reasonable justification (DL 7.107, *Fin.* 3.58).

Arcesilaus seems to have vandalized the Stoic system by defining right actions as they define appropriate actions. Having shown that there are no kataleptic impressions, it follows that there are no right actions, as defined by the Stoics. Consequently, if any actions are right, they must require something less demanding – not irrefutable knowledge, but a reasonable justification.

However, Arcesilaus is clearly not using the Stoic notion of reasonable justification. His account is meant to show how life is possible for one who suspends judgement. So acting in accordance with reasonable justifications involves no beliefs. By contrast, for the Stoics, a reasonable justification shows why a proposition is more likely to be true than false, and is meant to warrant the belief that this is so (see DL 7.76). So if Arcesilaus had appropriated the Stoic view of reasonable justification it would not explain how one can act while suspending judgement.

On the other hand, we may suppose that Arcesilaus is adjusting the notion of reasonable justification in accordance with his sceptical attack. If we are unable to identify which impressions are true, we will not be able to identify which impressions are more likely to be true either.

Whether or not Arcesilaus depends exclusively on Stoic commitments in developing his account of action and happiness, it is clearly antithetical to the Stoic view. As long as he is able to defend it with arguments that are as compelling as the arguments advanced in support of the Stoic view, he will have achieved his dialectical aim – he will have left his interlocutors with no better reason to believe one view than the other.

Some have objected, however, that Arcesilaus could have more easily discomfited the Stoics by pointing out that *apraxia* is actually their problem. The Stoics themselves are unwittingly committed to the notion that it is rational to suspend judgement, since there is nothing worthy of the sage's assent. If the *apraxia* objection shows that the Stoics are unable to act, Arcesilaus should applaud rather than respond (Maconi [110]). In responding as he does, Arcesilaus seems to acknowledge that *apraxia* raises a problem that he himself needs to solve (Ioppolo [108], Hankinson [68]). At the very least, as one who suspends judgement and leads others to do the same, he would have found it difficult to attract students if he refused to counter the claim that suspending judgement makes life unlivable.

It would not be necessary, however, for Arcesilaus to endorse the explanation he provides in response to the *apraxia* objection. We may suppose that he suspended judgement even here. But since his account is supposed to show how those who suspend judgement are able to remain active, he himself will be moved to act in accordance with what seems reasonable. Even if it is not the statement of an account that he believes to be true, it may still be a description of his practice. And in the meantime it admirably serves its dialectical purpose.

IV CARNEADES

Like Arcesilaus, Carneades refrained from writing, engaging instead in live discussion with the therapeutic aim of removing obstacles in the interest of advancing the pursuit of truth (Cicero, *ND* 1.11, *Tusc.* 5.11, but see also Eusebius, *Praep. evang.* 14.7.15).

On his famous embassy to Rome in 156–155 BCE, for example, Carneades defended a certain conception of justice on one day and overturned it the next. He did this not to disparage justice, but rather to show its proponents that they had no firm foundation for their arguments (Lactantius, *Epitome* 55.8, LS 68M). Although it is easy to sympathize with Cato that such a practice might have a corrupting influence on the youth, it would be uncharitable to suppose that Carneades was malicious.[15]

Similarly, he argued against Stoic theology not for the sake of doing away with the gods but in order to show the Stoics that their arguments had established nothing (*ND* 3.44). From the Socratic perspective it would be impious *not* to reveal the inadequacies in the Stoics' arguments. And Cicero reports that Carneades did so in a way that inspired the search for the truth (*ND* 1.4).

Carneades employs his ethical arguments to the same end. His target is not virtue itself, but rather the justifications offered in support of competing ethical theories. The lesson to draw is not that virtue does not exist, or even that no one is virtuous, but rather that there are no convincing accounts of what makes a person or an action virtuous, given the naturalistic assumptions informing his contemporaries' theories.[16]

This much is a continuation of Arcesilaus' method. On the other hand, two sorts of modifications are attributed to Carneades, one concerning the basic sceptical view that nothing can be known (*akatalêpsia*), and the other concerning the suspension of judgement (*epochê*).

According to Sextus, Carneades asserts that the truth cannot be apprehended. This is supposedly what sets him apart from the Pyrrhonists who neither affirm nor deny that the truth can be discovered (*PH* 1.1–4, 1.226). As far as Sextus is concerned, Carneades had given up on investigation since there is no point in searching for what cannot be found.

If Sextus is right, Carneades will have made a major modification in Arcesilaus' more agnostic stance with respect to the possibility of knowledge. This might have been the result of his expansion of the scope of the Academics' dialectical method. Carneades casts his sceptical net wider than Arcesilaus. With regard to the ethical issue of the highest good, for example, he argued not only against the positions that were actually held, but even against those that could be held (again given certain constraints, *Fin.* 5.16). And with regard to the central epistemological issue of the criterion of truth, he argued quite generally that all of the possible candidates fail since they sometimes deceive us (*M* 7.159).

We might take this expansion of targets to indicate that Carneades was not content with the relatively modest, Socratic conclusion that *so far* no one has successfully defended his view. If he wanted to show that knowledge is not possible, he would have to move beyond the Socratic method.

But this is unlikely. Such a confident conclusion is clearly at odds with his promotion of *epochê* and the spirit of open-ended inquiry. Furthermore, it is generally held that Carneades' students developed his views in two distinct ways, neither of which involves the dogmatic rejection of the possibility of knowledge. On the first, dialectical interpretation, Carneades merely expands the scope of Arcesilaus' method, but continues to promote universal *epochê*. On the second, fallibilist interpretation, Carneades restricts the scope of *epochê*, allowing for some, fallible beliefs.

The dispute regarding Carneades centers on his response to the *apraxia* objection. Carneades' practical criterion, the plausible or convincing impression (*pithanê phantasia*), provides a more detailed and powerful response than Arcesilaus'. As a fallibilist, Carneades would be proposing this view of action as his own. From the dialectical standpoint, it would simply further his project of refuting the Stoics, revealing nothing about his own position.[17]

V CARNEADES' PRACTICAL CRITERION

It is important to differentiate the issue of the content of Carneades' account of convincing impressions from the issue of the attitude he takes towards that account (Obdrzalek [186]). Before attempting to determine which attitude Carneades takes, we must clarify what is involved in acting in accordance with convincing impressions. In particular, we need to consider whether it involves the acquisition of beliefs and whether it indicates anything more than a merely subjective plausibility.

The root of Carneades' account is the distinction between impressions that are unclear and those that are inapprehensible (*Acad.* 2.32, Eusebius, *Praep. evang.* 14.7.15). The Academic attack on Stoic epistemology shows only that everything is inapprehensible. But that doesn't mean that everything is unclear. Some sense-impressions strike us as more clear than others, and we are more inclined to act on such impressions – we find them more convincing or plausible (*pithanon*) despite the fact that they lack any distinctive mark that guarantees their truth. So there is nothing really disconcerting about the absence of kataleptic impressions. Life would be completely overturned, as the Stoics objected, only if there were no convincing impressions.

Carneades develops his account both in descriptive and normative terms: we *should* trust convincing impressions despite their sometimes being false, since as a matter of fact, our actions and judgements are regulated by what applies for the most part (*M* 7.175). The general tenor of his account, however, suggests that he is merely describing how people act:

just as in ordinary life, when we are investigating a small matter we question one witness, when it is a greater matter, several witnesses, and when it is an even more essential matter we examine each of the witnesses on the basis of the mutual agreement among the others. (*M* 7.184)

In the first level of scrutiny, either not much hangs on whether we act in accordance with the impression, or we simply don't have time to examine it. In the second level, we inspect the impressions that come bundled with the one in question, seeking to falsify the original impression by seeing how well it coheres with the rest. And in the highest level, "on matters that contribute to happiness," we exercise even more caution, examining the general conditions in which we make the judgement, e.g. our own mental states, the distance of the object, the quality of the light, etc.

Although this description is applicable to everyone, we must remember that Carneades offers it specifically to show how one who suspends judgement is able to live an ordinary, active life. The problem is that ordinarily to find some impression convincing is simply to believe it is true, or probably true; and that appears to violate *epochê*.

Two types of solution are available: we may argue that (1) Carneades reduces the scope of *epochê*, allowing for beliefs that arise from following convincing impressions, or (2) Carneades preserves universal *epochê* by denying that following convincing impressions requires taking those impressions to be true. Either of these solutions may be derived from a distinction Carneades makes between two types of assent: when the sage follows a convincing impression, he assents to it in a sceptically acceptable sense, but withholds assent in a different sense (*Acad.* 2.104).[18]

For either interpretation, the sceptically acceptable assent reflects a positive attitude towards convincing impressions that does not involve the error of rash, or dogmatic assent. If we suppose that that error is simply taking the impression to be true, we will favor (2).

It is extremely hard, however, to understand how one can assent to a convincing impression without taking it to be true, or in general to make sense of the convincingness of an impression without appealing to the concept of truth. The examples proposed to make this case take the form of predictions or hypotheses that are merely entertained without, supposedly, accepting them as true.[19] But insofar as a hypothesis involves no commitment to the truth of what is hypothesized, it is not clear what one could find convincing about it. For example, I might hypothesize that a certain chemical compound will turn the litmus paper red. If I neither believe nor disbelieve that it will do so I will not find it convincing either. Contrast this example with my prediction that Big Brown will win the Kentucky Derby. The extent to which I find this convincing, and hence likely to be true, is revealed by the amount of money I'm willing to bet. I wouldn't have put any money on the litmus test since neither outcome seemed convincing.

In order for an impression to be convincing, there must be something about it that either inspires action or at least sets up a genuine expectation for things to turn out as predicted. This is why we are surprised when a convincing impression turns out false. We decide that things were not as they seemed. But if the approval of these impressions reveals no attitude on my part towards the way the world is, I should never be surprised at how things turn out. Nor is it clear why I should examine my impressions if not to improve the likelihood of getting things right. I don't poke the coiled object on the floor in order to get a more convincing impression, but rather to determine whether it really is the snake that it appears to be.

Consequently, we should suppose that assenting to convincing impressions is a matter of taking them to be true, or at least probably true. In that case, what distinguishes sceptically acceptable from dogmatic assent may be the degree of confidence with which one takes the impression to be true. The error of rash, dogmatic assent would then be to take oneself to know what one does not. To avoid this error we need not suspend judgement about everything; we only need to withhold the dogmatic sort of assent that leads us to believe we know what we do not. On this view (1), Carneades responds to the *apraxia* objection by reducing the scope of *epochê*, allowing for a modest sort of belief.

It is important to note that, as far as we know, Carneades' only examples of convincing impressions (with a few possible exceptions to be discussed below), deal with ordinary if not familiar situations: whether this is Socrates (*M* 7.176–78), whether to flee (*M* 7.186), whether a coiled object is a rope or a snake (*M* 7.187), whether to go on a voyage, get married, sow crops, etc. (*Acad.* 2.100, 109). All of these cases involve predictions of one sort or another, as well as tangible consequences. In deciding to go on a voyage, I predict that the ship will make the journey safely. Even if the ship sinks, I may still defend my choice on the grounds that a successful journey seemed convincing. The crucial point is that I will not have rashly assented with more confidence than the situation warrants.

By allowing for a modest, tentative sort of belief with regard to ordinary, practical matters, Carneades strengthens the Academic response to the *apraxia* objection while retaining what is, arguably, most important about *epochê*. The point of suspending judgement is not to avoid all errors – not even the Stoic sage is supposed to be omniscient – but rather to avoid the epistemic arrogance inherent in rash, dogmatic assent.

VI IS CARNEADES A FALLIBILIST?

Does Carneades personally think it is ever reasonable to form opinions? If, as I have argued above, his proposal is offered as a description of how everyone acts in practical matters, then it will, *a fortiori*, be a description of how he acts. Sextus confirms this point, remarking that the New Academics make use of the plausible in their lives (*PH* 1.231). Furthermore, given the degrees of scrutiny that can be employed, it will also be a description of how the sage acts – his deliberation is simply more thorough and exacting. Insofar as the figure of the sage is a normative ideal, it follows that Carneades thinks we *should* form fallible opinions in accordance with properly tested, convincing impressions. If the sage acts this way, then it is reasonable for all of us to do the same.

Again, Sextus' view can be taken to support this interpretation: Carneades grabs hold of the convincing impression in order to show how one who suspends judgement might attain happiness, since he was compelled, like Arcesilaus, to offer some such account (*M* 7.166). So there is at least prima facie evidence in support of Carneades' personal endorsement.

This is not to deny that Carneades promotes a fallible sage as part of a dialectical strategy as well. Having argued that there are no kataleptic impressions, Carneades presents the Stoics with a dilemma: either the Stoic sage suspends judgement (since nothing is worthy of his assent), or he assents to a non-kataleptic impression and thereby holds a mere opinion (*Acad.* 2.67). Of course, the Stoics would not agree with the initial arguments against kataleptic impressions, so the point of the dilemma is to emphasize just how much hangs on this fundamental issue. Suppose Carneades is able to show there are no kataleptic impressions. Since the Stoics believe that action requires assent, and that the sage would not assent in the absence of kataleptic impressions, they would be left with an inactive sage. So, in order for the sage to be active, he must assent. In that case he will assent to non-kataleptic impressions, i.e. he will form a mere opinion. But since the Stoics held that having a mere opinion is a moral and epistemic failing (let us refer to this as opinion$_S$), they would be left with an immoral sage.

It is only within the context of Stoic theory that opinions become such awful transgressions. Ordinarily, no one thinks it a sin to hold an opinion, especially a carefully examined one. So when Carneades speaks of the Academic sage following convincing impressions, and thus cautiously holding opinions, he must be referring to this more ordinary sense of opinion (let us refer to this as opinion$_A$). Although both types of opinion are fallible judgements of truth, opinion$_S$ must be understood as a deficient mental state in comparison to the firm grasp characterized by the sage's assent to kataleptic impressions.

It is clear that Carneades does not endorse the notion that the Stoic sage will ever have an opinion$_S$ – this would be incompatible with the very conception of the Stoic sage. So our question is whether Carneades endorses the notion that the Academic sage (or any other flesh and blood sage) will ever have an opinion$_A$; and by implication, whether it is ever reasonable for any of us to form an opinion$_A$.

The strongest evidence against such an endorsement comes from Cicero's report of a disagreement among Carneades' students.[20] Philo and Metrodorus took him to be sincere when he allowed that the sage would form opinions in the absence of kataleptic impressions. Clitomachus, on the other hand, took him to be advancing this view strictly for the sake of investigation, as part of his dialectical attack on the Stoics (*Acad.* 2.78, see also 2.59, 2.67, 2.148). Cicero sides decisively with Clitomachus on this issue, apparently rejecting the view that Carneades ever endorsed a fallible sage. Cicero even makes a point of affirming his belief that the sage will have no opinions – it is never reasonable, as long as one is in a state of uncertainty, to form opinions (*Acad.* 2.113). He also acknowledges that approving of falsehoods as truths is the worst thing one can do, and admits his weakness in being a great opinion-holder (*Acad.* 2.66), despite Carneades' Herculean labor of casting rash assent and opinion from our minds (*Acad.* 2.108). On this interpretation, Philo misunderstands Carneades, whether intentionally or not.

The problem with this reading of the *Academica* is that it forces us to attribute a fundamentally incoherent view of Academic methodology to Cicero. For in every other philosophical work, and even in portions of the *Academica* itself, Cicero unequivocally promotes the Academic method as a mitigated scepticism: by arguing pro and contra, Academics aim to draw out and give shape to the truth or its nearest approximation (*Acad.* 2.7–9).[21] Cicero frequently expresses and displays his view that it is reasonable to make fallible judgements of truth in accordance with a thorough and careful examination of the best arguments that can be found on both sides. It is equally clear that he thinks he is doing the state a great service in encouraging his fellow Romans to engage in this practice.

Since Cicero points his readers to the Academic books for an explanation of his allegiance,[22] it would be confusing, to say the least, if he were defending a view of the Academic method in the *Academica* that he fundamentally disagrees with elsewhere. It is therefore preferable to find an interpretation of Cicero's position in the *Academica* that is consistent with his overall view.[23] By doing so we will undermine the main support for the exclusively dialectical reading of Carneades.

The major obstacle is the reported disagreement between Philo and Clitomachus, along with the handful of passages in which Cicero appears to reject the claim that it is ever reasonable to form opinions. The resolution I propose is that Cicero is not sufficiently careful about differentiating the various senses of opinion and assent that are in play. So, for example, we may understand Carneades' Herculean labor as casting out the overly confident, dogmatic sort of assent – again, this is not merely a matter of taking something to be true, but also taking oneself to know that it is true. Cicero makes precisely this point when he says that nothing is more shameful than approving of falsehoods as truths, i.e. approving of falsehoods as if they were truths, or in the manner one would approve of something he knew to be true (*Acad.* 2.66). This is assenting *entirely*, and is the kind Carneades would have us withhold (*Acad.* 2.104). Philo would happily agree with this.

When Cicero proclaims himself a great opinion-holder, we should take him to be referring to the plausible truths he has drawn out by way of his cherished Academic method. Given his high estimation of himself, this remark should be taken as ironic self-deprecation (Görler [201], pp. 37–38). He is a great opinion$_A$-holder. He would hardly have accused himself of the reckless transgression involved in holding opinions$_S$.

His bold affirmation that the sage will have no opinions (*Acad.* 2.113) should be understood as part of the Academics' standard dialectical maneuver. What he means is that the Stoic sage will have no opinions$_S$. Similarly, when he agrees that the Stoics should not allow that the sage sometimes assents to what is uncertain, he is agreeing that this makes no sense on the Stoic view (*Acad.* 2.67).

Finally, we may see the disagreement between Philo and Clitomachus as the result of an undiagnosed equivocation on "opinion." Philo is right that Carneades sincerely proposed that the sage will form opinions$_A$. The passages from Clitomachus' books on Carneades (*Acad.* 2.99–104) may easily be read as confirmation of this sincerity since we have seen that sceptically acceptable assent to a convincing impression produces a fallible belief. On the other hand, Clitomachus is right that Carneades' claim that the Stoic sage sometimes forms opinions$_S$ is purely dialectical.

The benefit of reading the "disagreement" this way is that it preserves the coherence of Cicero's defense of the Academy. The cost is relatively minor: the equivocation I have hypothesized is the sort of error Cicero could have made given the speed with which he wrote the *Academica*. It is far less likely that, in the very dialogue in which he is defending his allegiance, he defends a view of the Academy that he fundamentally disagrees with everywhere else.

An additional benefit is that this interpretation allows Carneades to preserve the consistency of his view: like the Academic sage, he may hold the opinion$_A$ that nothing can be apprehended in the Stoic sense (*Acad.* 2.110). That is clearly the opinion that Cicero is driving his readers towards in the *Academica* as well. It would also be open to Carneades to hold the opinion$_A$ that the Academic sage will responsibly make fallible judgements of truth in the absence of certainty.

Whether or not Carneades availed himself of these philosophical applications of his practical criterion, it is clear that his successors did. But it appears that Carneades was indeed a fallibilist, at least with regard to practical matters.

NOTES

1   Fragments and testimonia for Arcesilaus and Carneades are collected in Mette [12] and [13] respectively. The most important texts are Sextus Empiricus *PH* 1.220–34 and *M* 7.150–89, 7.402–38, and scattered throughout Cicero's *Academica*. In this chapter I make use of the excellent translations of Annas and Barnes [40], Bett [42] and Brittain [56] respectively (with slight modifications). Next in importance are Diogenes Laertius' *Lives of Eminent Philosophers* 4.28–66, Numenius' remarks reported by Eusebius in *Preparations for the Gospel* 14.6–8, and various remarks in Plutarch's works. A good place to start is LS 68–69, which contains many of the central texts in translation.

2 See Schofield [188] for the former, Cooper [178] for the latter. I follow Cooper's interpretation closely in this section.

3 See Bett [143], pp. 132–40 for discussion of the similar hypothesis that Pyrrho's indeterminacy thesis derives from, or at least bears a striking resemblance to, Plato's account of Heraclitean flux in the *Theaetetus*, as well as the account of the indeterminacy of sensible things in *Republic* 5.

4 See also *Col.* 1121F–22A, *Acad.* 2.13–15, 2.72–75, and Brittain and Palmer [177].

5 See Lactantius *Div. Inst.* 3.6.7–15 for the charge of inconsistency.

6 They both attracted a large following by publicly deflating their interlocutors' intellectual pretences (*Ap.* 23c, DL 4.37, respectively).

7 Plutarch, *Alex. Fort.* 328A–B, DL 4.32, 1.16. In sharp contrast, Arcesilaus' contemporaries and predecessors were quite prolific, with the notable exception of Pyrrho who also wrote nothing (see DL 4.11–14, 5.42–50, 7.189–202, 10.26–28).

8 Compare Plato's criticism of writing in the *Phaedrus* (274c–278d). Arcesilaus is described as profusely inventive, able to meet objections and fit his discourse to every occasion (DL 4.37, see also *Acad.* 2.60). He is even supposed to have said that what is most distinctive of philosophy is knowing the fitting time (*to kairon*) for each thing (DL 4.42).

9 Consequently, Sextus is mistaken in attributing to Arcesilaus the view that *epochê* is the aim (*telos*) of inquiry, if that is supposed to mean the ultimate goal (*PH* 1.232). Alternatively, we might read the term *telos* in this remark to refer only to the outcome and not the goal, in which case Sextus would be right (see Hankinson [288] for a discussion of Sextus' use of the term *telos*).

10 DL 7. 31–32, 7.2–3, *Acad.* 1.35, Eusebius, *Praep. evang.* 14.5.11–12, 14.6.7. Themistius remarks (*SVF* 1.9) that Zeno was lured to the painted colonnade (*stoa poikilê*) at Athens and presumably to philosophy by reading an account of Socrates' defense speech.

11 Dillon [100], pp. 235–7 suggests that Arcesilaus was driven to his sceptical interpretation by the success of Zeno's new Stoicism, understood as an improved Platonism. It seems more likely, however, that Arcesilaus first found his sceptical interpretation of Plato's dialogues and then set his sights on the dogmatic claims of competing schools. See Long [184].

12 For a different perspective on the issues in this section and section V, see Katja Vogt, Chapter 8 "Scepticism and Action."

13 See Inwood [107], pp. 42–102 and Brennan [98], pp. 51–110.

14 This translation requires a slight emendation in the manuscripts, see Bett [42], p. 34.

15 Cato invokes Socrates as an example of this sort of corrupting influence (Plutarch, *Life of Cato the Elder*, pp. 22–23). Numenius retails an

uncharitable view of Carneades' character (*Praep. Ev.* 14.7). It is clear that Carneades was regarded by some as a sophist (Philostratus, *Lives of the Sophists*, p. 486).

16 See Annas [172], Algra [168].

17 Following Couissin [179], the majority of recent scholars have taken the dialectical view: Striker [190], Bett [174], [175], Allen [169], [170], Brittain [195]. Görler [83] is a notable exception. See also Obdrzalek [186] who argues that Carneades' theory is fallibilist, but his attitude towards it is not determinable from the evidence we have.

18 The distinction remains controversial, but see Frede [278] for one particularly influential view.

19 See Bett [175], 10 and Striker [190], p. 78.

20 For more on this disagreement in the interpretation of Carneades, see Carlos Lévy, Chapter 4 "The Sceptical Academy: Decline and Afterlife."

21 See also *Inv.* 2.9–10, *ND* 1.12, *Tusc.* 1.8, 2.9, 5.11, *Off.* 2.7, 3.20, *Div.* 2.150. In each of the passages Cicero uses his Latin terms *probabile* and *veri simile* for Carneades' *pithanon* to indicate the quality of a *belief* that has been tested dialectically, found to be more convincing, and accepted as probably true. Although Brittain [195], p. 200 n. 45 acknowledges that Cicero generally characterizes Academic philosophy as a modest fallibilism, he does not consider how odd it is for Cicero to espouse an utterly incompatible account in the *Academica*. See Görler [201] for defense of the view that Cicero's allegiance remained unchanged throughout his life.

22 *ND* 1.11, *Tusc.* 2.4, *Div.* 2.1, *Off.* 2.8.

23 For a more detailed defense of this interpretation see Thorsrud [193].

4   The sceptical Academy: decline and afterlife

It is always difficult to determine when an institution begins a process of decline, and philosophical institutions are no exception to this rule. What one can say, in the case of the Academy, is that the exceptionally long and brilliant scholarchate of Carneades – he was head of the school for several decades before leaving voluntarily in 137 BCE – marked the high point of the sceptical Academy, while at the same time revealing the fault-lines that would lead to its division, and then to its disappearance. There are several reasons for this two-sided legacy.

(a) Like his predecessor Arcesilaus, Carneades had not himself written any philosophical work. Oral teaching lends itself more than any other to contradictory interpretations. Carneades had a disciple, Zeno of Alexandria, who took notes during his courses, notes in which the master could at no time recognize his own thinking.[1] One may imagine that what was true for Zeno (in some sense Carneades' secretary) was all the more so for his other students, whose divergent notes must have given rise to disputes. It is not impossible that Carneades himself had incited a certain rivalry among his followers, like that which Cicero reports in *Orator* 51: he used to say that Clitomachus said the same things as him, but that Charmadas said them *in the same way* as he did.

(b) To the uncertainties inherent in oral teaching was added the fact that Carneades, as a good sceptic, saw to it that his thought could not be elevated into doctrine. His successor Clitomachus, despite having written a large number of books on his teaching (*Acad.* 2.16), declared, if one is to believe Cicero, that he had never been able to understand what his master had meant (*Acad.* 2.139). If Carneades took care to guard against the charge of negative dogmatism, asserting (*Acad.* 2.28) that the proposition "Nothing can be perceived with certainty" in no way constituted a dogma, his teaching nonetheless contained a structural ambiguity on which his followers would conflict. In his project of refuting Stoicism, he was led to put forward propositions such as "the sage will give his assent"; it was open to one to ask whether he was defending this solely to contradict the Stoics, or whether he was approving it himself, which would appear to be in conflict with the universal suspension of assent which was the Academy's mark of originality. The status of his utterances thus remained problematic, even for those who were close to him.

I THE SUCCESSORS OF CARNEADES

From here two main points of view would stand in opposition, one represented by Clitomachus, the other by Metrodorus and Philo of Larissa.

Clitomachus, of Carthaginian origin (his real name was Hasdrubal) was a faithful disciple through and through. Cicero describes him as shrewd and careful, staying at Carneades' side until his old age. This faithfulness, of which there can be no doubt, was nevertheless accompanied by an important decision that actually marked a break in the oral tradition begun by Arcesilaus and revived by Carneades. Contrary to this oral tradition which distinguished the New Academy from the Old, Clitomachus, who was scholarch from 127 to 110 BCE, wrote more than four hundred books developing his master's teaching.[2] He was not, like Zeno of Alexandria, a simple secretary, but a genuine author, who did not hesitate to publish his writings far from the milieu of the Athenian schools, as is shown by his dedication of works to the Roman satiric poet Lucilius and to L. Marcus Censorinus, consul in 149 BCE. He therefore gave priority to the genre of the written commentary, which was to achieve notable success in Middle Platonism and Neoplatonism. There were two ways of being faithful to Carneades: either by continuing, like him, the oral practice of universal refutation, or by laying out and justifying what Carneades had said. All the evidence suggests that Clitomachus inclined especially to the second. Thanks to Cicero, we have, in essence, several extracts that allow us to imagine what the contents of these books might have been. He put himself in the position of admiring disciple of a master considered as superhuman, just like Lucretius later did towards Epicurus.[3] He

claimed that in removing from the mind assent – comparable, according to him, to a savage beast – Carneades had accomplished a task akin
to that of Hercules, clearly an anti-Stoic metaphor, since this was the
heroic figure preferred by the Cynics and the Stoics. This symbolic
heroizing of Carneades, on Clitomachus' part, was in keeping with
something rather unusual in sceptical thinking, the defining of a sort
of orthodoxy, based on putting together two propositions:

(1)   the principles of Carneades' thought could not be known; and
(2)   Carneades made no exception to the rule of suspension of
      assent.

In this perilous enterprise – namely, exposition of the thought of
someone whom he declared he had never been sure he understood
perfectly – Clitomachus stressed the following points.

(a) In the work in four books that he devoted to suspension of
judgement (*Acad.* 2.98–99) he developed the Carneadean system of
differentiation among representations, based on two distinctions:
(i) representations that can be the object of a sure perception versus
those that cannot, and (ii) "probable" representations, that is, those
giving the feeling of corresponding to a real object, versus those not
giving this feeling. The goal of these distinctions was to show that the
Academy took account of the differentiated character of the realm of
phantasiai and used this as a basis for constructing their theory of
action. In reasoning like this, Clitomachus was responding to the
objection concerning the impossibility of action which was addressed
to the sceptics by the dogmatists, and especially the Stoics.[4]

(b) Carneades, according to him, had never maintained dogmatically that the sage would give his assent to an opinion.[5] In his eyes,
it was simply a proposition of dialectical force, which should only
be understood in the context of a refutation of Stoicism. Another
passage of Cicero, unfortunately very corrupt (*Acad.* 2.104), seems
to go in the same direction, since it says that the sage never gives his
assent, but that this does not prevent him from following probability
when it is present and from refusing to follow what is not probable.

This sceptical system, as we can fairly call it, set out by someone
who had been Carneades' closest companion and who had succeeded
him as head of the school, could have assured the permanence of the
sceptical Academy. In fact, it contributed to its decline, because of
the dispute it would arouse on the part of Carneades' other followers.

The debate is known to us through only a small number of testimonies, and it has given rise to disparate interpretations. It is nevertheless essential to try to understand it. If we are relatively well informed as regards Clitomachus, we are markedly less so with respect to those who did not share his interpretation of Carneades' thought. Some space is required to present them.

Metrodorus of Stratonicea is undoubtedly the one whose biography is least known. We know from the *Index Academicorum* and from Diogenes Laertius that he had been an Epicurean before becoming Carneades' student.[6] According to Cicero, he was considered to have been well acquainted with him, but the *Index* goes much further, stating that he judged himself the only one to have known the master's thinking.[7] If one accepts this information, that means that Metrodorus was a loner who had never tried to associate with any other disciple of Carneades to defend his point of view. This is consistent with a passage of Cicero's *De Oratore*,[8] in which the orator Crassus reports that at the time of his trip to Athens, in 100 BCE, the school was run by Charmadas, Clitomachus, and Aeschines. This text poses rather important problems about the history of the institution, but it seems to confirm Metrodorus' marginality.

Of Charmadas, we know that he studied for seven years in Athens under Carneades, and then left for Asia, before returning to Athens and creating his own school in the Ptolemaeum.[9] Endowed with a prodigious memory, very interested in problems of oratory, and himself oratorically gifted, he made Crassus work on the *Gorgias*.[10] If one tries now to define his philosophical position, the elements that one can hold on to are the following.

While he was Carneades' student, he did not display any originality since, as we have said, the master viewed him as being the one who, on the principles, but also in form, conformed the best to his teaching. The orator Antony says of him that he refuted everyone,[11] which confirms that he stuck to practising the type of dialectic that had been introduced by Arcesilaus and consolidated by Carneades. The fact that he claimed for philosophers a sort of exclusive right to eloquence in no way proves that he strayed from the orthodoxy defined by Clitomachus, since Sextus mentions the two philosophers together as resolute opponents of rhetoric.[12] In other words, nothing in the *Index Academicorum* nor in Cicero allows us to think that Charmadas' position was different from that of Clitomachus.

It is nevertheless true that, again in Sextus, in a text that amounts to a retrospective systematization of the history of the Academy,[13] there is the matter of the "fourth Academy," that of Philo and Charmadas, which would have succeeded Carneades' and Clitomachus' New Academy. Now, Sextus implicitly links this association with the publication of Philo of Larissa's Roman books, which, as we shall see, were produced in 88–87 CE. There are two ways of resolving this contradiction: either Sextus was mistaken, or Charmadas had, at a relatively late period in his life, advanced novel theses endorsing Philo's innovations. It is impossible to choose between these explanations. But what can be said in favor of the first is that the testimony of Cicero – who has some authority, having himself been a student of Philo of Larissa – affords no support to the second.

Of Philo of Larissa's biography we shall mention only the part that is relevant to the Academy's process of transformation. Born in Larissa, in Thessaly, around 159/8, he studied philosophy first in his native city, under the direction of Callicles, a former student of Carneades, before making his way to Athens in 134/3, where he studied under Clitomachus for fourteen years; at Clitomachus' death he was elected scholarch. In this career, which included associations with other teachers, there are two elements that no one has doubted[14]:

(a) Philo was initially an ardent defender of the sceptical system elaborated by Clitomachus. Numenius even says that he was a particularly fierce opponent of Stoicism.[15]

(b) At the time of the war against Mithradates, Philo left Athens, along with the Athenian aristocracy, to take refuge in Rome, where he undoubtedly already had some friends, since Plutarch says that he was among Clitomachus' companions, "The one the Romans liked best for his discourse and his manner."[16] Of all the Romans who followed his teaching at Rome, Cicero is clearly the best known. It is at Rome that Philo published, without doubt in 87, the books which caused a scandal, as much among his own friends as among his enemies.

At this point two closely connected questions arise:

(1) Had Philo, while still at Athens, already begun to renounce the scepticism elaborated by Clitomachus?

(2) What were the contents of the Roman books?

As far as the first question is concerned, there is absolutely no ancient testimony referring to any evolution by Philo before his departure for Rome. Moreover, the beginning of the second book of Cicero's *Academica* seems to run counter to this idea. When Antiochus, who had become Philo's main opponent within the Platonic tradition, received these Roman books at Alexandria, where he was located with the Roman general Lucullus, he was very angry at them, probably because in distancing himself from scepticism, Philo could compete on the terrain (which was his own) of a more dogmatic Platonism. But the more interesting point is that Antiochus, when he received the books, was accompanied by Heraclitus of Tyre, who was still faithful to the sceptical Academy, and had, as Cicero tells us (*Acad.* 2.11), listened to Clitomachus and Philo for a number of years. Antiochus begged Heraclitus to tell him if he had ever heard Philo or any other Academic holding similar views – which Heraclitus denied. If Philo had already begun his evolution at Athens, adopting even Metrodorus' position (which the latter claimed as an interpretation defended by himself alone), Heraclitus, as a faithful follower of Clitomachus, would probably not have continued to follow his teaching, and in any case, would not have displayed at Alexandria anything like the same surprise as Antiochus.

The evidence associating Philo with Metrodorus has allowed of being interpreted as a proof of the existence of a first, Metrodoran phase in Philo's life, which would have preceded the Roman books.[17] So we need to analyze the passages of Cicero where these two philosophers are alluded to. They entirely concern the question whether the sage will give assent to an opinion:

Acad. 2.59:   "We were hearing yesterday that Carneades sometimes went so far as to say that the sage would opine – in other words, make a mistake"; and

Acad. 2.78:   "It was nevertheless open [to the sage] to have no certain perception and yet have opinions – a thesis that is said to have been approved by Carneades. As for me, trusting more in Clitomachus than in Philo or Metrodorus, I think it was defended by him dialectically rather than approved."

The fact that philosopher A and philosopher B maintain a common thesis in their works does not necessarily mean that there was a period where A and B thought in exactly the same way. This thesis may be the meeting point of two different systems of thought, or a late, partial assimilation of one person's thought to that of another. Philo of Larissa found himself at Rome before an audience fundamentally different from the one he used to have at Athens, an audience much less interested in disputes (often technical in appearance) between rival schools than in the question what a human being can know and how he should live. This could have led him to a partial abandonment of Clitomachus' radical scepticism and a partial adoption of Metrodorus' interpretation. Numenius, a second-century Pythagorean, who was an admirer of Plato but ferociously hostile to the New Academy, said of Philo that "with the progress of time, he did not remain faithful to suspension of judgement; evidence (*enargeia*) and the agreement among impressions overturned him."[18] It is quite possible that there was a practice of *epochê* that, in the radical form given to it by Arcesilaus and Carneades, was not easy to maintain; but it is hard to see it as an accident that the break occurred when Philo had left the city in which the Academy had held its seat for several centuries.

If the total absence of any reference to a Metrodoran phase of Philo's thought preceding the Roman books makes this highly improbable, it is important to ask what these books could have contained that was so radically new.

The shortest text, that of Sextus, is very clear; it says that "for Philo, things are impossible to perceive with certainty, if one holds to the Stoic criterion, but that they can be perceived with certainty as far as the nature of things is concerned."[19] Philo's major innovation was to shift *epochê* from an absolute to a relative status. In asserting that things are in effect knowable in virtue of their own nature, he gave up the generalized suspension of judgement of Arcesilaus and Carneades, interpreting *epochê* as a weapon handy for the purpose of defeating a particular enemy, Stoicism. One can understand how such a position could have angered both the orthodox members of the New Academy, who considered absolute *epochê* as the heart of their philosophical thinking, and Antiochus of Ascalon, who had justified his dissent by declaring that Arcesilaus' and Carneades' radical doubt was in contradiction with the tradition of Plato and his immediate successors.

Certain recent interpreters have thought it possible to claim that Philo allowed that certain representations have an evident character that is a sign of their truth, yet without making of this the criterion of knowledge, as the Stoics did with their theory of the apprehensive representation.[20] This interpretation seems to me to rest on very fragile foundations. The evidence of Numenius cited above is polemical; it is much more a malicious interpretation of Philo's change of attitude than an objective account of what this change was. As for the passage most often invoked, *Acad.* 2.34, Lucullus, spokesman for Antiochus of Ascalon and hence an opponent of scepticism, here says, without once referring to Philo of Larissa nor any other precise group of sceptics, "They commit a similar error when, forced by the complaints brought against them by the truth, they wish to distinguish the evident from the perceived, and try to show that there is something evident and true that imprints itself on the soul and mind, but can be neither perceived with certainty nor understood." At bottom, this text says nothing different from what is stated in 77, a passage universally considered earlier than Philo's innovations. It is there stated that the whole debate between Arcesilaus and Zeno turned on the possibility of having true representations of which one would be absolutely sure that they are not identical with false representations. It is on this point that Antiochus mounted his critique, formulating an objection by which, Cicero says, Philo was greatly troubled[21]: when one claims that false representations are no different from true representations, that assumes that one has previously been capable of making the distinction between the two groups. On this point, Philo would really have been an innovator if he had accepted a kind of connection between truth and evidence; yet he never accepted that this was the criterion of a true representation. In affirming that reality is knowable, he opened himself up to questions about the character of this knowledge. Now, on this point his answer was basically no different from the one he had given along with Carneades: namely, that faced with certain representations, we can have the feeling of truth, but without ever being able to have the certainty of not being mistaken.

Philo's originality, then, was not in defining an alternative criterion to the Stoics' *phantasia kataleptikê*, but in asserting that *epochê*, in a restricted version, could be put in the perspective of a knowledge rooted in the very nature of things. Contrary to what has often been said, there is no indication that he renewed the doctrine of Forms[22]; but it is true that Cicero's decision to pass over in silence the contents of these books hardly makes the historian's job easy. Above all, this departure from the private conflict with the Stoics allowed him to affirm, better than his predecessors, the unity of the Academy's history, and hence openly to rejoin even those members of the Academy who had a non-sceptical interpretation of Platonism. Arcesilaus, when he gave the Academy its sceptical orientation, had taken care not to appear revolutionary, and he seems to have constructed an account legitimizing scepticism, in which Socrates and some Presocratics were included. We have no explicit testimony that Carneades continued this effort at historical justification, just as there is no text that says that these two scholarchs claimed to find themselves in Plato, despite breaking with his immediate successors. The least improbable hypothesis remains, after all, that Philo claimed that his theory of knowledge was not necessarily in conflict with earlier Academicians like Polemo and Xenocrates, to which the New Academy had never appealed before.[23] It is equally possible that he invoked Lacydes, a scholarch between Arcesilaus and Carneades, of whom current historians of the New Academy never speak, and yet who is the only one to figure in the Epicurean inscription at Oenoanda. The analysis I have made elsewhere of certain lines in the *Index Academicorum* gives a glimpse of a philosophical personality somewhat different from that of Arcesilaus and Carneades.[24] The continuum that we perceive between Arcesilaus and the Roman books of Philo is perhaps nothing but an optical illusion due to the fragmentary character of our sources.

11 TWO CONTINUATIONS OF THE ACADEMY, IN OPPOSITE DIRECTIONS

Aenesidemus

Aenesidemus, the founder of neoPyrrhonism, is a mysterious character, and in recent years has been the object of several studies, devoted in particular to what is probably the most mysterious aspect of his thought: his reference to Heraclitus' philosophy, which he conceived as the end-point to which scepticism must tend.[25] We know that it is because he was disappointed by the Academy ("especially," he said, "those now, who seem to be Stoics in conflict with Stoics"[26]) that he decided to break with this tradition and to appeal to a personality whom, if Cicero is to be believed, no one any longer remembered: Pyrrho, whom a tradition very probably arising from the New Academy presented as a moralist indifferent to everything other than the highest good. It is of little importance whether Aenesidemus officially belonged to the Academy; the essential point is that it was in opposition to the way it had developed that he devised his neoPyrrhonism. Recent studies have shown clearly that the fact that he appealed to Pyrrho does not signify any real continuity between them.[27] The mechanism of knowledge, on which there was such strong opposition between the Stoics and the New Academy, did not interest Pyrrho, for the good reason that he sought to "strip off humanity" – in other words, not to correct the errors in knowledge, but to get rid of the very project of knowing.[28] Aenesidemus, on the other hand, despite the disappointment the new Academy caused him, remained profoundly marked by its teaching. He not only transferred into his version of Pyrrhonism sceptical arguments that had become classic (the errors of the senses, the relativity of effects), but placed at the center of his reflections suspension of judgement – which was absent from the original Pyrrhonism but a fundamental concept for the New Academy. The famous Modes by which he systematized his scepticism were nothing other than organized arguments leading to suspension of judgement. Equally, he did not reject the theory of the *pithanon* ("probable") elaborated by Carneades, but (at least if he is Sextus' source in the remarks on the New Academy at *PH* 1.226 ff.) gave it a new sense, objecting that in the thought of the New Academy, the feeling of persuasion was accompanied by an inclination, whereas for him, it had to be a passive acceptance of the world of appearances. Because of a problem in the transmission of Sextus' text, we cannot know exactly what his position was in relation to Plato; according to the interpretation most often accepted today, Aenesidemus considered the founder of the Academy a stranger to the sceptical tradition.[29] However that may be, it is hard not to think of Aenesidemus' neoPyrrhonism as a partial, indirect, and unacknowledged survival of the Academy.

Middle Platonism

Middle Platonism is the period during which a dogmatic Platonism takes hold, which will end in Neoplatonism. Gradually, one stops speaking of Academics, and speaks instead of Platonists, the former term being restricted to the sceptical Academy.

Even before the death of Philo, the problem arose of what would be the philosophical beliefs of those who, while formed by the New Academy, had detached themselves from it. Cicero does not fail to report that Antiochus, who had broken with Philo, claiming to return to the dogmatism of the Old Academy, had himself been a faithful defender of scepticism, though he later became its uncompromising opponent.[30] Rightly or wrongly, Antiochus, one of the most complicated personalities in ancient philosophy, is considered one of the originators of Middle Platonism.[31] It is interesting, then, to consider what may have remained in his make-up from the teaching that he had pursued for so long. At first sight, nothing. Not only did he vigorously oppose the doctrine of *epochê*, but, as we have seen, he was opposed to Philo's evolution towards a more moderate position, preferring to continue attacking what had motivated his break-up. In Cicero's *Lucullus* (book 2 of the *Academica* in its surviving portions), the Roman general who gives his name to the dialogue appeals to Antiochus, who had followed him on his Eastern campaigns, to defend Stoicism against the New Academy's dialectic. It is this that has given rise to the image of Antiochus as a closet Stoic – an image promoted by Cicero in a context (this is often forgotten) of violent polemic against his old master, whom he accuses of being identical with the Stoics.[32] However, that Antiochus preferred Stoicism to scepticism in some debates does not necessarily mean that he genuinely adhered to Stoic doctrine. His claim that Stoicism was an attempt at correcting the thought of the Old Academy does not necessarily imply that he thought the attempt successful. The best proof of this is the vigor with which he takes on Stoic ethics in books 4 and 5 of Cicero's *De Finibus*, forcing the Stoics into a dialectical trap: either they must admit that they have brought only verbal changes to the perfect doctrine of the Old Academy and the Peripatetics, or they must recognize that they are fundamentally in agreement with the unorthodox Stoics (such as Aristo of Chios) who held that nothing besides perfect virtue had any value at all. In sum, Antiochus wanted to make the Stoics realize their inconsistency, at least in the ethical domain. Aside from the fact that, in his critical doxography of the ethical systems, he used the *divisio carneadea* (a classification devised by Carneades with plainly anti-Stoic intentions) it is notable that even the theme of the Stoics' lack of genuine innovation over the Old Academy is Carneadean. At the end of book 5 of Cicero's *Tusculan Disputations* (120), we actually find that for Carneades, the Stoics had done nothing but call "preferable" the things the Peripatetics had called "good." Antiochus, then, did not hesitate to make use of his training in the New Academy as anti-Stoic ammunition, in the service of the cause that was dear to him: the presentation and defense of an Old Academy whose doctrine he reconstructed with the inclusion of numerous later elements.

A text that currently holds a central place in debates about Middle Platonism (though it was long ignored or at least under-used, having been discovered in Egypt in 1901 and first published by Diels and Schubart in 1905) is the anonymous *Commentary on the Theaetetus*. The first problem is that of its dating, which continues to be debated. The first editors dated it, in a frankly rather intuitive manner, to 150 CE; others have argued for a much earlier date of 25 CE, but this has been challenged by several scholars.[33] I cannot undertake a detailed examination of the different arguments, the key here being to show the ways in which the New Academy's thinking survived. We shall focus on two topics: the transition from *oikeiôsis* to *homoiôsis* and the problem of the unity of the Academy.

On the first point, Carneades had tried to show dialectically that the Stoic doctrine of *oikeiôsis* – the adaptation of a human being to his nature and to society – so far from constituting the basis for ethics, as the Stoics thought, was such as to justify the worst excesses of egoism. In fact, the shift from the doctrine of *oikeiôsis* (which became a framework of ideas that went beyond Stoicism) to that of *homoiôsis*, "the assimilation to God as far as possible" (the formula that Plato used to define the highest good in the digression in the *Theaetetus*) is considered one of the surest signs of the transition from Hellenistic philosophy to Middle Platonism. Now, the Commentator, in explaining the foundations of justice, begins by criticizing the doctrine of *oikeiôsis*, showing that it is a principle not of justice but of egoism, and repeats Carneades' example (reported by Cicero in the *Republic*) of two shipwrecked people fighting over a single plank, which highlights the egoistic character of the instinct for life.[34] He concludes that the Academics have shown that neither the Stoics nor the Epicureans were able to provide a basis for the virtue of justice, and he adds: "This is why Plato does not introduce justice by deducing it from adaptation (*oikeiôsis*), but from the assimilation to God, as we shall show."[35] Plato is taken to have avoided the errors subsequently committed by the Hellenistic philosophers, and one can imagine that, in the Commentator's mind, the Academics had the mission of refuting those who had strayed down roads they would not have taken had they followed Plato's thought.

This obviously raises the problem of the type of relation he conceives between Plato and the New Academy, and this is the issue in another passage, where he says that some people have considered Plato an Academic, thinking that he espoused no doctrine – which is by no means his own opinion. In fact, he says that "with the exception of a very small number," the Academics had doctrines identical with Plato's, and thus he forcefully affirms the unity of the Academy throughout its history.[36] One wonders which philosophers are referred to by "a very small number"; this has sometimes been seen as an allusion to the entire sceptical Academy, sometimes as a reference to Carneades. It is not certain that the Commentator is referring to any precise group; he cannot deny that there was radical scepticism in the Academy's history, and he is trying to reduce its significance, mentioning in a very glancing manner some isolated individuals whom he avoids specifying. For him, the New Academy's anti-Stoic dialectic, as the shipwreck example shows, is nothing but a way for Platonists to undermine from within a doctrine built on immanence and virtually complete confidence in the senses.

The meaning of New Academic doubt in the Platonic tradition was again in question among those who took Plato as an authority in late antiquity; this is shown by the *Prolegomena to the Philosophy of Plato*, now attributed to the circle of Olympiodorus and Elias at Alexandria in the sixth century CE.[37] The Neoplatonic author of the *Prolegomena* wants to refute those who have attempted to make Plato into a sceptic and have used as arguments the frequency in his work of formulas expressing doubt, his tendency to adopt different positions on the same topics, the sceptical tone of the *Theaetetus*, or even the fact that the *Phaedo* downplays the ability of the embodied soul to achieve knowledge. This text is difficult to interpret, but is an important document for reconstructing Platonism's perception of its own history.

Philo of Alexandria (c.20 BCE–c.45 CE) is certainly one of the least well-exploited sources for the history of ancient philosophy. This is because philosophical information, in his work, is often inserted into biblical commentary, and because looking for it in a huge corpus is a lengthy and hazardous task. Still, Philo is a well-informed witness who enjoys a privileged position in the history of philosophy, since he is a contemporary both of neoPyrrhonism (we owe to him the oldest testimony on the Modes of Aenesidemus) and of Middle Platonism. His evidence is of interest because it gives us the point of view of a highly cultured man on what the New Academy meant at a time when it does not seem to have existed in an institutional sense. In addition, it is in Philo that, for the first time in surviving texts, the concepts forged by the New Academy were used for an end for which they were clearly not designed: the expression of a negative theology, which would give rise to an important current in the history of Western philosophy – fideism.[38]

The most important passage in terms of the history of philosophy occurs in *Questions and Answers on Genesis* 3.33, where, commenting on the passage in *Genesis* 16.12 in which the savagery of Ishmael is described, he writes:

He is like those who are now called Academics and Sceptics, who place no foundation under their opinions and doctrines and do not (prefer) one thing to another, for they admit those as philosophers who shoot at (the doctrines) of every school ... Therefore (Scripture) says, "Over against all his brothers he will dwell." For in truth the Academics and the Noncommittals take opposite stands in their doctrines, and oppose the various opinions which others hold.[39]

Unfortunately, we possess only the Armenian version of this text, so that there remain some linguistic uncertainties. The most interesting element from our point of view is that Philo distinguishes the Academics and the other sceptics, while also viewing them as two aspects of a single phenomenon, namely, contemporary incarnations of that sort of negative archetype in his eyes, the sophist. "Now," if one takes it literally, indicates that there were still in Alexandria, in Philo's time, representatives of New Academic scepticism coexisting with the neoPyrrhonians. This is the only evidence for a continuation of New Academic philosophers in this period.

As a believer, Philo might have thought that the philosophy of permanent doubt developed by the New Academy did not concern him. On the contrary, however, he fully adopted the concepts of the

New Academy – but to give expression to the feebleness of human judgement compared with divine omniscience. The most significant passage in this regard is where *epochê* becomes the expression of a renunciation of human reason, in what is undoubtedly the first expression of fideism (*On Flight and Finding* 136). It has to do with the allegorical commentary on the sacrifice of Isaac. At the point where the child is worried about where the lamb is for the burnt offering, Abraham responds "God will provide," and they find a ram caught by the horns in a bush. Philo explains that this animal represents *epochê*, because "The best offering is silence and suspension of judgement on the points where proofs are completely lacking," and he adds: "One can assert only this: 'God will see.' The universe is known to him, he illuminates it with a most dazzling light, namely himself. The created world can assert nothing else: thick darkness is spread over it, and in the darkness it is prudent to stay quiet." The significance of *epochê* here is no longer epistemological, but theological. Abraham literally discovers it as a gift of God, while he himself arrives at the sacrifice without it. He gives proof of *epochê* in saying "God will provide," but it is God himself who accepts these words as a substitute for the sacrifice of Isaac and who gives a visual representation of it (in Philo's allegorical interpretation) in the image of the ram entangled in a bush. In identifying suspension of judgement with the ram held fast in the bush, Philo signifies that the soul accepts the limits imposed on it by God, that it surrenders its autonomy, doubt thus being subordinated to faith. Equally, Philo is a great user of the Academic concepts of *eulogon*, "reasonable," and *pithanon*, "probable," which for him express humanity's limited possibilities in the area of knowledge as well as that of ethics.[40]

Plutarch studied at Athens under Ammonius, who figures in some of his works. His interest in the sceptical Academy is clear even in the titles of several of his works, which have unfortunately not survived.[41] For example, he wrote a book on the difference between the Academics and the Pyrrhonians (Lamprias Catalog 64) and a work dedicated to the question, central in the history of scepticism, of whether someone who suspends his assent on every occasion is condemned to inaction (Lamprias Catalog 210). No one now thinks that he was himself a true sceptic, so perfectly does he fit the image of the Middle Platonist who, while affirming the supremacy of Plato, willingly adopts a certain number of features from doctrines that he elsewhere criticizes.[42] In *Against Colotes*, Plutarch defended the New Academy against the attacks to which it had been subjected by this disciple of Epicurus. Two points have been the object of particular attention among scholars working on the New Academy: the historical justification of Arcesilaus' scepticism (1121f–1122a) and the argument that he attributes to him to refute the charge of making life impossible through *epochê*.[43] In the two anti-Stoic treatises, *On Stoic Self-Contradictions* and *On Common Conceptions*,[44] Plutarch shows how the Stoics are in conflict both with themselves and with common notions, the outcomes of experience, by which they claimed not to be cut off from the rest of humanity, despite their paradoxes. It is a matter for current scholarly debate whether his position on the problem of scepticism is the one defined by the innovations of Philo of Larissa. For this and other reasons, it seems certain that the work of Plutarch will allow a deepening of our knowledge of New Academic scepticism in the years to come.

III THE PERSISTENCE OF THE ACADEMY: THREE NON-STANDARD CASES

Favorinus

Favorinus has long been considered one of the most mysterious characters in ancient philosophy.[45] Still, the testimonies about him are relatively numerous, especially in Galen's *On the Best Teaching* and in Aulus Gellius, who shows great admiration for him, but also in Lucian and Philostratus. Born at Arles around 70 CE, he moved in his youth to Rome, where he had Dio Chrysostom as a teacher. He there engaged in polemic with Epictetus, and likewise at Athens with the Cynic Demonax, which explains why Lucian was so hostile to him. Back in Rome, he set up a school and had Aulus Gellius among his students. There is no doubt about his philosophical identity. Galen places him as close to the Academics, a point to which we shall return, and this is confirmed by the polemic of Lucian, who presents him as an "Academic eunuch"[46]; he is hostile to Stoicism, which he accuses in classic fashion of annihilating human freedom in defending their doctrine of providence and destiny, and uses Stoic vocabulary to criticize Stoicism from the inside; and he was friends with Plutarch, who was his teacher. The problem at the center of debates

about his philosophical profile is that of the connection in his thinking between neoPyrrhonism and the New Academy. A century after
Aenesidemus, the founder of neoPyrrhonism, who was profoundly
hostile to the New Academy, Favorinus seems, on the contrary, to
have wanted to reconcile these two factions. Not only was he an
ardent admirer of Pyrrho; he wrote a work in ten books laying out
in a new order the sceptical Modes that Aenesidemus had codified.
We know from Aulus Gellius that he distinguished the New
Academics and the Pyrrhonians by saying that the former practised
negative dogmatism, stating that nothing could be known with certainty, while the latter took their doubt even to this proposition.[47]
Basically, he is saying nothing different from Sextus Empiricus, but
while the latter put the emphasis on what he considered a crucial
difference, Favorinus seems, on the contrary, to have considered
this a mere detail – so that he is the first, to our knowledge, to have
thought of the sceptical tradition as more or less unified. But we still
need to understand what might have been the basis for his attachment to the New Academic tradition.

For Galen, in *On the Best Teaching*, Favorinus belongs among
the *neôteroi* or "newer" Academics (but is he talking about the
New Academy or does he mean "recent"?) which he contrasts with
the "old" ones. The latter, he says, had an oppositional discourse
leading to *epochê*, whereas these *neôteroi*, he says, adopt contradictory positions, sometimes practising radical *epochê*, sometimes
trusting in knowledge without reservations, to the point of imparting
to their students a form of learning devoid of scientific rigor. This
distinction of Galen's (and it should not be forgotten that he is speaking polemically) can be understood in two ways. One may think that
he is referring to the New Academy, distinguishing two periods
within it: one of sceptical rigor, probably that of Arcesilaus and surely
that of Carneades, and the other, that of Metrodorus and Philo, much
more lax in this respect. It is equally possible that by the "old" he
means the New Academy from Arcesilaus up to Philo (either including him or not), while the *neôteroi* are contemporary Academics,
who combine the practice of *epochê* with strongly dogmatic beliefs.
In the latter case, Galen must be identifying Favorinus with people
like Plutarch. An argument in favor of this reading could be that
Favorinus wrote an *On Plato*, of which nothing has survived, but
which there is no objection to thinking of as Middle Platonic in

character – which would make the connection with Plutarch even stronger. However, it is true that in this case, Favorinus' sympathy for Pyrrho becomes even harder to understand.

The solution perhaps lies in the fact that Favorinus saw as probabilities (*pithana*) everything that Galen accuses him of accepting as dogmas. We know that he had great sympathy for Aristotle, yet without being an Aristotelian. Galen criticizes him for contradicting himself by seeming to concede, in his *Plutarch*, that something can be known with certainty, while in his *Alcibiades* he considers it likely, on the contrary, that nothing can be known.[48] It is possible that Galen is right and that Favorinus' thinking did evolve, risking self-contradiction. But it is worth noting that about the *Plutarch* Galen writes "seems to concede" (*sunchôrein eoiken*), not "affirms," which sounds much more like an interpretation than a statement of fact. If Favorinus sided with Philo's innovations, how could he be sympathetic to neoPyrrhonism, which arose largely out of a rejection of them? No satisfactory response to this problem has been devised, partly no doubt because we do not have a chronology for Favorinus' works. It is not impossible that Favorinus thought in a general way that Pyrrhonism, as Acnesidemus had reformulated it, constituted a very strong defense of *epochê*, and made a point of showing a sort of sceptical solidarity with him, while at the same time reviving the topics and disputes that had belonged to the New Academy, following the line that led from the New Academy to neoPyrrhonism.

Augustine and the Academy

Augustine's *Against the Academics*, written just after his conversion in 386, is a surprising work. One might have thought that the new convert would have devoted himself to the study of Scripture, yet it is on philosophical questions that he focuses in the dialogues of this period. We know from *Confessions* 5.25 that in 384–385, after his Manichaean period, he went through a sceptical crisis. This was surely deeper than even he realized, since, as soon as he had converted, he undertook to refute the sceptical philosophers with philosophy, in a work in which, strangely, the name of Christ is mentioned only at the end. In his Letter 1, to Hermogenian, which is more or less contemporary with this work, he develops, in connection with *Against the Academics*, a surprising meta-argument:

(a)   Paradoxically, he recognizes that he has been completely
        unable to produce a line of argument capable of bringing down
        scepticism.
(b)   Being unable, then, to defeat people of such authority, he has
        imitated them (*imitatus sum*): the Academics had hidden the
        truth because they were in the midst of dogmatists and
        materialists, and he, describing himself as in a philosophical
        desert, has sought to arouse the desire for truth.
(c)   If he had let the sceptical image of the New Academy persist,
        he would have encouraged his contemporaries to believe that
        they could not discover what Carneades himself had been
        unable to discover. The letter ends by declaring that he is
        happy to have overcome his despair of attaining the truth,
        which had kept him away from philosophy.

In the *Handbook*, written in 422, Augustine again alludes to the
composition of *Against the Academics*. It is no longer a question of
leading others to the truth, but of casting off the doubts that were
assailing *him*.[49] He recognizes that he tried to cast off scepticism
utique, by every means. Relying on St. Paul's statement "The just
man lives by faith," he declares that withholding assent is withholding faith, and this justifies one casting off scepticism *utique*, by every
means. But did not maintaining that the Academics were in reality
Platonists, who concealed the truth, run the risk of suggesting that
pagans could have been in possession of the truth? On this point,
Augustine's position became more and more radical. Right at the end
of his life, in the *Revisions* (*Retractationes*), written in 426–427, he
will criticize himself for having so elevated those philosophers who
were after all nothing but impious pagans, and regret having called his
own argument *nugae*, "trifles," since, he says, he refuted the sceptical
arguments "with the most certain reasoning."[50] We may conclude
that the question of scepticism never ceased to haunt Augustine and
that his position in regard to *Against the Academics* never stopped
evolving.
    As for the work itself, we can give only its broad outlines here. The
first two books are dominated by what Augustine considers a major
contradiction: on the one hand, the Academics despaired of achieving
the truth, and on the other, they asserted that humans could attain
wisdom. What is this wisdom, then, which is not accompanied by

knowledge? The debate on this question is both epistemological and historical in character, and Augustine's method as a participant in the dialogue is very clearly stated in the second book: first he will discuss the scepticism attributed to the Academics, then he will expound the idea of esoteric dogmatism. The discussion on the likely and the probable, corollaries of suspension of judgement, therefore occupies an important part of this book, dominated by the question "How can one follow the likely, or 'truth-like,' while claiming not to know the truth?" This question, we should point out, only makes sense in terms of Cicero's concept of *verisimile*, literally "truth-like"; it could not be posed in the same way in terms of the *eulogon*, "reasonable," that we find in the texts on Arcesilaus, nor of the *pithanon*, "probable," in those on Carneades.[51] In the end, the whole debate is misrepresented by Augustine's belief that the Academics considered it likely that attaining wisdom was impossible. His friend Alypius confronts him with this argument: even when beaten the Academic is the winner, since his defeat confirms the fact that there exists absolutely no certainty – which makes the sceptic into a veritable Proteus, unable to be captured except with divine help. To this Augustine will first try to demonstrate the contrary, that a refutation of scepticism is possible, using both dialectical arguments: the wise person cannot not know *wisdom* with certainty, and this creates a certainty that can be the basis of all the others; and ethical ones: immoralism would be inherent in generalized doubt. The dialogue might have ended there. Instead of that, apparently against all logic, he will explain that in reality the sceptics whom he has so vigorously refuted were not sceptics. The thesis of esoteric dogmatism takes the form of a sort of explanatory myth. Arcesilaus, Augustine tells us,[52] taking account of the fact that Stoicism had foisted on a great many people a system based on confidence in the senses and material reality, concealed the Academy's doctrine, as one hides treasure, hoping that it will be discovered by successors who are a little less unworthy.

Many questions might be raised, in a longer treatment, about this startling reversal. However, what is clear is that Augustine's attitude to the New Academy is highly complex, and seems to be marked by the fear of letting stand a formidable enemy of faith, whom he decided needed to be attacked by every means. It would, in any case, profoundly determine the Christian West's attitude to scepticism.

Petrus Valentia and his Academica[53]

Though defunct as an institution, the New Academy continued to live in Western thought, in thinkers as eminent as John of Salisbury, Bayle or Hume, who, each in his own way, expressed some allegiance to the doctrine of suspension of judgement and probability. This many-sided reception cannot be examined here[54]; I will limit myself to a few words on a much less well-known thinker, Petrus Valentia, who in late-sixteenth-century Spain wrote an *Academica* that is of great interest. This work raises the question whether Petrus Valentia was a historian of the New Academy,[55] or an Academic, that is, someone who, though separated by many centuries, claimed to think and act according to the doctrine developed by Arcesilaus and Carneades. Petrus Valentia, who describes himself as a *grammaticus*, does not deny the pedagogical purpose of the work; it was designed to explain Cicero's *Academica* to D. Garcia de Figueroa, a gentleman at the court of Philip III, who was eager to understand this difficult text. He certainly assumes a pose of scholarly neutrality; but to do this, he uses the formula that Cicero himself uses to define his New Academic attitude: "we do not impose our judgement" – which shows how fluid the limit is between rigorous exposition of the New Academic doctrine and adherence to it. For him, there is no basic difference between Carneades and Philo of Larissa, two philosophers who never tried to deny the existence of reality and who protected themselves from error, thanks to the theory of the probable. By discreet touches, Petrus Valentia shows that it is in this direction that his sympathies lie. Certainly, at the end of his book, he adds (like many other Renaissance thinkers) a fideist declaration, condemning all Greek philosophers for not having understood that true wisdom is a gift from God; but the low estimation he displays for the Augustine of *Against the Academics* proves that this fideism, if it was sincere, fitted without difficulty, in his mind, with New Academic probabilism.

IV CONCLUSION

In closing, we can specify the link that exists between two apparently contradictory aspects: the disappearance of the Academy as an institution and its survival in multiple forms. In making the intellectually audacious decision, whatever its historical and personal motivations may have been, to leave Athens and the Academy, Philo of Larissa bequeathed this multifaceted tradition to a world that was not his own. Cicero understood this well and, while deploring the fact that Philo had no successor as scholarch, took over the succession in his own way. The demise of the institution allowed the autonomous development of two modes of thought that were undoubtedly already present in Philo's Roman books. Fidelity to Plato became Middle Platonism; mitigated scepticism was radicalized into neoPyrrhonism. Aspects of the New Academy survived in both of them, to the considerable enrichment of Western thought.

NOTES

Translated into English by Richard Bett.

1   See *Index Academicorum* 22.37.
2   DL 4.67.
3   *Acad.* 2.108. For other citations of Clitomachus, see *Acad* 2.31, 78, 98–99, 102–3, 137–39.
4   For more on this, see Katja Vogt, Chapter 8 "Scepticism and Action."
5   *Acad.* 2.78.
6   *Index Academicorum* 24.9–16, DL 10.9.
7   *Acad* 2.16, *Ind. Ac.* 26.4–11.
8   *De oratore* 1.45. See Görler [83], p. 907.
9   On Charmadas, see Görler [83], pp. 906–8; Brittain [195], pp. 312–13. The core of our information is in *Ind. Ac.* 31.35–32.10.
10 *De oratore* 1.47.
11 *De oratore* 1.84.
12 *M* 2.20.
13 *PH* 1.220.
14 For Philo of Larissa's biography, see Brittain [195], pp. 38–72.
15 Fragment 28 Des Places.
16 *Cicero* 3.1.
17 See especially Görler [83], pp. 920–21; Brittain [195], pp. 73–128.
18 Fragment 28 Des Places. On the interpretation of this fragment, see Lévy [204], p. 292.
19 *PH* 1.235.
20 See Glucker [198], pp. 77–78; Brittain [195], p. 107.
21 *Acad.* 2.111.
22 For an account of the range of interpretations that have been given of Philo's thought, see Glucker [198], pp. 70–75; Brittain [195], pp. 26–37.

Tarrant [206] has seen in Philo the beginning of Middle Platonism. His book, though very stimulating, is problematic in its methodology: the texts on which he relies are few in number and subject to contradictory interpretation.

23 On historical legitimation, see Brittain [195], pp. 169–219.

24 Diogenes of Oenoanda 5.3.14. See Lévy [167].

25 See in particular Decleva Caizzi [226]; Mansfeld [229]; Bett [143], pp. 198–232; Polito [231]; Pérez-Jean [230]; and R. J. Hankinson, Chapter 5 "Aenesidemus and the Rebirth of Pyrrhonism."

26 Photius, *Bibliotheca* 169b39.

27 Conche [154]; Bett [143], pp. 14–62.

28 For a partially different view of Pyrrho, see Svavar Svavarsson, Chapter 2 "Pyrrho and Early Pyrrhonism."

29 See Emidio Spinelli's contribution to Sihvola [86], esp. pp. 38–40, and the reservations of Lévy [224], pp. 311–13.

30 *Acad.* 2.4, and especially the violent invective at 69.

31 Glucker [198] remains an indispensable reference for all institutional and historical matters. See also Görler [83], pp. 938–80. As far as his philosophical profile is concerned, the forthcoming proceedings of the 2007 Cambridge colloquium will shed new light. On Antiochus' relation to Middle Platonism, see Dillon [99], pp. 52–106.

32 *Acad.* 2.132.

33 See Tarrant [206], pp. 66–68; Bastianini and Sedley [15], pp. 254–56; Opsomer [215], pp. 34–36; Brittain [195], pp. 249–54; Bonazzi [96].

34 Cicero, *Rep.* 3.26, *Comm. Tht.* 6.20–25.

35 *Comm. Tht.* 7.14–20.

36 *Comm. Tht.* 54.38–55.10.

37 On the *Prolegomena* see the introduction to Westerink [29] and Bonazzi [95], pp. 57–95.

38 On fideism see Penelhum [432]. For Philo's attitude to the Academy, see Lévy [213].

39 I use Ralph Marcus' translation (Marcus [59]).

40 For more on the Academics' use of these concepts, see Harald Thorsrud, Chapter 3 "Arcesilaus and Carneades" and Katja Vogt, Chapter 8 "Scepticism and Action."

41 The most complete treatment of Plutarch's attitude towards the Academy is Glucker [198], pp. 257–80. See also De Lacy [208], 79–85; Donini [209]; Bonazzi [95], pp. 216–40.

42 On Plutarch's relation to Stoicism, see Babut [207].

43 On this question see the divergent interpretations of Lévy [111] and Ioppolo [181]; see also Harald Thorsrud, Chapter 3 "Arcesilaus and Carneades."

44 See the excellent editions with commentary by Casevitz and Babut [16], [18], and Boys-Stones [17].
45 See Glucker [198], pp. 280–95 and *passim*; Barigazzi [9]; Ioppolo [211].
46 *Eunuch* 7.
47 *Attic Nights* 11.5.8.
48 *On the Best Teaching* I.41.6–12K.
49 *Handbook* 7.20.
50 *Revisions* 1.1.4.
51 On this point see Lévy [205], Glucker [200].
52 *Against the Academics* 3.17.38.
53 See Lévy [214].
54 On this topic (up to Descartes, and including John of Salisbury), see Luciano Floridi, Chapter 14 "The Rediscovery and Posthumous Influence of Scepticism."
55 As suggested by Popkin [353], p. 37; see also Schmitt [405], p. 75.

5 Aenesidemus and the rebirth of Pyrrhonism

I PRELIMINARIES

Some time early in the first century, Philo and Antiochus, the two leading philosophers of the Athenian Academy, had a serious philosophical falling out. Philo advocated an externalist epistemology, holding that it was reasonable to suppose that things could be known, even though they could not, individually, be known to be known; Antiochus responded that the only way one could know that one knew anything was by knowing of some particular thing that one knew it; and thus (according to Cicero: *Acad.* 2.44, 111) strayed perilously close to Stoic dogmatism.[1] Neither option appealed to their colleague[2] Aenesidemus:

The Academics, particularly those of today, sometimes adopt Stoic doctrines, and are, in truth, really Stoics quarrelling with Stoics. And they are dogmatic about many things; for they introduce virtue and vice, and posit good and bad, truth and falsity, persuasive and unpersuasive, existent and non-existent; and they firmly distinguish many other things as well; and, he [sc. Aenesidemus] says, it is only in regard to the cataleptic impression that they differ from them [sc. the Stoics]. (**1**: Photius, *Bibl.* 170a14–22 = 71C(9) LS)

Our knowledge of Aenesidemus is sadly restricted. For his views, we are indebted principally to a *précis* of his *Pyrrhonian Discourses* from Photius of Byzantium's library catalogue (from which **1** above is excerpted). As for direct references, Sextus refers to him by name some fifteen times (but some of these are problematic: see below, section IV), Diogenes a few times more; and that's about it.

On the other hand, he has often been supposed to be the source for, and inspiration behind, large tracts of Sextus' own work; and obviously, depending upon how just that assessment is, we might in fact possess a great deal more of Aenesidemus' intellectual remains than appears at first sight. Yet such speculations are inherently fragile; and for the purposes of this chapter I shall adopt a conservative strategy, ascribing to him only those particular ideas for which there is positive evidence in favor of the attribution. At all events, the *Pyrrhonian Discourses* seem to have been his major work[3]; and they covered a very broad range of topics, comparable to those dealt with by Sextus himself.

II THE GENERAL STRUCTURE OF AENESIDEMEAN SCEPTICISM

Aenesidemus began his *Pyrrhonian Discourses* by distinguishing Academic from Pyrrhonian sceptics, claiming that the former dogmatize, "confidently positing some things, unambiguously denying others" (*Bibl.* 169b36–40 = 71C(5) LS), a view partially echoed by Sextus, who contends that while the Academics make negative dogmatic claims, Pyrrhonists suspend judgement about everything (*PH* 1.1–2).[4] But Pyrrho wrote nothing; and he probably functioned for Aenesidemus (as he was to do for Sextus: *PH* 1.7), primarily as a model of a way of life rather than as a source of sceptical argument. But for all that, Aenesidemus attributed certain distinctive attitudes to him:

Aenesidemus says in the first of his *Pyrrhonian Discourses* that Pyrrho "determines nothing dogmatically (*ouden orizein dogmatikôs*) on account of disagreement (*antilogia*), but follows the appearances (*ta phainomena*)." He says the same things too in his *Against Wisdom* and *On Inquiry*... So the criterion, according to the skeptics, is the appearance, as Aenesidemus explicitly says. (2: DL 9.106 = 71A(1f)–(2) LS)

The "criterion" in question here is the practical criterion, not any "criterion of truth" (on the distinction, see Sextus, *PH* 2.314; *M* 7.29–30)[5]; and the background to the position presented is the perennial objection that scepticism renders life impossible: life requires action, and action presupposes belief, yet the sceptic supposedly eschews all belief.[6] The "disagreement" is either that between different sensory presentations (as a result of which, by way of a familiar sceptical move, we are rendered unable to say how things really are), or the doctrinal disputes among philosophers, or (more probably) both[7]; and, while Aenesidemus is here presented as reporting Pyrrho's position, he no doubt endorsed it. Diogenes also reports:

Pyrrhonian discourse is a sort of declaration of what appears (*phainomena*), or of things conceived (*nooumena*) in any way, on the basis of which they are all brought into confrontation with one another, and when compared are found to exhibit much disparity and confusion. This is what Aenesidemus says in the *Outline* to his *Pyrrhonics*. (3: DL 9.78 = 71B LS)

But one may still act on the basis of these appearances, and so life is not rendered impossible:

Aenesidemus says that while he [i.e. Pyrrho] philosophized in accordance with the principle of suspension of judgment (*epochê*), he did not however perform each action with any lack of foresight. (4: DL 9.62 = 1A(4) LS)

Yet at the same time the Pyrrhonist refuses to make any claims as to truth, and does so by collecting cases where the evidence (considered as offering a guide to how things really are) achieves an equal balance (*isostheneia*) between opposing and incompatible claims; and the result, explicitly ascribed to Aenesidemus, is *epochê*, the suspension of judgement as to how things really stand, upon which tranquility, *ataraxia*, supervenes (DL 9.107 = 71A(3) LS). This seems unequivocal enough, and perfectly compatible with the scepticism of Sextus.

But this picture is complicated by the testimony of Photius. No Pyrrhonist, according to Aenesidemus:

has said that everything is either inapprehensible or that it is apprehensible, but rather that they are (A) no more of this sort than that, or that they are (B) sometimes this way and sometimes not, or that they are (C) such for one person, not such for another and totally non-existent for a third. Nor do they say that all things in general, or some of them, are either accessible or not accessible to us, but rather that they are (A) no more accessible than inaccessible, or (B) sometimes accessible and sometimes not, or (C) accessible to some but not others. Furthermore, they do not say that anything is either true or false, plausible or implausible,[8] existent or non-existent; but rather the same thing is, in sum, (A) no more true than false, plausible than implausible, existent than non-existent, or (B) sometimes so and sometimes not so, or (C) so to someone and not so to someone else. For the Pyrrhonian determines nothing at all, not even this, namely that he determines nothing ("it is because," he says, "we have no way to express the thought that we put it like this"). (5: Photius, *Bibl.* 169b40–170a14 = 71C(6)–(8) LS)

The last parenthesis shows that Photius follows Aenesidemus very closely here; and it shows that he anticipated the characteristically Sextan maneuver of having "sceptical slogans" such as "I determine nothing" apply to themselves (*PH* 1.197; cf. 1.206, 2.188; *M* 8.480);[9] thus he was sensitive to the difficulties that threaten to undermine any sceptical discourse: how can a sceptic even express his own scepticism?

The negative component of **5** above, concerning what a sceptic cannot say, is also unimpeachably Pyrrhonian (in the sense of Sextus' Pyrrhonism). But difficulties arise with Aenesidemus' three types of sceptically-acceptable locution. Rather than expressly and unqualifiedly asserting or denying, the sceptic will adopt either all or some of the expression-types labelled "(A)," "(B)," and "(C)." A-type expressions are relatively unproblematic: although the formula "no more (*ou mallon*)" is not proprietorially sceptical (it was employed by Democritus Plato, and probably Pyrrho as well: DL 9.61; Eusebius, *Praep.evang.* 14.18.4; Aulus Gellius, *Attic Nights* 11.5.3), it figures as the first of the sceptical slogans discussed by Sextus, at *PH* 1.188–91, where Sextus emphasizes that for the sceptic the expression has no dogmatic significance, but rather simply "makes clear an affection (*pathos*) of ours: because of the equipollence (*isostheneia*) of the objects, we end in equilibrium" (190; cf. 213). But (B) and (C) sit less comfortably with genuine scepticism.[10] To say that something is sometimes F (or not-F), or F for someone, is apparently to make a claim about it (albeit a singular and not a universal one); and no decent sceptic should do that, as Aenesidemus himself implies when castigating the Academics for their dogmatism (**1** above).[11] Indeed:

The whole point of the book is to establish that nothing is firmly established, either by the senses or by reason; and so neither the Pyrrhonists nor any of the others know the truth in things; but while those who philosophize in other ways are ignorant both of other things ... and of this very fact, namely that they apprehend none of the things of which they think they have gained apprehension (*katalêpsis*). But he who philosophizes after the fashion of Pyrrho is happy both in regard to the other things and is wise in that he knows this above all, namely that nothing is firmly apprehended by him. And as for what he does know, he is smart enough to assent no more to the affirmation of such things than to their negation. (**6**: *Bibl.* 169b19–30 = 71C(1)–(3) LS)

The last sentence employs the *ou mallon* formula: but intriguingly it is applied to Aenesidemus' own second-order claims about knowledge, and as such exhibits the general fact that ancient scepticism in general recognized no important distinction between first- and second-order statements (or rather that they were not prepared to allow that one might make claims at the second order of a sort that sceptical propriety ruled out at the first). It is scepticism all the way down; which is why Sextus insists that the sceptical formulae apply to themselves in the manner of Metrodorus (see note 9).

Such a procedure, though, seems to involve saying something ("no one apprehends anything") and then taking it back, or at least assenting neither to its affirmation nor to its negation, as soon as one examines the claim itself. And anti-sceptics, from the earliest times, have not been slow to seize on such apparent incoherences. Aristocles says of Aenesidemus that:

One would have liked to ask him whether he was stating in full knowledge that this was the condition of things, or without knowledge. For if he did not know, why should we believe him? But if he did know, he was vastly silly for declaring at the same time that all things are uncertain, but yet that he knew as much. (7: Aristocles, in Eusebius *Prep. evang.* 14.18.12)

One reasonable riposte is to deny that the sceptic makes any claims *in propria persona*: all apparent assertions are simply moves in the dialectical game, positions that the opposition espouses (or at any rate ought according to their own canons to espouse), but about which the sceptic himself properly suspends judgement. Problems arise here too: can the sceptic enunciate such a strategy to himself or others undogmatically? If not, what (if anything) is he doing? Alternatively, one may insist that the sceptic is not really asserting anything at all, at any rate if (dogmatic) assertion involves making unequivocal claims as to the way things *really* are. Thus, Sextus will sometimes say that sceptical utterances are merely announcements (*appangeliai*) of their immediate affections, and hence do not qualify as assertions at all (*PH* 1.197, 200, 203).

In the face of these difficulties, and in response to certain clues to be found in Photius and elsewhere (notably in Sextus' presentation of ethical scepticism in *M* 11), Paul Woodruff and Richard Bett have argued that Aenesidemean scepticism should be distinguished from the mature Pyrrhonism to be found (for the most part) in Sextus.[12] Crucially, according to Woodruff, Aenesidemus' scepticism is *refutational*, and countenances the drawing of certain negative conclusions, paradigmatically of the form "*x* is not by nature *F*," construed as the denial of a general claim regarding *x*'s invariant nature (and not a claim about what *x* is of a nature *not* to be). The evidence for this would be precisely that it was *F* at some times but not others, to some people but not to others. This is an attractive suggestion, which dovetails neatly with the moderate reading of Sextus' scepticism, according to which the only real targets of the sceptic's fire are *dogmata* in the sense of "assent to one of the non-evident objects of scientific inquiry" (*PH* 1.13; cf. 1.193, 197).[13] But there may be no straightforward answer to the question of the scope of Sextan scepticism, and where there is, the boundary is to be drawn according to attitude rather than subject matter.[14]

However that may be, the principle

(P) if *x* is *F* by nature then *x* is *F* unrestrictedly,[15]

which may lie behind Aenesidemus' linguistic strictures in **5** above, is one that plays a prominent role in sceptical argument. Moreover, "unrestrictedly" is often interpreted as meaning (or entailing) "at all times," "in all conditions," "to all observers," and the like; and B- and C-type expressions (**5** above) will have a role in establishing (at least for the sake of argument) that there is no reason to think that anything is *F* by nature. Sextus repeatedly invokes such considerations, arguing, for example, that nothing is good by nature, since not everyone agrees on what is good, and alleged goods do not affect everyone in the same way, as fire invariably burns (*PH* 3.179–82; cf. *M* 11.69–89; for the general principle, see *PH* 3.190, 196, 220, 222, 226; *M* 8.37). Yet elsewhere, Sextus contends that fire does not in fact burn "from its own nature," since it does not do so invariably: there some things which it cannot consume (*M* 9.241–43; cf. *M* 8.197–99). The sceptic is quite happy to make one "claim" in one context (or relative to a particular comparison-class) and a quite different, indeed apparently contradictory, one elsewhere. This raises important issues regarding the nature (and consistency) of the sceptical method which I cannot pursue (although they obviously favor a "dialectical" reading of it).[16] Moreover, the conclusion that we cannot say, and hence are forced to suspend judgement as to, how things are as to their natures is equally common, indeed it figures regularly as the conclusion of Ten Modes attributed to Aenesidemus,[17] at any rate in Sextus' presentation (e.g. at *PH* 1.59, 78, 93, 123, 128, 134, 140, 163; and cf. 112, 144), and this too relies on (P).

So did Aenesidemus allow the drawing of unqualified negative conclusions?[18] In his brief summary of the remainder of *Pyrrhonian*

Discourses, Photius presents him as "dealing with truths,[19] causes, affections, motions, generations, destructions and their opposites, and showing by rigorous argument, or so he thinks, the problematic (*aporon*) and ungraspable (*akatalêpton*) in them" (Book 2: *Bibl.* 170b5–8 = 72L(1) LS). Similarly in Book 3 he deals with "thought[20] and perception and their particular species, and working carefully through a similar set of contradictory considerations, he makes them too inaccessible (*anephikton*) and ungraspable" (170b9–12 = 72L(2) LS). Equally the fourth book apparently claimed that "signs ... do not exist, and those who think they do are deceived by an empty enthusiasm," and similarly with "the standard difficulties concerning nature as a whole, the cosmos, and the gods, he says that none of them come within our grasp" (170b12–17 = 72L(3) LS). Turning to ethics, "the sixth book subjects good and bad, as well as chooseable and avoidable, and preferred and dispreferred,[21] to the same futile quibbling, excluding these things too ... from our grasp and knowledge" (170b22–6 = 72L (5) LS), while Book 8 "takes issue with the end, allowing that neither happiness, pleasure, wisdom, nor any other end conceived of by the philosophical schools exists, saying that the end which they all celebrate is wholly non-existent" (170b31–5 = 72L(7) LS).

So Photius portrays Aenesidemus as saying that some things are ungraspable, inaccessible, and non-existent, in apparent contradiction with the strictures of 5 above; moreover he presents these as *conclusions* of his various arguments. He plainly thought (like Aristocles) that Aenesidemus was simply inconsistent; and he concludes with a harshly dismissive assessment of the value of Aenesidemus' work: it is "emptiness and a lot of nonsense," readily refuted by Plato and a host of others, useless except possibly as providing argumentative exercises for those who are sensible enough not to be taken in by it (*Bibl.* 170b36–171a4). But there is no reason to accept Photius' questionable judgement: it is as easy to misunderstand the structure of scepticism as it is difficult to express it. All Pyrrhonism involves reams of negative argument (Books 2 and 3 of *PH* largely consist of it, as do the surviving parts of the longer treatise which we have as *M* 7–11); but its point is not to convince the reader of its conclusions, but simply to establish one part of the sceptical antithesis. And the fact that the negative portions are often much longer than their positive counterparts is to be accounted for by the demands of *isostheneia*. In discussing motion at *PH* 3.64–81, Sextus restricts his arguments in favor to one paragraph (3.66), but that is precisely because most people won't need much convincing that it exists (the same is true of the more detailed treatment of *M* 10.37–168). Indeed, the dialectical structure can be more complex still: in the course of considering the negative position, Sextus will both present and criticize the arguments, and will point out in grinding detail the internal disagreements among its partisans. There can be disagreement, and equipollence, at more than one level.[22]

So Aenesidemus anticipates Sextan Pyrrhonism in arguing on both sides of an issue to establish such equipollent disagreement, as a means to achieving *epochê*, which you cannot manage if you come out in favor of one side, even if it is the negative one. And while first-order *epochê* is compatible with second-order negative dogmatism, the evidence, when purged of its Photian (and Aristoclean) biases and misprisions, tends against such an interpretation. Even so, Aenesidemus *may* have argued (even supposed) that the mere fact that principle (P) is violated in the case of some x and some F shows that in that case x is not F by nature (although it does not of course show that x has no nature) which is something that Sextus would not endorse. Hence, Aenesidemus may admit weak negative conclusions of a certain restricted type consistently with his refusal to allow apprehension at any level, including second-order apprehension of this fact itself (at least if apprehension is construed as involving a firm grasp *of a nature*). But it would not warrant him in drawing a *general* conclusion, e.g. that nothing is good or bad by nature (cf. *M* 11.79, 95); the most it would support is the tentative "none of the candidates canvassed so far is good (or bad) by nature." And there is no real evidence that Aenesidemus went any further than that – if indeed he went that far.[23]

Which leaves the apparent relativism of the sceptically-acceptable B- and C-type locutions (5 above). Here, I think the operative word is "apparent," and in more than one sense. Sextus regularly says that, properly speaking, all sceptical language is the language of appearance, and that where a sceptic uses verbs with purported ontological or existential import, that is itself an appearance only: every occurrence of "it is" and the like should be mentally replaced with an "it appears" (cf. *PH* 1.135, 198; *M* 11.18; cf. *PH* 1.191, 1.193, 197). But sceptics will not insist on wrapping all their observations in the fussily formal garb their attitude requires (*PH* 1.195, 207), although

Sextus insists that this relaxed attitude should not be misinterpreted as a crypto-Dogmatism (which in turn suggests that such misinterpretations were common). This meshes nicely with the view I have been sketching of Photius and Aristocles, and in turn further suggests that Aenesidemus was not espousing an earlier, less consistently sceptical scepticism, even if he was perhaps less capable, at his earlier stage of terminological development, of expressing this clearly.[24]

III AENESIDEMUS IN SEXTUS

In what remains, I shall attempt to reinforce the (tentative) conclusions already established by a consideration of some of the particular passages in Sextus which refer to his Pyrrhonian predecessor. First, a precious direct quotation:

In the fourth book of his *Pyrrhonian Discourses*, Aenesidemus propounds the following argument… "if apparent things appear the same to all in a similar condition, and signs are apparent, then signs will appear the same to all in a similar condition. But signs do not appear the same to all in a similar condition, while apparent things appear the same to all in a similar condition. Therefore signs are not apparent." Aenesidemus seems here by "apparent things" to be referring to things perceived. (**8**: *M* 8.215–16; cf. 234)

That argument clearly relies on (P) (or some close relative); the context is a discussion of the Dogmatists' "indicative" signs, signs which are supposed to indicate how matters lie below the perceptible surfaces of things. In the canonical Stoic definition, an indicative sign is "an antecedently-established proposition in a sound conditional which is revelatory of the consequent" (*PH* 2.104). Sextus devotes a good deal of space to arguing against the availability of such signs on any Dogmatic account, while happily accepting an everyday reliance on "commemorative" signs, which simply serve to remind one of previously-observed conjunctions of phenomena.[25]

The restriction of "apparent things" to perceptibles is important. In the subsequent development of the argument (which may not be Aenesidemean), Sextus argues that, while evident things (such as whiteness and sweetness) do appear the same "to all those similarly constituted," the same is not true of alleged signs of non-evident internal conditions (*M* 8.217–19): the same symptoms in fever patients "seem to be signs of good blood to Herophilus, to Erasistratus of the transference of blood from the veins to the arteries, and to Asclepiades of the blockage of the imperceptible pores by imperceptible particles" (*M* 8.220). So (P) is not satisfied in this (or any other) case of alleged inference to hidden conditions. And while **8** above, and Sextus' subsequent elaboration, again suggest an Aenesidemus prepared to endorse a limited positive application of (P), this impression is clearly illusory in Sextus' case; and probably in Aenesidemus' too.

Relevant here is another view Sextus explicitly ascribes to Aenesidemus: "it is sufficient to point out, as Aenesidemus said, that while everyone considers what attracts them to be good, whatever that might be, still their particular judgments regarding it are in conflict (*M* 11.42)": you cannot take the claim that everyone considers what attracts them to be good as a valid instance of (P), since the referents of "what attracts them" are multiple and incompatible: all men agree that they find beautiful women attractive, but they disagree as to which are beautiful[26] (*M* 11.43).

Also pertinent are Aenesidemus' arguments in Book 5 of the *Pyrrhonian Discourses*:

He adduces doubt-inducing considerations regarding causes, allowing that nothing is the cause of anything, saying that the causal theorists (*aitiologountes*) are mistaken, and enumerating some modes according to which he thinks that the devotees of causal theory have gone astray. (**9**: *Bibl.* 212, 170b17–22 = 72L(4) LS)

The modes in question are the eight against the Aetiologists (*PH* 1.180–85);[27] the first effectively reiterates the argument for the non-apprehensibility of indicative signs, while the second notes that theorists often settle for one possible explanation for the data without bothering to consider any others (*PH* 1.181; the fourth and fifth make essentially similar claims: *PH* 1.182–83). The sixth contends that aetiologists are given to ignoring awkward anomalous data; the seventh says that their causal claims are often inconsistent both with their own assumptions as well as with the data (*PH* 1.183–84); the eighth avers that their "explanations" are often just as doubtful (*apora*) as the things they are supposed to account for (*PH* 1.184). Deployed both individually and collectively (as Aenesidemus urged they should be: *PH* 1.185) these modes offer a powerful challenge to the pretensions of theory.

We know a little more about Aenesidemus' arguments concerning cause and explanation. At *M* 9.218–26, in the course of a general sceptical assessment of the intelligibility of causal explanation, Sextus writes that "in this context Aenesidemus has treated of the difficulties concerning generation in a more intricate manner" (*M* 9.218). The argument (as Sextus presents it) consists of canvassing a highly (indeed almost unintelligibly) complex set of alternative ways in which generation might plausibly occur, and finding all of them wanting. The procedure is allegedly exhaustive, undeniably exhausting, and quite possibly mangled by Sextus or his source. But Sextus' summary of his argument against truth and reality (*M* 8.40–54) confirms that Aenesidemus did indeed handle complex dilemmatic forms: if anything real exists, it is either (a) sensible or (b) intelligible or (c) both (40); but not-(a) (41–43); and not-(b) (44–45) and not-(c) (45–47). This argument involves further complex subdisjunctions, and also invokes, *en passant*, principle (P) (*M* 8.45). Moreover, if the continuation of the argument from *M* 8.48–54 is also Aenesidemean, as the context perhaps suggests, then the considerations which Sextus advances against a relaxation of (P) in favor of some sort of majority rule (cf. *PH* 1.88–90; cf. 2.43–45) were also adduced by Aenesidemus (*M* 8.53–54), which in turn suggests he had given direct attention to the problem of the criterion.[28] But that must remain speculation. What is not speculative is the evident fact that Aenesidemus deployed the complex dilemmatic form of destructive argument that was to become so characteristic of Sextus' scepticism. He did not invent it: it was employed destructively by both Diodorus Cronus and Herophilus centuries earlier.[29] But it is reasonable to suppose both that he did so more vigorously and consistently than any of his predecessors; and that he did so not for the sake of destruction for its own sake, but in the service of establishing Pyrrhonian *epochê*.

IV AENESIDEMUS AND HERACLITUS

Finally, there is the matter of Aenesidemus' relations with Heracliteanism. There are two, interrelated issues to consider.

First, Sextus reports that:

Aenesidemus and his ilk said that the skeptical way is a road[30] which leads to the Heraclitean philosophy, since the idea that contraries seem to hold of the same thing leads to the idea that they actually do hold of it. (**10**: *PH* 1.210).

Sextus is unsympathetic: sceptics simply point to something agreed by everyone, namely that appearances apparently conflict; so scepticism no more precedes Heracliteanism than any other philosophy (or ordinary reflection for that matter) does (1.211–12).

The second issue concerns a recurrent, puzzling phrase. On a number of occasions (in fact the majority of those in which he mentions Aenesidemus by name), Sextus attributes a view to "Aenesidemus according to Heraclitus (*kat' Herakleiton*)." This cannot mean, of course, that the view was Aenesidemus', as reported by Heraclitus. But nor should it be taken to mean that Aenesidemus at some point *endorsed* Heracliteanism, as some have supposed. It is a contraction of a more complex locution, as expressed fully in the following passage: "Aenesidemus says that time is a body according to Heraclitus; for it does not differ from the existent and the first body" (*M* 10.216; cf. "the existent according to Heraclitus, as Aenesidemus says, is air; but time is nothing like air": *M* 10.233). In other words, the compressed phrase "Aenesidemus *kat' Herakleiton*" means "Aenesidemus says that, according to Heraclitus." How easy it is for this to get lost can be seen in the doublet passage in *PH* 3.138, which simply reads: "some have held it [sc. time] to be a body, like Aenesidemus and his followers, on the grounds that it does not differ from being and the primary body." Of course, no sceptic should avow anything like the latter; and Aenesidemus never did so, at least in his own voice.[31] The same holds for the places where Sextus apparently attributes Dogmatic claims to Aenesidemus.[32] Particularly relevant is the following:

Aenesidemus and his followers *kat' Herakleiton*[33] and Epicurus agreed in general in regard to the sensibles [sc. that they are the repositories of truth], but differed in specifics. Aenesidemus and his followers assert that there is a difference among the apparent things, saying that some appear in common to everyone, while others do so to one person separately, and of them those which appear in common to everyone are true, while those that do not are false. (**11**: *M* 8.8)

One might suppose that the second "Aenesidemus and his followers" indicates a claim they make in their own voice; but this is still part of the Heraclitean context. It is *Heraclitus* who is committed to the view that some things appear in common to all (and hence satisfy (P)), while others don't. The sceptic merely enunciates the principle, then applies it (dialectically) as a negative criterion.

Which brings us back to the route to Heracliteanism. Aenesidemus thought that Pyrrhonism might provide some suitable backdrop to Heracliteanism, in particular to the claim that contraries hold of the same thing. The Pyrrhonist, albeit dialectically, wields principle (P); and so too (according to Aenesidemus) does Heraclitus: things are true only if they appear the same way to everyone. The sceptic denies that they do; but the Heraclitean has a way of rescuing general consensus. All appearances have their basis in reality: if x appears F to O it is F; while if it appears not-F to O*, it is not-F too. There is a sense in which the appearances do not lie, and in which all appearances are true, even though they are apparently in conflict, and it does appear (collectively) to everyone that every x is both F and not-F. That is the route to Heracliteanism indicated by Aenesidemus. But it is not one he ever had any inclination to follow; and nor should he have done.

NOTES

1   See Hankinson [68], ch. 7, [203]; for Philo, see Brittain [195]; for Antiochus, see Barnes [194]; for the late Academy in general, see Glucker, [198], esp. pp. 393–98; see also Carlos Lévy, Chapter 4 "The Sceptical Academy: Decline and Afterlife."

2   For his dates, and the question of his Academic affiliation, see Decleva Caizzi [226]; Mansfeld [229].

3   Although several other titles are credited to him: see DL 9.78, 106 (3 and 2 below).

4   On this (possibly Aenesidemean) distinction, see Striker [191], and her Chapter 10 "Academics versus Pyrrhonists, Reconsidered"; Hankinson [68], pp. 141–45.

5   See Striker [118], [119].

6   For the classic formulation of this argument, see Hume, *Enquiry Concerning Human Understanding* XII.2; on the sceptic's "beliefs," see the essays in Burnyeat and Frede [79], also Casey Perin, Chapter 7 "Scepticism and Belief" and Katja Vogt, Chapter 8 "Scepticism and Action."

7   Cf. Sextus, *PH* 1.8: "the sceptical capacity is that of opposing appearances and thoughts in whatever manner you like, through which we come, because of the equal strength of the opposing objects and reasons, first of all to suspension (*epochê*), and then to tranquillity (*ataraxia*)"; cf. *PH* 1.31–33, and 3 below.

8   The categories Carneades allows at least for the sake of argument: *M* 7.166–75 (= 69D LS). On the status of the Academic *pithanon*, see LS

vol. 1, 457–60; Couissin [179]; Hankinson [68], ch. 6; and Harald Thorsrud, Chapter 3 "Arcesilaus and Carneades."

9   Although it is not clear whether he anticipates Sextus in thinking that by so doing they also flush themselves out like purgative drugs; Metrodorus of Chios got there earlier: "we know nothing, not even that we know nothing" (DL 9.58; *M* 7.88), a contention echoed by Arcesilaus: Cicero, *Acad.* 1.45 (cf. 2.73).

10 See Barnes [239].

11 As Malcolm Schofield has recently pointed out: [232], p. 293. My view of Aenesidemus' scepticism has been greatly influenced by this magisterial piece.

12 Woodruff [234]; Bett [41], [143].

13 Thus effecting a *rapprochement* between Aenesidemean and Sextan scepticism (*contra* Woodruff), by weakening the latter; for the debate as to the scope of Pyrrhonian scepticism, see the essays collected in Burnyeat and Frede [79]; see also Hankinson [68], chs. 17–18.

14 But see most recently Barnes [240].

15 The principle can be given a variety of different formulations; for a careful analysis, see Schofield [232], pp. 304–12; it is dubbed the "invariability condition" by Bett [143], who argues that Aenesidemus actually accepts the principle, while later Pyrrhonists, employing it only dialectically, do not.

16 See also Hankinson [287],   60–66; [68], pp. 129–31, 268–71; Decleva Caizzi [223].

17 On the Modes, see Paul Woodruff, Chapter 11 "The Pyrrhonian Modes"; and see also Striker [272]; Annas and Barnes [269]; Hankinson [68], ch. 9.

18 The negative conclusions are not construed by Woodruff as simple first-order denials of the form "x is not-F," but rather second-order (or "metadogmatic") rejections of the possibility of knowing one way or the other. But this sits uncomfortably with the obvious implications of 5 above, some of whose conclusions are apparently first-order.

19 Or, following Pappenheim's suggested emendation of "*archôn*" for "*alêthôn*," "principles"; but Aenesidemus certainly *did* deal with truth: section III below.

20 Reading "*noêseôs*" for "*kinêseôs*," again following Pappenheim.

21 The latter pair are drawn from Stoic action theory.

22 See Schofield [232], p. 303.

23 Thus, I am inclined to doubt Bett's contention that *M* 11 preserves an earlier, Aenesidemean, strand of ethical Pyrrhonism, distinct from that represented in *PH* 3; but see Richard Bett, Chapter 9 "Scepticism and Ethics."

24 Scc Polito [231], pp. 40–50, 89–101 (endorsed by Schofield [232], pp. 283 n.
    11 and 292–93 n. 26), who argues that Aenesidemus had not developed
    a generalized sceptical notion of appearance: cf. the last sentence of
    8 below.

25 Thus, the appearance of smoke is a commemorative sign of the existence
    of fire: *PH* 2.100, *M* 8.152, 157; for sceptical acceptance of such signs as
    "useful for life," see *PH* 2.102; *M* 8.156–58.

26 Cf. *PH* 1.108: "many men with ugly mistresses think them most
    comely."

27 On these, see Paul Woodruff, Chapter 11 "The Pyrrhonian Modes",
    section VII; see also Barnes [237], pp. 160–70; Hankinson [68], pp. 213–17.

28 On which see *PH* 2.14–79; *M* 7.29–37, 47–54, etc.; see also Striker [118],
    and [119], esp. pp. 155–59.

29 Herophilus: Galen *On Antecedent Causes* xvi 199–202: see Hankinson
    [323], pp. 146–49, 274–80; Diodorus: *M* 10.85–120; for a pointed anecdote
    linking Diodorus and Herophilus, see *PH* 2.245; and compare Gorgias *On
    Non-Being*.

30 On this metaphor see Polito [231], pp. 27–39; Schofield [232], pp. 276–84,
    322–38.

31 *Contra* Hankinson [68], pp. 129–31. See Viano [233].

32 Other cases: Aenesidemus *kata Herakleiton* places intellect (*dianoia*)
    outside the body, while some *kata Dêmokriton* place it in the whole of
    the body: *M* 7.349; Aenesidemus *kata Herakleiton* says that the part is
    both different from and the same as the whole: *M* 9.337.

33 This is Bekker's generally-accepted emendation of the MS. *kai
    Herakleiton*; it is supported (against Bett's linguistic objections: Bett
    [143], p. 223 n. 68) by Schofield [232], p. 272 n. 3.

6   Sextus Empiricus

I LIFE AND WORKS

Sextus Empiricus, who surely lived in the second and third centuries CE, is one of those rare Greek philosophers whose works we have more or less complete in the form in which he wrote them. Before the great commentaries and treatises of the Neo-Platonists at the end of antiquity, this is hardly the case except for Plato, Epictetus, Marcus Aurelius, and Plotinus. But should we place Sextus in such illustrious company? If his work had not been preserved, our knowledge of ancient scepticism would be much more limited; but, leaving aside the fact that he is an irreplaceable source, is Sextus "an obscure and unoriginal Hellenistic writer," as Richard Popkin says?[1] Or, on the contrary, did he introduce original elements into the philosophical debate of his time?

Of the life of Sextus Empiricus we know virtually nothing. We know that he was a doctor (he tells us himself, *M* 1.260, *PH* 2.238) and Diogenes Laertius lists him as the penultimate head of the sceptical school.[2] It seems that Sextus wrote some works that are now lost. He refers to his own *Medical Treatises* (*M* 7.202); one wonders whether or not this is the same work as the *Empiric Treatises* cited in *M* 1.62. The other books of his that Sextus himself appears to cite are probably ways of referring to passages from the works that have survived.[3] But that leaves us three works of his that seem (more or less) complete.

Outlines of Pyrrhonism (*PH*) is presented by Sextus as a sort of summary, in three books, of the sceptical doctrine. Very often he appeals to its "outline" character to justify his relatively brief treatment of some question. Book 1 is a general introduction to the sceptical philosophy; we shall discuss it in detail below. The two other books attack the "dogmatic" systems of thought, following the generally accepted plan for philosophical exposition: logic, physics, ethics. Book 2 deals with the "logical" part of philosophy, Book 3 with the physical and ethical parts.

The second work that has come down to us is a treatise *Against the Dogmatists* in five books: the first two (*Against the Logicians* 1 and 2) refute various philosophers' theses in the logical part, that is, various systems of logic and theories of knowledge; with *Against the Physicists* in two books and *Against the Ethicists* in one book, *Against the Dogmatists* thus covers the same ground as the last two books of *PH*. The opening lines of *Against the Logicians* allude to a general presentation of scepticism; this was long seen as an allusion to *PH*, but is more probably a back-reference to an introduction that has not survived. For the refutation of philosophers, Sextus thus offers two versions, with the same theses, often in identical or related terms, and relying on the same examples – one of them, however (that of *PH*), being more condensed. The first book of *PH*, on the other hand, has nothing corresponding to it in the version of *Against the Dogmatists* that has survived.

Then we have the treatise *Against the Learned* (or, more precisely, "against those involved with the sciences," hence sometimes called *Against the Professors*, and often designated by its Latin title *Adversus Mathematicos*) in six books: against the grammarians, the rhetoricians, the geometers, the arithmeticians (originally, no doubt, these last two books were together in one), the astrologers, and the musicians. Unfortunately, because of the arrangement of the manuscripts, the habit has arisen of citing these two last treatises under the same name, *Adversus Mathematicos*, a work that then comprises eleven books[4]: 1, *Against the Grammarians*, 2, *Against the Rhetoricians*, 3, *Against the Geometers*, 4, *Against the Arithmeticians*, 5, *Against the Astrologers*, 6, *Against the Musicians*, 7 and 8, *Against the Logicians*, 9 and 10, *Against the Physicists*, and 11, *Against the Ethicists*. In order to conform to standard usage, we will therefore cite the entirety of these texts by the title *Adversus Mathematicos*, abbreviated to *M*.

II A PROBLEMATIC TEXT

One cannot treat Sextus Empiricus like a "normal" philosophical author, and this for several reasons. First, there are historical uncertainties connected with the life of Sextus and the history of scepticism, which make it very difficult to determine exactly which "version" of scepticism Sextus adhered to: among the influences affecting him, which one, or which ones, turned out to be decisive? What place did he occupy in the philosophical arena? On his relations with his predecessors in scepticism, especially Aenesidemus, Sextus gives us a few basics, but here too we are largely reduced to conjecture. Since antiquity, to judge from Diogenes Laertius (9.116), there were two opposing views on the history of scepticism.[5] According to one, attributed by Diogenes to Menodotus of Nicomedia, Timon had no successor and it was only Ptolemy of Cyrene who "revived the sect." This Ptolemy was the teacher of Heraclides, who was the teacher of Aenesidemus. Others, on the contrary, speak of an uninterrupted tradition, but the list of names they give very probably includes a gap, which modern scholars have done their best to pinpoint in time. In the second case, too, the sceptical "school"[6] would have suffered an eclipse, and therefore a renaissance. Indeed, the difference between these two views is less important, in the end, than their agreement: whether or not it nominally survived throughout this time, the sceptical movement at some point lost its luster. Some modern interpreters have thought that this gap (in the first form or the second) was in some sense filled by the New Academy, and that it is not until after the disappearance, or the enfeeblement, of the latter that the sceptical movement regained its vigor. In any case, starting with Ptolemy, there was an uninterrupted succession of sceptical philosophers up to Saturninus Cythenas, the pupil of Sextus; if the list does not continue, it may be simply because Diogenes Laertius was a contemporary of Saturninus.

Sextus is therefore situated at the end of a movement of sceptical renaissance, a movement that drew its inspiration and took its name from Pyrrho. Aenesidemus, who was the main author of this revival, was perhaps the one who introduced the term "Pyrrhonian" (he wrote some *Pyrrhonist Discourses*, whose plan Sextus' *Outlines of Pyrrhonism* picks up on, at least in part) and was also the one who sharply separates the Pyrrhonian sceptics from the New Academy, a school to which he belonged for a time himself.[7] It is important to understand that Sextus represents the end of a movement of return to the source, and that in this sense Sextus is a "fundamentalist" sceptic. We shall see that he is more of one than is generally believed.

The reader of Sextus is faced from the start with numerous problems. Whether he is attacking philosophies, in *M* 7–11 and *PH* 2–3, or the arts in *M* 1–6, what Sextus prima facie offers the reader is a collection of arguments, among which he marks no differences – neither between those he borrows from other sceptics and those of which he is himself the author, nor between arguments that strike us as highly subtle and others that seem to us rather weak. (For instance, at *PH* 3.4 he suggests that it would be "silly" to say that God is incorporeal and blessed, since without knowing the essence of God one cannot know his attributes.) This lack of differentation is perhaps at its most extreme when he juxtaposes quite different *types* of argumentation, as in the case of the Modes.[8] It is understandable for a doxographer or a historian, like Diogenes Laertius, to report the Ten Modes of Aenesidemus and the Five Modes of Agrippa, for example, one after the other. But Sextus' procedure is exactly the same: in *PH*, having laid out at length the Modes of the "older sceptics" (1.36), which he elsewhere (*M* 7.345) attributes to Aenesidemus, he moves to those of Agrippa remarking simply "The more recent sceptics have left us five Modes of suspension of assent" (1.164). Since Sextus is not playing the role of a historian, but that of an advocate of scepticism, it is worth asking how he intends to make such different devices work together. Finally, let us note that Sextus' argumentation is often structured in "waves": what has just been ruled out is conceded, in order to show that *aporia*, or impasse, still remains. For example: there is no criterion of truth; but even if we admit that there is one, it is useless and empty, etc. This procedure is not peculiar to the sceptics; one can find it in Gorgias, for example (nothing exists; and even if something does exist, one cannot grasp it; and even if one can grasp it, one cannot communicate it). If one resists explaining these facts about the text by Sextus' stupidity or negligence, one needs to find a genuinely philosophical significance for them.

The first kind of non-differentiation indicated above is clearly of particular importance for the historian of philosophy: in the Sextan corpus, which parts are exposition of others' arguments and which exposition of Sextus' own material? The problem is largely insoluble, because along with his reticence about himself, Sextus is *theoretically* self-effacing to a degree unparalleled in history. So someone who wants to expound "the scepticism of Sextus Empiricus" is not in the same position as someone intending to analyze "Aristotle's physics" or "Chrysippus' logic"; one has to settle for expounding "the sceptic way" as it appears in the Sextan corpus, attempting occasionally to surmise innovations by Sextus.

III THE SCEPTIC WAY AND SUSPENSION OF ASSENT

To try to uncover these innovations, as well as to give point to the lack of differentiation (in its various forms) indicated above, we have to give special attention to the first book of *PH*, which, as noted, has no counterpart in *M*. Here, Sextus describes the "sceptic way" and situates scepticism in the ancient philosophical landscape. He insists, indeed, on the fact that the sceptics are not a philosophical school in the usual sense of the word (1.16–17). Still, one finds among the sceptics a central feature of philosophical schools, namely, strong relations between teacher and student, and Sextus himself alludes to this, saying "where my teacher held discussion, there I now hold discussion" (*PH* 3.120). To designate the manner in which the sceptics both manage their investigations and conduct their lives, Sextus uses the word *agôgê*, here translated "way." Besides literally "transporting" something, this Greek word signifies "conduct" in every sense of the term: the directing of an army, the conduct of political affairs, the manner of conducting one's life, the manner of conducting a piece of reasoning or intellectual research (*PH* 1.4, 6, 7, etc.). Sextus thus means to indicate that being a sceptic is a matter of conduct more than of doctrine. In *PH* 1, Sextus offers a general "account" (*logos*) of the sceptical philosophy, while the part that makes objections against the various parts of dogmatic philosophy is the "special" account (*PH* 1.5–6). This distinction between general and special accounts does not appear in the other major report on scepticism that we possess, that of Diogenes Laertius, and this is perhaps a case of innovation by Sextus. In any case, one should note the force, the rigor, and the elegance of this general account of scepticism. Many elements in this general account were no doubt collected by Sextus from the prior sceptical tradition, as he sometimes says himself. This is the case in his account of the Modes, in which, as we have seen, Sextus proceeds by accumulation rather than by construction. Nonetheless, it is in this first book of *PH* that we have the best chance of finding Sextus being "original."

PH 1 intends, in fact, to set up a portrait of scepticism. One can distinguish four parts. The first (chapters 1–12) traces the general contours of the sceptical position ("its conception, its principles, its arguments, its criterion and its end" (1.5)); the second (chapters 13–17) deals with the different sets of Modes of suspension of assent; the third (chapters 18–28) deals with the "sceptical expressions"; and the last examines the relations between the "sceptic way" and the main philosophical systems that could claim to be its rivals. Sextus actually gives a definition of scepticism (*skepsis*): it is the ability (*dunamis*) to place in opposition our impressions of sense-perception and intellect, "an ability by which, because of the equal force in the opposed objects and reasonings, we arrive first at suspension of assent and after that at tranquility" (1.8). There is another definition of scepticism that is latent in the whole work: scepticism is defined, that is, demarcated, against dogmatism. Modern historians of philosophy have often emphasized the fact that "dogmatic" for Sextus does not have the same pejorative connotation as in modern speech. Actually, the word is not exactly a compliment in his hands. The difference from modern usage is that, for the sceptics, a dogmatic person is one who holds an opinion that he takes to be true of the external world. But, unlike the dogmatic person in the modern sense, who professes his opinions in a tone of authority, and often derives them from irrational sources, the dogmatic person in Sextus' usage bases his convictions on rational discourse. The sceptic, by contrast, limits himself to describing his experiences as they appear to him: "he says what appears to himself and reports his own experience without holding opinions, making no firm pronouncements about external objects" (1.15). "External objects" here include what we call by this name, but also concepts that we form, and judgements that we make about these objects and concepts. Hence one falls into dogmatism as soon as one gives assent to an opinion.

For Sextus, then, the sceptic is defined as a searcher (that is why "zetetic," that is, "searching," is one of the labels for the sceptic "way" (*PH* 1.7)) who, like everyone, searches for the truth about things, and more precisely about the impressions or appearances (*phantasiai*) which present themselves to him. Sextus describes this attitude in these terms: the sceptic "was hoping to achieve tranquility by reaching a conclusion on the irregularities of things" (1.29). He then finds himself faced with a disagreement (*diaphônia*) between opposed opinions on every subject. Everyone finds these opinions both in himself and among others, notably among the philosophers called "dogmatic." Now, these opposed opinions on the same subject have an equal force of conviction (this is *isostheneia*, "equal strength"), which leads the sceptic to what is normally considered the decisive moment of the "sceptic way," suspension of assent (*epochê*). One may note here one of the features of the sceptic way that are peculiar to it, or at least, shared with very few other philosophies. It is after having searched for the truth in the manner of the dogmatists that the sceptic – who isn't yet really a sceptic – suspends assent. In other words, no one can be a sceptic who has not previously been a dogmatist and sought tranquility of soul in the manner of the dogmatists.

This equal strength is *experienced* by the sceptic, in that he is equally convinced by the opposing arguments. Thus, early in *PH* 3, Sextus concludes that "it is also necessary to suspend assent about the existence of cause, saying that cause no more is anything than it is not, as far as what the dogmatists say is concerned" (3.29), because he has laid out one by one the arguments for and against and has found them equally plausible. "Plausible" renders the Greek term *pithanon*, which comes from the verb *peithô*, "convince, persuade"; the point, then, is that the plausibility of the opposed arguments carries equal conviction for the sceptic who listens to them.[9]

Now, Sextus continues "when they had suspended assent, tranquility followed fortuitously, as a shadow follows a body" (1.29). This last image, which according to Diogenes Laertius (9.107) comes from Timon and Aenesidemus, and this word "fortuitously" are designed to stress that one cannot assert a rule; to assert a rule of the form "one who suspends assent finds tranquility" would amount once again to maintaining an opinion.

One of the key aspects of Sextus' philosophical enterprise is precisely that he takes seriously this notion of "suspension of assent" and extends its range to the maximum (perhaps to an impossible) degree. This very broad extension of suspension of assent goes hand in hand with a no less broad extension that Sextus gives to dogmatism – one sign, among others, of his "fundamentalism." In reviving the epithet "Pyrrhonian," following the sceptics at least since Aenesidemus, Sextus means to disqualify the New Academic tradition, now generally seen as belonging within ancient scepticism.

From the opening lines of *PH*, Sextus dismisses the New Academy as dogmatic, even if he notes that they are not dogmatists "in the proper sense" (*idiôs*, 1.3). There are in fact three possible attitudes for an inquirer: either one declares that one has made a discovery (Sextus might have added "or that one is sure that sooner or later one will do so"), which is the dogmatic position "in the proper sense"; or one declares that the matter is inapprehensible (Sextus means "*for ever* inapprehensible"), which is the position of (among others) the New Academy; or one continues the inquiry. Saying that how things are is inapprehensible, that the human mind cannot have an adequate conception of things, etc., belongs in the category that is today called "negative dogmatism" or, following Jonathan Barnes, "negative metadogmatism."[10] Saying that providence exists, or does not exist, would be an example of an opinion "dogmatic in the proper sense." A member of the New Academy will say, on the contrary, that it is impossible ever to settle the question. He will present himself, then, as equally an adherent of suspension of assent, in that he will suspend assent on either one of the two propositions – that providence exists or that it does not – *because* one cannot settle the question. According to Sextus, that too is giving one's assent to an opinion. The sceptic suspends assent not only on whether or not providence exists, but also on whether the answer to this question is within reach for human beings, and he continues to inquire, without pronouncing on the prospects for this inquiry having a successful conclusion. Hence the "nomenclature of scepticism" recorded by Sextus: the sceptic way is called "searching," "suspensive," "aporetic," "Pyrrhonian" (1.7).

This central notion of suspension of assent is therefore far from being an invention of Sextus. Pierre Couissin[11] showed that it is of Stoic origin and that, since Zeno, the Stoics maintained that one should suspend assent as long as one did not have a firm grasp of an object (even if it is not certain that the Stoics used the term *epochê*), and that Arcesilaus had subsequently made it one of the central strategies of his philosophy.[12] The first sceptic of the Pyrrhonian tradition to take hold of it is Aenesidemus.[13] He made a sweeping attempt to turn suspension of assent against his former colleagues in the Academy, reproaching them with claiming to be "in impasse" while holding certain things true and others false.[14] But, as has been shown,[15] what Aenesidemus refuses to assent to is the fact that one can determine that a thing is such and such by nature:

> none of them [the Pyrrhonists] has said that everything is absolutely inapprehensible, nor that they are apprehensible, but they say that they are no more of one kind than another, or sometimes of one kind and sometimes not, or that they are this way for one person and not this way for another, and for another completely non-existent. According to them things in general, or some of them, are neither accessible nor inaccessible, but no more accessible than inaccessible, or sometimes accessible and sometimes not, or accessible to one person and not to another.[16]

To be sure, Aenesidemus does not say that things are inapprehensible, as the New Academy does, but he does postulate the existence of a nature of things, which we cannot determine because we have access to it only *relatively*. Such a position is unacceptable to Sextus, who would without any doubt consider it an assertion about the nature of things, that is, a dogmatic position.

Hence the definition of suspension of assent in Sextus: "We use 'I suspend assent' in place of "'I am not able to say which of the things presented one should find convincing and which unconvincing'" (*PH* 1.196). But not being able to settle the question is not at all a fixed destiny for humanity. When he writes that "we act like historians and report according to what appears to us at the moment" (*PH* 1.4), Sextus wants to signify that neither is he able to say whether one day he *will* be able to settle the question. One could say, in fact, that the Stoics, the New Academy and even Aenesidemus practise a suspension of assent that is actually a refusal to give one's assent. For his part, Sextus is "unable to say if he should give his assent or refuse it" (*PH* 1.7).

IV SCEPTICAL DISCOURSE

Sextus will therefore take extraordinary precautions to prevent dogmatism from sneaking into sceptical discourse at the point where assent is suspended. Hence *PH* 1 goes to great lengths to *define the status of sceptical discourse*. It has been thought that, by doing this, it falls into dogmatism. Thus, as concerns the afore-mentioned equal strength of the dogmatists' opinions on each subject, does Sextus not introduce the *belief* that these dogmatic opinions are in equilibrium and cancel each other out?[17] This is what he seems to say at *PH* 1.12: "The overriding principle of the sceptical structure is that to every argument [or "discourse," *logos*] an equal argument is opposed; indeed it is from this, it seems to us, that we cease to dogmatize." In fact, Sextus was aware of this danger, and he addresses it in the chapters he devotes to the analysis of "sceptical expressions." Thus, in *PH* 1.203 he writes: "so when I say 'to every argument an equal argument is opposed,' I am implicitly saying this: 'to every argument I have investigated that establishes something dogmatically, it seems to me that another argument establishing something dogmatically is opposed to it, equal to the first in terms of conviction and lack of conviction' – so that the utterance of this discourse is not dogmatic."

How, in fact, is one not to dogmatize as soon as one speaks? Sextus answers: by adopting *non-assertive* speech. In the famous passage of Aristocles of Messene quoted by Eusebius of Caesarea, which is one of our main sources of knowledge for pre-Sextan scepticism, we read that it was Timon who gave the name "non-assertion" (*aphasia*) to the disposition of the sceptic who does not want to pronounce on the nature of the objects that his assertion is supposed to be describing.[18] Sextus not only declines to make "ordinary" assertions in saying "X is F," but when he is describing sceptical positions and procedures, he does so in a non-assertive manner: "Of none of what is to be said do we insist that it is entirely as we say, but for each thing we act like historians and report according to what appears to us at the moment" (*PH* 1.4). Sextus defines non-assertion as "an affect that precludes us from saying that we posit or deny anything" (*PH* 1.192). When he adds "Hence it is clear that we adopt non-assertion, too, not with the idea that things are by nature such as to drive us absolutely to non-assertion" (1.193), one cannnot help thinking that he is explicitly distancing himself from Aenesidemus. The sceptical expressions indicated by Sextus are, for example, "not more," "perhaps," "it may be," "it is possible," "I suspend assent," "I determine nothing," "I do not apprehend." When Sextus says: "concerning all the sceptical expressions one must understand from the start that we do not insist on their being entirely true, since we say that they can be canceled by themselves, falling into the same category as the things they are applied to, just as purgative remedies not only eliminate the humors from the body, but are themselves expelled with the humors" (*PH* 1.206), he means that the "sceptical expressions" are not meant to qualify the philosopher's discourse about things (as when, for example, Aristotle declares that regularities in the sublunary world hold only "for the most part") but to be "revelatory of the sceptical disposition and of our affects" (*PH* 1.187).

Hence a very important point of interpretation. In several well-known passages, Sextus specifies an aspect of the status of sceptical discourse. The sceptic "supposes that, just as the expression 'everything is false' states that it too, along with everything else, is false – and the same goes for 'nothing is true' – so too the expression 'no more'[19] says that it too, along with everything else, is no more this than that, and for this reason falls into the same category as all the rest. And we say the same thing about the other sceptical expressions. Besides, if the dogmatist posits as real that about which he dogmatizes, whereas the sceptic utters his expressions in such a way that they themselves in effect carry their own limitation, he cannot be said to dogmatize in uttering them" (*PH* 1.14–15). The word translated "carry a limitation" (*perigraphein*) has generally been understood as signifying "cancel,"[20] which has made commentators think that Sextus accepted the idea that his argumentation was self-refuting, and that he could accept this because sceptical arguments refute themselves only *after* having refuted dogmatic theses. This is how Sextus' images for sceptical critique, comparing it to purgative remedies that are evacuated with the humors they eliminate, to fire which consumes itself in burning combustible material, or to the ladder that one pushes away after using it to climb "to a high place" (*M* 8.481), have been understood. But perhaps Sextus should not be read as accepting that self-refutation applies to sceptical discourse and expressions, because "nothing is true," for example, is only self-refuting if one employs it dogmatically.[21] It is in fact the dogmatist who is reproaching the sceptic with self-refutation, and it is noteworthy that Sextus deals with the self-limiting of expressions like "nothing is true" in a chapter entitled "Whether the Sceptic Dogmatizes."

A particular case of this general problem of self-refutation is that of the "demonstration" that there is no such thing as demonstration. At *PH* 2.188, Sextus begins by refuting the dogmatists while adopting their own point of view. Their position is: if there is a demonstration, there is a demonstration; if there is no demonstration, there is a demonstration (since the non-existence of demonstration is *demonstrated*); but either there is one or there isn't; therefore there is one. Now, *according to them*, if the premise "if there is a demonstration, there is a demonstration" is true, the negation of the consequent must conflict with the antecedent; therefore the second premise is false. It should be noted that the sceptic, in assembling arguments, can put himself in the dogmatist's point of view and accuse him of incoherence. But the true sceptical position is different, and Sextus concludes his chapter on demonstration like this: "We offer this [i.e., the criticisms of the dogmatists from their own point of view] as an extra. For if the reasonings about demonstration are plausible – and let us suppose they are – and the attacks brought against demonstration are also plausible, it is necessary to suspend assent about demonstration too, and to say that it no more is than is not" (*PH* 2.192).

Sextus' response to the two accusations of self-refutation, one against the "sceptical expressions," the other against sceptical arguments like those directed against demonstration, is basically the same. It is based on *affect*. We have seen that Sextus defines non-assertion as "an affect that precludes us from saying that we posit or deny anything" (*PH* 1.192). This is applicable to all the "sceptical expressions": in uttering these expressions, the sceptic "reports" (*apangellei*, which one could render by "announce") the affect that strikes him at the moment. The same for the suspension of assent about demonstration: for it to occur, the sceptic must find equally convincing (*pithanos*) the arguments for and the arguments against, the latter no doubt being less readily convincing. Now at *M* 8.473 Sextus writes that the sceptics "will say that the argument against demonstration is merely convincing (*pithanon*) and that at this moment it convinces them and leads them to assent, but that they do not know if this will still be the case later, given the variability of the human mind." In saying "nothing is true" or in declaring himself convinced by the arguments put forward against the existence of demonstration, the sceptic thus reveals his own affect as he feels it at the instant when he reveals it. Insofar as it describes my present affect, the expression "nothing is true" does not apply to itself.

This matter of "affect" (*pathos*) is crucial, in that it also allows for a response to the major objection that, since antiquity, has continued to be made against scepticism, that of *apraxia*: how can the sceptic take part in any activity, especially social activity, if he proposes to live without opinion? To live at all, don't I just have to have the opinion that it is day and that it will soon be night, that cars can

run people over, or that tyranny is the worst kind of regime?[22] This
has given rise to a distinction (along with a debate) among some
current interpreters, between a "rustic" and an "urbane" scepticism,[23] the former rejecting absolutely all opinions, including those
about everyday things, and the latter attacking only the "technical"
opinions of philosophers and experts and accepting, by contrast, the
opinions of the ordinary person. It is interesting to note that this
distinction had been in a way anticipated, but on a practical level,
by Pyrrho himself, about whom the tradition gives us a twofold
picture. Sticking to the text of Diogenes Laertius (9.61–69), we see,
on the one hand, Pyrrho living an eccentric life (he took no precautions against cars, precipices, or dogs, and survived only by the aid of
his friends, he kept on talking to people who had departed, he disappeared to wander with companions at random, he passed by his
friend Anaxarchus who had fallen into a swamp, he talked to himself)
and, on the other hand, the same Pyrrho living a most orderly life –
living "in upright fashion" (9.66)[24] with his midwife sister and selling
chickens and pigs with her at the market, and so well integrated into
society that his city made him high priest, an office he does not
appear to have refused. In the end, the appropriate lesson to draw
from the doxography on Pyrrho is surely that the distinction between
rustic and urbane scepticisms is groundless. Pyrrho, as it were,
pushed indifference to the point of not choosing between the two.[25]
As for Sextus, a close reading of the texts appears to show that,
especially in *PH*, he combined an extreme (and in this sense fundamentalist and "rustic") sceptical position with an active life as an
individual and in society. And the main way in which he reconciles
this rusticity and urbanity is, precisely, affect.

In an oft-cited passage, Sextus writes: "So, attending to apparent
things, we live observing the rules of ordinary life without holding
opinions, since we cannot be completely inactive. This observation of
the rules of ordinary life seems to have four aspects: one consists in
the guidance of nature, another in the necessity of the affects, another
in the handing down of laws and customs, and another in the teaching
of the arts" (*PH* 1.23). Sextus' words by no means force us to decide
(as the "urbane" interpretation has it) that this important activity of
the sceptic requires him, in the domain of everyday life, to accept
having opinions and to confine his avoidance of opinion to "dogmas"
(which the opinions that accompany our everyday life are obviously

not). Besides, Sextus himself explicitly says that the sceptic does not take this position: he conducts his activities "without holding opinions" (*adoxastôs*). At *PH* 2.102 Sextus gives a striking example of the sceptic's attitude towards everyday life: "The commemorative sign is made trustworthy by ordinary life, since someone who sees smoke sees there the sign of fire, and having noticed a scar, he says that there was a wound. Hence not only do we not come into conflict with ordinary life, but we are on its side, giving our assent, without holding opinions, to what it trusts in, and setting ourselves in opposition to the fictions peculiar to the dogmatists." Sextus' claim, therefore, is that the sceptic, *without holding an opinion*, gives his assent not to the inference "no smoke without fire," which would be a general rule bearing on the external world, but to "relying on my past experience, it seems to me that what has struck me as smoke is a sign of what has struck me as fire." An inference of this kind does not go beyond the domain of the affects.

Now we can see the point of the expression "guidance of nature" (*huphêgêsis phuseôs*): when he emphasizes the points of contact between the "sceptic way" and Methodist medicine,[26] Sextus writes that this medical school, "following what is apparent, takes from it what seems to be beneficial, in this respect following the sceptics" (*PH* 1.237). The same passage also explains what Sextus means by "necessity of the affects": "by the necessity of the affects the sceptic is guided by thirst to drink and by hunger to food" (1.238). In the same way Methodist medicine is guided to the remedy *by the disease itself*, "by contraction and dilatation" (1.238). As for customs and laws, "following the rules of everyday life without holding opinions, we say that there are gods, we revere the gods and we say that they are provident" (*PH* 3.2). Sextus is not claiming that saying that gods and providence exist is not an opinion,[27] but that *he* says "gods exist" because it is the custom where he lives – that in doing so he follows the rules of ordinary life, and that opinion is not at issue. There is no question here of the hypocrisy of an atheist pretending to believe to avoid persecution, or simply to be like others, since Sextus is not an atheist – that would be to hold an opinion. One may, like Jonathan Barnes, find this "rustic" reading "forced."[28] But the "urbane" reading is much worse; it would ascribe to Sextus the view that the existence of the gods and providence are not dogmas. As for the arts, we know that Sextus was a doctor and thought that he could, like the

Methodist doctors, practise his art "without holding opinions." But the arts present special problems for the sceptic, which we shall consider below.

Sextus therefore kept his distance from the provocative indifference of a Pyrrho, in favor of a more conformist existence; but this shift was not at the cost of any weakening of the position – on the contrary. The Sextan sceptic lets himself be guided by his impressions and his affects, and this is enough for him to conduct himself in the world. Perhaps the extreme point of this attitude is reached when, at *PH* 1.198, Sextus specifies that "indeterminacy is an affect of thought by which we neither reject nor posit any of the objects of dogmatic inquiry." We should note right away the expression "affect of thought" (*pathos dianoias*), which indicates that thought too, like the senses, is affected in one way or another by the world on which Sextus refuses to make pronouncements. At this point, Sextus has completely broken with the approaches of the new Academy and of Aenesidemus: for him, indeterminacy and undecidability are not only not in the things – they are not in the subject, either. They merely appear in conjunction with one of his affects.

In this context, we can in a way verify the interpretation just advanced by considering one of the most famous examples in ancient philosophy, the proposition "honey is sweet." In a brilliant and subtle article, Jacques Brunschwig[29] puts forward what seems the best reading of this example. At *PH* 1.20, Sextus writes "Honey seems to us to have a sweetening action. But whether, in addition, it is sweet, *insofar as that follows from the preceding argument*, we continue to search." The subject of Brunschwig's paper is precisely the sense of the expression *hoson epi tôi logôi*, here translated by "insofar as that follows from the argument." It is possible that *logos* here designates the "notion" of honey, but it is more likely, as Brunschwig shows, that it has to do with an argument, probably one put forward by the dogmatists. The passage would then signify: the sceptic agrees – that is, gives his assent to the fact – that honey appears to him here and now to have a sweetening action, but as for knowing whether it is sweet, on the basis of (1) the phenomenon and (2) the principle that there is a conformity between phenomenal qualities and real qualities (a principle that, besides, he rejects), the sceptic does not agree.[30]

Within the framework of this production of arguments that rely in the last resort on affects presenting themselves, a certain number of the oddities noted above make sense. The accumulation of arguments of different force and type is an example. The important point is that they appear convincing to me in a given circumstance. Deciding that the Modes of Agrippa are more general, more refined, and/or more convincing than those of Aenesidemus is something that the Sextan sceptic cannot do. One should bear this in mind when approaching the problem of discrepancies in the work of Sextus.

V   UNITY OR SCHIZOPHRENIA?

There are several discrepancies between the texts in the Sextan corpus. At least three can be identified. The first has to do with two different ways of criticizing philosophers, one in *PH* 2–3 and the other in *M* 7–11. The second is a difference between *M* 11, *Against the Ethicists*, and the rest of the critique of philosophers in both *M* 7–10 and *PH* 2–3. The third is a difference between *M* 1–6, the treatise *Against the Professors*, and the rest of the corpus.

A number of recent studies have compared Sextus' treatment of the same questions in *PH* 2–3 and *M* 7–11, and they appear to have put into question one of the opinions that seemed most firmly established among interpreters of Sextus: the near-unanimous agreement that *PH* was earlier than *M* 7–11. Now, it has been observed that, although they take about three times as long to deal with the subjects tackled in *PH* 2–3, *M* 7–11 offer a text at once more chaotic, less refined, and above all less "advanced." It is once again Jacques Brunschwig who has shown this most brilliantly on one particular point, that of the critique of demonstration.[31] More specifically, to stress just one point, while both *M* 8 and *PH* 2 equally define demonstration by a series of dichotomies (demonstration is an argument, conclusive rather than non-conclusive, to a non-evident rather than an evident conclusion, etc.) the author of *M* 8 does not envisage the possibility of reasoning validly from false premises, and "he confuses an epistemological difference, which bears on the type of truth possessed by one of the premises, with a logical difference, which bears on the type of relation between premises and conclusion."[32] *PH* 2, by contrast, has neither of these defects.

There is another point concerning demonstration, also signaled by Brunschwig,[33] that should be discussed, incidentally because it reinforces the view maintained here of the more polished character of *PH*, but also because it raises an absolutely fundamental point for Sextus' scepticism. Brunschwig begins by pointing out that scepticism is not a form of eclecticism, eclecticism being characterized as an approach claiming that different philosophies are saying the same thing, their disagreements being purely verbal – they use the same words for different concepts and different words for the same concepts. "On the other hand, the sceptic must assume that dogmatists ... all have *the same notions* and use *the same words* to express them,"[34] otherwise there is no undecidable disagreement among them. But, says Brunschwig, the sceptic is also tempted to expose the disagreement among dogmatists when they give different definitions of the same term. And Brunschwig gives the example of *M* 8.300–36, where Sextus develops a critique of demonstration in which he takes all the philosophers to have the same conception of demonstration. But the Epicureans lay the following trap for the sceptic: either the sceptic has a notion of demonstration, in which case demonstration exists, or he does not, in which case he is in no position to critique it. Sextus replies first (332a–333a), in polemical manner, that the sceptic, far from being short of notions of demonstration, has lots of them – all the ones provided by the dogmatists. So he considers that the different definitions given by the dogmatists are indeed different. But he also accepts the following ontological implication: "If we had a single notion of the object of our inquiry, we would believe, guided by this notion, that there really exists an object of this nature" (333a). But immediately after (334a–336a), he adopts a completely different position, distinguishing the notion (*ennoia*), which is "a simple movement of the intellect," from the apprehension (*katalêpsis*), which includes recognizing the reality of its propositional content. These two strategies are incompatible with one another. This makes it all the more remarkable that the parallel passage of *PH* (2.9–10) adopts the second solution proposed by *M* 8 and rejects the ontological implication, while treating demonstration as a single concept. It is not far-fetched to think that Sextus, having noticed, by himself or with someone else's help, the absurdity of his position in *M* 8, corrected himself in *PH*.

Equally, the fact that *PH* 1 has nothing corresponding to it in *M* 7–11, even while *PH* borrows a lot of material from *M* 7–11, seems to be another indication of the later position of *PH*.[35] From all this a picture emerges of *M* 7–11 as a treatise put together from course notes, teacherly and a bit repetitive, and of *PH* as an incisive, terse summary written later, taking account of comments and objections to the version offered in *M* 7–11.

I move now to the case of *M* 11, *Against the Ethicists*. This book puts forward a somewhat different position from that of the ethical portion of *PH* 3, and the nature and degree of this difference has been a subject of dispute among interpreters. It seems that a close reading of *M* 11 leads inevitably to the conclusion that this treatise presents doctrinal characteristics that are incompatible with the "sceptic way" as it was expounded in *PH* 1. The third chapter of *M* 11 (42–109), having shown that the dogmatists are not in agreement in their preconceptions of the good, the bad, and the indifferent, claims to present the arguments of "the sceptics," only to end by maintaining that there is nothing good or bad by nature. When one reads in *PH* 3.235 that "the sceptic, seeing such divergence in things, suspends assent about the existence of anything good or bad by nature," one gets a measure of the difference. For *M* 11, everything is good or bad only *relatively* to persons or circumstances, which evidently recalls the position of Aenesidemus. In *M* 11, then, Sextus does seem to endorse opinions, notably the opinion that nothing is good or bad by nature. For lack of a better alternative, we can settle for admitting that *M* 11, rather than being in contradiction with Pyrrhonism as some have held, is (to a greater extent than *PH*) in agreement with an earlier phase of Pyrrhonian scepticism, which could be that of Aenesidemus. A similar interpretation is offered in somewhat more detail elsewhere in this volume.[36]

Finally, the case of *M* 1 6, which may correctly be called *Adversus Mathematicos*, *Against the Professors*. This work exhibits differences from the rest of the Sextan corpus of a kind that some have been tempted to interpret from a chronological perspective; the term "schizophrenia" or even "double schizophrenia" has been used.[37] In criticizing the different arts, on the one hand Sextus makes a distinction between arguments based on their lack of utility, arguments which he declares dogmatic (he attributes them mainly to the Epicureans) and therefore rejects, and properly sceptical arguments which show the "non-existence" of the arts (making them look more like Academic than Pyrrhonian arguments). On the other hand, though, Sextus sometimes has a less clear-cut attitude towards the arguments based on lack of utility, to the point of mentioning them without criticizing them at all. The most striking example is *Against the Musicians*, where Sextus juxtaposes the two sorts of argument, the first being called "somewhat dogmatic" and the second "somewhat aporetic" (*M* 6.4–5). He offers a justification whose exact sense is obscure, although the general point is clear enough: it involves heading off the objection that anything has been left out of the refutation. It must be recognized that Richard Bett's conclusion is not absurd, according to which *M* 1–6 reflects an earlier stage of Pyrrhonism, perhaps that of Aenesidemus – also the one described by Diogenes Laertius, who actually says that the Pyrrhonists "did away with" certain notions (9.90, 94, 97, 100). Thus, *M* 1–6, along with *M* 11, would constitute the Aenesidemean side of Sextus' scepticism. But an alternative, more unified reading of *M* 1–6's relation to *M* 7–10 and *PH* is also possible, and in the remaining space I shall offer a few brief remarks in support of it.[38]

The argumentation to the effect that some art, or some essential component of an art, does not exist is explicitly presented as "aporetic," that is, sceptical; but is it not itself dogmatic? The question is all the more difficult in that *M* 1–6 itself asserts that deciding on the existence or the non-existence of something is a dogmatic attitude (1.28). A first response to this question could be that in the rest of the Sextan corpus one can find affirmations of the form "X does not exist" without it being a question of existence in the dogmatic sense. Terms like *anuparktos* or *anupostatos*, commonly translated "non-existent," indicate not non-existence in the ontological sense, but inconsistency or lack of foundation (as when, in *Against the Musicians*, Sextus says that "sound does not exist" (6.58)). But there is more to the story than this.

The position of Françoise Desbordes seems fundamentally sound: "Sextus speaks differently than in other works because he is speaking of a different thing."[39] More precisely, he is no longer speaking of philosophy. In the introduction to *M* 1–6, Sextus says that the arts present "equal difficulties" (*M* 1.7) to those encountered in examining philosophical theories. But "equal difficulties" are not necessarily *the same* difficulties; "equal" may just mean "equally serious." The difficulties are fundamental ones concerning the very validity of the arts; it is not a matter of the equal strength of opposing theses, as in the case of philosophy. In acquiring an art, a student is taught a whole theoretical apparatus that claims to inform us about the nature of certain things; for example, grammar purports to decide on the nature of the elements of discourse. Now, the introductory passage (*M* 1.6–7) is very clear that the end-point in philosophy is suspension of assent, whereas in *M* 1–6 it is arguing *against* the arts; the goal is plainly that of refutation or destruction, which is not the case in philosophy. And it seems to be this overturning of the pretensions of an art to possess a theoretical structure, and especially, principles (cf. *M* 1.40), that Sextus calls *anairein*, "overturning" or "destroying" an art.

Let us return to the arguments based on lack of utility. We have seen that sometimes Sextus not only does not criticize them, but even seems to make them his own. All this suggests that Sextus is talking of two distinct sorts of non-utility. Richard Bett is quite right to point out that, since the arts are defined by their utility, arguments attacking their utility are *one type* of argument for their non-existence – since if an art is not useful, it ceases to be an art.[40] So why accuse Epicurus of dogmatism when he holds their lack of utility against them? Sextus' statement of the Epicurean position is this: "the arts are useless for attaining wisdom (*sophia*)," and it is this that is labeled "dogmatic" (*M* 1.5). In other words, Epicurus' assertion has more to do with wisdom than with the arts, namely, that learning the arts taught in his time will not produce wisdom. He is taking a position in a recurring debate among ancient philosophers about the value to assign to intellectual culture in the philosophic life. In other passages, by contrast, it seems that drawing attention to the non-utility of the arts amounts to a critique of their very existence; and here the arguments advanced by various dogmatists, including the Epicureans, can be used by the Pyrrhonian sceptic. The Pyrrhonians and certain dogmatists, who had irreconcilable positions about philosophy, find common ground concerning the arts, namely in undermining one of their fundamental elements – in this case utility. The "somewhat aporetic" part of *Against the Musicians* then just continues that work of annihilation.

It remains true that Sextus thinks it is possible to practise certain arts, and at a high level, without holding opinions. This was especially the case in medicine. Sextus' relations with medicine are a complicated subject, which is examined elsewhere in this volume.[41] It is difficult to determine to what extent the influence went from scepticism to the medical schools and to what extent they exerted an influence on scepticism. In any case, it is in Sextus' sceptical milieu that antiquity has bequeathed its one attempt at a non-metaphysical use (in Auguste Comte's sense) of reason in the natural sciences.

NOTES

Translated into English by Richard Bett.

1   Popkin [354], p. 19. (But see the partial reassessment in Popkin [355], p. 18.)
2   See House [235].
3   Cf. Brochard [61], pp.319–20, with some doubt about the treatise *On the Soul* mentioned at *M* 10.284.
4   On this issue, see also the Introduction, section II.
5   Unlike many in this volume, I generally reserve the term "scepticism" for the Pyrrhonist tradition alone. (On the more common usage in which it also includes certain Academics, see the Introduction, section II.)
6   Diogenes thinks naturally in terms of a "school" (or "sect," *hairesis*), a label that the sceptics reject, as we shall see.
7   For more on this, see R. J. Hankinson, Chapter 5 "Aenesidemus and the Rebirth of Pyrrhonism."
8   See Paul Woodruff, Chapter 11 "The Pyrrhonian Modes."
9   One must remember that the *pithanon* was the criterion by which Carneades rebutted the accusation of "inactivity." See Bett [174], also Harald Thorsrud, Chapter 3 "Arcesilaus and Carneades" and Katja Vogt, Chapter 8 "Scepticism and Action." Sextus' account probably incorporates a critique of the dogmatism of the New Academy.
10 Editor's note: neither the author nor Jonathan Barnes could trace the source of this quotation, but both are comfortable with the attribution.
11 Couissin [247].
12 See further Harald Thorsrud, Chapter 3 "Arcesilaus and Carneades."
13 That Aenesidemus recommended suspension of assent is attested to by Sextus himself when he presents the Ten Modes of Aenesidemus, although we cannot be completely sure that Aenesidemus used the term *epochê*. According to Diogenes Laertius, Aenesidemus said that Pyrrho "philosophized in terms of the method of suspension of assent" (9.62) and for Timon and Aenesidemus "the end is suspension of assent, which tranquility follows like its shadow" (9.107). The passage of Photius' *Library* which forms the most complete testimony on Aenesidemus' *Pyrrhonist Discourses* (cf. note 16) speaks of "freedom in relation to all dogma."
14 Photius, *Library* 170b28.
15 See e.g. Bett [143], p. 199.
16 Photius, *Library* 169b41–170a11. For more on the significance of the Photius text, and for a different view of Aenesidemus, see R. J. Hankinson, Chapter 5 "Aenesidemus and the Rebirth of Pyrrhonism"; the passage just quoted forms part of text 5 in that chapter.
17 Burnyeat [276]'s objection.

18 For more on this, see Svavar Svavarsson, Chapter 2 "Pyrrho and Early Pyrrhonism" in this volume.

19 The expression "no more" (i.e. no more one way than the opposite) is in Sextus' hands an expression of suspension of assent between opposing alternatives (*PH* 1.188–91).

20 E.g. Annas and Barnes [40].

21 For a convincing case along these lines, see Castagnoli [246]. For the usual position see Hankinson [68] and especially McPherran [256].

22 For more on the *apraxia* objection and sceptical responses to it, see Katja Vogt, Chapter 8 "Scepticism and Action."

23 It was Galen who coined the term "more rustic sceptics" (*On the Differences in Pulses*, 8.711K).

24 This detail no doubt derives from the sceptics' (like the Cynics') questioning of social conventions, including incest.

25 For a different reading of this evidence, see Svavar Svavarsson, Chapter 2 "Pyrrho and Early Pyrrhonism."

26 For more on this, see James Allen, Chapter 12 "Pyrrhonism and Medicine."

27 To avoid attributing such a position to Sextus, one must take *adoxastôs*, "without opinions," with *katakolouthountes*, "following," not with *phamen*, "we say."

28 Barnes [238], p. 2646.

29 Brunschwig [244].

30 Brunschwig [244], p. 120 (p. 257 in the English translation).

31 Brunschwig [242].

32 Brunschwig [242], p. 158.

33 Brunschwig [243].

34 Brunschwig [243], p. 147.

35 At least, if *M* 7–11 was not preceded by a now lost general introduction; but see above.

36 See Richard Bett, Chapter 9 "Scepticism and Ethics." For a fuller picture, see also the introduction and commentary to Bett [41].

37 See Bett [298]; before him Barnes [297].

38 I have developed this reading in more detail in Pellegrin [312]. For another strongly "unified" reading of the place of *M* 1–6, see Emidio Spinelli, Chapter 13 "Pyrrhonism and the Specialized Sciences."

39 Desbordes [306].

40 Bett [298], p. 21.

41 See James Allen, Chapter 12 "Pyrrhonism and Medicine." See also Pellegrin [347].

II Topics and Problems

7 Scepticism and belief

Ancient scepticism, in its most radical forms, calls into question the place of beliefs, or at least beliefs of a certain kind, in the best life. For the Academic scepticism of Arcesilaus consists in part in the claim that one ought not to have any beliefs at all. And Pyrrhonian scepticism, as Sextus Empiricus describes it in his *Outlines of Pyrrhonism*, is a way of life characterized above all by the absence of beliefs of a certain kind. Some of the most difficult problems in the interpretation of ancient scepticism are the result of the ancient sceptic's claim that one ought not to have any beliefs at all or that he himself does not have any beliefs of a certain kind. Here I consider two of these problems. Ordinarily a person claims that p – that it is raining, that the wine is corked, that his wife will be at the party – because he *believes* that p, and in claiming that p he expresses his belief that p. In the first part of the chapter I examine whether, and how, Arcesilaus can claim that one ought not to believe anything without thereby doing just what he is claiming one ought not to do, namely, believing something. According to Sextus Empiricus the Pyrrhonian sceptic is someone who lacks not all beliefs but all beliefs of a certain kind. In the *Outlines of Pyrrhonism* Sextus relies on a distinction he does not explicate between beliefs of the kind the Pyrrhonian sceptic, in virtue of his scepticism, lacks and beliefs of the kind his scepticism permits him to have. In the second and longer part of this chapter I try to make sense of this distinction and to identify those beliefs that are, and those beliefs that are not, compatible with Pyrrhonian scepticism.

I ARCESILAUS

According to Cicero at *Acad* 1.45 Arcesilaus claimed *both* that

(NK) Nothing can be known

and that, *since* this is so,

(USJ) A person ought not to assent to anything but suspend judgment about everything.

If believing something is a matter of assenting to it, then (USJ) – the principle of universal suspension of judgement – is equivalent to the claim that one ought not to believe anything at all. Cicero in the same passage also tells us that Arcesilaus claimed that one ought to assent to a proposition p, and so believe that p, only if by assenting to p one thereby comes not only to *believe*, but also to *know*, that p.[1] The claim that one ought to believe that p only if doing so satisfies the conditions for knowing that p together with the claim (NK) that nothing can be known – that in no case does believing that p satisfy the conditions for knowing that p – entails the claim the one ought not to believe anything.

Cicero represents Arcesilaus as assenting to, and so believing, both (NK) and (USJ). But other ancient sources suggest that Arcesilaus at least claimed to suspend judgement about *everything*, and so would have claimed to suspend judgement about (NK) and (USJ).[2] So on one possible line of interpretation – call it *the dialectical interpretation* – Arcesilaus did *not* believe either (NK) or (USJ).[3] Instead, Arcesilaus argued that it is the Stoics who, in virtue of certain philosophical doctrines they hold, are committed to both (NK) and (USJ). For the Stoics claimed that knowing, rather than merely believing, something about the world is a matter of assenting to a particular kind of impression they called a "cognitive impression."[4] Arcesilaus argued that there are no cognitive impressions and that, consequently, anyone who takes knowledge to consist in assent to a cognitive impression, as the Stoics do, is committed to the claim that nothing can be known, that is, that no instance of believing something about the world can be an instance of knowledge.[5] Moreover, on the dialectical interpretation it is the Stoics, not Arcesilaus, who claim that one ought to assent to, and so believe that, p only if doing so satisfies the conditions for knowing that p. Since the Stoics accept this norm for giving and withholding assent, and since (Arcesilaus has argued) they are committed to the claim that no instance of believing that p satisfies the conditions for knowing that p, the Stoics are also committed to (USJ), that is, to the claim that a person ought not to assent to anything but suspend judgement about everything.

On the dialectical interpretation, then, Arcesilaus argues as a critic of the Stoics and in that role he simply identifies certain implications of Stoic doctrine. His criticisms leave the Stoics with two options. They can retain their view that knowledge consists in assent to a cognitive impression but alter the norm they take to govern giving and withholding assent. They can do this by claiming that in fact it *is* permissible to assent to non-cognitive impressions since, as Arcesilaus' argument against the existence of cognitive impressions has shown, mere belief is the best epistemic condition a human being can attain. Alternatively, the Stoics can abandon the view that knowledge consists in assent to a cognitive impression, and in this way detach the possibility of knowledge from the existence of cognitive impressions. If they were to excercise either option, however, the Stoics would be making significant revisions in their epistemology.

One motive for the dialectical intepretation, and so for dismissing Cicero's testimony at *Acad* 1.45 as inaccurate, is that Arcesilaus as Cicero presents him there is, it is claimed, inconsistent. For Arcesilaus is said by Cicero to assent to something – namely, to the proposition, (USJ), that one ought not to assent to anything – while also believing, as a result of assenting to that very proposition, that one ought not to assent to anything. Moreover, Arcesilaus is said by Cicero to assent to several other propositions – that nothing can be known and that one ought to assent to something only if doing so satisfies the conditions for knowledge – while also believing (as a result of assenting to (USJ)) that one ought not to assent to anything. Strictly speaking, however, Arcesilaus, as Cicero presents him at *Acad.* 1.45, is *not* guilty of inconsistency.[6] For inconsistency, at least in the usual logical sense of that term, is a matter of two statements being incompatible, and two statements are incompatible if and only if it is not possible for both statements to be true. Someone who claims or believes that p is guilty of inconsistency in this sense if and only if he claims or believes something else q such that it is not possible for both p and q to be true. But Arcesilaus, as Cicero presents him at *Acad* 1.45, does not make incompatible claims or hold incompatible beliefs.[7] He simply does something – assent to a proposition – that he believes he ought not to do.

By itself this is an all-too-human phenomenon. In this case, how-ever, it indicates a significant problem for anyone who, like Arcesilaus as Cicero describes him, assents to, and so believes, (USJ). For it seems as though it is not possible for someone who assents to, and so believes, (USJ) to avoid doing something that, as a result of assenting to (USJ), he believes he ought not to do. A person who assents to (USJ) believes, as a result of doing so, that he ought not to assent to anything. Yet if he believes this, then he believes that he ought not to assent to (USJ). So Arcesilaus cannot assent to (USJ) without thereby violating it – with-out, that is, doing just what (USJ) says, and Arcesilaus himself believes, he ought not to do. He can satisfy (USJ) – that is, do what (USJ) says he ought to do, namely, suspend judgement about everything – only if he withholds assent from and suspends judgement about (USJ) itself. As Cicero presents him at *Acad.* 1.45, then, Arcesilaus is in the unsatis-factory position of assenting to, and so believing, a principle, (USJ), that he violates by assenting to, and so believing, it. Cicero's testimony here, therefore, raises without answering the following question. Is there a stance or attitude Arcesilaus can take toward (USJ) such that (1) as a result of taking that stance or attitude toward (USJ) Arcesilaus is not indifferent to it, and yet (2) by taking that stance or attitude toward (USJ) Arcesilaus does not thereby violate it?

There are at least two ways to answer this question in the affirma-tive. The first way is to draw a distinction between two kinds of assent: strong vs. weak assent. On this line of interpretation (USJ) is to be understood as the thesis that one ought not to give *strong* assent to anything. Arcesilaus, as Cicero presents him at *Acad.* 1.45, does not give strong assent to (USJ) or to anything else. But he does give *weak* assent to (USJ) and to much else – including (NK) and the claim that one ought to give (strong) assent to something only if doing so satisfies the conditions for knowledge. Yet in giving weak assent to (USJ) Arcesilaus does *not* thereby violate it. For (USJ) prohibits one only from giving strong assent to itself or to anything else.

How, though, is strong assent different from weak assent? Michael Frede has proposed that strong assent to a proposition, unlike weak assent, involves taking that proposition to be true.[8] But what is it to take a proposition to be true? Frede seems to give more than one answer this question. Sometimes he writes as though taking a proposition p to be true is a matter of *explicitly* or *consciously* think-ing the thought that it is true that p.[9] I give strong assent to the proposition "It is raining" if and only if I give weak assent to that proposition (and so believe that it is raining) *and* explicitly or consciously think the *additional* thought that it is true that it is raining. But this way of distinguishing strong from weak assent is implausible for two reasons. First, it would be very odd to believe that it is raining and then to think as an additional thought – as a thought that is distinct from, rather than an expression or manifestation of, one's belief that it is raining – that it is true that it is raining.[10] Second, and more importantly, on Frede's view giving weak assent to a proposition *p* is compatible with *implicitly* or *unconsciously* thinking that it is true that *p*. If this is so, then the difference between strong and weak assent to *p* is just the difference between thinking explicitly and implicitly, or consciously and unconsciously, that it is true that *p*. Yet *this* difference, real as it is, is utterly irrelevant to (USJ). For there is no reason to think that (USJ) is to be understood as the thesis that, for any proposition *p*, one ought not to think *explicitly* or *consciously* that it is true that *p*. There is no reason to think, that is, that (USJ) is supposed to prohibit one from thinking explicitly or consciously thoughts of the form "It is true that *p*" while permitting one to think implicitly or unconsciously thoughts of the very same form.

Frede also describes strong assent as "active acceptance as true."[11] If Frede is here using "acceptance" as a synonym for "belief" (as he appears to be doing), then on his view weak assent to a proposition *p* is a matter of believing that *p without* believing that *p* is true.[12] This is, at a minimum, a non-standard conception of belief. For on the standard conception of belief, believing that *p* is equivalent to believing that *p* is true – even, as is almost always the case, in the absence of the *additional* thought, implicit or explicit, that *p* is true. Frede cannot reject this standard conception of belief without providing a good argument for doing so, and this he does not do.[13]

A more promising way to go is to appeal not to a distinction between two kinds of assent but to the distinction between assenting to, and so believing, a proposition and merely treating that proposition as true – in the way we do when we assume or pretend or hypothesize that *p*. On this line of thought Arcesilaus does not assent to (USJ) but he does treat it, and a host of other propositions, as true. Now the distinction between assenting to a proposition and merely treating it as true might have an Academic pedigree. For elsewhere in the *Academica* (2.104) Cicero attributes to the Academic

Clitomachus (who, in turn, is presumably following an argument as he understands it made by his teacher Carneades) a distinction between assenting to an impression and merely "approving" of it. Clitomachus uses this distinction to reply to the *apraxia* charge made by the Stoics against the Academics – the charge, that is, that anyone who assents to nothing and so suspends judgement about everything will be incapable of action and, for that reason, reduced to complete inactivity.[14] Clitomachus argues that, contrary to the Stoic theory of action, action does *not* require assent to, but only approval of, an impression. The relevant point for our purposes is that Clitomachus' (or Carneades') distinction between assent and approval can be interpreted as the distinction between assenting to, and so believing, a proposition and merely treating that proposition as true.[15] In any case, questions remain even if Arcesilaus is to be understood as not assenting to (USJ) but merely treating it as true. When *we* treat a proposition as true in one way or another (by making an assumption or engaging in pretense or forming a hypothesis) we do so while retaining a vast body of beliefs about the world. We treat a proposition as true in the course of, and possibly as a consequence of, assenting to, and so believing, many other propositions. Is it possible to treat some propositions, but not others, as true while assenting to nothing and suspending judgement about everything? And if this is possible, why is it that Arcesilaus treats some propositions, but not others, as true? Why, in particular, does he treat (USJ) rather than its negation as true? Until these questions are given answers we won't have a plausible account of how Arcesilaus, or anyone else, can be more than indifferent to (USJ) without thereby violating it.

II SEXTUS EMPIRICUS

Scepticism as Sextus Empiricus describes it in his *Outlines of Pyrrhonism* has a scope, and its scope is the range of candidates for belief about which the Sceptic, in virtue of being a Sceptic rather than a non-Sceptic, suspends judgement.[16] Suspending judgement about a candidate for belief p is a matter of withholding assent both from p and from its negation, and so of lacking both the belief that p and the belief that not-p.[17] The scope of Scepticism is unrestricted if the Sceptic, in virtue of being a Sceptic, suspends judgement about *everything* and so has *no* beliefs at all. Sextus, however, places a restriction on the scope of Scepticism, and by doing so he claims that there are some beliefs the Sceptic can have without thereby compromising his Scepticism. For in a passage that requires, and has received, much careful explication Sextus writes that:

When we say that the Sceptic does not have beliefs we are not using "belief" in the more general sense in which some say that belief is acquiescing in something. For the Sceptic assents to the conditions forced on him in accordance with an appearance. For example, the Sceptic when warmed or cooled would not say "I think I am not warm (or cool)." Rather, we say that the Sceptic does not have beliefs in the sense in which some say that belief is assent to some non-evident matter investigated by the sciences. For the Sceptic does not assent to anything non-evident. (*PH* 1.13)[18]

Sextus tells us here that there are some things to which the Sceptic assents. If that is so, then there are some things about which the Sceptic does *not* suspend judgement. Moreover, in this passage Sextus implies something he does not explicitly state, namely, that by assenting to some things the Sceptic thereby acquires *beliefs*. For Sextus reports that the term "belief" (*dogma*) is used in two different ways and so has two different senses. Sextus says that in one sense of "belief" – where it is used to denote "acquiescing in something" – the Sceptic does *not* deny that she has beliefs. He then says that there are some things to which the Sceptic assents. In saying *this* he is offering an *explanation* for why it is that the Sceptic does not deny having beliefs in the sense of "belief" where a belief is "acquiescing in something."[19] Yet – and this is the implication Sextus does not make explicit – the fact that there are some things to which the Sceptic assents explains why the Sceptic does not deny having beliefs in one sense of "belief" only if the Sceptic acquires beliefs in this sense by assenting to these things. So according to Sextus in this passage (1) there are some things to which the Sceptic assents, (2) the Sceptic acquires beliefs by assenting to these things, and (3) insofar as the Sceptic acquires these beliefs the Sceptic's suspension of judgement, and so the scope of Scepticism, is restricted. Now Sextus in *PH* 1.13 also says that there is a sense of "belief" – where it is used to denote assent to something non-evident – in which the Sceptic does not have any beliefs. As a result, an interpretation of the scope of Scepticism is adequate only if it draws a distinction between two kinds of belief such that beliefs of the first but not of the second kind are compatible with Scepticism.

Call beliefs of the kind the Sceptic, in virtue of his Scepticism, lacks *dogmatic beliefs*, and beliefs of the kind that are compatible with Scepticism *non-dogmatic beliefs*. There are two general ways to understand the distinction between dogmatic and non-dogmatic belief. The first way to understand it is as the distinction between belief about how things *are* and belief about how things merely *appear* to one to be. If the distinction between dogmatic and non-dogmatic belief is understood in this way, then the Sceptic has no beliefs about how things are. Nonetheless, the Sceptic has, and perhaps cannot avoid having, beliefs about how things merely appear to him to be, and it is beliefs of this kind that are compatible with Scepticism. The notion of a belief about how things merely appear to one to be is easiest to grasp in connection with familiar perceptual illusions. An oar in the water appears to me – it looks to me as if it is – bent. If I am asked whether it *is* bent, however, I will say, because I believe, that it only appears to me to be bent. I believe that things appear to me to be a certain way (that it appears to me that the oar is bent) without believing that things are the way they appear to me to be (that the oar is bent). In the same way the Sceptic believes that things appear to him to be a certain way (that it appears to him (for example) that the tower is square or that the honey is sweet) without believing that things are the way they appear to him to be (that the tower is square or that the honey is sweet). Moreover, beliefs about how things appear to one to be are not restricted to beliefs about how things *perceptually* appear to one to be. If I can detect no flaw in an argument of great complexity, it might be the case both that the argument appears valid to me and that, being aware of its complexity (or of my inability to detect subtle fallacies), I do not yet believe that it is valid. The Sceptic, then, can have beliefs about how things appear both perceptually and non-perceptually to him while suspending judgement in each case about whether things are as they appear to him to be.

The second way to understand the distinction between dogmatic and non-dogmatic belief is not as the distinction between belief about how things are and belief about how things appear to one to be but rather as a distinction between two kinds of belief about how things are. On this line of interpretation, Scepticism permits the Sceptic to have not only beliefs about how things appear to him to be, but also, and more importantly, at least some beliefs about how things are. For the Sceptic, in virtue of his Scepticism, lacks only one kind of belief about how things are: dogmatic beliefs. Now, understanding the distinction between dogmatic and non-dogmatic belief in this second way obviously raises the question: if a dogmatic belief is *not* a belief about how things *are* rather than merely *appear* to one to be, what exactly is it? I want to consider briefly, and to reject, a particularly influential answer Michael Frede has given to this question.[20] I then turn to the details of *PH* 1.13 and argue that, according to Sextus, the only beliefs that are compatible with Scepticism are beliefs about how things appear to one to be.

Sextus says at *PH* 1.13 that the Sceptic does not have any beliefs if a belief is taken to be assent to some non-evident matter investigated by the sciences. For Sextus the sciences include, above all else, philosophy. So it might seem that for Sextus a dogmatic belief is simply a philosophical or scientific belief, that is, a belief that is part of a philosophical or scientific doctrine. The Sceptic would then be someone who, in virtue of his Scepticism, has no beliefs of this sort.[21] Frede, however, has a more inclusive conception of dogmatic belief. For Frede's view seems to be that a belief is dogmatic if it is held because its truth is taken to be a consequence of some philosophical or scientific doctrine that is itself taken to be true.[22] The Sceptic withholds assent from, and so suspends judgement about the truth of, any philosophical or scientific doctrine. There is no philosophical or scientific doctrine the Sceptic accepts, and it follows that, though the Sceptic has beliefs, and these are beliefs about how things *are* rather than merely *appear* to the Sceptic to be, there is nothing the Sceptic believes *on the basis of* a philosophical or scientific doctrine he accepts. This is one important respect in which the dogmatist (that is, someone who has dogmatic beliefs) differs from the Sceptic. The dogmatist also differs from the Sceptic in having some beliefs the Sceptic lacks, namely, those beliefs that constitute a philosophical or scientific doctrine the dogmatist accepts. But the dogmatist and the Sceptic will also share many beliefs, and with respect to these beliefs the dogmatist differs from the Sceptic not in what he believes but in the grounds or basis upon which he believes it.

The problem is that Frede's conception of a dogmatic belief as only one kind of belief about how things are – a belief that is either part of, or held on the basis of, a philosophical or scientific doctrine – has no basis in Sextus' text. Frede appeals first to *PH* 1.20 where, he claims,

Sextus places an explicit restriction on the Sceptic's suspension of judgement (and so on the scope of Scepticism). For Sextus there writes that:

When we investigate whether existing things are such as they appear, we grant that they appear, and what we investigate is not what is apparent but what is said about what is apparent – and this is different from investigating what is apparent itself. For example, it appears to us that honey sweetens. We concede this – for we are sweetened in a perceptual way. But we investigate whether, *as far as the argument goes*, it is sweet. And this is not what is apparent but something said about what is apparent.

Sextus says that the Sceptic investigates, and suspends judgement about, whether honey is sweet "as far as the argument goes." Frede, however, construes the Greek phrase standardly translated as "as far as the argument goes" as meaning instead "to the extent that this is a question for reason."[23] For Frede's view seems to be that Sextus uses this Greek phrase to refer to a special dogmatic notion of reason.[24] He writes that for the dogmatist reason is the faculty "that can lead us beyond the world of appearances to the world of real beings; and thus for [the dogmatist] it is a matter of reason, what is to count as real and as true, and what is to count as appearance."[25] According to Frede the dogmatist believes not only that honey is sweet but also that reason, as the dogmatist understands it, can establish it as true that honey is sweet. But reason, as the dogmatist understands it, is the faculty by which we acquire, if we do, philosophical or scientific knowledge. For it is the faculty by which we come to know self-evident philosophical or scientific first principles and to deduce from these first principles various truths about the world. The Sceptic, in virtue of his Scepticism, suspends judgement about whether there are any self-evident philosophical or scientific first principles. Consequently, he suspends judgement about whether anything he takes to be a truth about the world (for example, that honey is sweet) can be validly deduced from principles of this sort. But without lapsing into inconsistency the Sceptic can suspend judgement about *this* while also believing that honey is, and does not merely appear to be, sweet. On Frede's view the Sceptic believes that honey is sweet and does so not because this is something reason establishes as true but because, for example, the honey appears to him to be (that is, it tastes) sweet.

There is, however, no textual evidence to support Frede's claim that Sextus uses the Greek phrase standardly translated as "as far as the argument goes" to refer to a special dogmatic notion of reason and that, consequently, the Sceptic's suspension of judgement is restricted to how things are "to the extent that this is a question for reason." Frede cites *PH* 1.215 where Sextus, discussing the differences between Scepticism and Cyrenaicism, writes that "we [Sceptics] suspend judgment *as far as the argument goes* about external objects while the Cyrenaics assert that these objects have an unknowable nature." Frede claims that the restriction on the Sceptic's suspension of judgement expressed by the phrase standardly translated as "as far as the argument goes" is "not that the sceptic suspends judgment about how things are but not about how they appear; the restriction, rather, is that the sceptic suspends judgement about how things are in a certain respect. That, however, implies that there is another respect in which the sceptic does not suspend judgement about how things are."[26] There is, however, no reason to think that Sextus' use in this passage of the Greek phrase in question has this implication. And in fact it is much more plausible to think that Sextus uses the phrase standardly translated as "as far as the argument goes" to indicate (1) that when the Sceptic suspends judgement about a matter, he does so on the basis of a particular argument, and (2) that, given what the Sceptic takes to be the force of this argument, he regards his suspension of judgement as subject to revision. If the Sceptic suspends judgement about whether, for example, honey is sweet, he does *not* do so on the basis of an argument whose conclusion is that there is not and cannot be any reason to believe that honey is sweet. For that conclusion is equivalent to the conclusion that it is not possible to know whether honey is sweet. These are conclusions that, at least according to Sextus, the Cyrenaic accepts, and these conclusions are each an instance of negative dogmatism. For negative dogmatism is the view that knowledge or reasonable belief of one sort or another is impossible. But the Sceptic's suspension of judgement, as Sextus describes it, is not supposed to be based on any form of negative dogmatism. The Sceptic suspends judgement about whether honey is sweet on the basis of an argument that purports to show only that he does not *now* have any reason to believe that honey is sweet. But the fact that the Sceptic now lacks a reason to believe that honey is sweet is compatible with there being, and the Sceptic at some later point in time coming to have, a reason to believe that honey is sweet. That is why the Sceptic's suspension of judgement is understood by the Sceptic himself to be subject to revision. So when Sextus writes at *PH* 1.215 that the Sceptic suspends judgement "as far as the argument goes," he is claiming only that a particular argument whose conclusion falls short of negative dogmatism is the basis upon which the Sceptic suspends judgement about whether, for example, honey is sweet. *That* claim does *not* imply that there is, as Frede claims, some respect in which the Sceptic does not suspend judgement about whether honey is sweet. *PH* 1.215, then, provides no support for Frede's claim that Sextus in using the phrase standardly translated as "as far as the argument goes" is referring to a special dogmatic notion of reason and, by doing so, restricting the Sceptic's suspension of judgement to how things are "to the extent that this is a question for reason."[27]

There is, in addition, a passage from the *Outlines of Pyrrhonism* (a passage Frede does not discuss) that is difficult to reconcile with the claim that the Sceptic suspends judgement about how things are *only* "to the extent that this is a question for reason." At *PH* 1.27 Sextus argues that the belief about *anything* that it is good is a source of anxiety or distress (and so an obstacle to the achievement of the tranquility that Sextus, in line with Hellenistic philosophy more generally, identifies with happiness).[28] For, according to Sextus, if I believe that *x* is good, but I fail to possess it, I will believe that my failure to possess *x* is itself something bad, and so I will be distressed by it. Yet if I possess *x*, I will fear losing it – for I will fear the loss of anything that I possess and believe to be good – and I will be anxious about doing whatever I can to prevent its loss. In both cases the distress or anxiety I experience is the indirect result of my belief that *x* is good. For it is because I believe that *x* is good that I believe that my failure to possess *x* is bad and that, if I do possess *x*, I fear losing it. Now Sextus' argument at *PH* 1.27 does *not* target any belief that is compatible with Scepticism – that is, it does not target any non-dogmatic belief. For, otherwise, the argument would have what is for Sextus the unwelcome consequence that Scepticism does not remove, as Sextus claims it does, all of those *beliefs* that are obstacles to tranquility.[29] Sextus' argument at *PH* 1.27 is supposed to show that *only* the dogmatic belief that *x* is good – a belief the Sceptic, in virtue of his Scepticism, lacks – is a source of distress and anxiety.

Now, on Frede's interpretation of Sextus it is possible to have either a dogmatic or a non-dogmatic belief that x is good: the dogmatist has the former while the Sceptic has only the latter. According to Frede, moreover, the dogmatic belief that x is good differs from its non-dogmatic counterpart only with respect to the grounds on which it is held. For the belief that x is good is dogmatic if and only if it is held on the basis of a philosophical or scientific doctrine. If this is so, however, why would Sextus (or anyone else) think that it is *only* the dogmatic belief that x is good, and not its non-dogmatic counterpart, that is a source of distress and anxiety? Why, that is, would Sextus think that it is the grounds or basis upon which I believe that x is good that determines whether, and to what extent, I am distressed by my failure to possess x or, if I do possess x, anxious about losing it? The problem for Frede is that while it is not difficult to see how the belief that x is good is, or can be, a source of distress or anxiety, it is difficult to see how this distress or anxiety is the result of the grounds on which I believe that x is good rather than the strength of my belief that x is good or the amount of value I attribute to x in believing that it is good. If I believe strongly that x is good, or if I believe that the goodness of x is especially great, then it is plausible enough that I will be distressed by my failure to possess x or, if I do possess x, anxious about losing it. Yet if we accept Frede's account of the distinction between dogmatic and non-dogmatic belief, then we must read Sextus at *PH* 1.27 as claiming that it is the grounds on which I believe that x is good – more specifically, the fact that these grounds are philosophical or scientific rather than mundane   that is the ultimate source of my distress and anxiety. And this reading of the argument at *PH* 1.27 deprives it of any plausibility it might otherwise have had.[30] So, to sum up, Frede gives us no reason to think that for Sextus the distinction between dogmatic and non-dogmatic belief is a distinction between two kinds of belief about how things are rather than, as I shall now argue, the distinction between belief about how things are and belief about how things merely appear to one to be.

At *PH* 1.13 Sextus identifies the kind of belief the Sceptic, in virtue of his Scepticism, lacks – a dogmatic belief – as assent to something non-evident. The distinction between the evident and the non-evident is a distinction between two ways in which something is known, if it is known at all. This distinction is drawn by someone (call him the philosophical dogmatist) who, unlike the Sceptic, has a philosophical theory of knowledge. Sextus reports elsewhere that for the philosophical dogmatist something is *evident* if and only if it is known without being known on the basis of, or as a result of, an inference from something else that is known. In contrast, something is *non-evident* if and only if it is known, if it is known at all, as the result of an inference from something else that is known.[31]

Although he tells us at *PH* 1.13 that there are some things to which the Sceptic assents, Sextus does not say that the Sceptic assents to something evident. There is, however, good reason to think that, according to Sextus, the Sceptic does assent to something evident. For at *PH* 1.13 Sextus claims *both* that the Sceptic assents to something *and* that the Sceptic does not assent to anything non-evident. Yet the dogmatic philosophical distinction between the evident and the non-evident is exclusive and exhaustive: something is either evident or non-evident, and it cannot be both. So if, as Sextus claims, the Sceptic assents to something, and yet, as Sextus also claims, the Sceptic does not assent to anything non-evident, then according to Sextus the Sceptic assents to something evident.

Now at this point, there appear to be at least two problems with trying to understand the scope of Scepticism in terms of the dogmatic philosophical distinction between the evident and the non-evident. First, there are some passages where Sextus says that the Sceptic suspends judgement about those things that are evident no less than about those things that are non-evident. If this is so, then the Sceptic does not assent to anything evident and, consequently, a non-dogmatic belief cannot be characterized adequately as a belief about something evident. This first problem, however, is easily solved. At *PH* 2.95, for example, Sextus writes:

Criteria of truth having appeared perplexing, it is no longer possible to make strong assertions, so far as what is said by the Dogmatists goes, either about what seems to be evident or about what is non-evident. For since the Dogmatists deem that they apprehend the latter from what is evident, how, *if we are compelled to suspend judgment about what they call evident*, could we be bold enough to make any assertion about what is non-evident.[32]

Here and in similar passages, Sextus says that the Sceptic suspends judgement not about those things that are evident but about those things that the philosophical dogmatist regards as evident. The philosophical dogmatist thinks that certain matters are evident, and Sextus tells us that *these* matters are not evident to the Sceptic and that the Sceptic suspends judgement about them. But – and this is the important point – it does not follow that *nothing* is evident to the Sceptic. Hence, it does not follow that there is nothing to which the Sceptic assents because it is evident to him. Sextus, in describing the scope of Scepticism, makes use of the philosophical dogmatist's distinction between the evident and the non-evident. But he can do so while disagreeing with the philosophical dogmatist, as he does, about what is non-evident and what, if anything, is evident.[33]

The second, and more serious, problem is that by itself an account of the scope of Scepticism in terms of the distinction between the evident and the non-evident is uninformative. For it simply raises without answering the question what it is a dogmatic belief is about in being about something non-evident. *This* question, it seems to me, is best answered by considering what it is a non-dogmatic belief is about in being about something evident. Sextus at *PH* 1.13 says that the Sceptic assents to his own *pathê* (singular *pathos*), a term that I shall leave untranslated. A *pathos* is a state or condition the Sceptic is in as a result of being affected by something else. If, as I have argued, the Sceptic assents to and only to what is evident to him, then the Sceptic's own *pathê* are evident to him. The fact that his own *pathê* are evident to him explains, in turn, why, as Sextus also says at *PH* 1.13, the Sceptic does not deny having these *pathê*. There is, in other words, a range of states or conditions such that if the Sceptic is in one of these states or conditions, he does not deny that this is so. Thus, at *PH* 1.13 Sextus explains that if the Sceptic is warm or cool, he will not say "I think I am not warm (or cool)," that is, he will not deny that he is warm or cool. Moreover, Sextus indicates at *PH* 1.22 that the state or condition of its appearing to one that *p* (call this state or condition an *appearance*) is a kind of *pathos*.[34] If, for example, it appears to the Sceptic that honey is sweet, then its appearing to him that honey is sweet is a *pathos* the Sceptic has and so a state or condition he is in. If the Sceptic does not deny that he has this *pathos*, and so does not deny that he is in this state or condition, then he does not deny that it appears to him that honey is sweet.

However, it does not follow that the Sceptic *believes* that it appears to him that honey is sweet. For it is possible to fail to deny that p without believing that p. Yet if the Sceptic's own *pathê* are evident to him, then – given what it means for something to be evident to one – he has (non-inferential) knowledge of his own *pathê*. Further, it is an implication of Sextus' remarks at *PH* 1.215 on the differences between Scepticism and Cyrenaicism that the Sceptic has knowledge of his own *pathê*. For Sextus writes that "Some say that the Cyrenaic way of life is the same as Scepticism, since it *too* says that we apprehend only *pathê*." Sextus here reports that someone else has identified Cyrenaicism with Scepticism and that they have done so on the grounds that both the Cyrenaic and the Sceptic claim that we have knowledge only of our own *pathê*. Sextus rejects the identification of Cyrenaicism with Scepticism, but he does *not* do so by rejecting the claim that the Sceptic, like the Cyrenaic, claims that we have knowledge only of our own *pathê*. He instead explains that Scepticism differs from Cyrenaicism in *other* respects. (For the Cyrenaic, but not the Sceptic, pleasure is the end or goal of life; and the Cyrenaic, but not the Sceptic, asserts that some things – the natures of external things – cannot be known.) Now, if the Sceptic's *pathê* include his appearances (the states or conditions in which it appears to him that something is the case) then the Sceptic has knowledge of his own appearances. If it appears to the Sceptic that p, then the Sceptic knows that it appears to him that p. If this is so, and if belief is a constituent of knowledge, then if it appears to the Sceptic that p, the Sceptic not only does not deny, but also believes, that it appears to him that p.

Consider next Sextus' remark at *PH* 1.22 that an appearance is a kind of *pathos* and, as such, is *not* an object of investigation. This is so because an appearance, as a *pathos*, is something evident to the Sceptic, that is, something of which he has non-inferential knowledge. The object of any investigation the Sceptic undertakes is something that can be known, if it can be known at all, only on the basis of an inference from something else that is known. Whether honey *is* sweet is, according to Sextus at *PH* 1.19–20, something non-evident to the Sceptic, and so something the Sceptic investigates and comes to suspend judgement about. Sextus says that the Sceptic "concedes" or "agrees" that it *appears* that honey is sweet. Now the Sceptic's suspension of judgement is supposed to be the product of an investigation: the Sceptic suspends judgement about all and only those matters he investigates. If the Sceptic does not investigate whether it appears that honey is sweet, then he does not suspend judgement about whether this is so. The Sceptic's failure to investigate, and so to suspend judgement about, whether it appears that honey is sweet, together with his concession or agreement that it does appear that honey is sweet, is best explained by the fact that it is evident to the Sceptic, and so something the Sceptic knows, that it appears to him that honey is sweet.

So here, in summary, is what Sextus has to say at *PH* 1.13 about the scope of Scepticism. The Sceptic assents to his own *pathê*. The fact that he does so explains why the Sceptic does not deny having beliefs in one sense of "belief," namely, the sense in which a belief is a matter of "acquiescing in something." But the fact that the Sceptic assents to his own *pathê* explains why the Sceptic does not deny having beliefs in this sense only if the Sceptic, by assenting to his own *pathê*, acquires beliefs in the sense of "acquiescing in something." But what exactly is it to have a belief in this sense – what is it "to acquiesce in something"? Sextus at *PH* 1.13 does not give us an explicit answer to this question. But he does say that the Sceptic does not have beliefs in the sense of "belief" in which belief is assent to something non-evident. Since the dogmatic philosophical distinction between the evident and the non-evident is exclusive and exhaustive, it follows that if the Sceptic assents to something, he assents to something evident. But, as we have seen, Sextus at *PH* 1.13 tells us that the Sceptic does assent to something – his own *pathê*. It follows, then, that the Sceptic's own *pathê* are evident to him. If that is so, then, given what it is for something to be evident to one, the Sceptic has knowledge of, and so beliefs about, his own *pathê*. The Sceptic's *pathê* include, above all else, his appearances – the states or conditions in which something appears to him to be the case. Since this is so, the Sceptic's beliefs about his own *pathê* include beliefs about his own appearances, that is, beliefs about the ways things appear to him to be. If this is right, then for Sextus a non-dogmatic belief – the kind of belief that is compatible with Scepticism – is simply a belief about how things appear to one to be. And if this, in turn, is so, then a dogmatic belief – a belief about something non-evident and so a belief of the kind the Sceptic, in virtue of his Scepticism, lacks – is a belief about how things *are* rather than merely appear to one to be.

NOTES

1 At *Acad.* 1.45 Cicero attributes to Arcesilaus the claim that "nothing is more shameful than for one's assent or acceptance to outrun knowledge or apprehension" (*neque ... quicquam esse turpius quam cognitioni et perceptioni assensionem approbationemque praecurrere*). See also *Acad.* 2.77 where Cicero tells us that Arcesilaus accepted the claim made by Zeno the Stoic that it is necessary for the wise person not to have opinions, that is, mere beliefs. Since what the wise person does, or must do, is what those of us who are not wise ought to do, Zeno's claim is equivalent to the claim that one ought not to have opinions or mere beliefs – where that, in turn, is the claim that one ought to believe that *p* only if doing so satisfies the conditions for knowing that *p*.

2 See especially Sextus Empiricus, *PH* 1.232 as well as Diogenes Laertius, 4.28 and 4.32.

3 For the dialectical interpretation, see especially Couissin [179], pp. 32–42.

4 For the Stoic doctrine of cognitive impressions, see the texts collected in LS sections 39–40; and, for commentary, see Frede [103] and Perin [115].

5 For Arcesilaus' argument against the existence of cognitive impressions, see Perin [187].

6 Despite the fact that commentators regularly charge Cicero's Arcesilaus with inconsistency (or, what amounts to the same thing, self-refutation). It is particularly misleading to say, as Cooper [178], p. 87 n. 11 does, that Arcesilaus, as Cicero presents him, "contradicts himself" and so fails to preserve what Cooper calls "logical consistency."

7 As he would if, e.g. Cicero had presented him as claiming both that nothing can be known and that he knows that this is so (and, therefore, that something is, and so can be, known).

8 See Frede [278], pp. 134–36.

9 See the references in Frede [278], pp. 135–36 to "the further thought that it is true that *p*" along with his example of the craftsman who, in practicing his craft, relies on his *implicit* expert beliefs.

10 For this point, and other important criticisms of Frede's version(s) of the distinction between two kinds of assent (or, equivalently, two kinds of belief), see Fine [250], 84.

11 Frede [278], p.138.

12 See also Striker [190], p. 113.

13 Here I am very much in agreement with Fine [250], 82–88.

14 For the *apraxia* charge, see Katja Vogt, Chapter 8 "Scepticism and Action."

15 But, since Cicero gives us very little to go on, this is not the only way the distinction between assent and approval can be interpreted. For a different interpretation, see Bett [175].

16 For ease of exposition I use "Scepticism" and "Sceptic" to designate the form of Pyrrhonian scepticism described by Sextus in the *Outlines of Pyrrhonism*. I discuss the scope of Scepticism at greater length in Perin [259], ch. 3.

17 See *PH* 1.10 for Sextus' definition of suspension of judgement.

18 I use (often modified) the translation of the *Outlines of Pyrrhonism* in Annas and Barnes [40].

19 Sextus' use of the particle *gar* to introduce the claim that there are some things to which the Sceptic assents indicates that he is offering this claim as an explanation for the fact that the Sceptic does not deny having beliefs in one sense of "belief." See Fine [250], 94.

20 In fact, it is not easy to make sense of Frede's views on the scope of Scepticism in his [278] and [279]. For a more extensive discussion of his views than I can give here, see Perin [259], ch. 3.

21 This is the way that, e.g. Barnes [273] reads *PH* 1.13; see pp. 73–75 of the reprint in Burnyeat and Frede [79].

22 See especially the difficult remarks in Frede [279], pp. 18–19.

23 On Sextus' use of this Greek phrase, see Brunschwig [244].

24 See Frede [279], pp. 9–11 – though here, again, Frede's discussion is obscure.

25 Frede [279], p. 10.

26 Frede [279], p. 11.

27 It is worth noting, as Brunschwig [244], p. 244 (in the English translation) does, that the phrase standardly translated as "as far as the argument goes," and on which Frede places so much weight, occurs very rarely in Sextus: only four times in *PH* (1.20, 1.227 (a passage Frede does not cite), 3.48, and 3.72). Frede also appeals to Sextus' discussion of signs (*PH* 2.97–103) as support for his claim that the Sceptic suspends judgement about how things are only "to the extent that this is a question for reason." Sextus says there that though the Sceptic suspends judgement about one kind of sign (the so-called "indicative sign"), the Sceptic does not deny the existence of another kind of sign (the so-called "recollective sign"). There is not, as Frede suggests there is, a single kind of sign such that in one respect the Sceptic believes that there are, while in another respect he suspends judgement about whether there are, signs of this kind. So, as far as I can see, Sextus' discussion of signs offers no evidence that he restricts the Sceptic's suspension of judgement in the way Frede claims.

28 For a discussion of Sextus' argument at *PH* 1.27, see Perin [259], ch. 1. This argument differs in certain important respects from the argument for a connection between Scepticism and tranquility given at *M* 11.111–14. On that argument see especially Bett [41].

29 Though Sextus does not claim that Scepticism removes *all* obstacles to tranquillity (and so he does not claim that the Sceptic does, or can, achieve *complete* tranquility). For, as he concedes at *PH* 1.29, the Sceptic, no less than anyone else, is subject to those bodily conditions (e.g. cold, hunger, and thirst) that are sources of distress.

30 See Burnyeat [276] for a similar point against Frede (p.52 of the reprint in Burnyeat and Frede [79]).

31 *PH* 2.97, 2.99, *M* 8.141, 8.144.

32 See also *M* 7.25 and 8.141–42.

33 Burnyeat [277] has argued that the fact, as he sees it, that the Sceptic does not practice what he calls *insulation* renders the distinction between the evident and the non-evident irrelevant to the scope of Scepticism; see pp. 115–16 of the reprint in Burnyeat and Frede [79]. For a discussion of, and response to, Burnyeat's argument (something I can't undertake here) see Perin [259], ch. 3.

34 For this point see especially Fine [250], 90–91.

8 Scepticism and action

If the sceptic holds nothing to be true, his dogmatic opponent argues, he is not able to act. This is the core of the famous Apraxia challenge, arguably the best known anti-sceptical argument in antiquity.[1] Several versions of this argument figure in ancient scepticism. At least for the most part, these arguments rely on core assumptions of Stoic epistemology and theory of action: that we have impressions (*phantasiai*), some of which are practical, i.e. prescribe an action as to be done, and that we either assent to our impressions or not. In assenting to an impression, we hold something to be true. For fools (i.e. almost everyone), this amounts to having an opinion. For the wise person, every instance of holding something to be true is a piece of knowledge. In the case of practical impressions, assent (*sunkatathesis*) is further identified with impulse (*hormê*). If there are no external impediments, impulse sets off action.[2]

The sceptic's explanation of his actions most importantly consists in his response to the Apraxia challenge, and more particularly, in his critical engagement with the Stoic claim that, in action, we assent and thus hold something to be true. Our interpretation of his response to the Apraxia challenge, however, relates to a broader framework of questions. First, how closely does the sceptic's life resemble ordinary life? Are the sceptic's actions, in the end, like everybody's actions? Secondly, does the sceptic consider his way of life as an attempt at living *well*? Is suspension of judgement, perhaps, a safer road to happiness than adherence to a (potentially false) philosophical account of what is good and bad? Thirdly, we need to consider the sceptic's core activity: searching. Is sceptical investigation *genuine* investigation? What would it *mean* for the sceptic genuinely to investigate? This chapter will be devoted almost exclusively to sceptical replies to the Apraxia challenge. But our ultimate view of how well a certain reply fares will depend on a broader picture of what kind of endeavor the sceptic's life of investigation is.[3]

I shall begin with a tentative list of versions of the Apraxia challenge, as well as with an outline of what I take to be basic elements of sceptical replies (section I). I shall then turn to the two figures in the Academy whose arguments have been most influential, Arcesilaus and Carneades (section II), and to the one Pyrrhonian who wrote extensively, and whose works survive: Sextus Empiricus (section III).

I THE APRAXIA CHALLENGE: OBJECTIONS AND REPLIES

(a) Versions of the Apraxia challenge

Let me assign names to a number of problems regarding the sceptic's ability to act (this list, however, by no means aims for completeness). Note that, most generally, sceptical action must be explained in a way which is consistent with sceptic philosophy, i.e. it must be consistent with the way in which a sceptic explains his suspension of judgement. Secondly, the opponents of the sceptics might formulate several versions of the objection. Thirdly, a sceptic might *interpret* the challenge he is confronted with, and this interpretation might already be part of his reply. I have indicated in square brackets where, I think, the particular problem is most prominently addressed:[4]

Self-destruction charge: Suspension of judgement leads to self-destruction [Pyrrho]

Animal charge: Action without assent is not the action of a rational being; at best it is the behavior of a non-rational animal [Academics]

Plant charge: Without assent, the sceptic is reduced to complete, i.e. plant-like, inactivity [Sextus]

Inconsistency charge: No matter what the sceptic professes, he at least sometimes assents [Sextus]

Paralysis charge: Without a practical criterion, the sceptic may not be able to choose one particular course of action. There is no way to settle on any one of several, mutually incompatible actions available at a given time [Academics and Sextus]

Eudaimonist charge: The sceptic cannot live a good life [Academics and Pyrrhonism]

(b) The sceptic's options

Much of ancient scepticism seems to be worked out and presented in so-called dialectical fashion. The sceptic envisages himself, or indeed is, in a controversy with philosophers from other schools, whom he calls dogmatists. In the most general sense, everyone who holds philosophical views is a dogmatist. But when a sceptic speaks of "the dogmatists," this expression often simply refers to the Stoics. When explaining how they can act, the sceptics make dialectical use of the Stoics' technical vocabulary and some of their assumptions. While there is broad scholarly agreement that we find some such dialectical element both in Academic and Pyrrhonian Scepticism, there is considerable disagreement on the details of this picture, and individual sceptics may employ their opponents' assumptions in different ways. A sceptic's arguments might, as it were, exclusively target the dogmatist, leading *him* to a certain view. Alternatively, we might think that the sceptic is *himself* developing a philosophy – his *own* philosophy – through dialectical engagement with the dogmatist's views. Thirdly, a sceptic could be committed to the idea that we must rely on reason as our guide in life (in a way that we might call Socratic), but act on this commitment by investigating the philosophical theories of *others*.[5]

Most generally put, sceptics engage with at least two elements of the Stoic account of action. First, they push the dogmatist's views on what assent actually *is*, *how it comes about*, and whether one needs to *assent* to an impression in order to become active, or can somehow *adhere* to it without assenting to it. Secondly, they characterize the *kind of impression* that figures in action. By addressing these two issues, the sceptic can formulate a so-called practical criterion: an explanation of what it is that makes the sceptic active rather than inactive, performing one action rather than another.

II ACADEMIC RESPONSES TO THE APRAXIA CHALLENGE[6]

(a) Arcesilaus: action without assent

Arcesilaus discusses what are, according to the Stoics, three movements in the soul: impression, assent, and impulse. Apparently appealing to Stoic assumptions, he argues that we can avoid only one of these movements, assent (Plutarch, *Col.* 1122A–D). Impression and impulse arise without us performing a cognitive act. But as movements of the mind, they can "move us." Impulse for action is generated without assent to the impression.

To the Stoics, action without assent is not the action of a rational being. Arcesilaus is robbing people of their minds (Cicero, *Acad.* 2.37–39). Insofar as Arcesilaus' arguments aim to explain the sceptic's ability to act, Arcesilaus is thus faced with the kind of objection I am calling the Animal charge. But the claim that one can act without assent is also vulnerable to the Eudaimonist charge – that, if the sceptic's action does not involve assent, he cannot lead a *good* life (a life in which one chooses to perform better rather than worse actions, etc.) (Cicero, *Acad.* 2.39). Apparently in response to this, Arcesilaus argues that someone who suspends judgement about every-thing will regulate his actions in accordance with "the reasonable" (*to eulogon*) (Sextus, *M* 7.158; cf. 7.150). This reply is difficult to interpret in two respects. First, what is "the reasonable"? Secondly, is "regulat-ing in adherence with" a weaker kind of acceptance than assent?

(b) The reasonable I: reasonable impressions

Arcesilaus might be exploiting either of two Stoic uses of the term "the reasonable." Let us first consider the Stoic use that scholars traditionally see in play here.[7] The Stoics distinguish between a number of different kinds of *axiomata*, "statements," which are the linguistic counterparts of impressions. One kind of *axioma* is called "*eulogon*," with the explanation that such *axiomata* have a greater tendency to be true than they have not to be true, e.g. "I shall be alive tomorrow" (DL 7.76). It is assumed that today, I do not actually know whether I shall be alive tomorrow, and I am thus not able to determine the truth-value of the *axioma*. But the *axioma* is such that its tendency to be true is greater than its tendency to be false.[8] If Arcesilaus uses "reasonable" in this sense, his practical criterion responds to the Paralysis charge. Acting on the basis of impression and impulse alone is not an uncontrolled response to just *any* impression. In the absence of a cognitive impression, and without assenting to the non-cognitive (thus avoiding opinion), the sceptic can adhere to a certain type of impressions, namely reason-able impressions.

(c) The reasonable II: reasonable justifications

The way in which Sextus portrays Arcesilaus' criterion, however, suggests that Arcesilaus exploits a sense of *eulogon* which is more directly concerned with virtuous action and leading a good life (and thus with the Eudaimonist charge). Arcesilaus seemingly argues that the sceptic who regulates his actions in accordance with the reasonable acts *correctly* (*katorthôsei*), leads a good life, and thus will be *happy* (Sextus, *M* 7.158). Is Arcesilaus refering to a different Stoic use of *eulogon* from the one mentioned above?

The Stoics define an appropriate action as an action that can, in retrospect, be given a reasonable (*eulogon*) justification.[9] Appropriate action is not correct action; however, both are closely related insofar as the perfect agent, who acts correctly, does so by *consistently performing only appropriate actions*.[10] Scholars disagree on the interpretation of the definition of appropriate action. The more widespread interpretation holds that, since appropriate action falls short of being *correct* action, and since fools can perform appropriate actions, a reasonable justification is a "more-or-less reasonable" justification (even very conscientious fools, who are on the path to virtue – so-called progressors – do not reason perfectly).[11] Against this interpretation, Brennan argues that an appropriate action is an action for which one can give a genuinely *well*-reasoned justification.[12] This is compatible with fools performing appropriate actions insofar as the definition does *not* say that, whenever one performs an appropriate action, one deliberates perfectly. Rather, the point is that, *ex post facto*, a reasonable justification could be given, and the definition does not state that such a justification would be given by the agent *herself*.

It seems unlikely that Arcesilaus would not have been aware of this rather prominent Stoic use of the term. Further, this notion is much more directly associated with Stoic thought about a *good life* than the category of reasonable impressions (or *axiomata*). But on the other hand, Arcesilaus seems to be primarily concerned with characterizing impressions that are, for the sceptic, practical criteria. An *ex post facto* justification cannot play the role of a criterion. Perhaps Arcesilaus is alluding to both Stoic notions of the reasonable, and attempting to exploit different aspects of them.

(d) Carneades' criterion: the persuasive

Before we turn to the idea of "regulating one's life," let us examine Carneades' criterion: the persuasive (*pithanon*, translated by Cicero as *probabile*).[13] The term *pithanon* is employed by the Stoics to describe the psychological effects that impressions have on us, and it seems that Carneades uses the term in this sense as well (Cicero, *Acad.* 2.99, 104). According to the Stoics, impressions can be more or less persuasive, pulling us towards assent or not (Sextus, *M* 7.242–43). In everyday contexts, Carneades says, it is fine to adhere to the persuasive. But he develops a complex account of how impressions can be thoroughly examined. An impression which is persuasive, undiverted (by another impression), and fully explored, constitutes his *general* criterion. This criterion must be employed in weighty matters of happiness (*M* 7.166–75 and 176–84). From this account, we can gather that Carneades takes himself to be responding not only to the charges that the sceptic cannot act, and cannot decide which action to perform, but also to the Eudaimonist charge. The sceptic's life, lived according to persuasive impressions which are scrupulously explored, is assumed to be a good life.

(e) Approval versus assent

Our surviving sources do not explain Arcesilaus' notion of *regulating* or *guiding* one's life. Carneades, however, seems to have explicitly argued that there is a difference between assenting and "following" or "approving of" an impression (Cicero, *Acad.* 2.104). He holds that it is possible to adhere to a persuasive impression without assenting to it (*Acad.* 2.59, 99, 108). What would it mean for the sceptic to adhere to an impression without assenting to it? Scholars have explored various ways of explaining this distinction. Frede suggests that the sceptic may "have a view" (and be guided by it) in a way which does not involve "taking a position."[14] Bett argues that the sceptic can call into question the plausibility of the Stoic assumption that, in everything we do, we judge things to be so-and-so.[15] Perhaps the sceptic, in merely "adhering" to impressions, is actually rather like everyone else, and it turns out to be a dogmatic fantasy that action ordinarily involves assent (e.g. in walking down the street, assenting to the impression that this is a street, this is a man, etc., in such a way as to walk down the street, not bump into the man, etc.). The questions surrounding these issues are manifold. Most importantly, it does not seem to me that the Academics argue for, as it were, a "rationally blind" way of being active; their actions are guided by conscious engagement with impressions. In this way, their practical criteria take care of what I am calling the Paralysis charge. They can readily explain why the sceptic adheres to this impression rather than to that one (i.e. the sceptic is not, by letting go of assent, but retaining impression and impulse, faced with an impossible stalemate among multiple conflicting impressions). They also address the Animal charge. Action that follows the reasonable or persuasive is action for which the agent assumes responsibility, and which she ascribes to her own, rational decision-making.[16]

III SEXTUS EMPIRICUS

(a) Actions or activity?

The Academics, it seems, are happy to describe the sceptic as performing *actions*. And it may indeed seem that their adherence to reasonable or persuasive impressions retains essential traits which various philosophical schools think that the actions of human beings display. Adherence to reasonable or persuasive impressions leaves room for something like decision-making and accountability. The agent performs one action rather than another because it seems more reasonable or more persuasive to her to do so.

But when we come to Sextus matters are different. For he is careful to present the Apraxia challenge *not* as the claim that the sceptic cannot *act*, i.e. not as the Animal charge. Rather, he presents it as the charge that the sceptic cannot *be active*, the Plant charge. It is not his objective to show that Pyrrhonian action has the traits which are traditionally ascribed to the action of rational beings who are accountable for their actions. Rather, his aim is to show that the sceptic, as it were, goes *through the motions* of an ordinary life.[17] Sextus' sceptic is *active*, but he is not *acting* in the robust sense of the dogmatist's theory of human action.

Sextus' most elaborate presentation of the Apraxia charge is at *M* 11.162–66. According to the critics whom Sextus cites, the sceptic is either confined to inactivity (*anenergêsia*) or to inconsistency.

To inactivity, because not desiring one thing and avoiding another is virtually to reject life, and to be reduced to a plant (scc also *PH* 1.226–27), and to inconsistency, because, if faced with a tyrant's command to do something unspeakable, each available option (choosing voluntary death for non-compliance, or going along with the command) is a deliberate choice, i.e. a choice which, according to the anti-sceptical argument, involves assent to the impression that *this* (accepting the penalty of death, doing the unspeakable deed) is what one should be doing. In *PH* 1.21–24, where Sextus explains his practical criterion (a passage which we shall focus on below), he mentions the charge of inactivity (Plant charge), but not the Inconsistency charge. Here, however, he says that the sceptic needs a *criterion* according to which he can perform some actions and abstain from others. I take this remark to indicate that Sextus addresses what I call the Paralysis charge – the problem how the sceptic can discriminate between various alternative actions, so as to perform *one particular* action, rather than being pulled towards several actions at once.

(b) Appearances

The practical criterion of Pyrrhonism, according to Sextus, is "that which appears" (*to phainomenon*); the sceptic adheres to appearances (*phainomena*) (*PH* 1.21–22). But how can adherence to appearances make the sceptic perform some actions, and not others? Would it not seem, in particular from the sceptic's *own* point of view, that there are regularly several conflicting appearances? The attempt to act on all of them would indeed seem paralysing. Let us look more closely at Sextus' explanation, and at the Pyrrhonian notion of appearances.

The term "appearances" is at the center of Pyrrhonian Scepticism, and probably already played an important role in Pyrrho's response to the Apraxia challenge. Part of the evidence we have about Pyrrho, the eponymous hero of Pyrrhonian Scepticism, consists of biographical anecdotes. These anecdotes focus on the seeming self-destructiveness of Pyrrho's philosophy. Famously, Pyrrho needs to be protected by his friends so as not to be run over by oncoming wagons (DL 9.62). However, the anecdotes might well be hostile fabrications; it is likely that other sources, which attribute to Pyrrho a certain kind of reliance on *appearances*, are on balance more trustworthy.[18]

Sextus speaks of appearances in a number of related, but different ways. (i) He defines scepticism as the ability to put things into opposition: thoughts with thoughts, appearances (*phainomena*) with appearances, and thoughts with appearances. At this point, Sextus says, he takes *phainomena* to refer to perceptible things (*aisthêta*) (*PH* 1.8–9). (ii) When explaining the sceptic's mode of speech, Sextus takes care to use the cognate verb, *phainesthai* (to appear), elliptically: "A now appears F to me [the sceptic]" (rather than: "A now appears to be F to me"). He says that an appearance is an affection (*pathos*) of the sceptic, something he passively undergoes (*PH* 1.15). Here, "appearance" need not be limited to cases of perceptual appearing. (iii) In his account of sceptical action, Sextus defines the term *phainomenon* as co-extensive with the term "impression" (*phantasia*), saying that an impression is an involuntary affection (*pathos*) and therefore not open to question (*PH* 1.22). As we saw, according to the Stoics, impressions can (but need not) be practical. Sextus' account of adherence to appearances depends on a wide conception of appearances, according to which appearances can, in a similar fashion, be either practical or not. However, Sextus also needs to narrow down the notion of appearances that he uses when explaining the sceptic's criterion – otherwise, it would simply not be a practical *criterion*, i.e. something according to which some actions are performed, and other actions are *not* performed. He does so by tying the notion of appearances to the notion of "ordinary life," explaining that ordinary life seems to have four aspects:

Thus, attending to the appearances, we live in accordance with the ordinary ways of life, without holding opinions – for we are not able to be utterly inactive. These ordinary ways of life seem to be fourfold, and to consist in guidance by nature, necessitation by affections, the handing down of laws and customs, and instruction in expertises. By nature's guidance we are naturally capable of perceiving and thinking. By the necessitation of affections, hunger conducts us to food and thirst to drink. By the handing down of customs and laws, we regard piety as good and impiety as bad in a practical, everyday kind of way. Through instruction in expertises we are not inactive in those kinds of expertise which we adopt. (*PH* 1.23–24, tr. Annas and Barnes [40] with modifications)

Adherence to appearances is here explained as adherence to the normal ways of life – to the ways in which life happens to be lived in the communities that the sceptic is part of. The notion of appearances is thus importantly narrowed down. Not every passively experienced impression guides the sceptic's actions. Rather, only those passively experienced impressions that go along with an ordinary way of leading one's life do so. Thus, appearances can do the work of a practical *criterion*.

(c) Necessitation of the affections, customs, and training

Necessitation of affections is, at other points in the *Outlines*, associated with the sceptic's forced assent (cf. *PH* 1.13, 19, 29–30, 193, 237–38). Hunger, for example, necessitates our assent, and thus moves us to eat. Note that Sextus does not claim that the sceptic "adheres" rather than assents, or assents to something like "it is persuasive that I am hungry." Rather, he assents to the impression that he is hungry. Why is his assent not inconsistent with suspension of judgement? First, and this applies to Sextus' discussion of appearances as the sceptic's criterion as a whole, because, insofar as assent is given, it is given to *appearances*. Secondly, and this applies specifically to necessitation of the affections, the sceptic's assent is *forced*. It is not in the sceptic's power and does not involve the view that, indeed, one should perform this action. The notion of "forced assent" is quite ingenious. It turns the Stoics' theory upside down. According to the Stoics, it is the mark of assent that it is "in our power." Sextus here devises a kind of assent that lacks precisely this core feature. "Forced assent" seems like a pun on the Stoic conception of assent.

The sceptic adheres to the value judgements of his community, without adopting them or endorsing these values. Customs and laws are appearances. We grow up with a certain way of doing something, and it thus appears to us that this is how it should be done. The sceptic "falls in" with the ways of life in his community. Similarly, the sceptic adopts ways of doing things that require expertise. In the course of his life, he receives instruction in many areas, some of them part of ordinary life (e.g. being able to fix himself breakfast), some of them part of professions (e.g. if he is trained as a doctor, which medications to prescribe for which illnesses). Custom and training explain why the sceptic does some things, but not others (thus responding to the Paralysis charge). In *M* 11.166, Sextus says that the sceptic's actions are "by chance" (*tuchon*). The point of this, however, is not that he performs random actions (adhering by mere chance to this rather than to that impression). Rather, his actions are "random" in the sense that it just happens to be the case that he was raised and trained in this way rather than in that way. When complying with the tyrant's demands, or resisting him in what looks like bravery, the sceptic will adhere to the ideas his parents raised him with; and it is a matter of chance what these ideas are. The sceptic thus is able to discriminate, and to perform one rather than the other action. At the same time, even "hard cases" can be accounted for without ascribing any kind of assent (in the dogmatist's sense: i.e. regarding what is valuable, to be done, the case, etc.) to the sceptic, thus saving him from the Inconsistency charge.

In *PH* 1.21–24, Sextus does not address the question whether adherence to custom and technical instruction involve any kind of assent. However, at *PH* 2.102, Sextus says that the sceptic undogmatically assents to the things that ordinary life relies on, and we might thus think that *undogmatic assent* figures in these aspects of the sceptic's life.[19] Like forced assent, this notion is, from the point of view of the Stoics, nonsensical. Perhaps there are no further features of Stoic assent that are as central as these two: that assent is in our power, and that assenting is holding something to be true. For the Stoics, "undogmatic assent," i.e. assent by which one does not come to hold something as true, simply is not assent.

(d) Nature's guidance

Let us now turn to the first point in the sceptic's list of adherence to appearances: nature's guidance. From the immediate context, it is not clear how this fits in.[20] Why is the fact that the sceptic can perceive and think a result of nature's guidance? And why does it need to be explained within the reply to the Apraxia challenge? First, I suggest, we should note that it is a dogmatic idea that nature makes us acquire the abilities to perceive and think.[21] According to both the Stoics and the Epicureans, human beings acquire reason in the early years of their lives. Reason is here understood in a substantive way. To have reason means to have acquired so-called preconceptions and thus to have mastered a certain amount of content. Having a preconception of a tree, for example, involves being able to identify (most) trees as trees, and to frame as well as to answer certain questions about trees (such as "what distinguishes a tree from a bush?"). It is through the formation of preconceptions that we perceive trees as trees, and that we are able to think and investigate.

One of the major activities in the sceptic's life is investigation. In order to respond to the Apraxia challenge, the sceptic must not only explain how he can cross the street or eat his breakfast. Perhaps more than anything else, he must explain how he can persist in his investigation – without this, he would cease to be a sceptic. But why is the sceptic's search problematic? Traditionally, scholars have emphasized that it is difficult to see how the sceptic might still "seek the truth," even though, after his conversion to scepticism, he applies an arsenal of argumentative modes that intentionally and reliably produce suspension of judgement.[22] Further, the sceptic's tranquillity might seem like an all-too miserable substitute for the quietude that he initially sought by trying to find answers to troubling questions.[23] There is, however, a third problem to consider. According to Hellenistic assumptions, *understanding* the questions that are under discussion, and the concepts they employ, involves mastering a certain amount of content. But this might appear to involve assumptions (such as "dogs have legs"), which would be inconsistent with suspending judgement.

While Sextus does not refer to this problem in *PH* 1, he begins Book 2 of the *Outlines* with an elaborate account of it, and discusses it again in *M* 8.337 *et seq.*, saying that it is a charge *commonly brought against the sceptics*. I shall add this charge to my list of versions of the Apraxia challenge, and call it the Search charge. The sceptic cannot be a sceptic, i.e. engage in investigation (*skeptein*), if investigating involves assumptions in a way that is inconsistent with suspension of judgement. However, the *naturally* acquired assumptions that come along with preconceptions do not have this feature: they are acquired without assent (assent being a capacity which reason only has once one *already* has acquired preconceptions). The sceptic thus can understand and employ concepts. He is able to ask, for example, whether there is anything good by nature, and to have some understanding of what this question amounts to, without having assented to any assumptions about what the good is, or what nature is.

We can now see why the first aspect in the sceptic's adherence to appearances is vital to Sextus' response to the Apraxia challenge. Sextus needs to explain the sceptic's ability to think, an ability that his dogmatic interlocutors do not view as a merely *formal* one.

According to his opponents, being able to think involves the mastery of a certain amount of *content*. The sceptic's ability to investigate is an extension of his ability to think. In order to explain his investigative activity, Sextus might dialectically employ the dogmatic view that a certain amount of content is acquired via a natural process – a process that does not involve assent and thus is consistent with suspension of judgement. *PH* 1.23–24 does not mention this line of thought. However, it is only in the context of the dogmatists' substantive theories of reason that the sceptic needs to explain why his cognitive abilities and their exercise are consistent with suspension of judgement. With a view to Sextus' engagement with these issues in *PH* 2 and *M* 8, we can thus speculate that, if he were to explain the sceptic's abilities to think and perceive in more detail, he might argue along these lines.

(e) The Pyrrhonian life

Sextus begins the *Outlines* with the remark that, while certain others hold doctrines, and still others state that nothing can be known, the sceptic continues to investigate (*PH* 1.1). In the early chapters of the account that follows, Sextus tells us a story about the Pyrrhonist's conversion to scepticism – how he discovers the quietude of suspension of judgement as it were by chance.[24] Once he has become a sceptic, he regularly produces suspension of judgement, armed with argumentative modes apparently tailored so as to be the perfect tools for achieving this end. The details of this story need not concern us here. Rather, we will confine ourselves to one question – a question that relates to sceptical investigation on the one hand, and to whether the sceptic, in the end, leads a rather ordinary life after all, on the other. Perhaps we should believe Sextus when he says that the sceptic does not call into question, but rather adheres to, ordinary life. Perhaps it is the ideal Stoic agent who is an odd figure, remote from life. The sceptic's response, which tradition portrays as radical, might in fact depict a much more plausible way of life – a life in which there is ample room for customary, learned action, and in which agents do not actually see themselves as fully accountable for their actions, and do not act with the conviction that their actions are what should be done.

However, no matter how much credit we give to Sextus' story, there is at least one reason why we might hesitate to adopt this interpretation. The sceptic's life seems to be a life which only people who are troubled by *philosophical questions* would adopt. Sextus' threefold distinction between those who hold doctrines, those who say that nothing can be known, and those who continue to search, does not encompass everyone. Indeed, most people are (in a way which philosophers sometimes find difficult to comprehend) rather unreceptive to what might be disturbing about unsettled questions. This observation does not seem to me to arise from our own culture. Rather, it would seem that this is what Socrates runs into all the time, and what the sceptics will have studied in Plato's dialogues: that people first need to undergo skillful interrogation before they finally come to be worried about their own unquestioned assumptions and the many inconsistencies which may lurk in them. Thus, it seems to me that the Pyrrhonian sceptic, even though he professes to adhere to ordinary life, does so in a highly unordinary way: he arrives at this adherence not from an unquestioning acceptance of things, but in the rather roundabout way of being first worried about all kinds of questions and delving into a highly specialized technique of investigating them, which, in addition to suspension on theoretical matters, supplies him with what seems an oddly uncommitted adherence to the way people ordinarily do things.

Sextus' account of the sceptic's investigative activities is also central to his reply to the Eudaimonist charge. As Sextus argues, the sceptic actually lives "correctly" and thus well (and in a sense, better than everyone else).[25] Early on in the *Outlines*, Sextus raises the question of whether the Pyrrhonist has a *hairêsis*. In the sense in which this term is often used in such contexts, he does not: he does not adhere to a set of doctrines associated with one particular "school." However, the sceptic has his own way of life, which coheres with an account. This account (i.e. his outline of Pyrrhonism), Sextus suggests, shows that the sceptic can live correctly (*orthôs*), but only in a loose sense of the term, "where 'correctly' is taken not only with reference to virtue, but more loosely, and extends to the ability to suspend judgment" (*PH* 1.16–17, tr. Annas and Barnes [40]). The sceptic's way of life thus involves an *ability* (*dunamis*) (most likely, the argumentative abilities that Sextus describes and demonstrates at great length) which leads to suspension of judgement. An explanation of the sceptic's ability to *think* is, as it were, a first step in giving this account, which eventually, or so we are invited to believe, lays out a *good* way to live.

1 *Apraxia* can be translated as "inactivity," or as "lack of action." The term *apraxia* is used in this context in Plutarch, *Col.* 1122A.

2 It is a difficult question whether assent *generates* opinion, knowledge, and impulse, or whether assent *is* opinion, knowledge, and impulse. Key passages are: Origen, *On principles* 3.1.2–3 = LS 53A; Stobaeus 2.86,17–87,6 = LS 53Q; Plutarch, *On Stoic Self-Contradictions* 1037F = LS 53R; Stobaeus 2.88,2–6 = LS 33I.

3 Two recent papers which explore these issues are Striker [264] and Cooper [178]. See also Sedley [71].

4 Striker [190] distinguishes two versions that roughly correspond to what I am calling the Plant and Animal charges, on the one hand (that without assent the Sceptic cannot act), and the Paralysis charge, on the other hand (that the sceptic will not be able to decide what to do). See also Gisela Striker, Chapter 10 "Academics versus Pyrrhonists, Reconsidered."

5 A classic discussion of the sceptic's dialectical mode of argument is Couissin [179]. The first and second option accord with different readings of Pyrrhonism. The third option is Cooper's interpretation of Arcesilaus' scepticism. Cooper argues that Arcesilaus' scepticism "is the expression of his Socratic commitment to living according to reason as our life's guide" (Cooper [178], p. 103). On Arcesilaus' dialectical method, cf. also Brittain [56], "Introduction," and Brittain [176].

6 For more on the issues considered in this section, see Harald Thorsrud, Chapter 3 "Arcesilaus and Carneades."

7 That "the reasonable" is a Stoic term was already noted by v. Arnim [173].

8 It is a difficult question whether this notion of reasonable impressions is the one that figures in a famous anecdote about Sphaerus, one of the earliest third century Stoics (DL 7.177 and Athenaeus 8.354E = LS 40F).

9 Stobaeus 2.85,13 f. = LS 59B.

10 Stobaeus 5.906,18–907,5 = LS 59I.

11 Striker [190], p. 101.

12 Cf. Brennan [97].

13 Cf. Allen [171] and [169] and Bett [174].

14 Frede [278], p. 143.

15 Bett [175].

16 According to Obdrzalek [186], assent to the *pithanon* involves "belief in the truth of one's impressions," 259. Accordingly, she opts for the translation "probable," rather than "persuasive" (which is in disagreement with most recent views, but in agreement with a long tradition of translating Cicero's *probabile* as "probable").

17 I discuss these issues in more detail in Vogt [284]. See also Gisela Striker, Chapter 10 "Academics versus Pyrrhonists, Reconsidered."

18 Bett [143], ch. 2, esp. pp. 92–93. See also Svavar Svavarsson, Chapter 2 "Pyrrho and Early Pyrrhonism."

19 Cf. M 8.156–58. Another class of appearances the sceptic adheres to is the ordinary usage (sunêtheia) of language. While he disputes the theses of grammarians, the sceptic must adhere to these appearances (which also have a normative side – think of "speaking well"; M 2.52) in order to be able to speak and investigate (M 1.172, 193, 206, 218, 229, 233; M 2.52–53, 58–59). On Sextus' claim that the sceptic accepts commemorative signs, cf. Allen [89], pp. 87–146. For discussion of aspects of ordinary life not mentioned in PH 1.21–24, see Vogt [284], pp. 166–172.

20 For discussion of various interpretations of the passage cf. Vogt [265], and Vogt [284], pp. 157–65.

21 Cf. Frede [339], p. 95. Note that, with respect to this problem, the Epicureans seem to play a rather important role. In M 8.337, Sextus explicitly refers to them. Key passages for the theory of preconceptions are: Aëtius 4.11.1–4 = LS 39E (Stoics); DL 10.31 = LS 17A and DL 10.33 = LS 17E (Epicurus).

22 Striker [264]; see also Perin [260].

23 Cf. Striker [120].

24 I adopt Striker's expression here, calling it a story [190].

25 For more on the purported advantages of the sceptic's life, see Richard Bett, Chapter 9 "Scepticism and Ethics."

9   Scepticism and ethics

Ancient Greek scepticism has an inherently practical character; in this respect it is unlike some of its modern counterparts, but typical of ancient Greek philosophy. This practical aspect is explicit in the Pyrrhonist tradition, all of whose leading members emphasized the tranquility (*ataraxia*) the sceptical outlook supposedly engendered, by contrast with the mental turmoil associated with a dogmatic outlook. But it is apparent in the Academic tradition as well. Both Arcesilaus and Carneades are reported to have offered means by which it would be possible, consistently with sceptical suspension of judgement, to engage in choice and action of a recognizably human type; and in both cases these strategies are described as capable of generating happiness (*eudaimonia* – Sextus, *M* 7.158, 184), which ancient Greek ethics generally took to be the mark of a well-lived human life. The Greek sceptics, therefore, have their eye on the question whether and how scepticism can be *lived*; and so one can speak, in a broad sense, of an ethical dimension that is always in the background in Greek scepticism, whatever the topic under discussion at any given time. However, it is also true that the topics discussed by the sceptics are sometimes themselves ethical. That is, they have to do, precisely, with how to live one's life; they concern such matters as the good and the bad, justice, or the goal (*telos*) of human life. In what follows, I focus mostly on the treatment of these issues in Sextus Empiricus, for whom our evidence, here as elsewhere, is by far the best.

At the beginning of *Outlines of Pyrrhonism*, Sextus distinguishes between "general" and "specific" sceptical discussions (1.5–6, cf. *M* 7.1). The general discussion is the characterization of scepticism itself, while the specific discussion deals with the three standardly recognized parts of philosophy, subjecting to sceptical scrutiny the theories offered by dogmatic philosophers in each of those parts. One of the three parts was, of course, ethics, and so Sextus takes up ethical topics both in the third book of *PH*, which is divided between physics and ethics, and in a complete book, *Against the Ethicists* (*M* 11), which concludes the surviving portion of the longer work that originally covered all of the same ground as *PH*.[1] The central questions in both works are whether anything is by nature good or bad, and whether there is a "skill relating to life" (*technê peri ton bion*). There is also some attention to ethical matters in *PH* 1, the only surviving specimen in Sextus of the general discussion. The last of the Ten Modes[2] is concerned with disagreements (mostly, though not entirely, between cultures) on ethical matters (*PH* 1.145–63). In addition, *PH* 1 contains an account of the sceptic's *telos*, including an account of why the sceptic is better off than the non-sceptic (*PH* 1.25–30); the latter issue also appears in the specific discussion, both in *PH* 3 (235–38) and, at much greater length, in *M* 11 (110–67). I now consider these various topics one by one.

Given Sextus' normal procedures, as outlined at the beginning of *PH* 1 (especially 1.8) and as exhibited in most of his surviving books, one would expect his discussion of the question whether anything is by nature good or bad to take the following form. He would assemble arguments in favor of there being things that are good and bad by nature, and arguments against this; these arguments might be taken from dogmatic philosophers, who actually believe in them, or they might be devised by Sextus himself or by others in the Pyrrhonist tradition, purely for dialectical purposes. And the intended result of being confronted with these opposing arguments would be that one would suspend judgement about the existence of anything by nature good or bad. In fact, neither *PH* 3 nor *M* 11 conforms precisely to this model.

The *PH* 3 discussion does at least conclude with the expected outcome; Sextus says that the sceptic "suspends judgement about anything's being by nature good or bad or in general to be done" (*PH* 3.235). But the bulk of the arguments that are supposed to motivate this outcome are not arguments for or against the general proposition that there exist things that are by nature good or bad. Rather, they consist in a multitude of conflicting positions concerning *what* things are by nature good or bad. The clearest example is an extensive series of conflicting practices and views about how to behave or not to behave (197–234); the conflicts are primarily between cultures, but also occasionally between philosophers. (This section is reminiscent of the Tenth Mode, to which I will return.) However, this departure from the expected pattern is minor. For it is not hard to see how an inability to settle on a definite answer to the question *what* things are by nature good might lead one to wonder whether *anything* is by nature good.

But Sextus does also explicitly address the latter question, and this raises a more serious puzzle. In addition to the arguments mentioned so far, the chapter includes several arguments to the effect that *nothing* is by nature good, bad, or indifferent, and some of these rely on precisely the kinds of disagreement just mentioned, concerning what things are really good (or bad or indifferent). These arguments depend on a principle that is repeated several times (*PH* 3.179, 182, 190, 193, 222, 226): if something is *by nature* a certain way, it must affect everyone in the same way. So, in order for something to be by nature good, it must strike everyone as worth pursuing (and the same applies, *mutatis mutandis*, to the bad and the indifferent). And since, as the disagreements show, there is nothing of which this is true, nothing is by nature good (or bad or indifferent).

It might seem that such arguments fit nicely with Sextus' normal procedures. If arguments that nothing is by nature good are juxtaposed with arguments for certain things being by nature good (many of which, as we have seen, do make an appearance), will this not generate suspension of judgement concerning whether anything is by nature good? But this is not how Sextus operates in this chapter. The competing positive views concerning what is really good are not placed in *opposition* to the conclusion that nothing is by nature good. Rather, as noted just above, they are the *data* that *generate* that conclusion, given the principle concerning what it is to be by nature a certain way. The conclusion that nothing is by nature good is therefore in an uncomfortable relation to the suspension of judgement that is the supposed outcome of the chapter. If it is a conclusion Sextus endorses, then his scepticism seems in question; but if he is not endorsing it, what is it doing in the discussion?

Sextus signals in two ways that he recognizes there is a difficulty. First, he twice indicates that the arguments that nothing is by nature good, bad, or indifferent are not his own arguments (178, 179), but those of other unnamed people. Secondly, immediately after laying out an argument from disagreement to the non-existence of anything by nature good (179–182), he appeals to the *same* disagreement to generate suspension of judgement about what is by nature good (182) – as if the conclusion that nothing is by nature good should not be allowed to stand on its own. The trouble is that the status of that conclusion, and its relation to the suspension of judgement that immediately follows it, is still left quite unclear. And, to return to the first point, that unclarity is only heightened when, alongside the attributions of the arguments for this conclusion to unspecified others, he also occasionally claims them as his own (179, 190). So although he does seem to see that a difficulty exists, he does not properly resolve it.

The arguments in *PH* 3 concerning things by nature good, bad, or indifferent are, then, problematic; both their relation to one another, and the consistency of some of them with sceptical principles, appear to be in question. Now, at this point it may be helpful to turn to the corresponding discussion in *M* 11. Here, too, there is a chapter about whether anything is good or bad by nature (42–109). And, although this chapter is considerably longer, it uses much of the same material. Clearly this is a case, of which there are many in Sextus, where *PH* and the longer, incomplete work of which *M* 11 is a part are drawing on the same source material. However, there is no internal conflict in *M* 11. The arguments issue straightforwardly in the conclusion that nothing is by nature good or bad (the indifferent is not mentioned here); there is no mention of suspension of judgement on this topic at all. One might try to explain this by saying that the negative arguments are intended to be juxtaposed with positive arguments of the dogmatists, with suspension of judgement as the eventual outcome. But Sextus makes clear in the next chapter that the negative arguments are indeed arguments the sceptic is supposed to have endorsed; for the sceptic's goal of *ataraxia* is here said to be a direct consequence of accepting their conclusions – not of suspending judgement as between them and other, opposing arguments. The best example is perhaps *M* 11.130: "When reason has established that none of these things is by nature good or by nature bad, there will be a release from disturbance and a peaceful life will await us."[3]

But if the position in *M* 11 is internally consistent, there is still the question how Sextus, as a sceptic, can consistently advance it. The answer, I believe, is that *M* 11, unlike any other book of Sextus, contains a pure specimen of an earlier version of Pyrrhonism (earlier, that is, than the version to be found in *PH* and in most of Sextus' surviving writings) in which such negative conclusions were normal and expected. There is reason to associate this version of Pyrrhonism with Aenesidemus; the central piece of evidence for Aenesidemus' philosophy (Photius, *Bibliotheca* 169b18–170b35 = LS 71C, 72L) attributes to Aenesidemus several key conclusions in which the existence of something is denied.[4] This passage also suggests that Aenesidemus was prepared to make positive claims about things, so long as they were relative to specific circumstances. And this too is something we find Sextus doing in *M* 11: while he denies that anything is *by nature* good, or to be chosen, he does ascribe to the sceptic the view that things may qualify as to be chosen *at one time and not another*, or *in relation to one person but not another* (*M* 11.114, 118). Again, the background assumption is that anything *by nature* good would be so invariably and for everyone; relativized statements thus have no implications concerning how things are by nature. And this, in turn, suggests how this position could be considered sceptical: it refrains from any attempt to specify how things are by nature.[5]

M 11, then, presents a consistent version of Pyrrhonism distinct from Sextus' usual version. And this, in turn, may help to explain what is going on in the discussion in *PH* 3. *PH* 3, as we have seen, does officially put forward Sextus' usual version of Pyrrhonism, in which suspension of judgement is the outcome of balancing opposing views. But it looks as if Sextus has tried, with limited success, to incorporate arguments that had their original home in the earlier version of Pyrrhonism. The arguments that nothing is by nature good, bad, or indifferent thus make an appearance, but are not properly integrated into the later outlook to which *PH* is committed. This is not, of course, a philosophically satisfactory solution; but it does offer a historical explanation of how the major problem in the *PH* 3 discussion could have arisen.

I have already mentioned the common ground between the Tenth Mode and the passage in *PH* 3 on differences in values between cultures. Now, Sextus elsewhere (*M* 7.345) attributes the Ten Modes to Aenesidemus, and so one might wonder whether traces of Aenesidemus' version of Pyrrhonism can be found here as well. No such traces are apparent in Sextus' actual treatment of the disagreements in the Tenth Mode. However, the conclusion, while it does mention suspension of judgement between alternative views, also includes the following statement: "Since so much variation in objects has been shown by this mode too, we will not be in a position to say what the underlying thing is like in its nature, though we will be in a position to say how it appears in relation to this way of life or in relation to this law or in relation to this custom, etc." (*PH* 1.163). Again we have the contrast between how things are by nature and how things are relatively speaking, with absence of variation as a requirement for anything to be true by nature. This is not the only one of the Ten Modes to include statements of this kind. What is distinctive about this final, ethical mode is that this statement fits into a wider pattern apparent in Sextus' treatment of ethical topics. For reasons that may now be impossible to determine, his ethical writings (especially, but not only, *M* 11) have retained much more pervasive signs of Aenesidemean heritage than his writings on other subjects.

As noted earlier, the other main topic in both *PH* 3 and *M* 11 is whether there is a "skill relating to life" (*technê peri ton bion*). The answer actually given in both books (although more outspokenly in *M* 11) is "no," not "this is something on which we must suspend judgement." One might see this as further evidence of a different version of Pyrrhonism from Sextus' usual one. But Sextus offers no explicit statement about the status of what he is doing, and we can equally read him as intending the latter answer, with the dogmatists' positive conception of a "skill relating to life" as the unexpressed opposing position. The notion of *technê* in ethical contexts has a long history in Greek philosophy, going back to Plato's Socrates. A *technê* is a systematic body of knowledge directed to some practical end. And Socrates' frequent recourse to what has been called the "craft analogy" reflects in part an aspiration towards a form of ethical knowledge, applying to life as a whole, that would have the same systematic and reliable character as the knowledge displayed in *technai* such as pottery or ship-building. The Stoics, in particular, developed this strand of Platonic thinking and made explicit the notion of a *technê* applying to life as a whole, a *technê* that their ideal sage would possess (e.g. Stob. 2.66, 15–67, 2, Cic., *Fin.* 4.16). And it is fundamentally this Stoic notion that Sextus is opposing, even though he makes occasional efforts to include other dogmatists within the scope of his criticism.

Sextus' arguments in these parts of *PH* 3 and *M* 11 are not without interest. Unfortunately for our present purposes, they mostly have nothing to do with ethics. One could well imagine a sceptical treatment of this topic that addressed matters of enduring concern in ethics, such as whether there can be such a thing as ethical knowledge, and if so, what it might look like. But Sextus' arguments mostly either revolve around the concept of *technê* itself, with no particular ethical implications, or have to do with the supplementary question whether, even if there were a *technê* for life, it would be teachable. And when they do have ethical import, they largely take the form of quotations from the Stoics designed to highlight their sanctioning (in special circumstances, though of course Sextus does not say so) of promiscuity, incest, and cannibalism (*M* 11.190–96, *PH* 3.245–49). It is hard not to feel that, as Julia Annas has put it, "a golden opportunity to discuss central ethical issues is frittered away in trivialities."[6]

I turn now to Sextus' description of the sceptic's own practical stance and its advantages. An important issue in this area, which has received attention in several recent articles,[7] is that of the sceptic's *telos*. In the opening segment of *PH* 1 (25–30) Sextus tells us that the sceptic's *telos* is "tranquility in things involving opinion and moderate feeling in things that are inevitable" (*PH* 1.25).[8] The "inevitable" things, as the subsequent discussion makes clear, are things such as hunger, thirst, and pain, over which we have no control; by contrast, "things involving opinion" (*tois kata doxan*) are matters about which there can be arguments and beliefs – matters one's attitudes to which can be affected by scepticism. Sextus thus concedes that there are limits to the extent of the sceptic's tranquility, and this may be a response to incredulity at the stories in Diogenes Laertius (e.g. 9.67) about Pyrrho's extraordinary insensitivity to pain and other physical hardships. However, as we shall see, Sextus does claim that, even with regard to these things, the sceptic is in a certain way better off than other people.

One might wonder how a sceptic can even be in the business of offering a *telos*. Sextus defines a *telos* in the standard way as "that for the sake of which everything is done or contemplated, whereas it is not itself done or contemplated for the sake of anything; or, the ultimate thing desired" (*PH* 1.25). And the positing of a *telos* was certainly one of the central moves in standard (that is, dogmatic) ethical theory. Now, the *telos* was usually understood as the end for which all human beings should, or by nature do, strive; the *telos* was also referred to as the highest good, and so belief in a *telos* typically committed one to the clearly non-sceptical belief in things that are good by nature.[9] But Sextus does not have to be understood as committing himself to any such belief. First, in saying what the sceptics take as the *telos*, Sextus deliberately avoids any claim about how things are by nature; his wording is "We say up to now that the *telos* is ...," and the phrase "up to now" (*achri nun*) is one of Sextus' regular ways of indicating that he is merely recording the impressions of himself or his sceptical colleagues. Secondly, the definition of the *telos* itself contains no implications concerning the nature of things. All we need understand Sextus as saying is that tranquility and moderate feeling are what the sceptics in fact seek; there is no suggestion that they or anyone else *ought* to seek these things, or that there is any justification in human nature for their doing so.

One might also wonder what basis Sextus has for seeking *this* particular *telos*. Does this not presuppose some view to the effect that tranquility and moderate feeling are better states to be in than various alternatives? But there is no reason why Sextus should hold any such view; tranquility and moderate feeling may simply be what he and his friends happen to prefer – one is not required to have a basis for one's preferences. Sextus does tell us that the origin of scepticism is the search for tranquility by means of the discovery of the truth (*PH* 1.12, 26), though in fact the sceptic achieves tranquility through suspension of judgement, a route different from the one initially pursued. Now, it is sometimes thought that there is something illegitimately non-sceptical in his retaining the same *telos*, tranquility, that he is said to have had prior to becoming a sceptic; but this suspicion is unfounded. At the earlier stage, no doubt, he held the belief that tranquility was a good (as did the Epicureans, for example) and he may have held this belief on some kind of theoretical grounds. But from this it does not follow that now, as a sceptic, he has any such belief, or that his preference for tranquility has any grounds at all. He desires tranquility, and he thinks he has a way to produce and maintain it: end of story. That this desire may once have been buttressed by beliefs, or that it is the kind of desire that only a philosopher would have, is neither here nor there. (Sextus might in any case contest the second point; in discussing the troubles induced by beliefs about good and bad, he gives the impression that release from trouble is what humans in general are ultimately seeking.)

There remains the question whether Sextus' positing of tranquility as the *telos* is consistent with his self-description as an inquirer, a *skeptikos*. For if his ultimate goal (with regard to matters involving opinion) is tranquility, and if the route to tranquility that he finds to have been successful is through suspension of judgement, what is left of his claim (used at the opening of *PH* to distinguish himself from both positive and negative dogmatists) that he is still searching for the truth? Several scholars have concluded that his claim to be an inquirer is disingenuous, or that "inquiry" has to be understood in a special way, as referring to the assembly of opposing arguments rather than any attempt to discover the truth.[10] Against this, it has been argued that Sextus can quite consistently seek the truth for its own sake in addition to seeking tranquility.[11] But although nothing in the text formally contradicts that idea, and although it makes good sense of the strand in Sextus' writing that portrays him as an inquirer, it is difficult to reconcile with his description of the sceptic (*PH* 1.8) as an expert at assembling opposing arguments, or with the tenor of most of his works. Someone as apparently single-minded as Sextus is at constructing oppositions among arguments with a view to tranquility is just not believable when he claims to be still seeking the truth; for the two activities cannot be pursued simultaneously or in the same frame of mind.

Sextus' introductory characterization of Pyrrhonism (*PH* 1.8) makes it sound as if the sceptic's tranquility is attained by suspending judgement about the nature of things on all topics; and some of what he says about tranquility as the sceptic's *telos* (1.26, 29, cf. 1.31) seems to support this. But whenever he specifically addresses the question *why* scepticism produces tranquility whereas dogmatism does not, he limits himself to just one topic, the good and the bad; this occurs both in the chapter on the *telos* (*PH* 1.27–28, 30), and in *PH* 3 (235–38) and *M* 11 (110–67). The central idea in all three passages is that belief in things that are by nature good or bad leads to intense turmoil; one is obsessed with obtaining the good things, or with keeping them if one already has them, and with avoiding the bad things, or with getting rid of them if one has them. The sceptic, who lacks any such beliefs, is therefore rid of a huge source of anguish and psychic instability that afflicts other people (and not only philosophers – at *PH* 1.30 it is "ordinary people" (*idiôtai*) who are said to be afflicted with belief in things good and bad by nature). To return to a point discussed earlier, the sceptic of *M* 11 holds that nothing is by nature good or bad, whereas the sceptic of *PH* suspends judgement as to whether anything is by nature good or bad. But either way, the sceptic is free from a type of belief that is a special source of worry, and this explains both his tranquility and his moderate feeling. As far as the beliefs themselves are concerned, he is tranquil (because he does not have them). And as far as conditions such as hunger, thirst or pain are concerned, his level of feeling is moderate and not intense. For the sceptic merely feels hunger, pain, etc., whereas the non-sceptic also has the belief that this condition is bad – which, as we have seen, drastically raises the anxiety level.

The idea that one may be more troubled if one believes certain things to be good or bad than if one does not is sometimes plausible. But the opposite is sometimes plausible as well; those with firm beliefs about the moral order of things are often calmer than those whose minds on such matters are not made up. Sextus' arguments on the subject, elaborated at far greater length in *M* 11 than in *PH*, have a myopic, one-sided quality that makes them not particularly convinc-ing – even assuming one were to agree with the sceptic in valuing only tranquility.[12] One may also ask whether a sceptic is entitled to put forward as a universal truth that beliefs of this kind lead to anguish and turmoil; is this not a dogmatic claim? Moreover, the idea that beliefs as such, regardless of their truth-value, are a source of mental anguish is puzzling in itself. For all that is said in these passages, the non-sceptics' beliefs about good and bad might actually be correct (and even known to be so); but this would supposedly make no differ-ence to their anxiety-inducing character. It is hard to square this with the picture of the sceptic initially hoping to achieve tranquility through discovery of the truth, and then achieving it through the impasse in that search; for the problem with these beliefs about good and bad is simply their content, irrespective of their truth or of one's cognitive relation to them. Finally, as already suggested, the notion that beliefs about good and bad specifically are what the sceptic achieves tranquility by avoiding stands in an uneasy relation to the idea that tranquility is achieved by suspension of judgement across the board. The chapter on the *telos*, especially, seems to switch back and forth between the two. It is no doubt possible to construct an account of how the two might be combined; but we might at least have hoped that Sextus would have addressed this explicitly.

Either way, though, beliefs on ethical subjects will be among those that the sceptic lacks. And this leads to the question what kinds of ethical attitudes and practice, if any, are open to a sceptic on Sextus' account. This is not unrelated to the question how the sceptic can act and make choices at all[13]; so it is no surprise that his answer to the question of the sceptic's ethical outlook occurs in the context of his treatment of this broader question. First, we are told that one of the major categories of "appearances" that shape how the sceptic acts consists of the laws and customs prevalent in the society in which he was raised (*PH* 1.23–24, cf. 237). Broadly speaking, then, the sceptic does what his society conditions him to do. He acts in this way not because he believes this is the *right* way to act (although he may have believed this prior to becoming a sceptic). It is simply a matter of habit; given the way he was raised, he will have an inclination to act in certain ways in certain situations, without claiming to justify this inclination. And the same applies when he is faced with a situation that a non-sceptic would describe as an ethical dilemma. In *M* 11 (164–66) Sextus uses the example of a sceptic forced by a tyrant to do some appalling deed or face torture and death. The example appears in support of the imagined objection that the sceptic is inconsistent; the reason seems to be that whatever the sceptic chooses, the choice must be based on a definite belief that this is the best thing to do in the circumstances. But Sextus answers that this is not so; instead, the sceptic's choice simply reflects "the preconception which accords with his ancestral laws and customs" (166). For example, some societies encourage subservience to authority more than others; some encourage perseverance through thick and thin more than others. The sceptic might act either way in the situation envisaged – Sextus does not presume to say how he will or should respond in this situation. But either way, it is simply the result of the various societal influences that have shaped his particular repertoire of dispositions; no beliefs about good or bad need enter the picture.

Whether anyone could really react so passively in such highly charged circumstances, without identifying with any of the values that might dictate a choice either way, is clearly open to question. For action to be determined by habitual responses may be perfectly feasible in much of everyday life; but the kind of case Sextus describes does seem to demand that one "take a stand" – that is, bring some set of personal beliefs to bear on the decision. (And this is especially true if the decision is the harder one, to challenge the tyrant; I return to this point below.) Secondly, even if what Sextus describes is possible, many will find it peculiarly unappealing. Naturally, Sextus is not interested in reassuring the reader that the sceptic will do the *right* thing (by the reader's lights) in tough situations; for the belief that there is some right thing to do is precisely the kind of belief that, as we saw earlier, he takes to be the root of the malaise that scepticism cures. But it is not only believers in fixed ethical standards who may find Sextus' picture unattractive; an existentialist, for example, might well feel the same way. Compare Sextus' tyrant example with Sartre's example of the young man faced with the choice between joining the Resistance or staying to comfort his mother.[14] What the young man had to do, according to Sartre, was simply to act one way or the other, and thereby make of himself a certain type of person through that commitment. Sextus' account is, in a certain sense, the exact opposite; one's choice will reflect whatever type of person one has been made by the influences around one – commitment has nothing to do with it.

For this reason, too, on Sextus' account, sceptics are not likely to be social reformers; for that would seem to presuppose attachment to a moral vision at odds with the dominant one. Sextus does perhaps exaggerate the extent to which the sceptic's dispositions are shaped by conventional mores; there might be other influences on his psychological make-up (such as radically unconventional parents) that overrode the influence of the society's prevailing values. But still, the sceptic's stand-offish attitude towards whatever values have in fact shaped his dispositions would surely limit his tenacity in challenging the status quo. (Could one imagine a sceptic doing what, say, Nelson Mandela did?) And this is another unsatisfactory aspect of Sextus' treatment of the tyrant example; it is hard to believe that, in the absence of all convictions, the sceptic is as likely to take the harder way as the easier way.

Yet neither is the sceptic simply an ordinary adherent of his society's values. Sextus sometimes presents himself as on the side of the ordinary person, as against the rarefied theories of the philosophers; and there is a hint of this in the tyrant passage, where he says that the sceptic's decision will be an instance of "non-philosophical practice" (*M* 11.165). However, as we saw, in the case of ethics Sextus is quite explicit (*PH* 1.30) that the ordinary person, as well as the philosopher, is afflicted by the belief in things by nature good and bad. And it is surely correct that ordinary and conventional members of society do not share the sceptic's stand-offish attitude towards the values on which they act, any more than do ardent believers in social change.

If tranquility is one's *telos*, and one sees suspension of judgement as the means to it, then the attitude that Sextus describes makes good sense. But someone with that attitude does not seem to be, in the usual sense, an ethically involved agent. And this perhaps sums up what is, from several perspectives, unpalatable about it.

I close with a word on the Academics' treatment of ethical topics. We saw at the outset that Arcesilaus and Carneades both address the question how one could live while maintaining a sceptical outlook. It is, however, a much disputed question whether they are arguing merely dialectically, showing their opponents how *they* could live with a sceptical outlook (to which the Academics' critiques supposedly force them), or whether these ways of living are intended for the Academics' own use.[15] In any case, the Academics make no claim comparable to the Pyrrhonists about practical benefits stemming from scepticism. However, Carneades is attested as addressing numerous topics within, or with a bearing upon, ethics – the *telos*, free will, justice, divination, and the existence of the gods.[16] The spirit of these discussions is usually critical; but, in keeping with the Academics' usual methodology, the purpose is not to persuade one of the truth of the conclusions and the falsehood of the positions being attacked, but to subvert assent from those positions, leaving one without definite beliefs on either side. Sometimes Carneades himself constructs both sides of the opposition; on the subject of justice, he famously argued in its favor one day and against it the next. And sometimes he constructs a schema of dogmatic positions, along with additional positions devised by himself, so as to exhibit their relations with one another and, one may assume, their vulnerability to one another; this seems to be the case with the *telos* and with free will. There is little or no direct evidence of Arcesilaus' engagement with ethical topics; but given his reported willingness to debate on all topics (e.g. Cic. *Fin.* 5.10), we can presume that ethics came under his scrutiny. For both Arcesilaus and Carneades, however, it looks as if ethics is treated in the same way as other topics; it does not raise any special issues of its own, as it sometimes does for Sextus. The situation appears to be rather different for Philo of Larissa, who is reported to have devised an ethical system (Stob. 2.39,20–41,25). This is not in itself surprising, since Philo was in general much more willing to put forward views than were his Academic predecessors. But both the spirit in which the system was offered, and its specific content, are hard to reconstruct from the surviving clues.[17]

1 On this work and its relation to *PH*, see Pierre Pellegrin, Chapter 6 "Sextus Empiricus" and the Introduction.

2 On these and other groups of sceptical Modes, see Paul Woodruff, Chapter 11 "The Pyrrhonian Modes."

3 Translation from Bett [41]; cf. *M* 11.140.

4 A somewhat different perspective on Aenesidemus is offered in R. J. Hankinson, Chapter 5 "Aenesidemus and the Rebirth of Pyrrhonism." A more detailed presentation of the view offered in this chapter is Bett [143], ch. 4; see also Woodruff [234].

5 "Nothing is by nature good" does not break this rule; from this statement nothing follows about what qualities things *do* have by nature. (In particular, given the invariability requirement, it does not follow that anything is by nature non-good.)

6 Annas [92], p. 356 n.11.

7 Moller [292]; Grgic [286]; Perin [260].

8 He adds (1.30) that some sceptics propose suspension of judgement as an additional goal. On this see Brunschwig [222], p. 482; Perin [260], 339–41.

9 The *telos* was also regularly identified as *eudaimonia*, "happiness." Interestingly, Sextus equates his candidate for the *telos* with *eudaimonia* in *M* 11 (apparently following both Timon and Aenesidemus), but not in *PH*. I have discussed possible reasons for this in Bett [221].

10 Palmer [257]; Striker [264]; Grgic [286].

11 So Perin [260].

12 The arguments in *M* 11 are analyzed in detail in Bett [41].

13 On this subject see Katja Vogt, Chapter 8 "Scepticism and Action."

14 Sartre [435], pp. 35–38.

15 See further Harald Thorsrud, Chapter 3 "Arcesilaus and Carneades."

16 E.g. Cic. *Fin.* 5.16–20 (the *telos*), Cic. *De fato* 20–33 (free will), Lactantius *Div. inst.* 5.14.3–5 = LS 68M (justice), Cic. *De div.* 2.9–10 (divination), Sextus *M* 9.139–41, 182–84 (the gods).

17 An excellent attempt at a reconstruction is Brittain [195], ch. 6. On Philo see also Carlos Lévy, Chapter 4 "The Sceptical Academy: Decline and Afterlife."

10 Academics versus Pyrrhonists, reconsidered

When I first wrote a paper about the difference between Academic and Pyrrhonist Sceptics[1] a long time ago, I was less interested in the differences than in the commonalities. My point was to get away from the Humean distinction between moderate Academics and radical Pyrrhonists. I argued that both were radicals – not, as they came to be seen in early modern times, dogmatists who denied the possibility of knowledge more or less generally, but in the ancient sense of having no philosophical doctrines. They used the same method of arguing for and against any given thesis or belief, declaring the debate undecided, and suspending judgement. The "mitigated" sceptic, who believes that nothing can be known though one may have more or less well-founded opinions, was a figure invented by Carneades in order to refute the dogmatists' objection that suspension of judgement on all matters will make life impossible. Ironically, this figure later became the model of modern versions of scepticism

Up to this point I still think I was right – at least as far as the early sceptical Academics Arcesilaus and Carneades were concerned. Arcesilaus argued that, given their conception of knowledge and wisdom, the Stoics themselves ought to suspend judgement on all matters. Carneades offered an alternative epistemology to counterbalance the impressive Stoic theory. But these philosophers did not maintain that they were right and the Stoics wrong, or that one should accept their own proposal. The only salient difference that seemed to me to be left between those Academics and their Pyrrhonist successors was the curious claim of the Pyrrhonists that their so-called "way of life" would lead to the goal that other Hellenistic schools were also endorsing – tranquility.

I have never found this claim either convincing or attractive, since the Pyrrhonist version of tranquility, as far as I can see, would rid us (if successful) not only of most worries, but also of most joys in life. Wouldn't that be depressing rather than liberating? So I took this innovation as a negligible and superfluous addition to what was essentially the same sceptical position.

But when I returned to Sextus in a seminar many years later and looked at his vigorous polemic against "the followers of Carneades and Clitomachus," I began to see that things were probably more complicated, and that tranquility might have a more important role in Pyrrhonism than I had been willing to believe. In the opening paragraph of his *Outlines of Pyrrhonism*, Sextus Empiricus distinguishes three types of philosophers: positive dogmatists who claim to have found the truth; negative dogmatists who declare that the truth cannot be discovered, and those – the Sceptics – who are still searching. He describes "the followers of Carneades and Clitomachus" as negative dogmatists, but he does not include the first and oldest of the Academic Sceptics, Arcesilaus, and at the end of the book he actually says that Arcesilaus seems to him to have many arguments in common with the Pyrrhonists, so that his school and theirs are virtually the same (*PH* 1.232). So Sextus describes only the later Academics as negative dogmatists. And although I would exclude Carneades himself from this group, we can see from Cicero's *Academica* that there were indeed negative dogmatists among the followers of Carneades and Clitomachus – followers who claimed to hold Carneades' own position. So Sextus' classification is not as unfair as it might seem at first, and it may well reflect the perspective of Aenesidemus, who was probably a contemporary and fellow student of these later Academics. We can see from the summary of Aenesidemus' book in Photius (*Bibl.* 169b18-171a4) that he was dissatisfied with the turn toward a modest version of dogmatism in the Academy of his time – but why? What is so good about being a "real" sceptic, or what is so bad about being a modest dogmatist? And why did Aenesidemus choose Pyrrho as the figurehead of his movement – Pyrrho rather than, say, Socrates or Arcesilaus? The feature that sets Pyrrho apart from other philosophers seems to be his supreme detachment and equanimity, allegedly based on a total indifference to all questions about true and false, right and wrong. Sextus tells us (*PH* 1.7) that the sceptics call themselves Pyrrhonists "from the fact that Pyrrho

appears to us to have attached himself to scepticism more systematically and conspicuously than anyone before him."[2] By choosing
Pyrrho as their figurehead, the Sceptics thus emphasized the importance of tranquility and presented themselves as competitors to the
dogmatic schools of philosophy. By contrast, the sceptical Academics
never advertised their own philosophical method as a way to reach
happiness, not even after they had to all appearances accepted the
Carneadean epistemology.

The difference brought about by this change emerges clearly if one
looks at the different replies that Academics and Pyrrhonists gave to an
objection that any ancient sceptic had to face: the argument that
suspension of judgement on all matters will leave the sceptic unable
to act and to lead the life of a human being, rather than that of a mere
vegetable. When one compares the respective replies of the two schools
to this objection, it becomes clear, I think, both that the Pyrrhonists
were indeed descendants of the earlier sceptical Academy (as one
should expect), and that their opposition to the Academy was motivated by their declared hope of reaching tranquility.

Let me briefly remind you of the inactivity (apraxia) argument[3]:
the oldest version I know of occurs in Aristotle's *Metaphysics* (4.4,
1008b13–19), as an argument against people who claim to be able to
believe both of two contradictory propositions, p and not-p, for any
given p: Aristotle argues that if they take care to stay away from a well
or a ravine into which they might fall, they show by their actions that
they do not believe that it is equally good or not good to fall in. In
other words, action implies belief, and so a person who professes to
have contradictory beliefs, or indeed no beliefs at all, will be either
paralyzed or dishonest.

The Stoic version of this argument that appears in the reports
about the Hellenistic sceptics is more complicated because it is formulated in terms of the Stoic psychology of action. Instead of simply
saying that action implies belief, the Stoics say that any action presupposes an impression or thought (phantasia) to the effect that it
would be appropriate or good to do so-and-so. Action ensues when a
person assents to such an impression. A sceptic who (as we tend to
say) suspends judgement is therefore described as refraining from
assent. Since a sceptic will not have a view as to what is appropriate
or not, she will never be able to decide whether doing something will
be right or wrong, good or bad, and so she will be unable to act.

As Aristotle's example already shows, action often involves strictly speaking at least two beliefs or acts of assent (corresponding to the contemporary pair belief and desire): the agent believes that there is a ravine, and also that the ravine is dangerous and should be avoided. I mention these complications because the Academics' defenses of sceptical suspension of judgement address both of these beliefs.

I THE ACADEMICS: ARCESILAUS AND CARNEADES

We have two ancient reports about Arcesilaus' response to the inactivity argument. The first comes from Plutarch's treatise against the Epicurean Colotes who, in his polemic against Arcesilaus, "brought in from the Stoa like some Gorgon's head the argument from inactivity." Plutarch then reports Arcesilaus' reply as follows:

The soul has three movements: sensation, impulse, and assent. Now the movement of sensation cannot be eliminated, even if we would: instead, upon encountering an object, we necessarily receive an imprint and are affected. Impulse, aroused by sensation, moves us in the shape of the action towards a suitable goal ...

So those who suspend judgement about everything do not eliminate this second movement either, but follow their impulse, which leads them naturally to the things that appear suitable.[4]

Then what is the only thing that they avoid? That only in which falsity and error can arise, namely forming an opinion and thus interposing rashly with our assent. (Plutarch, *Col.* 1122B–C)[5]

According to Arcesilaus, then, action requires no assent at all. His argument seems to apply the model of animal activity to humans, and so it dispenses with assent altogether. But if so, the model leaves no room for considerations of what might be good or bad, right or wrong: the distance between impression or thought and decision to act, introduced by the notion of assent, has been eliminated.

At this point it may be useful to remember that Arcesilaus did not begin his philosophical studies in the Stoa. He was a contemporary of the founder Zeno, and according to Diogenes Laertius' biography (DL 4.29), he was sent first to the Peripatos to study rhetoric with Theophrastus and later changed over to Plato's school. He is said to have been a great admirer of Plato and to have owned a private copy of

Plato's books. So the conceptual framework of Stoic psychology was not something with which he had (as it were) grown up, and he might indeed have considered the notion of assent as superfluous.

The second report is from Sextus Empiricus' books *Against the Logicians*, where he relates the polemic between the Stoa and the Academy about the existence of a criterion. Sextus says that after having argued that a wise man will suspend judgement on all matters, Arcesilaus still had to offer a criterion "for the conduct of life." So Arcesilaus said that:

He who suspends judgment about everything will regulate his choices and avoidances, and his actions in general, by the standard of the reasonable (*to eulogon*), and by proceeding in accordance with this criterion he will act rightly. (Sextus, *M* 7.158)

Unlike the passage from Plutarch, this statement might well be understood to imply assent, though it is cautiously formulated in terms of "regulating" one's actions by means of a criterion. But the use of a criterion clearly introduces reflection intervening between impression and impulse or action. In fact, the terminology Arcesilaus uses in this and the following sentences shows that he borrowed his account of action from the Stoics themselves. According to their doctrine, if the wise man does not know what is going to happen (and what will, therefore, be the right thing to do), he will do what he thinks is reasonable – more exactly, he will opt for the action that, when done, can be given a reasonable justification in terms of what it would be natural for a human being to do in the circumstances. Arcesilaus was reacting to the claim that the wise man will only assent to what he recognizes as evidently true, and pointing out that even the Stoic sage will often have to be content with less than certain truth – so, the suggestion is, why not do so all the time?

Note that Arcesilaus here does not address the question how a person can act at all without assent, but how she might determine what she should do, thus making room for the reflection and decision that the first reply to the inactivity argument seemed to declare as superfluous. What he says leaves open the question of assent: will the agent assent to a proposition of the form "it is reasonable that I should do x," or will he just do x, refraining from assent to "I should do x"? If he does not assent, but still decides to do one thing rather than another, he can hardly be said simply to act instinctively, as the first passage suggested. But we do not have any further information on this point, and it may well be that Arcesilaus' defense of the sceptical position was purely *ad hominem* and did not add up to an alternative philosophical view. In the first case, he probably relied on Aristotle's account of animal activity; in the second, he used the Stoics' own premises to show that action does not require certain knowledge. He may not have found it necessary to provide his own account of rational action without judgement or belief.

Things are very different in the case of Carneades. He had carefully studied the books of Chrysippus, the greatest of the Stoic philosophers, who was said to have restored his school after the devastating criticism of Arcesilaus (see Plutarch, *Comm. not.* 1059B). Carneades used to say, parodying a famous line about Chrysippus: "Had there not been Chrysippus, there would not be me."[6] Carneades countered Chrysippus' arguments against the sceptical position by a detailed account of how one could live without either knowledge or assent, availing himself of Chrysippus' own theories.

Like Arcesilaus, he took up both the claim that there can be no human action at all without assent, and the charge that a person who suspends judgement on everything would have no way of deciding what to do. Addressing the first Stoic claim, he introduced a distinction between two kinds of assent[7]: there is assent in the strong Stoic sense, which consists in taking a proposition or impression to be true, and there is a weaker version, which consists in "approving" of a proposition or taking a positive attitude to it without, however, committing oneself to its truth. There are then also two different senses in which one can be said to refrain from assent. Cicero reports, quoting from a book by Carneades' student and successor Clitomachus, that:

The wise man is said to suspend assent in two senses: in one sense, when this means that he won't assent to anything at all; in another, when it means that he will restrain himself even from giving responses showing that he approves or disapproves of something, so that he won't say "yes" or "no" to anything. Given this distinction, the wise man accepts the suspension of assent in the first sense, with the result that he never assents; but he holds on to his assent in the second sense, with the result that, by following what is persuasive wherever that is present or deficient, he is able to reply "yes" or "no". (*Acad.* 2.104; tr. Brittain [56])

Thus, a sceptic may accept a plausible or persuasive impression as a basis for decision or action, for example as an informed guess, without actually being convinced of its truth. Sextus Empiricus presents the plausible impression in the same way as Arcesilaus' alleged criterion of the reasonable:

yet as he (sc Carneades), too, himself was required to offer a criterion for the conduct of life and for the attainment of happiness, he was practically compelled to give his own account of it, adopting both the plausible impression (*pithane phantasia*) and that which is at once plausible and uncontroverted and tested. (Sextus, *M* 7.166)

With regard to the second Stoic objection, then – that the person who suspends judgement on all matters will have no way of deciding what to do – Carneades, drawing once again on Chrysippus' works, developed an elaborate account of the ways one can try to make sure that an impression one finds persuasive is also reliable. But at every step he also pointed out that no amount of plausibility, checking of the circumstances and consistency with other beliefs can amount to a guarantee of truth.

The plausible impression was introduced by Sextus as a criterion of action, but the examples given in the subsequent exposition are mostly not of the action-prompting kind (e.g. "This man is Socrates" (178), "Some enemies are lying in ambush over there" (186), "This thing is a snake" (187)) though the second and third do lead to action, namely running away without further ado. But a few paragraphs into his exposition, Sextus calls the plausible impression a criterion *of truth* (173).

Indeed, taken together, the theory of the plausible, tested and uncontroverted impression and the conception of approval as opposed to full assent amount to a philosophical alternative to Stoic epistemology, covering both factual and action-guiding impressions.

Whether Carneades endorsed this theory as his own philosophical view is a question that was debated already among his own students.[8] Given his stance as a philosopher who would argue for and against every thesis, it seems more likely to me that he proposed the theory only in order to show that the Stoic view, according to which humans can acquire certain knowledge and eventually reach the blessed state of wisdom, is no more convincing than the Academic view, according to which certainty cannot be achieved, and philosophers would do better to suspend judgement about this theory as about any other. But it is perhaps not surprising that most Academics in the generations after Carneades ended up accepting his theory as the official epistemological position of their school. It is also not surprising, however, that Aenesidemus, their contemporary, described the continuing debate between those later Academics and the Stoa as "Stoics fighting Stoics" (Photius, *Bibl.* 170a16). Carneades' theory was indeed a variant of the Stoic one.

II   THE PYRRHONISTS: SEXTUS EMPIRICUS

The Pyrrhonists, like the Academics, suspended judgement on all matters. But they did not take over Carneades' appeal to plausible impressions as a guide to action for those who cannot decide with certainty what is true and what is false. Faced with the argument from inactivity, Sextus offers an account of "the criterion of scepticism," distinguishing it emphatically as a criterion of action from the criteria proposed by his dogmatic opponents that are used to decide what is or is not the case:

We say, then, that the criterion of the skeptical way of life is appearance, implicitly meaning by this the impression, for it lies in passive and involuntary affection and is not an object of investigation. Hence no one, presumably, will raise a controversy over whether something appears this way or that; rather, they investigate whether it is such as it appears.

Thus, attending to appearances, we live in accordance with everyday observances, without holding opinions – for we are not able to be utterly inactive. These everyday observances seem to be fourfold, and to consist in guidance by nature, necessitation by feelings, handing down of laws and customs, and teaching of kinds of expertise. By nature's guidance we are naturally capable of perceiving and thinking. By the necessitation of feelings, hunger conducts us to food and thirst to drink. By the handing down of customs and laws, we accept, from an everyday point of view, that piety is good and impiety bad. By teaching of kinds of expertise we are not inactive in those crafts which we take up. (*PH* 1.22–24)

Sextus does not speak of right action in this passage, but he has said a few paragraphs earlier (*PH* 1.17) that the Pyrrhonist story (*logos*) suggests to its followers a way of living correctly, with the significant qualification that "correctly" is to be taken in a loose sense, not just in the sense of "virtuously." But I think Sextus is probably right not to bring in correctness here, because it emerges from his description that questions of right and wrong do not arise for a person who simply

follows appearances. The very word "criterion," used no doubt
because Sextus' general account of scepticism is organized according
to the standard topics in expositions of philosophical doctrine, is
somewhat misleading to the extent that it means an instrument of
judging: Sextus' text makes it abundantly clear that the Sceptics' way
of following appearances does not involve a judgement or decision.

Now while one might think that the first two items on the list of
"everyday observances" describe adherence to appearances as simply a
matter of instinctive response to external influences, it has often been
pointed out that the last two items can hardly be seen as anything but
beliefs. If the Sceptic accepts piety as good and impiety as bad, and if he
learns technical skills and applies them in the exercise of a profession
(remember that Sextus was a doctor!), surely this shows that he shares
the moral beliefs of his community and has acquired the knowledge
that guides his practice as a professional? I think this is correct, but it
does not refute the Sceptic's claim to live without opinion. All four
parts of the "everyday observances" are covered by the initial remark
that they arise as passive and involuntary affections, and hence are not
subject to critical examination. Moral beliefs, for example, are inculcated in us through our upbringing, and technical skills can be acquired
by simply following the instructions of a teacher. Once one has
absorbed these, one may then act on them in the same way as one
responds to feelings of hunger and thirst. Following appearances in this
way never requires a decision as to what is true or false, nor endorsement of what appears to be the right way of proceeding. Such decisions
the Sceptic feels unable to make – but as it turns out, they are not
needed in order to lead an ordinary life. Sextus is thus drawing a
distinction between what we might call judgements – the voluntary
and reason-based acceptance of something as true – and mere beliefs
that we find ourselves having involuntarily and without any critical
reflection. There need not be a difference in content between the
beliefs of a dogmatist and those of a Sceptic; the crucial difference
lies in the way those beliefs are acquired. What it means to act following appearances in this last way is illustrated later in the book by the
example of the Methodic doctor:

By the necessitation of feelings Skeptics are conducted by thirst to drink, by
hunger to food, and so on. In the same way Methodic doctors are conducted by
feelings to what corresponds to them: by contraction to dilatation (as when

someone seeks refuge in heat from the compression due to intense cold), and by flux to checking (as when those in the baths who are dripping with sweat come to check it and so seek refuge in the cold air). And it is clear that things foreign to nature force us to proceed to remove them: even a dog will remove a thorn which has got stuck in his paw. (*PH* 1.238)

It is significant that Sextus assimilates the performance of the doctor to the instinctive actions triggered by hunger or thirst, and that he compares these to the behavior of an animal: no reasoning is involved in either case, and the physician's actions should presumably be seen as a kind of conditioned reflex.

This reply to the inactivity argument was no doubt inspired by the Pyrrhonists' Academic predecessors. But it sounds a lot more like the first reply of Arcesilaus than like the distinction between two kinds of assent introduced by Carneades, because it eliminates assent altogether. And indeed in a later passage, where he argues against the view of those who identify the Pyrrhonists with the Academics, Sextus explicitly rejects Carneades' proposal:

The members of the New Academy, then, prefer plausible and scrutinized appearances to those which are merely plausible, and to both they prefer appearances which are plausible and scrutinized and undistracted. Even if both Academics and Skeptics say that they go along with certain things, the difference even here between the two philosophies is clear.

For "go along with" is used in different senses. It means not resisting but simply following without strong inclination or adherence (as a boy is said to go along with his chaperon); and it sometimes means assenting to something by choice and, as it were, sympathy (as a dissolute man goes along with someone who urges extravagant living). Hence, since Carneades and Clitomachus say that they go along with things, and that some things are plausible, in the sense of having a strong wish with a strong inclination, whereas we say so in the sense of simply yielding without adherence, in this respect too we differ from them. (*PH* 1.228–30)

"Going along" (Greek *peithesthai*) here corresponds to Cicero's "approve" (*adprobari*) and indicates the weak kind of assent distinguished from dogmatic assent by Carneades. However, the Pyrrhonists go a step further: they reject even the modest appeal to greater or lesser plausibility and refuse to discriminate among impressions in any way. Approval, even if it does not amount to dogmatic assent or judgement, will still be voluntary, and the

Academics no doubt adopted it in the hope that a plausible view was more likely to be true than an implausible one. The Pyrrhonist considers such hopes to be groundless – he sees no reason to think that there might be a link between persuasiveness and truth (cp. DL 9.94). His way of "going along" with appearances is entirely passive and unquestioning, not based on any reasons at all.

We have, then, a distinction between three kinds of belief, in descending order of strength: there is, first, dogmatic assent or judgment, accepting something as true and fully justified; second, there is approval, based on considerations of plausibility and coherence with other beliefs or impressions, but without the presumption of truth; and third, there is the purely passive acquiescence of the Pyrrhonist.[9]

What emerges from these passages is that the Pyrrhonist has abandoned not just philosophical argument as a means of arriving at a judgement, but ordinary reasoning as well – and this, I should say, is no longer in agreement with "everyday observances." But why should the Pyrrhonist insist on only this minimal kind of belief, comparable to the kind we might even ascribe to animals? What lies behind this is, I think, his concern for tranquility. Sextus describes the way the sceptical Academics "go along" with plausibility as being accompanied by a strong inclination and sympathy. And such strong inclination (or aversion) is exactly what, according to Sextus, characterizes ordinary people's beliefs about values:[10]

> Those who hold the opinion that things are good or bad by nature are perpetually troubled. And when they have acquired these things, they experience more troubles; for they are elated beyond reason and measure, and in fear of change they do anything so as not to lose what they believe to be good. When they lack what they believe to be good, they take themselves to be persecuted by natural evils and they pursue what (so they think) is good. But those who make no determination about what is good or bad by nature neither avoid nor pursue anything with intensity, and hence they are tranquil. (*PH* 1.27–28)

The Pyrrhonist prefers to "go along" with the beliefs he finds himself having without reflection, taking as it were the attitude of a neutral observer even to his own inclinations. He will treat piety as good and impiety as bad; he will be disturbed by pain, since he is a sentient creature, but he will not aggravate matters by adding the judgement that pain is really bad, or piety really good. By distancing himself from his own reactions and beliefs, he preserves his peace of mind – or so at least Sextus invites us to think.

This elaboration of the sceptical attitude takes the model of animal activity to cover human action as well; and it is, I think, the main innovation introduced by Aenesidemus when he left the Academy and decided to choose Pyrrho as the figurehead of his new radical version of scepticism. No doubt there were further developments during the time between him and Sextus (for example, someone introduced the so-called Modes of Agrippa), but this is difficult to trace for us in the absence of detailed sources. Still, the emphasis on tranquility must have come with the adoption of Pyrrho as a model Sceptic.

And I think this change in direction also explains why the Academics returned to the philosophical mainstream of more or less dogmatic philosophy after Carneades, while the Pyrrhonists remained outsiders. Carneades' epistemology could be adopted as a philosophical alternative to Stoicism, and those who endorsed it could still claim to be sceptics in some sense by insisting that they put forward their views only as plausible ones, not as certain truths.

Not so the Pyrrhonists, who refused to make even a judgement of greater or lesser plausibility. So we find Sextus spending an extraordinary amount of effort on explaining how it is that Pyrrhonists can engage in argument with other philosophers and also recommend their own way of achieving tranquility without making any serious assertions. Sextus' chapters on the sceptical pronouncements (PH 1.187–209) show that there must have been a large number of proposals. Sextus mostly prefers the line that the sceptic is merely expressing the way he happens to be affected, but he also, and understandably, likes the retort to the argument that when the Sceptic says, for instance, "no more p than not p" he undermines his own statement. Sextus happily concedes that his pronouncement applies to itself as well as to any other, for if nothing is more true or false than its contradictory, then it is also no more true than false that nothing is more true or false … (PH 1.206, cp. also PH 1.14).

The problem is that in order to get rid of philosophy, the Sceptic himself has to engage in philosophy.[11] As Aristotle famously argued in his Protrepticus: "if one ought to philosophize, one ought to philosophize, and if one ought not to philosophize, one ought to philosophize: therefore, one ought to philosophize in any case."[12] Sextus' reply to this may be found at the end of his long series of arguments against the existence of proof: "Just as it is not impossible that a man who has used a ladder to climb up to a high place should overturn the ladder with his foot, so it is not unlikely that the Skeptic, having used the argument that shows that there is no proof as a kind of scaffolding to establish his thesis, should then destroy that argument itself" (*M* 8.481).

NOTES

1 Striker [191].
2 Translations from *PH* I are from Annas and Barnes [40], with occasional modifications.
3 Compare Katja Vogt, Chapter 8 "Scepticism and Action." I have discussed the Academics' reaction to this argument in more detail in Striker [190].
4 The word translated here as "suitable" is the Greek *oikeion* – "what is familiar" or "what belongs to one." Arcesilaus was no doubt alluding to the famous Stoic doctrine of *oikeiosis*, according to which all animals, including human children, instinctively pursue what is beneficial to their survival and hence suitable for them.
5 Loeb translation with modifications.
6 The original line was: "Had there not been Chrysippus, there'd be no Stoa." See DL 4.62.
7 On this distinction see Frede [278]. Frede goes too far, I think, in assuming that the Pyrrhonists simply took this over from the Academy; see below pp. 204–5.
8 Compare Harald Thorsrud, Chapter 3 "Arcesilaus and Carneades" and Carlos Lévy, Chapter 4 "The Sceptical Academy: Decline and Afterlife."
9 Compare Casey Perin, Chapter 7 "Scepticism and Belief."
10 For more on this, see Richard Bett, Chapter 9 "Scepticism and Ethics."
11 On this point see also Striker [264].
12 Cited in Elias, *proleg. phil.* 2, Commentaria in Aristotelem Graeca XVIII. I, p. 3, 17–23.

11   The Pyrrhonian Modes

The Pyrrhonian Modes are argument schemata for general use against dogmatism. We have records of two main lists of Modes, the Ten and the Five, which were used at various times in the history of ancient scepticism, either independently or in some sort of systematic connection. These Modes use strategies with ancient roots in such thinkers as Protagoras, Democritus, Plato, and Aristotle, but users of the Modes were not committed to positions held by those thinkers. They were compiled long after Pyrrho (the Ten probably by Aenesidemus[1] and the Five by a shadowy figure named Agrippa) during the first phase of the Pyrrhonian revival.[2] In addition, we have a list of eight causal Modes attributed to Aenesidemus.

The second and final phase of Pyrrhonism occupies most of the works of Sextus Empiricus (apart from *Against the Ethicists, M* 11). Although he has different strategies from Aenesidemus, he lays out the Ten Modes in some detail and makes extensive use of the Five. His account of the Ten is sometimes at odds with his general practice, and this is most likely due to his use of sources from the first phase of the revival.

Besides Sextus (*PH* 1.36–163), we have two main sources for the Ten Modes:[3] Diogenes Laertius (9.78–88) and Philo of Alexandria (*On Drunkenness* 169–202), both of whom seem to have a source independent of Sextus. Diogenes is just reporting what he knows, whereas Philo appropriates eight of the Modes for his own purpose[4] and leaves out the other two (the Third and Ninth in the list according to Sextus). Brief mentions by Aristocles[5] and Herrenius do not add to our understanding.

The Modes have in common a general aim to disarm dogmatism in whatever form it might take. The tools of Academic scepticism were parasitic on Stoicism – using Stoic principles and Stoic logic against

Stoic claims. Such tools are effective only if their dogmatic targets are systematic philosophers such as Stoics. But the Pyrrhonian revival aims to save us all from dogmatism, and, indeed, that revival comes at a time when systematic Stoics are thin on the field.

The Ten Modes are discussed extensively by Annas and Barnes [269] and by Hankinson [68] (pp. 155–83), and the Five are the subject of a book by Barnes, who is chiefly concerned with their philosophical merits [270]. This chapter cannot pretend to the same level of detail about specific Modes, but will explore instead general questions about the working of the Modes in Pyrrhonian contexts.

I EPOCHÊ AND PYRRHONIAN HYGIENE

The aim of Pyrrhonian practice is *epochê*, a suspension of belief that benefits us by relaxing our minds. This aim may concern all beliefs, or it may concern only a subset of beliefs that turn out to be dogmatic. In the former case, Pyrrhonians will seem to have a hard time living their scepticism, as action seems to imply some form of belief on the part of an agent. But in either case, Pyrrhonians will have a hard time giving arguments in favor of *epochê*. The problems about action and belief belong to a general problem I will call the problem of hygiene: how to do what Pyrrhonians set out to do without stressing their minds with the sorts of belief they set out to avoid.

What counts as dogmatism was a major issue for the Academics, who considered a distinction between stronger and weaker forms of assent.[6] The Pyrrhonian revival appears to have worked with broad and narrow understandings of dogmatism. On the broad view, assent to any belief would be dogmatic. On this view, negative assertions of the form "P is false" and "P is unknowable" would be dogmatic. Sextus, who mostly takes the broad view, generally does not succumb to either positive or negative demonstrations, but holds back. The narrow view takes as dogmatic only those beliefs that are held to be true in virtue of the natures of things. Such a belief has the form "X is G in virtue of the nature of X" (where "in virtue of the nature of X" functions as a modal operator). The Ten Modes often explicitly aim to guard us against falling into beliefs that are dogmatic in this narrower view, which was probably held by Aenesidemus.[7] A Pyrrhonian of this kind may safely accept the conclusion of a relativistic argument that refutes a claim to truth by nature.[8]

The Ten Modes are often understood as tools to induce relaxation of the mind in anyone who is inclined to dogmatism, regardless of prior philosophical commitments. If one Mode will not do the trick, another is at hand; hence the proliferation of Modes and lists of modes. The Modes ought to capture what it was that Pyrrhonians did as philosophers. But Sextus makes little use of the Ten Modes, and shows some disquiet over his use of the Five. An air of discrepancy hovers between the Modes and Sextus' actual practice of scepticism.

We may think of the Modes either as strategies of rhetoric or of demonstration. A rhetorical strategy would induce relaxation of mind without introducing any beliefs. If such a strategy works, it works whether or not its premises are true, and whether or not its inferences are valid. And its conclusion is not a reason to believe anything – not even a reason to believe that you should withhold belief. It simply comes to a stop at the point at which the interlocutor (a person formerly vulnerable to dogmatism) has become likely to suspend belief. The argument would compel agreement by making its interlocutor feel that he or she must suspend belief, without demonstrating that a rational person would in this case suspend belief.

Sextus introduces his long discussion of the Modes by proposing to show "how suspension of belief arises for us" (PH 1.31). This strategy is therapeutic: it aims not at getting things right, but at leaving us in a state of suspension. Thus, it is supposed either to help a dogmatist recover from the stress of dogmatism and become a Pyrrhonian, or to strengthen a Pyrrhonian in resisting felt temptations to dogmatize.

A demonstration would draw a conclusion from premises known to be true, by means of logical rules known to be truth-preserving. The difficulty about a demonstration is that it entangles you in beliefs – beliefs in your premises, in your rules of inference, and then in your conclusion. Indeed, a successful demonstration requires you to believe its conclusion, on pain of irrationality. It thus requires that you be committed to certain views about what rationality requires. If sceptics aim to abstain from belief, therefore, they cannot consistently subscribe to demonstration. This is a central problem posed by the Modes: How may we construe them consistently with sceptical hygiene? The most obvious answer is to take the Modes as therapeutic rhetoric. But this answer will not apply to all cases; sometimes the Modes are plainly demonstrative, as we shall see.

The users of the Modes may not have thought through this problem when they cast them as demonstrations. More likely, however, they preserved hygiene by one of two devices: First, they may have eschewed not all beliefs, but only those that are dogmatic in the narrower view – beliefs about how things are in their natures. In that case, the users of the Modes may have felt that the beliefs utilized by the Modes are not dogmatic, because those beliefs do not concern how things are in their natures. Or, second, they may have intended the Modes as demonstrations to which only dogmatists – and not sceptics – need subscribe.[9] It would be as if they were coaxing dogmatists up a ladder that will turn out to be treacherous – a ladder of the dogmatists' own making. When it breaks, it will leave the dogmatist in *epochê*.

II RHETORIC VERSUS DEMONSTRATION

Each strategy seems to have been in play at one time or another. Indeed, Sextus gives evidence for both. In his preface to the Modes, he holds back from any claim as to whether they are powerful or weak (literally "rotten," 1.35) – apparently as demonstrations – and in presenting the first Mode he alludes to a credible case against any sort of demonstration (1.60). This would seem to leave only the possibility of rhetorical strategy, and this fits the causal language of some of the conclusions: "it is reasonable to expect[10] that suspension would take hold on these grounds" (*PH* 1.87, Second Mode).

Sextus' favored strategy outside of the Modes is the appeal to *isostheneia* (equipollence), the equal power of opposed arguments that are supposed to leave one's mind poised in suspense between the force fields of the two arguments (*PH* 1.8, 10). This strategy uses arguments without subscribing to them; its overall aim is rhetorical. This strategy does not care about the truth of the premises or the logic driving the inferences, so long as the arguments on either side wind up having an equal grip on the mind.

We are led to expect the Modes to appeal to *isostheneia*, and this is consistent with Sextus' introduction of the Ten (*PH* 1.31–35). But although Sextus identifies conflicts in the appearances, he does little in his presentation of the Modes to make us feel that both sides are equally compelling.[11] Instead, we find in each Mode, not a pair of balanced arguments, but a single argument with a conclusion that is apparently intended to be compelling: "So if their sensory impressions differ in accordance with variation among animals, and there is no way to judge among them, then it is necessary to suspend judgment about what is real externally."[12] Sextus may suppose that the necessity here is psychological, or he may mean that it is the force of the argument that is necessary, i.e. that the argument is a demonstration and that the Mode is a schema for refuting claims of a certain kind.[13] And, indeed, the Modes have the appearance of refutations.

Refutation, on the face of it, is incompatible with *epochê*. An effective refutation leaves you convinced that the hypothesis in question is false. Could Pyrrhonians have indulged in refutation? The Pyrrhonian revival apparently took more than one form, and its activists may have entertained different versions of the sceptical goal.[14] Sextus offers four terms as nomenclature for sceptics.

Ephectic Pyrrhonism. Two of Sextus' terms fit a therapeutic practice: *ephectic*, after the experience of suspended judgement that comes to the sceptic after his inquiry, and *Pyrrhonian*, after the man they regard as founder of their practice, Pyrrho. The practice as Sextus introduces it (*PH* 1.8), is to balance perceptions and thoughts against one another (any pairing will do) in such a way that a pair is equipollent, that is, equally credible or incredible while still in some sense opposed to one another. Suspension of judgement evidently just happens to the sceptic (it is a *pathos*, rather than a conclusion), and leads to undisturbedness (*ataraxia* – but see the ghost of a contrast between these at the end of *PH* 1.12), and this, although it may not be deliberately sought, is the goal of the sceptic.

Aporetic Pyrrhonism. The other two names for the sceptic, *zetetic*, "engaged in seeking," and *aporetic*, "engaged in refutation," are appropriate to a more argumentative form of scepticism, one that works more actively towards its goal.[15] These are, interestingly, epithets that belong to Plato's Socrates in view of qualities he had, which actually distinguish his work from the therapeutic scepticism I outlined in the preceding paragraph. Therapeutic sceptics, by contrast, do not seek further, once they have found a way to a balanced opposition between two thoughts or perceptions. Seeking is a very small part of their practice. Socrates, however, is never content after a failed inquiry (*Euthyphro* 15e–16), but always proposes to go on with his quest: "I do not advise us to let ourselves remain as we are [without an answer to our question]" (*Laches* 201a6).

An *aporia* is an impasse; it is a kind of argument that closes off, by refutation, all the avenues of thought we have considered.[16] Therapeutic sceptics balance positive arguments against refutations and then, finding no way to choose between them, find themselves in a state of suspension of belief about the matter in dispute.[17] The *aporetic* sceptic, by contrast, would be one who works by way of refuting dogmatic positions. But refutation is a form of argument; its premises and its conclusions are to be believed and therefore arguably dogmatic. The conclusion that an account is false could be dogmatic, albeit negatively so. For that reason, *aporia* could be at most something that therapeutic sceptics play at, along the way to suspended judgement.[18]

For this reason, *aporetic* is quite wrong as a descriptor for the therapeutic sceptic and quite right for Socrates or for anyone who followed the tradition of Socratic refutation. It is a synonym for "Pyrrhonian" in Aenesidemus' usage, if we are to judge by the report of Photius.[19] Truly zetetic and aporetic sceptics would, like Socrates, seek answers to questions and determine that all available answers are wrong, and therefore that they ought to have no positive beliefs on the matters in question. They have found reasons for suspending belief. The outcome would be the same for them as for therapeutic sceptics with two differences: the aporetics at the end hold certain negative beliefs (that the hypotheses in question are all wrong) and are still committed to seeking better answers. As a result, they may not experience the calm that descends on the mind of the therapeutic sceptic.

Now the Platonic Socrates may well have been an influence on Aenesidemus, who probably began in the Academy and rebelled against it, rejecting both Platonic and Stoic lines of thought. Platonic argument strategies seem nevertheless to have been part of his armory. Aenesidemus appears to have practiced refutation on a large scale,[20] and to have distinguished the result from the negative dogmatism he eschewed,[21] whereas Sextus generally uses refutation and negative dogmatism to balance positive argument, while distancing himself from both *aporia* and negative dogmatism as if they were inseparable from one another.

We cannot be sure that Aenesidemus is the author of the Ten Modes, but we can say that they suit his argument strategy very well. Most sources present the Ten Modes in the form of refuting arguments, and Diogenes Laertius actually calls them *aporiai*, meaning refutations (9.79). While the Modes may be given a therapeutic use, they are best suited to be used as demonstrations. And this goes for the Five as well as the Ten. In what follows, I shall treat them as demonstrations.

III THE TEN MODES

The first seven Modes show the relativity of perceptual appearances in various ways; these are summed up in the Eighth Mode, Relativity, which may also go beyond the seven to argue for the relativity of all things. The Ninth and Tenth Modes deal with issues of value. Although the Five were introduced after the Ten, argument strategies from the Five may be used in support of the Ten. The Eight Causal Modes were probably contemporary with the Ten; they serve to undermine any attempt to reason from appearances by reference to cause and effect.

Here is the list in the order in which Sextus presents the Ten, with references in parentheses to other relevant sources. I have provided capsule summaries for each, based on Sextus.

(1) From differences among animals (*PH* 1.40, cf. 2.26, First also in Philo 171, in DL 9.79–80, and in Aristocles). Different animals have different sensory receptors; the same object will probably have different effects on different receptors; so different animals will probably receive different sensory impressions. As party to the issue, we humans cannot judge between our impressions and those of other animals, so the matter is undecidable; therefore we must of necessity hold back from judgement about external objects.

(2) From differences among human beings (*PH* 1.79, also 2 in Philo 175, DL 9.80–81, and Aristocles). The same thing may affect different people differently and so give them different impressions. From here we follow the same route to *epochê* as in the First Mode.

(3) From differences among the senses (*PH* 1.91, DL 9.81). The same object may affect different senses differently (honey seems pleasant to the taste but not to the eyes). An object possibly has qualities that cannot affect our senses; therefore the nature of the object is not evident to us, and *epochê* as to external objects follows.

(4) Contrasting circumstances (*PH* 1.100; this is Third in Philo 181.3 and in DL 9.82; Sixth in Aristocles). The same object may affect a single observer differently in different circumstances. We have no criterion for preferring one circumstance to another, and *epochê* as to external objects follows.

(5) Contrasting positions, distances, and places (*PH* 1.118; Fourth in Philo 181.3; Seventh in DL 9.85–86, and Fourth in Aristocles). An object looks different from different distances or locations; any object that is observed is observed from a distance and location; if we judge this location to be best, either we give no proof or we give a proof that is subject to the regress argument; therefore we cannot say what an object is in its nature, but only as it appears to us.

(6) Contrasting mixtures (*PH* 1.124; Seventh in Philo 189 and Sixth in DL 9.84–85). External objects affect us always in combination with other objects; change the mix and you change the resulting impression. Therefore we are unable to say what an object is in its external nature and come by necessity to *epochê*.

(7) Contrasting quantities and compositions (*PH* 1.129; Fifth in Philo 184; Eighth in DL 9.86, Fifth in Aristocles). The same stuff in different concentrations or quantities affects the same observer differently. Therefore we are unable to say precisely what the external stuff is in its nature.

(8) From relativity (*PH* 1.135; Sixth in Philo 186, Tenth in DL 9.87–88, and Seventh in Aristocles). All things appear relative, because, as the preceding Modes show, all appearances involve relativity. All things are relative because, for example, all things belong to species and genera, and these are relative to each other. Therefore we cannot state the nature of external objects with precision.[22]

(9) According to constant or rare concurrence (*PH* 1.141, also Ninth in DL 9.87). Objects seen rarely seem more wonderful or valuable than those seen often. Therefore we cannot say how the external objects are.

(10) Contrasting ways of life, customs, laws, myths, and dogmatic assumptions (*PH* 1.145; Eighth in Philo 193; Fifth in DL 9.83, Third in Aristocles). There are conflicts among customs, laws, and traditional beliefs as to the value of various actions. These conflicts leave us unable to say what the external nature of objects is.

Rather than discuss each Mode at length, which is not suitable for this brief study, I will discuss the range of interpretive strategies available for most of the Modes. Each Mode is an argument schema, but may admit interpretation as any of three different schemata, which I will sort out in the next section. The Eighth Mode (Relativity) presents special problems of interpretation, which I will take up when it reappears as one of the Five.

IV ARGUMENT SCHEMATA

I will take the Second of the Ten Modes as my main example, although it is not typical of all of the Ten. Based on human differences, the Second Mode invites three different readings, depending on whether its governing principle is taken to be (A) causal invariability, (B) variability of appearance, or (C) undecidability. In addition, each depends on one of the following assumptions about rationality. I list them in order from the easiest to the hardest to accept:

(R1)   One should hold back from believing what has been shown by forceful arguments not to be the case.

(R2)   One should hold back from accepting an appearance that has been shown to be not trustworthy.

(R3)   One should hold back from believing either of a pair of undecidable alternatives.

In what follows I will argue that the Ten Modes are most compelling if read in terms of causal invariability (CI) and the first rule. The weakness of this reading is that it allows the Modes to protect its users against only the narrower form of dogmatism (dogmatism about the natures of things). But we have textual reasons as well for accepting this interpretation for the early versions of the Modes.

A. Causal invariability (CI). If it is the nature of x to be F, then x will have F effects, and no effects contrary to F, on anyone on whom it has an effect.[23]

For example, if the sun is by nature hot, it will warm everyone and not cause anyone to be cold. But the sun apparently chills Alexander's butler, causing him to shiver, and the poor man must seek the protection of the shade in order to warm himself (*PH* 1.82). Again, if it were the nature of hemlock to cause death, then it would kill anyone who takes it. But an elderly Attic woman was unharmed by a large dose (*PH* 1.81). This argument schema works for many of the Modes, most obviously the Seventh, the Mode of quantity. Small amounts of wine are healthy, large amounts not, and the same for most foods (*PH* 1.131).

(A1)   The same thing, X, makes some people F and other people G, where F and G are opposites.

(A2)   Therefore (by CI) it is not the case that X is either F or G by its own nature.

(R1)   One should hold back from believing what has been shown by forceful arguments not to be the case.

(A3)   Therefore, by A2 and R1, we ought to hold back from ascribing F or G to the nature of X.

This schema is well suited to support the position that Sextus takes in *Against the Ethicists* (*M* 11.118), that being untroubled will come of thinking that nothing is good or bad by nature (Bett [41], p. 137). But it will support this kind of thinking only point by point, thing by thing, unless it persuades us that all supposed goods and evils will succumb to this strategy. Note that the conclusion is only weakly dogmatic, in that it makes no positive claim about the nature of X. Contrast it with the strongly dogmatic "X is such by its nature that it cannot be either F or G." Indeed, wine and food can be good or bad, depending on circumstance, but, since their natures cannot depend on circumstance, these effects are not due to their natures. So on the CI reading the Second Mode leaves us not claiming to know anything about their natures.

Even strict Pyrrhonists would not balk at R1 as it is expressed; R1 is, after all, merely one-half of the procedure for achieving equipollence. But what right has a Pyrrhonist to use CI, which appears to have a dogmatic pedigree? It is not a metaphysical claim, because it is consistent with there being nothing with a nature that satisfies CI. CI appears to be a postulate for the meaning of "nature," and it is the right postulate to express a feature we have in mind for the goods and evils we are most inclined to worry about: they are the ones that bring benefits or harm with them no matter what the circumstances. The

Second Mode will allow us to see, for each thing we are inclined to fear or desire, that it does not inevitably have the consequences that concern us. On this reading, the Second Mode is a demonstration, but one that does not ensnare its users in dogmatism, either by way of premise or conclusion (on the narrow view of dogmatism). The origins of CI, however, are in Plato's arguments for the forms, as we shall see below, and these do lead to dogmatic conclusions.

B. *Variability in appearance (VA)*. Appearance p is trustworthy as to the nature of its object if and only if p appears true to everyone.[24]

Most scholars take the Second Mode as based on differences in the way things appear to people.[25] We may reasonably suppose that the old lady and I perceive hemlock differently if it poisons me but not her. But the examples given are strictly causal, and we must infer differences in conscious perception (as Sextus does from difference in choice, *PH* 1.87). Differences in opinion will loom large enough in other Modes, however, that we must investigate this line of argument thoroughly.

(B1)   The same thing, X, appears F to one person and G to another, where F and G are opposites.

(B2)   Therefore, by VA, neither appearance is trustworthy as to the nature of X.

(R2)   One should hold back from accepting an appearance that has been shown to be not trustworthy.

(B3)   Therefore, by B2 and R2, one should hold back from accepting either appearance as true of the nature of X.

Although R2 is harmless, the principle governing this argument, VA, needs a supporting argument. Sextus will support it by appeal to undecidability. But he does not need to do so, and the appeal imports risks of its own. Other reports of the Modes do not take this tack. For the First Mode (differences between humans and animals) Diogenes says simply that "*epochê* follows such a conflict" and Philo evidently thinks his work is done when he has established such a conflict.

Why should recognizing a conflict among appearances lead rationally to *epochê*? Surely one person, or one kind of animal, might perceive things wrong. I offer two explanations that do not appeal to undecidability. First, if the same method – seeking to know how something appears to creatures – yields inconsistent results, then we know that the method yields at least one result that is false. But if so, we have good reason for doubting that the method could ever yield results that are trustworthy. If my lab experiment gives different results on Monday and Tuesday, I had better try a different method, or at least an improved one. This method has been found wanting.

Secondly, on a causal theory of perception of the sort that prevailed in antiquity, VA reduces to CI. If X causes me to have a desirable appearance, and you to have an undesirable appearance, CI tells us to conclude that it is not the nature of X to cause either kind of appearance.

Later Pyrrhonists such as Sextus were not satisfied by invariance arguments, probably because they did not accept the implicit Platonism of its basis in CI. Aenesidemus evidently held the semantic postulate that, if X had a nature, its nature would be invariant, without ever finding that there are invariant entities such as Plato's Forms. But his successors shied away even from this and sought refuge in undecidability.[26]

C. Undecidability (U). When appearances conflict, and at most one of them may be true, there is no decision procedure for deciding between them.

(C1)   The same thing, X, appears F to one person and G to another, where F and G are opposites.

(C2)   At most, one of the appearances in C1 can be true.[27]

(C3)   Therefore, by U, no decision procedure will decide whether X is F or G; the matter is undecidable.

(R3)   One should hold back from believing either of a pair of undecidable alternatives.

(C4)   Therefore, by C3 and R3, one should hold back from accepting either appearance as true of X.

To return to our example, if the sun appears warm to me and cool to the butler, and if at most one of us could be right about the sun, then, in the absence of a decision procedure, rationality requires us to withhold judgement. But why should we believe that there is no decision procedure to resolve a conflict in the appearances? We decide such conflicts frequently among our own perceptions: The oar in the water looks bent, but it looked straight in dry air, and I decide for the dry appearance; or the dish looked foul but tasted delicious, and I decide to go with taste. Conflicts involving others may also be easily resolved: My friend thinks the oar is bent, but

I have more experience of the effects of a water line on vision, so I rightly decide for the appearance of the oar to me.

The difficulty with R3 is that rationality sometimes requires us to accept reasons for believing one of two alternatives even when neither reason is decisive. And what rationality requires it must also permit. When I can plant only one of my two fields, it would be irrational to plant neither one because I find no decisive reason for preferring one to the other. I should make the best choice I can in view of the information available.

Sextus defends U in his account of the First Mode (*PH* 1.59–61): We would have no place to stand to make a decision between two appearances; deciding to use my appearance as a criterion would be begging the question. "We will not be able to judge the sensory impressions – ours and those of the animals – as we are ourselves party to the dispute and therefore are more in need of a judge than able to judge for ourselves" (59). In his account of the Second Mode, he fleshes the argument out at *PH* 1.87–89: If we try to appeal to the experience of the majority we will be stymied by our inability to canvas all the peoples of the world. Sextus will bolster U-based arguments also by appeal to the Reciprocity and Regress Modes of Agrippa (Reciprocity at *PH* 1.61, 91, and 112–17; Regress at 121–22).

The Modes probably made no use of undecidability in their early versions,[28] but Sextus or his source introduces undecidability in five of the Modes, numbers 1, 2, 3, 4, and 5 (*PH* 1. 59–61, 90, 98, 112–17, and 121–23). The Fourth is deceptive: Sextus and Diogenes report an argument premised on the claim that sane and crazy people are both in natural conditions (*PH* 1.103, DL 9.82); this probably goes back to an Academic reply to the Stoics who appealed to the natural perceptions of people in good health. The argument does not leave it undecided which group is in the natural state; both are, and therefore the process that produces different impressions from the same object in different people is natural, and the conflict between them undermines any claims we might make about the object on the basis of such impressions. If the same thing produces contrary effects, even by natural processes, neither effect represents its true nature. This result is not based on undecidability but on causal invariability (CI), but Sextus will bring it under U at the end (*PH* 1.112–17).

Undecidability is the weakest of the three principles. The invariability principles rest simply on an understanding of what is meant by the nature of something that has a nature. But undecidability has to be shored up against all of the obvious ways that we decide cases of conflicting appearances: appeal to the majority, to normal conditions of perception, and so on. These decision procedures work for most purposes, giving us reasons, acceptable to rational people, for acting on some appearances in preference to others. A modern sceptic might say that these decision procedures do not yield certainty, but rationality does not require that we withhold belief from all propositions that fall short of certainty, and neither does Sextus. Sextus says instead that undecidable propositions do not go beyond appearances to the natures of their objects. But if Sextus wants to bring in the concept of nature, he would do better to rest his case on invariability, as early versions of the Ten Modes probably did.

V THE PLATONIC MODE

I will give a brief account of the Platonic or Socratic Mode of refutation that may be the root of the Pyrrhonian Modes. Members of the Academy solved the problem of sceptical hygiene by framing their arguments in terms that Stoics would accept. The Academics could thus confound a Stoic without committing themselves to premises or to rules of logic; in particular, they needed no commitment to criteria of knowledge. Stoics brought all of that with them to the fray. The Pyrrhonians, taking on a more general crowd of dogmatists, needed more general strategies.

As heirs of the Academics, Pyrrhonians are also heirs of Plato, and the earliest users of the Modes may well have gone back to Plato to escape Stoic influences and, indeed, to draw on the resources of Socratic arguments that were aimed at unsophisticated people who did not know what they thought about philosophical subjects.

Accordingly, I will introduce here an argument strategy I will call the Platonic Mode. Socrates uses this to show that his partner can say how something appears to him, but not say how it actually is. The result of repeated applications of the Mode is summed up at *Republic* 5, 479a as follows:

"Of these many fine things, my good friend, shall we say that any of them will not appear foul? Or that any of the just things will not turn out to be unjust? Or of the holy things unholy?" – "No, but by necessity even the fine things will themselves appear foul, and the same with the others."

Socrates' aim is to induce a limited *epochê*: the hearers are supposed to suspend judgement about the many fine things that they love to hear or see, and seek instead to know the one Fine form, which, by contrast with the many fine things, will never appear foul. What are the many things to which the argument applies? The matter is controversial, but I suppose that they include all the things to which Socrates has applied the Mode. I give two examples:

(1) *Hypothesis*. A beautiful woman is the really fine thing.
(2) Next to a goddess, a beautiful woman appears foul.
(3) The really fine will never appear foul (unstated).
(4) A beautiful woman is not the really fine thing.
(5) Therefore the hypothesis is false; the woman only appeared to be fine, in certain situations, and therefore is "no more fine than foul."
                                                        (*Hippias Major* 289c)

(a) *Hypothesis*. Returning what you borrowed is the real justice.
(b) Returning what you borrowed appears unjust in one situation.
(c) The real justice will never appear unjust.
(d) Returning what you borrowed is not the real justice.
(e) Therefore the hypothesis is false; the rule about borrowing only appeared to be justice in certain situations. (*Republic* 1, 331e)

The Platonic Mode turns on the principle of opposites:

PO. If X is really G it will never appear to be F, where F is the opposite of G. It follows that if X appears to be G in one situation and F in another, then X is not really G.

By "really" I translate Plato's *akribôs* or *eilikrinôs*, which seem to have the same usage, and which turn up in Pyrrhonian contexts to make the same contrast between the way things appear and the way they really are. By "appear" I do not mean to introduce subjectivity; the fineness of the woman and the justice of the rule about borrowing will vary in appearance, so long as they are considered with respect only to the particular situations in which they had been first brought forward. Socrates and his partners agree about these things, and they will agree that they appear different in a new situation.

Plato leaves PO undefended, but I would propose to treat it as an application of the principle of synonymy, if an appearance is taken to be an effect:

PS. If X is G, then it cannot cause any effects that are opposite to G.

Add to this the invariability condition (I) and a causal account of appearances (C), both of which Plato appears to hold:

I. If X is G by its own nature, then it is always G and never F, where F and G are opposites.
C. If X appears to be G to you, then X is causing you to have a G appearance.

From PS and I we can infer first causal invariability (CI) and then, by way of C, the invariability of appearance, from which PO follows.

If all you can say about X is how you find it to be in certain situations, then we can probably find a situation in which it appears the opposite way, and then the Platonic Mode would require you to recognize that your first judgement was only a matter of appearance, so that you would suspend judgement about the real nature of X. What Socrates proposes to do to anyone who is devoted to the many fine things, a Pyrrhonian might propose to do to anyone on any topic. The Platonic Mode is *aporetic* and *zetetic* – and these epithets are, as we saw above, used for some earlier Pyrrhonists such as those who devised the Modes.

Of course, the Platonic Mode may not be quite right for a Pyrrhonian, for four reasons. First, it is essentially a refutation of a hypothesis, and not all Pyrrhonians allow themselves to use refutation outside of balancing contexts. Secondly, it leads not to a relaxation of mind but to a determination to seek the real nature of its subject. And, thirdly, it gets there on the basis of a strong (and arguably dogmatic) assumption about what it is for something to be really a certain way. Fourthly, Plato uses this Mode to support a two-world theory, according to which the Forms, being precisely what they are, are accessible only to knowledge and never through appearances, while appearances are never reliable about the Forms and are therefore outside the scope of knowledge. Pyrrhonians do not use their Modes to support any theories whatever.

VI THE FIVE AGRIPPAN MODES

The Five Modes, with the Ten, show "more variety and completeness" than the Ten do alone (*PH* 1.177). They are dissonance, regress, relativity, hypothesis, and reciprocity (1.164–77, Diogenes, 9. 88–89).

The formal ones, regress, hypothesis, and reciprocity, have an especially long history in epistemology, both before and after
Pyrrhonism.[29] Although Sextus gives pride of place to the Ten
Modes, he almost never uses them; the Five Modes, by contrast,
show up frequently in his arguments. In various combinations, the
Five work as a system: if you escape the toils of one Mode, you fall
into the trap of another, as we shall see below. The Five have been
discussed thoroughly by other scholars,[30] so I will offer here a brief
summary of each, with remarks about its usage by Sextus.

   First Mode, Dissonance (PH 1.165). Also known as "dispute" or
"disagreement" (*diaphonia*) it is the least compelling by itself. Many
propositions are under dispute, but it would be irrational not to accept
them for that reason alone; if dispute about a proposition sufficed to
throw us into *epochê*, we would hardly need the other Modes.
Hankinson and Barnes both treat this Mode as coming into play for
undecidable disputes (supported by *PH* 1.178, 2.19, 2.56–57, 2.85, and
2.182) or ones declared equipollent (*PH* 3.139); in some cases Sextus
moves from dispute to undecidability by way of other Agrippan Modes
such as regress and reciprocity (as in *PH* 2.85, 2.182, and 3.23), and in
one case he appeals to the Ten (*PH* 3.50) in order to reach undecidability. Sometimes, however, Sextus treats disagreement as an independent Mode leading directly to a denial of apprehensibility; if the
matter were apprehensible, it would have made a clear, direct impression that left no room for dissonance (*PH* 2.8, see also 3.3, 3.13, 3.30).
This use of dissonance could harp back to causal invariability (above
p. 216): if the object really were a certain way in its nature, it would not
cause us to have different impressions of it.

   Second Mode, Regress (*PH* 1.166). This Mode comes into play when
a claim or argument derives its credibility from another, and that from
another, and so on to infinity. Pyrrhonians claim that it is impossible to
judge or prove an infinite series of arguments (*PH* 2.78, 85, 89, 182, 3.8,
3.53). The same or an analogous Mode is used against an infinite series
of signs (*PH* 2.124), of definitions (*PH* 2.207), and of causes (*PH* 3.24).

   Third Mode, Relativity (*PH* 1.167). Some scholars would prefer to
banish this from the Five, because they take it to be essentially
dogmatic.[31] A strict Pyrrhonian would hold back from the dogmatic
belief that things are relative. Protagoras is supposed to have claimed
that contrary impressions are true for the individuals who have them,
but in that case neither individual should withhold belief. Sextus or

his source takes Protagoras to be proposing a criterion for what is the case, and that is dogmatic (*PH* 1.219).

Sextus allows that relativity is fundamental to the first seven of the Ten Modes and assigns it a central position in the Five, but, although he often appeals to relativity against dogmatic positions, he does not use the Relativity Mode in his argument.

Different sources give different versions of the Relativity Mode in the context of the Ten Modes, and these may hark back to earlier stages of the Pyrrhonian revival.

Sextus may use an argument for relativism that is a fallacy. Anything can be found to have attributes that are in some way relational, but having some relational attributes does not entail having only attributes that are relational. Any human being is some-one's child, but, for all that, any human being is, non-relationally, human.[32] Sextus has a better case for the relativity of appearances to observers (*PH* 1.135–36), which runs through several of the Modes, especially the First and Second of the Ten, and which, as we have seen, can be understood as a failure of causal invariability (CI): if the object were of a certain sort by nature, it would affect its observers in a way that is consistent with that nature (above p. 216).

Fourth Mode, Hypothesis (*PH* 1.168). In its simplest and most plausible form, this throws you into *epochê* when you are reduced by the other Modes to asserting the starting point of your argument "simply and without demonstration." That is because a hypothesis by itself has no more authority than whatever it is supposed to support. But Sextus has more complex and less plausible ways of deploying this mode (*PH* 1.173–74).[33] Sextus refers to this Mode rarely by name, but he uses it often nevertheless.[34]

Fifth Mode, Reciprocity (*PH* 1.169). Reciprocity kicks in when the proof of a matter depends on the matter in question (*PH* 2.9, 2.20). Sextus offers an argument from the reciprocity of knowledge for cause and effect: if you have C in mind as a cause, you must first know of E as an effect; but to have E in mind as an effect, you must first know of C as a cause. But then you could never get started (*PH* 3.22).

Sextus is interested in using this Mode against an odd mix of deduction with induction: If you deduce that Socrates is not four-footed from the general claim that no man is four-footed, you may not also induce that general claim from particular claims including the one about Socrates – that he is not four-footed (2.197, 2.199).

Sextus sometimes seems to confuse a particular supporting claim with an entire genus of supporting claims. There is no circularity in the following (*PH* 2.36, 2.92, 3.35–36, 3.53): "A supports B, while C (which is merely of the same kind as B) supports A."

System of the Five Modes. Sextus claims that the Five may be deployed to undermine any dogmatic claim whatever, and reduce the claimant to *epochê* (*PH* 1. 169–77, cf. 2.18–21). His system of Five Modes plays objects of perception (*aisthêta*) against objects of thought (*noêta*). Whatever is at issue, it will be subject to dispute. If the claimant admits that the dispute is undecidable, then the First Mode leads straight to *epochê*. If, however, the claimant contends that the matter can be decided, then it will be decided by appeal either to another of the same sort (a percept by appeal to a percept) or by appeal to the other sort of thing (a concept to a percept). If the appeal is to the same sort of thing, the claimant will be driven to an infinite regress by the Second Mode. If he seeks safety by appealing to a different sort, then he will be led to reciprocity by the Fifth Mode: to defend the concept he appeals to a percept, and to defend that percept he either starts a regress by appealing to another percept or appeals to the original concept and so falls foul of reciprocity. If the claimant takes refuge in a hypothesis, he will be trapped by the Fourth Mode, unable to offer a defense for his claim. In any case, whether the claim is about percepts or concepts it will succumb to the Third Mode, since both percepts and concepts can be shown to be relative. Thus, the Third Mode does not function as part of the system, but works on its own.

The Two Modes in Sextus are a systematic application of Modes One, Two, and Four: If the claim is self-supporting, use Dissonance by bringing the claim into dispute; if the claimant offers independent support, attack that support with an iteration of Dissonance, or drive the claimant into Regress or Reciprocity (*PH* 1.178–79).[35]

VII THE EIGHT MODES AGAINST CAUSAL EXPLANATION (PH 1.180–85)

Aenesidemus provided Eight Modes for refuting causal explanations (*aitiologiai*). In introducing his brief summary of the Eight, Sextus makes it clear that they are designed to refute by using cognates of *elenchus* and *aporia* (*PH* 1.180–81). What they are designed to refute, however, is not a general claim such as "color emerges from the combining of atoms." On such matters – that is, on actual causes – Aenesidemus would hold back from refutation. His Modes are supposed to refute any claim for the truth of a particular explanation; many explanations are possible, and none may be conclusively proved, and, by implication, none may be conclusively ruled out.[36]

Aenesidemus has in mind the explanation of appearances by appeal to the non-apparent natures of things. Much of ancient science and philosophy appealed to a non-apparent reality, but the most notorious appeal of the sort was to atoms and void, the explanatory entities of Democritus and the Epicureans. The First Causal Mode uses the Epicurean term for confirmation (*epimarturêsis*), and Hankinson plausibly draws from this the hypothesis that Aenesidemus has atomism as one of his main targets.[37] Atomism cannot be the only target, because Aenesidemus uses the diversity of dogmatic explanations effectively in the Second Mode.

The First Causal Mode is designed to show the dogmatists that they cannot confirm their causal hypotheses from observations of the non-apparent. As Hankinson points out, this Mode needs help; if we had only one coherent explanation available, or precisely one that was more coherent than all others, then the dogmatists could claim that they do not need confirmation by further observation. But, as the Second Causal Mode insists, we have a rich supply of possible explanations and no good way to choose among them.[38] The Third Causal Mode points out that it would not be enough to explain particular events; dogmatists would have to explain also the order or arrangement in which the events occur. In the Fifth Causal Mode, an underlying concern of all these Modes comes close to the surface – the unresolved differences among dogmatic theories. Each theory uses the elementary substances it has posited, but the theories do not agree on what the elements are. The remaining Modes bring up general difficulties about appeals to the non-apparent (Causal Modes Four and Eight), along with problems about consistency that seem to be targeted against specific theories (Causal Modes Six and Seven).

If fully successful, his Eight Causal Modes would leave all appearances unexplained. Then all we have to assert would be appearances, and, since all appearances are relative to the perceiver, we have nothing to assert but what is relative – and that is precisely where Aenesidemus wants the Modes to leave him.[39]

NOTES

1 The Ten Modes are associated with Aenesidemus or his followers in Sextus, *M* 7.345 and by context in Diogenes Laertius 9.78 and Aristocles. As Aenesidemus is the founder of the Pyrrhonian revival, he is most likely in any case to have been the author of the Modes.

2 Woodruff [234] and Bett [143] have argued that there were two distinct phases of the Pyrrhonian revival, with Aenesidemus being the primary representative of the first, while Sextus (most of the time) speaks for the second. Hankinson holds that Diogenes Laertius in his presentation of the Mode of Relativity "looks back to an earlier, less developed Pyrrhonism" ([68], p. 178). Schofield [232] has marshaled arguments to show that Aenesidemus was a Pyrrhonist in precisely Sextus' sense. Although my view of the matter is not changed, my interpretation of particular Modes does not depend on the two-phase hypothesis.

3 On the sources see Hankinson [68], p. 155 and Annas and Barnes [269], pp. 26–30.

4 So, rightly, Schofield [232], p. 298.

5 Aristocles in Eusebius, *Praeparatio Evangelica* 14.18.

6 For more on this, see Harald Thorsrud, Chapter 3 "Arcesilaus and Carneades."

7 Aenesidemus is reported to have been a relativist. On the evidence, which comes mainly from Photius, see Woodruff [234], 158–61. For the case that Aenesidemus was an orthodox Pyrrhonian like Sextus, who carefully held back from relativism, see Schofield [232].

8 Such are the arguments for relativism (*PH* 1.135, 140, 167), which supply the general strategy for the first Seven Modes (*PH* 1.136). There are two ways of being a negative dogmatist. If you deny any position whatever you are a negative dogmatist on the broad view. On the narrow view, you would be a negative dogmatist if you asserted anything in the form, "The nature of X is such that X cannot be G." By contrast, you could assert, "'X is G' cannot be supported by appeal to knowledge of the nature of X," without risk of dogmatism on the narrow view.

9 An interpretation proposed by many scholars, e.g. Hankinson [68], p. 192.

10 As a sentential adverb, *eikotôs* here implies not that it is reasonable to suspend judgement, as Bury's version (Bury [39]) suggests, but that it is reasonable [to expect] that suspension will occur in these circumstances. See for a parallel the use of the adverb in Thucydides, 1.77.5.

11 See Bett [143], pp. 208–9; *pace* Annas and Barnes [269], pp. 24–25, who conflate undecidability with equipollence. They are not the same. Equipollence is equal credibility (*PH* 1.10); undecidability obtains when, credible or not, the two positions do not admit of a decision

procedure. Schofield [232], p. 297 *et seq.* makes a strong case against Woodruff [234] that the Modes aim at *epochê*.

12 *PH* 1.61, cf. 78; for an even more argumentative conclusion, see 1.140, for the Eighth Mode, Relativity.

13 The consensus of scholars, Annas, Barnes, and Hankinson, is to treat this Mode and others like it as demonstrations.

14 The ephectic does not need to be committed to truth-functional logic. In equipollence, the oppositions of one thought or perception to another need not be by way of affirmation or denial. That is, they are not truth-functional: if A is opposed to B it does not follow that an affirmation of A entails a denial of B. Instead, the pair are just "in battle" with one another, apparently like two sides in a contest, in which the contestants on each side do not affirm the positions on which they stake their hopes for victory. Taking a position in such a contest is rather like betting on a horse in a race.

15 The two terms are found together also at *M* 7.393 and 8.156.

16 An *aporia* is not a doubt or a confusion, and, in Sextus' work, it is not a problem. It is a refutation, and as such is negatively dogmatic. See *PH* 2.9, 2.197, 3.22, 3.242. That aporetics refute: see *M* 8.76, 78, 99, 160, 9.207, 10.68, 240, 340.

17 So Sextus, *PH* 3.80–81, *M* 8.159–60, 9.207.

18 So Woodruff [234], p. 141 *et seq.* Schofield [232] has argued vigorously for a broader view of *aporia* in Sextus (pp. 287–89). He appeals to *M* 9.207, but this does not support his view; there Sextus finds equipollence between the arguments of the dogmatics (cause exists) and those of the aporetics (cause does not exist). Aenesidemus is responsible for the aporetic arguments (9.218), but from this alone we cannot tell whether or not he used the aporetic (here, "refuting") arguments with the sole aim of equipollence.

19 Photius, *Library* 169b40 and elsewhere. See also Galen *Adv. Jul.* 18A. 268K (Barnes [270], p. 7).

20 See Photius in 170b3–35 = LS 72L. For a somewhat different view, see R. J. Hankinson, Chapter 5 "Aenesidemus and the Rebirth of Pyrrhonism."

21 If Aenesidemus held the narrow view of dogmatism, his *aporetic* refutation of the sentence "X is G" would conclude simply that it is not in the nature of X to be G. Schofield rightly points out an ambiguity in our word "refutation." Aenesidemus could have practiced refutation as part of a program of reaching *epochê* through equipollence (Schofield [232], p. 295).

22 Sextus quotes an earlier account here, which claims that all things are relative; but Sextus corrects for this at the start by asking us to

understand "appears" wherever the argument uses "is." For a brief discussion of the special issues raised by this Mode, see below pp. 224–5. For the tradition that Aenesidemus was a relativist, see note 7.

23 Causal invariability follows from Bett's invariability principle (Bett [143], p. 118) with the principle of synonymy of cause and effect. See below, on the Platonic Mode.

24 Modified from Hankinson [68], p. 159. I have added "as to the nature of its object." Argument B concerns only the natures of things; argument C (which Hankinson rightly takes to be Sextus' interpretation) is more general.

25 Annas and Barnes [269], p. 57; Hankinson [68], esp. p. 166.

26 Such is the argument of Bett [143], which I find highly plausible.

27 In C2 I am following Hankinson [68], p. 156. C2 is explicit in Sextus and necessary to forestall the "Protagorean" conclusion that the two conflicting appearances are equally true.

28 Sources other than Sextus do not appeal to undecidability, and some of the modes – the Seventh Mode (Quantity), for example – cannot be understood in this way. We can decide that certain foods are bad for us in large quantities; problems arise only concerning the *natures* of those foods. In Sextus' version we find arguments similar to those in other sources, but with undecidability arguments apparently patched in, as in the Fourth Mode. The best explanation for this is that Sextus (or his source) is trying to accommodate Modes from an aporetic tradition into his more ephectic form of Pyrrhonism.

29 They were known to Aristotle, as has been widely recognized (e.g. Barnes [270], pp. 12–21, Hankinson [68], pp. 186).

30 Barnes [270] and Hankinson [68].

31 Barnes labels it a "strange beast" that does not belong with the other four Agrippan Modes (Barnes [270], p. 113). Hankinson does not use it as part of the system (Hankinson [68], p. 191). On the dogmatism of relativism in the view of a Pyrrhonian such as Sextus, see Barnes and Annas [269], pp. 97–98 and 144–45, where they outline different forms of relativism, some of which are compatible with Pyrrhonism. On the alleged relativism of Aenesidemus, see above note 7.

32 Hankinson [68], pp. 180–81.

33 On this see Barnes [270], pp. 90–112.

34 So Barnes [270], pp. 96–97.

35 Barnes [270], p. 120 offers a system of Three Modes that avoids the weakness of Mode One (Dissonance) and the dogmatism of Three (Relativism). Hankinson [68], p. 191 offers a system of four that is closer to Sextus.

36 The second of the Eight Modes presupposes that for any proposed explanation there are many that are not ruled out (*PH* 1.181).

37 Hankinson [68], pp. 213–17, where Hankinson constructs an effective line of argument from Sextus' severely abbreviated report. His account is the basis for my briefer one here.

38 Hankinson [68], p. 213.

39 See Bett [143], pp. 200–7. I am grateful to Richard Bett for thoughtful comments on this chapter.

12 Pyrrhonism and medicine

Sextus Empiricus, the best known to us of the Pyrrhonian sceptics and the only one whose works have survived substantially intact, was, as his name indicates, a member of the Empirical school of medicine. Other evidence also points to a close and long-sustained relation between medical Empiricism and Pyrrhonian scepticism. Diogenes Laertius' list of Pyrrhonists includes at least three Empiricists apart from Sextus himself: Menodotus, Theodas, and Sextus' student, Saturninus (9.115–16). Some of the others may also have been Empiricists, and there are figures not included on DL's list who seem to have been members of both schools.[1]

In his *Outline of Empiricism* (*Subfiguratio empirica*), where he adopts the point of view of an Empiricist (Deichgräber [20] 43, 20–22), Galen maintains that the Empiricist is to medicine as the Pyrrhonist is to the whole of life (82, 28 *et seq.*), and he criticizes Menodotus harshly for failing to live up to the ideal represented by Pyrrho, whom he (Menodotus himself) had held up to his fellow Empiricists as a model (84, 13 *et seq.*).[2] Sextus mentions empirical forms of the arts with approval: grammar (*M* 1.49–53, 61); astronomy, navigation, and farming (*M* 5.1–2). He wrote a work on Empirical medicine (*M* 1.61), which is not extant, and his surviving works contain many expressions of sympathy for the Empiricists and their ideas (*PH* 2.246, 254; *M* 5.104; *M* 8.191, 288, 291).

There was, then, an affinity between the two schools that amounted, in the eyes of some of their members, to an identity of outlook.[3] This brings into focus one of the principal problems posed by Pyrrhonian scepticism. How is the sceptic, who avowedly suspends judgement about absolutely everything, whose watchwords are "everything is inapprehensible" and "no more this than not

232

this" and the like, in a position to make discriminations and choose one course of action over another, as it seems a human being must if he or she is to live at all, let alone practice an art as complex and demanding as medicine?[4] If we were able to understand how some Pyrrhonists practiced medicine as members of the Empirical school, it might throw light on the general problem. There is, however, a further complication. When he tackles the question whether, as some say, Pyrrhonism is the same as medical Empiricism (*PH* 1.236–41), Sextus' answer is a stern criticism of Empiricism together with the suggestion that the Pyrrhonian sceptic would be better advised to practice medicine as a member of the so-called Methodist school.

If we attend closely to Sextus' words, the puzzle is somewhat reduced. It appears that his complaint against the Empiricists is conditional. "One must realize", he maintains, "that if this [i.e. medical] Empiricism really is firmly convinced of the inapprehensibility (*akatalêpsia*) of non-evident matters, then neither is it the same as skepticism nor would it be fitting for a skeptic to adopt it" (*PH* 1.236). Unsceptical firmness about the inapprehensibility of non-evident matters was the charge brought in the *Subfiguratio empirica* against Menodotus, who is sternly rebuked for claiming to know with certainty that all the views of Asclepiades of Bithynia, a Rationalist physician active in the first century BC, are false even though he holds that the Empiricist's attitude toward assertions about the non-evident should be that perhaps they are true, perhaps not (*Subfig. emp.* Deichgräber [20] 84, 11–85, 3; cf. 82, 20–28). Sextus' complaint appears to be an especially strong form of the same internal criticism, and the assertion that the sceptic would be better advised to pursue the so-called Method may apply only on the same condition, i.e. that medical Empiricism really is firmly convinced of the inapprehensibility of non-evident matters.

Indeed there is no evidence of relations between Methodism and Pyrrhonism of the kind that obtained between Empiricism and Pyrrhonism. Sextus, who usually speaks of "our" views and what "we" Pyrrhonists think, seems to indicate that the praise he bestows on Methodism is his own personal opinion (*PH* 1.237). And however high Sextus' opinion of Methodism was, it did not prevent him or his student, Saturninus, from being Empiricists. Nonetheless, even if we are not obliged to suppose that Sextus or any other Pyrrhonian doctors changed their allegiance to Methodism, the problem is lessened and not eliminated, for as we shall see, Sextus' view of Methodism's positive features is extremely favorable.

Before we can tackle this problem and assess the merits of the two medical schools from the Pyrrhonian perspective, however, we need to acquaint ourselves with the debates in medicine that gave rise to and shaped the two schools' outlooks. Medical Empiricism, which arose in the middle of the third century BC, defined itself in opposition to the pervasive rationalist tendency that its founders detected in the medicine of their time. Although elements of both Empiricism and Rationalism were already present in the medical literature of the fifth century, the debate between the two presupposed a framework of assumptions that cannot automatically be attributed to earlier thinkers. In particular, it presupposed a sharp distinction between what is given in experience and what lies beyond its reach that was not obvious or uncontroversial. The framework may owe something to the philosophers. In any case, it is in Plato and Aristotle that we find its first explicit formulations.[5] In the *Gorgias*, using medicine as an example, Socrates maintains that a true art (*technê*) selects the measures it will employ on the basis of an understanding of the nature of the object upon which it acts, and he insists that its master be able to give an account of what he does in the light of this understanding. Experience, by contrast, can never rise above the level of a knack (*tribê*). Such an ability is, Socrates says, mute (an *alogon pragma*); its practitioners can give no reason for what they do beyond the brute fact that things have been seen to happen as they do (465a, 501a; cf. *Phaedrus* 270b, *Laws* 720b, 857c).

Though he sets a higher value on experience as an indispensable stage on the way to art and science, Aristotle is of the same opinion. Experience, he maintains, can grasp only *that* certain facts obtain; the causes explaining *why* they do, which it is the task of an art or science to understand, forever elude it (*Metaphysics* 1.1, 981a28–b6). Experience arises out of the memory of many episodes of perception, and this conception of experience crucially depends on a view about the objects and properties accessible to perception. On the view in question, the facts grasped by perception are, as such, brute or discrete (1.1, 981b10–13). Experience adds to perception the power to discern patterns of conjunction and sequence among types of perceived events and to form expectations on this basis.

According to this way of thinking, to know the causes requires that one grasp that, given certain truths, others cannot fail to obtain because of the nature of the matters at issue, while still others are necessarily excluded. Reason, when it opposed to experience, is, then, above all, the faculty which furnishes insights into *why* things could not be otherwise, at the same time as it shows *that* they must be as they are. Thus, in Galen's account of Rationalism a place of central importance is occupied by an intellectual faculty able to grasp natural or rational relations of consequence and exclusion (*Subfig. emp.* Deichgräber [20] 87, 7; 89, 12–15).

Regardless of who first formulated the issues in this way, from roughly Aristotle's time, medical thinkers were occupied with questions about the relative contributions of experience and causal explanation to medical knowledge. Unlike medical Empiricism, medical Rationalism was not in a strict sense a single school, but a tendency, identified by the Empiricists, common to many schools whose substantive views about physiology and pathology often differed.[6] By "Rationalists" the Empiricists understood physicians who hold that correct treatment of patients at least some of the time requires a grasp of the hidden, underlying causes of health and disease of the kind that can only be obtained by reason (Celsus, *Proem.* 12, 62.[7]) For their part, the Empiricists dispensed with the appeal to causes entirely and set themselves the task of demonstrating that experience unaided by reason is a sufficient basis for art. Although they developed their position with the practice of medicine itself chiefly in view, the Empiricists took it to apply to the other arts as well (Celsus, *Proem.* 31–32; Galen, *Subfig. emp.* 86, 23–87, 4 Deichgräber [20]; *MM* X 126, 15–127, 1 K).[8]

They explained their position along roughly the following lines. Experience is the knowledge one has when one has observed something happening in the same way many times, e.g. that symptom X follows or accompanies or precedes symptom Y or that therapy A is followed by the alleviation of syndrome B. The knowledge one has at this stage can be expressed as a theorem, which states that X follows or accompanies Y always, for the most part, roughly half the time, or rarely (Galen, *Subfig emp.* 45, 25–30 Deichgräber [20]; cf. *On Medical Experience*, 95, 112 Walzer; [Galen] *Def med.* XIX 354 K). In another sense, "experience" refers to the knowledge had by the master of an art as a whole, which consists of many such theorems. Ultimately, every theorem belonging to the art owes its place there to repeated observation, but the artist will derive some of his knowledge from his own observation (autopsy), some of it from the records of others' observations (history). What is known by autopsy to the observer is history to the practitioner who learns from him (Galen, *Sect. ingred. SM* III 3, 17–20).

Where Empiricism relies on observation and the memory of what has been observed, Rationalism goes beyond observable symptoms to grasp the unhealthy affections that are their cause and which *indicate* the appropriate therapies. The physician who relies on indication (*endeixis*) draws a rational inference based on the causes at work in the diseased patient and leading to a conclusion about the proper treatment. If humoral theory is correct, for example, the unhealthy condition will be, at bottom, an imbalance of the humors, and the indicated therapy will be the restoration of the proper balance. Since effective therapy has to be adjusted to take account of the season, the age and sex of the patient, and the like, the Rationalists also admitted subordinate indications from these factors (*Sect. ingred. SM* III 5, 16–6, 26). The patient's underlying condition, which furnishes the basis for the indication of the therapy, is itself grasped by an inference from the evident symptoms that remind the Empiricist of the therapy which he or his colleagues have seen to be effective in past practice (*Sect. ingred. SM* III 7, 20–25; cf. [Galen] *De optima secta* I 119–21 K = fr. 277 Tecusan [28]).[9]

Within the framework that the Empiricists shared with the Rationalists, their opposing positions exhausted the possibilities. Either expert artistic knowledge is confined to phenomena and what can be known about them by long observation of the sequences and conjunctions obtaining among them, or it embraces the hidden underlying natures of things grasped by a special faculty of reason as well.

These assumptions were rudely rejected by the Methodists, who advocated the third main position in ancient medicine and the last to emerge. The method from which they took their name had no more use for hidden causes than did the Empiricists'. Like the Empiricists, the Methodists claimed to rely wholly upon the phenomena. At the same time, however, they maintained that observation, as it was practiced by the Empiricists, was of little or no value (Celsus, *Proem.* 57; Galen, *Sect. ingred. SM* III 14, 10–17; [Galen] *De optima secta* I 119 K = fr. 277 Tecusan [28]; Soranus, *Gynecology* I 4).

Without agreeing about how to distribute the credit between the two, our sources assign the leading parts in the formation of Methodism to Themison of Laodicea, active in the first part of the first century BC, and Thessalus of Tralles, active about a century later. Themison was a student of Asclepiades (the object of Menodotus' ire) whose physiology and pathology were a paradigm of Rationalist theory.[10] According to him, the body contains passages through which flow minute particles; both passages and particles are imperceptible and must be grasped by reason. This bodily system is in a healthy state when a proper, balanced flow of particles prevails. Diseases are caused by departures in the direction of excessive or deficient flow (though Asclepiades seems to have emphasized the latter). The Methodists take all diseases to be instances of three common conditions or "generalities": one of flux or excessive flow, one of constriction or deficient flow and a third that is a mixture of the two.[11] They also recognized therapeutic and surgical generalities, e.g. an alien presence in the body such as a thorn requiring surgical excision ([Galen] *Introductio* XIV 680–81 K = fr. 283 Tecusan [28]). Although the Methodists may have gone beyond Asclepiades by making flux, constriction, and the mixed condition responsible for all diseases, their most striking innovation was to regard these conditions as evident or apparent. Thus, they define the medical art as "knowledge of apparent generalities," to which they append "that accord with the end of medicine," because, like the Empiricists, they viewed their account of medicine as just a special case of an account of expert artistic knowledge in general (*Sect. ingred. SM* III 13, 23–14, 8).

The Methodist position provoked consternation. Galen complained that the Methodists' generalities were apparent only if the Methodists legislated a new sense for "apparent" opposed to its ordinary meaning (*Sect. ingred. SM* III 24, 19–22; cf. [Galen] *De optima secta* I 176 K = fr. 279 Tecusan [28]). He recognized two classes of phenomena, those apparent to the senses, and those apparent to the intellect (*MM* X 36 K = fr. 161 Tecusan [28]). The latter consist of indemonstrable axioms, e.g. that two quantities equal to a third are equal to each other. The contingent bodily condition of a patient can hardly be one of these, and Galen takes the Methodists to be asserting that the manifest generalities are grasped by the senses (*Sect. ingred. SM* III 24, 9 *et seq.*). To be sure, the Methodists do speak of "seeing" them, but, according to another source, they took the manifest generalities to be evident in

the sense of being grasped directly without inference but not necessarily by sense perception ([Galen] *De optima secta* I 176 K = fr. 279
Tecusan [28]). By this they seem to have meant that the three conditions can be grasped by means of a non-inferential sensitivity of the
kind that sets seasoned practitioners apart from laypeople.[12]

The Methodists differ from the Empiricists not only by recognizing
a wider range of phenomena, in the way that dogs hear higher fre-
quencies than humans, however. As Galen puts it, the way in which
they are occupied with the phenomena is different (*Sect. ingred. SM*
III 14, 12 *et seq.*). The apparent generalities retain all the pregnancy
and richness of the non-evident conditions from which they are
somehow descended. Thus, it is not because they have repeatedly
observed patients suffering from fluent conditions recovering after
constrictive therapy, according to the Methodists, that they prescribe
constriction. Rather, it is because flux *indicates* treatment by constriction. The indications on which the Methodist physician relies
are evident apart from observation in the way that elementary truths
of reason are.[13] They neither need, nor stand to benefit by, empirical
confirmation. This is why, on the Methodists' view, patient observation of the kind practiced by the Empiricists is largely beside the
point. It is enough to see that someone is suffering from flux to
know that he requires therapy by constriction. It is here that the
Methodists break most radically from the framework of assumptions
shared by the Rationalists and Empiricists, according to which the
only relations that obtain between phenomena as such, are those of
brute conjunction and sequence.

Since the Methodists do not share these assumptions, they reject
the charge that they must really be Empiricists or merely another sect
of Rationalist (Celsus, *Proem.* 57, 62–64; Galen, *Sect. ingred. SM* III
13, 19–14, 17). They are not Rationalists, they insist, because their
attention is confined to phenomena; they are not Empiricists because
their choice of therapies is not based on the observation and memory
of the phenomena, but on the indications they derive from them (cf.
Sect. ingred. SM III 14, 15–17; [Galen] *Introductio* XIV 683 K = fr. 283
Tecusan [28]).

Let us now return to the question we put aside earlier, i.e. what
recommended the two medical schools to Pyrrhonism? As I noted at
the outset, one reason for investigating Pyrrhonism's medical connections is the light they promise to throw on how the sceptic can

carry on life and practice an art. The problem is that both Empiricists and Methodists seem to do what they do by violating the sceptical principle of universal suspension of judgement. In their different ways, both schools claim to adhere to the phenomena, disclaiming knowledge only of non-evident matters. Empiricists, Methodists, and Rationalists seem, then, not to have disagreed about the possibility of knowledge quite generally, as sceptics and dogmatists did, but rather about the precise scope and limits of human knowledge.

To be sure, the Pyrrhonists also claim to live by adhering to the phenomena, and their answer to the charge that the sceptic will be reduced to complete inactivity is that he too has a criterion, the phenomenon (*PH* 1.5, 19–24, 238; *M* 7.29–30; DL 9.106). Like the verb "appear" and related words like "apparent," the Greek verb *phainesthai*, which it translates, and "phenomenon" differ in meaning depending on which of two contrasts they stand in. In one sense, "phenomenon" is synonymous with "evident," and the phenomena are the objects of knowledge immediately given to evident apprehension, most obviously by the senses but perhaps in other ways as well. Phenomena in this sense are contrasted with non-evident matters, knowledge of which is possible, if at all, only indirectly through inference. In the second sense, talk of phenomena signals a contrast between the way things appear and the way they are in reality, which may be quite different. It is in the first sense, it seems, that phenomena figure in the three-sided debate in medicine, but it is phenomena in the second sense that furnish the Pyrrhonists with the criterion on the basis of which they select some actions and reject others.

Sceptical adherence to the phenomena, Sextus continues, is a matter of living undogmatically in accordance with everyday observance (*biôtikê têrêsis*), which has four parts: the guidance of nature, the compulsion of the affections, the tradition of laws and customs, and the discipline of the arts (*PH* 1.23–24, 237). The phenomena, understood along these lines, belong to a family of ideas with the aid of which the Pyrrhonists attempt to explain their distinctive way of life. Thus, there is a sense in which the sceptic *assents* to his impressions: he yields or acquiesces to them, i.e. he does not deny that things seem a certain way to him as they can hardly fail to do; as a result, he has *beliefs*, in a sense (*PH* 1.13, 19, 193; *PH* 2.102; cf. DL 9.103–5).

The Pyrrhonists also tried to explain the difference between what they, in a sense, accept and what they suspend judgement about in terms of the contrast between phenomena and non-evident matters already familiar to us from the medical debate. It is only about the latter, we are assured, that they raise questions and suspend judgement (*PH* 1.13, 193, 197, 198, 200, 201, 208; cf. DL 9.103–5). The contrast the Pyrrhonists mean to draw is not, however, that between, say, macroscopic bodies and their sensible properties, on the one hand, and atoms and intelligible pores, on the other. Rather, they suspend judgement about non-evident matters in a sense of "non-evident" that complements the sense of "phenomenon" that figures in their account of the criterion. Whether things are in reality or by nature as they appear is non-evident, and even the most apparently manifest matter becomes non-evident when made the object of philosophical investigation.

This attitude toward the phenomena is strikingly different from the one attributed to the Empiricists in much ancient medical literature. According to Galen, they liked to contrast the endless disagreements in which the Rationalists are enmeshed, with the agreement that can be reached in the realm of phenomena, where the fact that "each thing has appeared as it is confirms the correctness of those who are right and refutes those who are not" (Galen, *Sect. ingred. SM* III 11, 20–12, 4; cf. *On Medical Experience*, 103, 133–35 Walzer; Celsus, *Proem.* 28; Sextus, *M* 8.188, 220). In sharp contrast, Pyrrhonists concede that things appear a certain way, but "investigate whether the real object is such as it appears" and find it impossible "to be sure regarding the phenomena whether they are as they appear" (*PH* 1.19, *M* 8.142, cf. 357).

These passages show how wide the gap between the two schools could be. But they also gives us a clue about how this gap might be reduced, as it must have been if relations between Pyrrhonism and medical Empiricism were as close as we know they were. When Sextus expands on the sceptical criterion he appeals, as we have seen, to everyday observance or common life. The idea that, by adhering to the phenomena, the sceptic will somehow lead a life like that of common, ordinary human beings is supported by several other passages in Sextus (*PH* 2.102, 237, 244, 246, 254; 3.151, *M* 8.158; 11.165). In some of these, the life the sceptic and the ordinary human being will lead is conceived in empirical terms. "It is sufficient to live empirically and undogmatically in accordance with common observances and conceptions, suspending judgement about things said out of dogmatic subtlety (*periergia*) and furthest from the usages of life" (*PH* 2.246, cf. 256).

Sextus' most vehement assertion of Pyrrhonian affinity for common life is in his discussion of sign-inference, however (*PH* 2.97–133; *M* 8.141–299). The discussion is couched in terms of a distinction between commemorative and indicative signs. The latter, which are said to signify that of which they are signs by their own nature and constitution, are the means by which naturally non-evident matters are apprehended. The former serve to remind us of other evident but temporarily non-evident items with which they have been conjoined in past experience. Smoke, for example, is a commemorative sign of fire. Commemorative signification is not only broadly empirical in character, but was embraced by the medical Empiricists and very likely introduced, under this name, by them (cf. *M* 8.156–57; *PH* 2.102; [Galen] *Def. med.* XIX 396, 12–14 K).[14] The Pyrrhonists, Sextus maintains, direct their fire wholly against the indicative sign, which is the contrivance of dogmatic philosophers and Rationalist physicians (*M* 8.156; *PH* 2.102). The commemorative sign is, on the other hand, trusted in common life and far from having any quarrel with common life, Sextus assures us, the Pyrrhonists join in advocating it (*M* 8.158; *PH* 2.102).

It comes as no surprise that the Pyrrhonists' affinity for common life should draw them closer to medical Empiricism. The Empiricists saw themselves as simply extending and refining forms of knowledge available to all human beings. Consider, for example, their response to the argument that since the mark of the true artist that sets him apart from the layman is the apprehension of non-evident truths, medicine as conceived by the Empiricists cannot be a genuine art because it requires no special powers beyond those that are part of every human being's natural endowment. To this they replied "we find that of the bulk of mankind each individual making use of frequent observations gains knowledge not attained by another" (Galen, *On Medical Experience* 98–99 Walzer; cf. [Galen] *De optima secta*, I 110, 14–16 K; Sextus, *M* 8.280, 291).

The Empiricist's attachment to the impressions he largely shares with the Pyrrhonists and with ordinary people, according to this way of thinking, can, as we have seen, harden into dogmatic certainty and be coupled with the dogmatic conviction that non-evident matters are unknowable. But it is also open to him to adopt the Pyrrhonists' attitude. To leave questions open, to make do with what appears to one, without knowing whether it is as it appears, because, so far as one can see, doing so "works," is something the two schools have in common, and very likely part of what recommended medical Empiricism to the Pyrrhonists in the first place.

Galen's report of the views held by some Empiricists about the pulse throws light on the way in which Empiricism could lend itself to scepticism (*De dign. puls.* VIII 780, *et seq.* K = fr. 74 Deichgräber). According to these Empiricists, one should not say the pulse is the expansion and contraction of the artery. Rather it should be described as a blow (felt by the physician). Naturally, Galen disagrees, but he is chiefly concerned to convince the Empiricists that they ought to admit that the artery *seems* to expand while remaining uncommitted about whether it does so in nature. So, for example, he says, they claim not to know that there is a sun, a moon, an earth, a sea, whether we are awake, even whether we are thinking, *by nature*, yet they do not deny that these things seem to be so. And they should, he insists, adopt the same attitude toward the expansion of the artery. It looks very much as if Galen is citing Pyrrhonian chapter and verse.[15] To judge by this evidence, then, it was open to Empiricists to adopt the Pyrrhonian attitude to the phenomena and, in Galen's view at least, they should be moved by considerations that have their home in Pyrrhonian scepticism.

It is the Methodists' noncommittal attitude toward non-evident matters that Sextus emphasizes first in his praise of their school. But there is also much about the positive side of Methodism – the Methodists' attitude to the phenomena of which they make use – that recommends it to Sextus. By following the phenomena, Sextus tells us, the Method arrives at a conclusion about what seems to be beneficial in conformity with the sceptical way. He refers back to the discussion of the sceptical criterion, the phenomenon, and reminds us that the common life, of which the sceptic makes use, has four parts, and he maintains that what the Methodists say can be assimilated to one of them, the compulsion of the affections (*PH* 1.23–24, 237, 239). Just as the sceptic is led, under the compulsion of the affections, to drink by thirst and to food by hunger, Sextus tells us, so the Methodist physician is led by the affections to the corresponding therapies, e.g. by constriction to relaxation. It is evident, he continues, that things that are by nature alien compel one to their

dissolution; thus, even a dog pricked by a thorn proceeds to remove it
(238). These are apparently meant to be specimens of Methodist
indication, and Sextus maintains that the Methodists and
Pyrrhonists have in common the undogmatic and indifferent use of
terms, employing "indication" to mean "the guidance by apparent
affections in accord with or contrary to nature to what seems to
correspond to them" (240).

Medical Empiricism saw itself, and was viewed by many
Pyrrhonists, as nothing more than the result of ordinary everyday
ways of observing the phenomena pursued more systematically and
persistently than they are in everyday life. But medical Empiricism
also contains, at least potentially, an epistemological theory.
According to this theory, knowledge is confined to perceptible
objects and what can be known of them by perception and memory.
It further holds that what is grasped in this way, by itself, never
implies anything substantively different from itself. It can be the
basis of an inference only in connection with an empirical generalization founded on long observation.

Methodism does not share these assumptions. It treats states like
constriction and dilation that are not obviously perceptible as evident
or apparent. What is more, by embracing indication, it accepts that
the grasp of an evident matter of fact may put one in a position to infer
something different from it, not because items of this observable type
have been conjoined with those of a second type in past experience,
but because it somehow seems obvious, e.g. that constriction should
be countered by dilation. Methodist indication, then, participates in
the power to illuminate or explain which is the mark of Rationalist
inference and which sets it apart from Empirical reasoning; to grasp
that a patient is dilated is to see that, and at the same time to have an
insight into why, the proper therapy could not be other than
constrictive.

Apparently these features of Methodism, which could not fail to be
objectionable to Empiricism, were not equally objectionable to
Pyrrhonism. I should, then, like to suggest that Methodism, or
Methodism as Sextus conceives it, had a better, more sceptical attitude toward the phenomena than Empiricism, or a form of it. This
attitude would have contrasted favorably, in Sextus' eyes, with that
on display in the views about the pulse described by Galen. There, as
we have seen, the phenomena are equated with evident matters

immediately grasped by sense perception. And they are granted a uniquely privileged epistemic status, which justifies obsessive efforts to isolate the immediate perceptual given from speculative additions. This is not the attitude of the Pyrrhonists, who fall back on or make do with the way things seem to them. "We agree that we see and recognize that we think, but we are ignorant how we see and how we think" they say (DL 9.103). That the impressions with which the Pyrrhonist is left in this way are not confined to the phenomena admitted by the stricter forms of Empiricism and that the inferences they draw from them will not all be on strictly Empirical lines is highly plausible.

The same result seems to follow when matters are considered from the point of view of ordinary life. Pyrrhonists were not attached to ordinary life because they believed that it enjoyed an epistemic advantage over philosophical theory or because they thought that philosophy is under an obligation to vindicate common sense. Rather, they turned to ordinary life because it seemed to them that the impressions they were left with correspond on the whole to those of ordinary human beings and because this furnishes an answer to the challenge with which they were constantly confronted. The sceptic is able to live by relying on impressions much the same as those that serve ordinary people as they go about their lives without the benefit of philosophy. Yet, though many of the impressions and forms of reasoning on which ordinary human beings rely may lend themselves to an empirical account, others will not. Indication, in the stripped down form that Sextus ascribes to Methodism, may accommodate them better. Given phenomena of a certain kind, certain other things seem to follow, even though one is in no position to provide the kind of backing for this thought that dogmatic philosophers and Rationalist physicians demand, or account for the intellectual faculty in virtue of which one thinks it. It is noteworthy that the Methodists faced an objection like that directed against the Empiricists, i.e. that their indications are obvious to laymen, even irrational animals, and cannot therefore be the mark which distinguishes a true art ([Galen] *De optima secta* I 173 K = fr. 279 Tecusan [28]).

If the suggestion defended above is on the right lines, Methodism appealed to Sextus because it had a more generous conception of the phenomena and the reasoning that is possible on their basis than did Empiricism or a version of it. A position does not become more sceptical by imposing tighter restrictions on the objects about which it permits beliefs, if it does so on the basis of purported knowledge that items falling outside these limits are unknowable and a firmly held theory of the appearances that does violence to the way things actually appear to human beings. The Methodists' generous views about the content or extent of the phenomena is preferable from the point of view of scepticism if the character of their attitude toward the phenomena is as undogmatic as Sextus maintains it was.

There are, however, problems with the view as Sextus presents it (or the interpretation on which he holds this view that I am defending). As we have seen, Methodism stood accused in ancient medical circles of being nothing more than another form of Rationalism (Celsus, *Proem.* 62–64, cf. 57). The Methodists responded by claiming that they are not Rationalists because they are wholly occupied with the phenomena. This effectively sets Methodism apart from Rationalism as it is understood in the ancient medical debate, where a concern with non-evident items is treated as a defining feature of Rationalism. As we have also seen, however, Methodist indication shares certain characteristics with reason as the Rationalists conceive it, characteristics which are enough to make Methodism unacceptably Rationalist in the eyes of a medical Empiricist. I have argued that there are good reasons for Pyrrhonism to view this feature of Methodism with sympathy, yet Sextus' opening to Methodism does not take the form we might expect of a simple move in the direction of an accommodation with reason, however non-dogmatic.

Sextus wants to assimilate all that the Methodists say to the compulsion of the affections. In support of this, he cites the fact that even a dog will seek to remove a thorn from its paw. The removal of a thorn was used by the Methodists as an example of a surgical generality, the presence of an alien body that indicates its own removal ([Galen] *Introductio* XIV 681 K = fr. 283 Tecusan [28]; [Galen] *De optima secta* I 121 K = fr. 277 Tecusan [28]). The mention of the dog, however, which appears to be due to Sextus (and resembles a complaint lodged against Methodist indication, i.e. that it is available to non-rational animals), seems to change the character of the example. The affection by which the dog is moved, like the hunger that leads the human being to food, is its own, whereas the Methodist physician, as a rule, will be led by an affection that he detects in one of his patients to prescribe the corresponding therapy.[16]

There is a revealing ambiguity in Sextus' observation "it is evident that things that are by nature alien compel one to their dissolution; thus even a dog pricked by a thorn proceeds to remove it" (238). Is the compulsion at issue rational? Is the thinking of a trained physician being compared to the non-rational behavior of a brute, or is it the evident truth – one is tempted to say of reason – that alien items compel their own dissolution by which the physician is guided? The example certainly lends itself to a strongly non-rational interpretation. But apart from being exceptionally implausible, this will hardly fit Sextus' account of indication as "the guidance by apparent affections in accord with or contrary to nature to what *seems* to correspond to them" – if it is the being moved by the indication, the physician, and not an outside observer to whom it *seems* so (240). Here, it seems, an inference is plainly in view. A thought – that a patient apparently suffers from an unhealthy affection – leads the physician to think something else – that a therapy seems to correspond to it.

If, as I suspect, Sextus is not drawing, as he usually does, on a long tradition of scholastic Pyrrhonism, this may explain the conflicting signals this passage gives. I suggest that Sextus' remarks do point, as I have argued, to a move away from Empiricism in the direction of an accommodation with reason, but that Sextus is at pains to emphasize the passive, unreflective, if you will phenomenal, character of this kind of reasoning, a character that makes it like, even perhaps an instance of, the compulsion of the affections. If this is right, it is paradoxically the Empiricist in this debate who plays the part of the active innovator by revising the appearances, while the partisans of reason – the Pyrrhonist and the Methodist – passively yield to them.

However we interpret Sextus' account of Methodism, his strongly favorable attitude towards it is hard to square with his own and other Pyrrhonists' ties to medical Empiricism. I have argued that Sextus' remarks can be read as criticizing a certain tendency in Empiricism rather than an unqualified repudiation of the school. The praise that Sextus bestows on Methodism puts this proposal under a certain amount of strain. But Sextus' conclusion is perhaps not a unqualified endorsement of Methodism: "whence it is necessary for us [when] arguing from these and similar considerations to say that the Methodist school has an affinity with skepticism and more of one than other medical schools" (*PH* 1.241). This may leave room for the possibility of other arguments from other considerations to other conclusions. Yet even so, and allowing for the highly polemical context, where Sextus is at pains to distinguish Pyrrhonism from schools which it is popularly supposed to resemble, Sextus' praise for Methodism raises questions about whether and how a form of Empiricism less objectionable to scepticism might have accommodated Sextus' criticisms and earned the same kind of praise that he bestows on Methodism. For this reason, the loss of his work on Empiricism is especially to be regretted.

NOTES

Michael Frede has done more than anyone else in recent times to reveal the philosophical riches contained in ancient medicine. News of his untimely death reached me as I was writing this chapter, which owes an immense debt to his work, and I dedicate it to his memory.

1   See Deichgräber [20], p. 19; Barnes [237], pp. 189–90 n. 14; Brunschwig's annotated translation of DL 9 in Goulet-Cazé [57], pp. 1143–45.

2   A bibliographical guide to the works by Galen cited in this chapter appears in the Bibliography, under 4.5 "Scepticism and medical theory."

3   Academic sceptics also noticed the Empiricists (Cicero, *Acad.* 2.122). Mudry [346] argues that the Empiricists were influenced by Academic scepticism.

4   On this issue see also Katja Vogt, Chapter 8 "Scepticism and Action."

5   Cf. Deichgräber [20], pp. 272–74.

6   See von Staden [351].

7   Aulus Cornelius Celsus, a Roman Encyclopedist of whom eight books on medicine (*De Medicina*) survive. The Preface (*Proemium*) is of considerable philosophical interest. The text with English translation may be found in Spencer [26], vol. 1.

8   See again note 2.

9   Some Empiricists wanted to deny they employed reason not only in the sense that defined Rationalism, but also in a broader sense that covers reasoning quite generally. See Frede [339], [340]; Allen [89], p. 110 ff.

10   Cf. Vallance [352].

11   Cf. Vallance [352], pp. 131–43.

12   Though this issue, controversial from the start, remains so. See Frede [338], pp. 11–13; Lloyd [344], p. 196; Pigeaud [349], pp. 23–28; Van der Eijk [337], p. 310.

13   Frede [338], pp. 4–8.

14   Philippson [348], p. 65 ff.; Allen [89], p. 107 ff.

15   Including a verse of Timon's (cf. *M* 7.30; DL 9.105). Elsewhere in the same work about the pulse, Galen mentions "others" influenced in another way by the "sceptics and aporetics" (VIII 708 ff. K = fr. 75 Deichgräber [20]). These doctors, afraid to assert anything about an external existent, prefer to speak only of "a perception of their own affections of touch." Galen proposes to ignore them, remarking that soon, influenced by the so-called "rustic Pyrrhonists (*agroikopurrôneioi*), who say they do not have knowledge of their own affections, they will not even dare to say a motion *appears* to them."

16   Cf. Mates [45], p. 263.

13 Pyrrhonism and the specialized sciences

I A PRELIMINARY AGENDA

"Having said this much against the principles of music as well, basing ourselves effectively on factual data (*pragmatikôs*), at this point we bring to an end our disquisition against the objects of instruction in the liberal arts (*mathêmata*)."[1] These are the closing lines of the compact set of treatises Sextus Empiricus devotes to the demolition of the so-called liberal arts[2] (*M* 1–6, or more precisely: *M* 1, *Against the Grammarians*; *M* 2, *Against the Rhetoricians*; *M* 3, *Against the Geometers*; *M* 4, *Against the Arithmeticians*; *M* 5, *Against the Astrologers*; *M* 6, *Against the Musicians*). Before confronting problems of some importance concerning the placing of this work and its type of scepticism, it is worth at least touching on two questions.

The first has to do with whether or not it is possible to attribute to Sextus an already systematized version of the "canon" of liberal arts, divided into a *trivium* (grammar, rhetoric, dialectic) and a *quadrivium* (arithmetic, geometry, astronomy, music). Although the way he presents the object of his analysis (see *M* 1.7) has opened the way to various interpretations, we have to recognize[3]:

(a)   In Sextus we do not have the traditional *seven* liberal arts; we find only *six* of them. Although the absence of one of them, dialectic, has been explained by appeal to the fact that its treatment had already been included in the sections of *PH* and *M* 7–8 dedicated to the more general area of logic,[4] it seems beyond doubt that he does not have before him, nor is he the first to create, the schema of the *trivium*, which emerged only later, perhaps with Porphyry.

(b)   As for the *quadrivium*, it is true that it makes an appearance
       in Sextus; it also happens to be true that the order in which he
       examines the arts that make it up is the same one adopted
       later by Martianus Capella. But first, this order is not the one
       uniformly attested in the tradition, and second, it answers to
       the internal logic of Sextus' argument, guided by philosoph-
       ical motivations, certainly not literary ones as will be the case
       in Martianus Capella.

In light of these considerations it is perhaps best to adopt a very
cautious position, well formulated by Pierre Pellegrin: "it is reasonable to think that, as regards both the epistemological and the pedagogical arrangement of the arts, Sextus is attacking a way of
proceeding that was dominant in his time, or at least, that he considered 'more complete' than the others."[5]

Without wishing to enter into the details of the concept of *technê*,
its development, and the different ways in which it was understood in
the ancient world, the second requirement, in discussing *M* 1–6, is that
of shedding light on Sextus' targets in the case of each individual art.[6]

Regarding "complete" grammar (*entelês, M* 1.44) or linguistic
theory, which in its origin is traced back to Crates of Mallos,
Aristophanes of Byzantium, and Aristarchus of Soli, Sextus tries first
to destroy its standing by means of the critical examination of some
important definitions supplied by Dionysius Thrax, Ptolemy the
Peripatetic, Asclepiades of Myrleia, Chares, and finally Demetrius
Chlorus (*M* 1.41–90).[7] Next, using either material already developed
by Asclepiades of Myrleia (perhaps with an Epicurean source as critical
intermediary), or arguments drawn from the Epicurean tradition,[8] he
attacks the various parts of grammar (*M* 1.91–320): technical (letters,
syllables, names, parts of discourse, orthography, alleged good Greek
usage or *hellenismos*, etymology), historical (characters, places, poetic
inventions in general), and more specific (*idiaiteron*) or "hermeneutic"
(examination of verse or prose texts).

Starting from a definition of rhetoric that seems to blend Platonic,
Aristotelian, and Stoic considerations (*M* 2.9), and privileging a
strictly Stoic concept of *technê* (*M* 2.10), Sextus first gives it a general
refutation. He shows not only its theoretical inconsistency, but at the
same time its lack of utility – indeed, its harmfulness, repulsiveness,
obscurity, inability to persuade, and lack of positive outcomes, either

for the individual or for the city (*M* 2.10–87). In the second part of the treatise, given the Aristotelian division of rhetoric into deliberative, laudatory, and forensic kinds, he raises difficulties of detail (*M* 2.88–105), to conclude then with a broader criticism, which denies (by means of arguments also used in some passages of *PH* 2 and *M* 8) the very possibility of any demonstration, either in a generic or a specific sense (*M* 2.106–13).[9]

The attack directed against geometry in *M* 3, too, follows a precise scheme. After a preface designed to illustrate the various senses, and the possible philosophical and also mathematico-geometrical use of hypotheses (whose connection with reliable demonstration nonetheless remains indemonstrable (*M* 3.1–17)), Sextus devotes himself to demolishing the fundamental principles (namely: point, line, surface, body, as well as certain theorems or notions that depend on such principles, relating in particular to the straight line, angles, the circle, the bisector, etc.) at the basis of a type of geometry that recalls Euclidean elements, even if occasionally concepts or theories seem to surface that are closer to Old Academic, Epicurean, and Stoic positions (*M* 3.18–104).[10]

In the much shorter treatise against the arithmeticians, the object of criticism is above all the notion of number as a discontinuous quantity, which is tackled by calling into question definitions and explanations ultimately of Pythagorean origin, but probably traceable to Platonic circles, perhaps those of Speusippus and/or Xenocrates (*M* 4.1–2). After a reference to the doctrine of the tetrad (*M* 4.3), the critique is directed especially against the monad or unit, the foundation of arithmetic and perhaps, on the Platonic-Pythagorean perspective just mentioned, of all reality. It is analyzed not only in itself (*M* 4.4–20), but also in its relations with the dyad and the other numbers, which are described particularly in terms of the traditional operations of addition and subtraction (*M* 4.21–34).[11]

One of the high points (and perhaps also the most agreeable) of the many-sided attack on the liberal arts is *Against the Astrologers*.[12] Sextus here attacks the doctrine of "nativities," immediately examining its theoretical basis: the dogma of universal sympathy, according to which influences from the heavens affect terrestrial events, in view of the role of efficient causes attributed to the seven planets, aided by the parts of the zodiac (*M* 5.1–5). Sextus then offers a schematic description of some elements of the art of astrology: the circle of the zodiac, the means of observing and registering the horoscope at the moment of birth, the planets and their essential powers in relation to the signs of the zodiac (*M* 5.5–42). An initial set of objections from other unnamed authors or schools is also reported (*M* 5.43–48), before moving to the Pyrrhonian position, which is concentrated on the horoscope, "principle and, so to speak, foundation" of the astrologers' activities (*M* 5.50–54). Sextus first registers original objections of a "technical" or "scientific" character (*M* 5.55–85), then a series of standard, even classic anti-astrological moves (which go back to Carneades: *M* 5.86–102). He ends with a criticism (*M* 5.103–5) stemming from the form of scepticism typical of the entirety of *M* 1–6 (more on this in section III).

Finally, in the last treatise the target is music understood as "a science dealing with melody, notes and rhythmic compositions" (*M* 6.1), according to a definition here linked with the name of Aristoxenus of Tarentum. It is attacked in two different ways, one dogmatic (or Epicurean) and one more properly aporetic or, we must suppose, genuinely Pyrrhonian (*M* 6.1–6). Leaving aside for now the peculiarities of these different polemical strategies,[13] Sextus underscores the division of the rest of the treatise into two distinct parts: first he shows how music cannot be assimilated to philosophy and is also useless as therapy (*M* 6.7–38), then he moves on to eliminate those elements that constitute the theoretical framework of musical doctrine (sound, note, interval, rhythm, with significant reflections on the notion of time as well: *M* 6.39–68).

Now that the contents of each book of *M* 1–6 have been summarized, we must deal with some outstanding problems: first the chronological position of this work, and then the precise character of its philosophical outlook.

II CHRONOLOGY

Returning to the closing formula at *M* 6.68, cited at the start, it seems reasonable to ask whether we are *also* dealing with the last words of the entire corpus of Sextus' works. Do we have here the final theoretical account of Sextus' neo-Pyrrhonism?

Answering this question undoubtedly means trying to offer, at least in a purely hypothetical way, an ordering of the relative chronology of Sextus' writings. However, such an answer cannot be separated from a more general analysis of the whole nature of *M* 1–6, the coherence of its composition, and the possible changes in theory indicated by its structure.

Once the field has been cleared of some hasty judgements on the "exoteric" character of *M* 1–6,[14] the first question to pose concerns its relations with Sextus' other works. Among scholars, beginning at least with Brochard, the opinion seems to have prevailed that the treatment of the "liberal arts" represents the final work of Sextus.[15] Many different reasons have been put forward for this conclusion. In the first place, there seem to be considerations of content and theoretical layout: after having devoted two entire works (*PH* and *M* 7–11) to his radical attack against the three canonical parts of dogmatic philosophy (logic, physics, and ethics), Sextus would have decided to close his Pyrrhonist enterprise, as if by way of appendix, with a detailed polemic, using a different philosophical approach, against the individual "liberal arts." However, of definitely greater weight are several possible internal cross-references: one thinks above all of some arguments "against the physicists" recalled in *M* 1.35 and 3.116, which perhaps refer back, respectively, to *M* 9.195/10.310 and 9.279.[16]

Leaving aside other considerations,[17] the traditionally accepted relative chronology (*PH*, *M* 7–11, *M* 1–6) seems, finally, to be confirmed and reinforced by the minute stylistic and philological analyses of Karel Janáček, with its discovery of an evolution in Sextus' methods of writing.[18]

III SCEPTICAL "FLAVOR"

If the placing of *M* 1–6 at least after *M* 7–11 appears settled, another pressing question arises: that of the type of scepticism Sextus uses in his polemic against the liberal arts. Or rather, to put it even more clearly: can we continue to speak of Pyrrhonian scepticism in approaching *M* 1–6? And if we can, is this scepticism single, coherent, and fixed in character, or are there multiple approaches, distinct from one another and not always compatible?

Reflecting on the stylistic peculiarities of *M* 1–6, for example, the disappearance of some technical terms belonging to the language of suspension (especially *epechô*, "suspend judgement," itself), or again the frequent presence of expressions that make one think of forms of

negative dogmatism (connected with the prevalence of the vocabulary of *antirrhêsis*, "refutation"), Janáček already insisted on the non-
sceptical character of this work, leaving open the possibility of an
evolution in Sextus towards the principles of medical empiricism.[19]
At many points in his treatment, in fact, Sextus does not seem to
want to construct an opposition of arguments with equal force so as
to lead to *epochê*; he seems rather to formulate strong assertions,
which deny the very existence of the object of examination. How
should we interpret this apparent prevalence of the language of elimination or *anairein*, "doing away with"?

The answer to this question is made even more complicated by
another undeniable fact. Right from the introductory paragraphs of
M 1–6, to which we will turn in a moment, Sextus presents a double
mode of attack against the various liberal arts. On the one hand, he
records (and does not hesitate to use) objections of dogmatic, and
more precisely Epicurean, origin; Epicurus himself and his followers
had often and in various contexts argued against the utility of some
subjects discussed by Sextus. But on the other hand, he distinguishes
such objections from those formulated in a more aporetic or sceptical
mode,[20] which put into question not only the utility of this or that
liberal art, but more generally the existence of its theoretical principles or its objects. A good way to confront these problems is perhaps
to re-examine certain pivotal statements of methodology at the opening of *M* 1–6.

In the first place, it seems significant that the specific analysis of
the individual *technai* is preceded by a section (*M* 1.1–40) which is in
two ways introductory in character. It serves, in fact, to clarify two
important points about Sextus' enterprise:

(a)   its motivations, the uniqueness of his approach compared
       with other possible types of attack, and finally the relation
       it holds to the rest of Sextus' work (this by way of methodo-
       logical preface, *M* 1.1–8); and

(b)   a very general opening plan of attack, which demolishes the
       very idea of the transmission of knowledge, whatever its
       object, teacher, student, or method may be (*M* 1.8–40); this
       form of second-level reflection is a sort of negative meta-
       pedagogy, which, joining a well-established tradition on the
       basic topic of unteachability,[21] exploits a series of impasses to

deny its very object. Nor can one forget that (uniquely in his output, and perhaps in a further sign of the lateness of *M* 1–6) Sextus offers a parallel treatment of the same theme in both his other works, in *PH* 3.250 ff. (though with some difference in the organization of the material)[22] and especially in *M* 11.216–56.

While the arguments of *M* 1.8–40, too, "give the impression of having been institutionalized within the sceptical tradition itself,"[23] and hence reinforce the opinion that *M* 1–6 is genuinely faithful to the Pyrrhonist tradition, the programmatic introductory section *M* 1.1–8 requires much more delicate discussion.[24]

Here, indeed, Sextus distinguishes, with some polemical exaggeration, between the Pyrrhonists' own negative attitude towards the liberal arts and that of Epicurus. The objections advanced by the latter, he suggests, not only deny all utility to these arts in terms of true knowledge, but also seem driven by somewhat shabby motives: actual ignorance; envy at comparisons with much more sophisticated fellow-philosophers (like Plato, Aristotle, and others); and hate, fed by the desire to present himself as a complete autodidact, against one of his teachers, Nausiphanes, who by contrast was particularly well versed in many sciences and especially rhetoric.[25]

The Pyrrhonists' point of view is quite different; they do not claim unequivocally that the liberal arts are either useful or useless from the perspective of acquiring wisdom. In addition, they are represented as absolutely outstanding men, possessed of great culture and even greater experience than their other "colleagues," in no way slaves to the opinions of the many and entirely devoid of envy and malevolence; on the contrary, their spirit is one of *praotês*, "mildness," an important virtue in the sceptical outlook.[26] Against the background of this positive self-presentation, Sextus then supplies the real reason for his interest in the liberal arts. The Pyrrhonists examine and refute them because:

they had in some sense/almost[27] the same experience in the case of the liberal studies as they had with all of philosophy. For just as they approached philosophy wishing to get at the truth but when confronted with the equipollent conflict and the irregularity of things they suspended judgment, in the same way they set out to grasp the liberal studies and sought to learn the truth here as well and when they discovered equal difficulties they did not hide them. That is why we too, who follow the same school of thought as they,[28] shall attempt without any spirit of competitiveness to select and put the effective arguments against the liberal studies.[29]

This passage is fundamental for at least two reasons.

In the first place it puts forward a sort of story of the origin of the Pyrrhonian philosophical attitude, with images and explanations that can also be found in the opening paragraphs of *Outlines of Pyrrhonism* (*PH* 1.12, 26–29). Sextus declares explicitly that he wants to attack the liberal arts according to the same "rules of engagement" that have already been made to work for anti-philosophical polemic in general: the impossibility of reaching the firm terrain of truth appears in both cases connected to the equal force of opposing claims. I take it as methodologically correct to interpret the whole of *M* 1–6 in light of this clear, programmatic preface.[30] And in doing so, one can reasonably take account, as we shall see in a moment, of all those numerous passages in which Sextus seems to affirm the non-existence or, better, inconsistency of one of the *technai* examined or of one of its principles.

In the second place, at the close of the passage, after presenting the reasons tending *de iure* towards *epochê*, there also appears a hint at the strategy to which Sextus will *de facto* return: selecting all the counter-arguments that are really effective at demolishing the dogmatic pretensions of the supporters of the liberal arts. In this case too, the continuity with the Pyrrhonist method consistently adopted by Sextus, which we can call "chameleonic," is evident. He feels quite free to appropriate others' opinions and conclusions, whether dogmatic or sceptical, without for this reason having to defend them in his own person.[31] This justifies the presence in *M* 1–6 of diverse voices, among which, apart from the Pyrrhonian (to which we must shortly turn) and those of other philosophical schools and movements, the Epicurean, as already noted, stands out. This is by no means incompatible, if used for polemical purposes and for the sake of argument, with the Pyrrhonian; nor is it such as to incite Sextus to disagree with or even refute it.[32]

Moreover, this co-presence of diverse attitudes is in some cases explicitly recognized and indeed deliberately underlined by Sextus himself; he does not, then, seem to be acting like an mechanical compiler or, worse, like an obtuse copyist. The most obvious case is surely the opening section of *Against the Musicians*. Here, after presenting three different meanings of music and selecting as his target only the idea of music as "a science concerned with melodies, notes, rhythmic compositions, and parallel subjects,"[33] Sextus explicitly recalls the similarity with his attack against the grammarians and therefore distinguishes between two different ways of refutation: the first (Epicurean in its essence) was dogmatically oriented to denounce the harmfulness of music, while the second, more aporetically (*aporêtikoteron*), "in shaking the principal suppositions of the musicians thought to abolish the whole of music."[34] Sextus indicates here a further element of continuity with the polemic he employs not only in *M* 1–6,[35] but all the time in his other works as well. There is no shortage of strategically relevant passages in his works, in which he insists on the special character of sceptical attacks. Described by means of images taken from the military world, as for example that of the siege, and distinguished from the polemical practices of, for example, the sceptical Academy,[36] such attacks aim not so much to strike home on matters of detail or those peripheral to this or that dogmatic system of philosophy, but rather to demolish its fundamental principles and essential elements. This then becomes the target of Sextus' critiques: according to a principle of Ockham-like economy, one needs to concentrate the fire of one's polemic against the foundation of the dogmatic edifice, since only by totally knocking them down will the collapse of all the other theoretical aspects that depend on them also be guaranteed. From this perspective too, then, we can explain Sextus' recourse to arguments that emphasize the destructive aspect, the complete elimination of a dogmatic thesis; on condition, however, that we never forget we are here dealing with the "explicit recognition of the general principle that, even though the sceptical arguments conclude to non-existence, they are none the less instances of equipollent arguments."[37]

The presence of diverse voices, in this as in other writings of Sextus, thus seems justified and justifiable, in line with a steadfast Pyrrhonist strategy. Nonetheless, in the case of *M* 1–6 it has given rise to a lively interpretive debate and has been explained by scholars in different ways. One of the best known and most interesting proposals is that of Jonathan Barnes. He has spoken of a sort of "schizophrenia" in Sextus' treatment of the liberal arts, marked by the possibility of making use, for therapeutic purposes, of arguments either of more markedly dogmatic origin or of genuinely Pyrrhonist sceptical design.

In short, Sextus would be selecting from inside a full and most diverse pharmacy (following a medical metaphor that Barnes prefers to the judicial or the military one), equipped with medicines of varied intensity, strength and force, depending on the dogmatic malady in need of cure.[38] Without wishing to deny the attractions of this reading of Barnes, it is worth recalling other elements that are useful for framing the distinctive character of Sextus' polemic.

In this connection, the polemic's new target marks a genuine difference from the strictly philosophical terrain of *PH* and *M* 7–11, and this has prompted some scholars to deny a *complete* uniformity in the two treatments.[39] Having carried to a conclusion "the entire exposition of the sceptical method" (*M* 11.257), Sextus seems to turn to arts or *technai*, instead of specific aspects of philosophical reasoning, and these have different features. Although they too do indeed claim to be anchored to a theoretical structure that aims at an alleged incontrovertible truth, which is the object of Sextus' destructive critiques in the various books of *M* 1–6, it seems that they are additionally, and especially, dangerous in another direction. Such *technai*, in different ways and to different degrees, are in fact not only a source of dogmatic rashness at the level of abstract argument, but represent a threat to the one moral and behavioral frame of reference accepted by the sceptic: the appearances related to ordinary life or *koinos bios* (*PH* 1.17). Here, then, is the explanation for the dichotomy of approaches noted earlier, as well as the tactical, temporary alliance with some Epicurean critiques of the liberal arts' lack of utility. In particular, though, it becomes easier to understand Sextus' many remarks in defense of the legitimacy of some *technai* and the possibility of practising them, sometimes in explicit contrast to liberal studies. A careful look at *M* 1–6 yields a sizeable list[40]: we have basic grammar or *grammatistikê* (*M* 1.44, 49 ff. and perhaps 2.13), but also poetry (*M* 1.278, 299); "astro-meteorology," founded on the observation of the phenomena (*M* 5.1–2), just like agriculture (*M* 5.2) or the art of the pilot (*M* 1.51, 2.13, 5.2; see also *M* 8.203); and again, in addition, perhaps, to sculpture and painting (*M* 1.182), music as the simple playing of instruments (*M* 6.1), and obviously medicine (*M* 1.51, 2.13, and see below); and perhaps, finally, philosophy, if understood in a genuinely Pyrrhonian sense (again *M* 2.13, but also 1.280, 296, and 2.25).

These arts do not claim to formulate a doctrine about the real nature of their objects, nor do they impose dogmatic beliefs on their

practitioners. What characterizes them (in the context of an adherence to custom or *sunêtheia*, many times referred to in *M* 1–6) is
rather their utility or their ability to satisfy some needs related to
everyday life.[41] They allow even the Pyrrhonist, who rejects robust
theoretical devices for achieving tranquility and happiness, to operate
in the world. Here we see the centrality of that teaching of the
arts or *didaskalia technôn*, which Sextus in *Outlines of Pyrrhonism*
(*PH* 1.23–24) presents as one of the fundamental elements of the
fourfold division in the observance of the rules of life.[42]

Once again, then, Sextus' strategic choices in *M* 1–6 and his inter-
ventions in the first person, in quite a range of contexts, appear
coherently related to the basic outlines of the Pyrrhonian philosophical attitude. This is also clear in the course of the arguments developed on individual points in *M* 1–6: they in fact rely on traditional,
well-worn devices of Pyrrhonist sceptical polemic, such as (to list
just a few) the so-called Modes of Aenesidemus and especially those
of Agrippa (seeing that "every object of investigation can be referred
to these Modes,"[43]) or the undogmatic choices of language peculiar to
the sceptical "philosophy of language."[44]

IV SCEPTICAL, OR RATHER SCEPTICAL-EMPIRICAL, CONCLUSIONS

In light of the foregoing considerations, it would seem we are bound
to reject any accusation of "negative dogmatism" against Sextus as
author of *M* 1–6; this work seems to show itself as coherent on the
level of composition, homogeneous in the construction of its arguments against the liberal studies and largely faithful to Sextus'
Pyrrhonist method of attack as applied in his other works.
However, one point still needs to be better explained. Some ideas in
M 1–6, in particular the acceptance of specific *technai*, lead one to
wonder about the epistemological model that even a Pyrrhonist
sceptic like Sextus feels entitled to adopt. And it is in this context
that, with suitable qualifications of course, Janáček's hypothesis of a
tendency towards medical Empiricism that marks Sextus' scepticism
in *M* 1–6 perhaps regains strength (though in my opinion such a
tendency may be detected in all of Sextus' works).

Rather than multiplying references, I would like to concentrate just
on the closing sections of *Against the Astrologers*.[45] From *M* 5.103 on,

Sextus seems to concede the meaningfulness of the stars: they are signs; but what kind of signs? And what is the relation between the arrangement of the stars, on the one hand, and the various events in human life, on the other? Since our future life comes under the heading of non-evident things – if not absolutely, at least by nature – one would expect that it could be known solely by means of *indicative* signs[46] (as to whose existence and effectiveness there is, however, an undecidable dispute), certainly not by means of *commemorative* signs[47] (it is indeed quite impossible to see the stars and their arrangement as having this status). Besides, even conceding what the astrologers claim, to succeed in formulating a really sound prediction and to know the *causal relation* between a determinate arrangement of the stars and a determinate effect on earth, we have to be in a position to observe both these aspects together repeatedly, in a constant connection *in all possible observed cases* (*epi pantôn*). The arrangement of the stars, in sum, has to be the object of empirical observation not just one time, but "often in many cases" (*pollakis epi pollôn*), in order to be able to function as an indication or sign revealing a certain kind of life. The paradigm positive instance here turns out to be Empirical medicine, whose principles Sextus appears to accept. It verifies and confirms the constant, lethal connection that exists between a wound inflicted on the heart and the onset of death *in a multiplicity of cases* (Dion, Theon, Socrates, "and many others," *M* 5.104), to the point that we can consider the first as cause of the second.[48] Yet the need to discover a general regularity on the basis of experience, a constant connection between *explanans* and *explanandum*, is precisely what cannot be satisfied in astrological observation, because of a series of obstacles (from the length of the Great Year to the recurring destructions of the cosmos, for example) polemically recorded by Sextus (*M* 5.105).

Aside from the specific objections, behind Sextus' attack an alternative model of explanation seems to be operating: the medical one, in its Empiricist version. The stars, like other celestial or terrestrial phenomena, could be legitimately investigated, if one did not yield to the dogmatic temptation to establish compelling and necessary inferential connections, but rather contented oneself with exploring and exhibiting just those connections guaranteed by repeated and constant empirical observation, very probably supported by an implicit faith in the regularity of nature. In a context of this type, the insistence on the role of *têrêsis*, "everyday observance," and memory seems hard to interpret as a mere dialectical diversion; it is better understood "as an untheoretical account of how we come to have expert knowledge," without requiring recourse to any type of rational inference in the strict sense.[49]

A similar conclusion does not, however, apply across the board; nor should it make us forget that even the sceptic (close to the position of medical Empiricism) can accept a form of empirical generalization only within well defined limits. These, in a testament to the abiding validity of this model of explanation in Sextus' eyes, are clearly expressed in a passage from *Against the Logicians*:

but even if we allow that the human being differs from other animals in discourse, and appearance that involves transitions, and a conception of following, we will *not* agree that he is this way when it comes to unclear things and things that are matters of undecided disagreement. Rather, when it comes to apparent things, he has an awareness of following based on watching (*têrêtikên tina … akolouthian*), in virtue of which he remembers which things were observed with which, which before which, and which after which, and so from his encounters with earlier things renews the rest.[50]

These considerations taken together produce a scepticism that is by no means "rustic" or extreme, but rather one sustained by a positive, even refined acceptance of "an Empiricist alternative to the Rationalist constructions of grammarians and rhetoricians and the rest."[51] We must, however, remain cautious and always remember that Sextus never once, in any of his anti-dogmatic polemic, relies on theses concerning the essential nature of reality or sets down "how things truly are."

NOTES

Translated into English by Richard Bett. I would like to thank Richard Bett, who kindly translated and simplified my complicated Italian, and Mauro Bonazzi, Riccardo Chiaradonna, Diego Machuca, and Francesco Verde, who read an early version of this chapter, offering valuable advice and suggestions; naturally I am solely responsible for the final product and for any errors it may contain.

1   *M* 6.68. For the translation of *pragmatikôs* see esp. Blank [44], pp. XLI and 84; see also Desbordes [306], 171 and Bett [298], p. 22 ff. For different interpretations, see however Delattre [304], pp. 131–32; Delattre [303], pp. 135–37 and 144.

2   For Sextus' own use of the expression *eleutherai technai,* "liberal arts," see *M* 2.57.

3   What follows is a concise *résumé* of Hadot [105], esp. pp. 168–72 and 293, criticized however by Barnes [297], p. 56 n. 8 and Blank [44], pp. 84–85.

4   E.g., Barnes [297], pp. 56–57; Hankinson [68], p. 251; Blank [44], p. 85.

5   Pellegrin [50], p. 30.

6   For a useful *résumé* see also Pellegrin [50], pp. 34–47.

7   On the introductory section of *M* 1 (1–40), see section III.

8   See Blank [44], esp. pp. XLV–L; Delattre [303].

9   On *M* 2 see at least Barnes [296a] and Sluiter [315]; for both the Epicurean and the sceptical attitude towards rhetoric see Longo Auricchio [310].

10 On this question see esp. Mueller [311]; also Pellegrin [50], pp. 23–25; contra see, however, Dye-Vitrac [306a]. For a commentary on *M* 3 see Freytag [308].

11 On *M* 4 see Brisson [299].

12 For a detailed commentary on *M* 5 see Spinelli [54]; other scholars too seem to give a special relevance to it within *M* 1–6: see, e.g. Hankinson [68], pp. 256–60 and Pellegrin [50], pp. 42–45.

13 See section III. Apart from the critical edition, with translation and detailed commentary, by Davidson Greaves [6], on *M* 6 and its Epicurean "flavour" see Gigante [66], esp. pp. 215–21; Rispoli [314]; Delattre [303].

14 See Pappenheim [258], esp. pp. 16–17, who therefore considers *M* 1–6 a work written by Sextus in his youth; compare Zeller [123], III/2, p. 51 n. 2.

15 Brochard [61], pp. 318–19; also, e.g. Barnes [297], p. 55; Hankinson [68], p. 251; Blank [44], p. XVI; Pellegrin [50], p. 10.

16 For discussion of other possible cross-references see Blomqvist [37].

17 As, for example, the importance given by Sextus to different sources, or even his alleged audience: see Blank [44], p. XVI n. 14.

18 Apart from his many short but very significant articles (now collected in Janácek [32]), see Janácek [30] and esp. [31].

19 Janácek [31], pp. 87, 132–34; on the relations between Pyrrhonism and Empiricism, see also James Allen, Chapter 12 "Pyrrhonism and Medicine."

20 For *aporêtikos* as one of the names of the sceptical *agôgê* see *PH* 1.7, also Pellegrin [50], p. 453.

21 On this history see Bett [41], pp. 225–26; Hankinson [68], pp. 252–53.

22 Some of these differences are examined by Bett [41], pp. 266–71, whose conclusions about the chronological position of *PH* in comparison with *M* 11 and *M* 1, however, are not fully convincing and in many cases highly speculative.

23 Bett [41], p. 226.

24 Apart from Decleva Caizzi [317], pp. 318 ff., 293–96, for commentary and further references see Blank [44], pp. 70–85.

25 On this last topic see Warren [121], ch. 7 (specifically pp. 189–91).

26 Cf. *M* 6.6 and especially DL 9.108.

27 This is a double way of rendering the *ti* in the text; see also Pellegrin [312], p. 38.

28 This translation is indebted to Barnes [297], p. 59.

29 *M* 1.6–7, trans. Blank [44], p. 4, slightly modified.

30 Unless we accept Janáček's conclusion that *M* 1.1–40 is "extraneous matter in *M* I-VI" (Janáček [31], p. 133). Richard Bett also tries to argue for a disunified picture of *M* 1–6 in light of his theory of successive phases of ancient Pyrrhonism; he explains the destructive conclusions in *M* 1–6 as a form of "historical schizophrenia," due to the survival of Aenesidemean arguments inconsistent with the version of Pyrrhonism later adopted by Sextus elsewhere, especially in *PH*. See Bett [298]; against this, very reasonably, see Pellegrin [312].

31 See also Hankinson [68], p. 252.

32 *Pace* Bett [298], pp. 21–22.

33 *M* 6.1, trans. Davidson Greaves [6], p. 121.

34 *M* 6.4, trans. Davidson Greaves [6], p. 127.

35 See especially *M* 5.3, 49, with other references in Spinelli [54], pp. 34 and 138, and Hankinson [68], p. 259; see also *M* 1.39–40, 144 (with commentary in Blank [44], pp. 107–8), 2.113, 3.18, 92–3, 108, 4.1, 6.5.

36 See esp. *M* 9.1–3; *PH* 2.84, 3.1; *M* 8.337a, 11.257.

37 Blank [44], pp. LIV–LV; see also, in the same vein, Pellegrin [50], pp. 20–21 and 27; *contra* Bett [298].

38 See Barnes [297], pp. 72–77; for a critical reappraisal of his interpretation see now Pellegrin [50], pp. 26–27, while on Bett's hypothesis of a "double schizophrenia" in *M* 1–6 see note 30. The Pyrrhonian philanthropic attitude is clearly attested in *PH* 3.280–1.

39 See, e.g. Cortassa [300], pp. 717–21; Desbordes [306], p. 170; Pellegrin [50], pp. 13–14; also for Hankinson [68], p. 251, *M* 1–6 is surely "more restricted in scope."

40 See Barnes [297], pp. 62–63; Pellegrin [50], pp. 17–18; for a partially overlapping list in Philodemus see Blank [44], p. XXXII.

41 On their distinctive Pyrrhonian features see Barnes [297], pp. 63–66; Blank [44], p. XXXIV and Bett [298], pp. 19–20; on their being a peculiar form of "know-how" see useful observations in Desbordes [306], pp. 176–77.

42 On the central role of this passage for Sextus' practical attitude see Spinelli [72], p. 138 ff., with further references.

43 *PH* 1.169, tr. Annas and Barnes [40]. For a list of relevant examples see Machuca [51], 507.

44 In this last case see Sextus' polemic against grammarians and rhetoricians, where he seems to apply the linguistic "rules" specifically discussed in *PH* 1.187–208: on this see Sluiter [315].

45 I summarize here some of my observations in Spinelli [72], p. 97 ff., where, in addition to further references, I tried also to explore a possible parallelism between Sextus' position and the first formulation of Hempel's "covering law model."

46 It is therefore significant that Sextus uses, right at the beginning of *M* 5.103, the verb *endeiknumai*, related to *endeiktikos*, "indicative"; for the same usage see *M* 8.195, 208, 263 (twice), 264, 274 (twice).

47 The verb, used three times in *M* 5.103–4, is accordingly *sumparatêrô*, "observe together": Sextus uses it always in order to present the feeble inferential mechanism at work in the case of commemorative signs (see *PH* 2.100–1; *M* 8.152, 154 and also 143); useful remarks on this question in Desbordes [306], p. 178; see also Pellegrin [347].

48 For the correct text in *M* 5.104 see Spinelli [54], p. 97 n. 35. The example of the mortal wound in the heart occurs also in *M* 8.254–55; see also *M* 8.153, 157 as well as Galen, *Subfig. emp.* Deichgräber [20] 58, 18–20; Deichgräber [20] 44, 4–51, 9; Quintilian V 9.5 and 7. One should remember, in addition, that "the Empirical doctors ... were quite happy to speak (non-theoretically) of causes" (Hankinson [68], p. 349 n. 15).

49 Frede [340], p. 249; see also Barnes [297], p. 72; Blank [44], pp. 212–13; and, more generally, Spinelli [262].

50 *M* 8.288, trans. Bett [42], p. 146. For a *technê* that acts solely inside the horizon of *ta phainomena* it is even possible to create a system of theorems or "rules" (*theorêmata*), based on "things often watched or examined": see *M* 8.291 and Pellegrin [50], pp. 460–62.

51 Barnes [297], p. 70; for a comparison with Menodotus' refined form of "memorism," see Frede [340], esp. pp. 248–49.

III Beyond Antiquity

14 The rediscovery and posthumous influence of scepticism

I INTRODUCTION

The history of the transmission, recovery and posthumous influence of ancient scepticism is a fascinating chapter in the history of ideas. An extraordinary collection of philosophical texts and some of the most challenging arguments ever devised were first lost, then only partly recovered philologically, and finally rediscovered conceptually, leaving Cicero and Sextus Empiricus as the main champions of Academic and Pyrrhonian scepticism respectively. This chapter outlines what we know about this shipwreck and what was later salvaged from it. It cannot provide many details, given its length. And, being a review, it does not try to solve the many puzzles and mysteries still unsolved. But, as an introduction, it does seek to give a general idea of what happened to ancient scepticism in the long span of time occurring between Augustine and Descartes. It covers a dozen centuries of Western philosophy, so a few generalizations, some schematism and a good degree of abstraction from specific information will be inevitable.[1]

II LATE ANTIQUITY AND THE MIDDLE AGES

Our story begins with a dramatic loss of memory, roughly in the fourth century. By the time Augustine was writing *Contra Academicos*, Academic scepticism, transmitted in Latin, had become the brand of scepticism known to philosophers and theologians, at the expense of Pyrrhonism in general and Sextus Empiricus' Greek texts in particular. There may still be some sporadic references to the Pyrrhonians at the beginning of the fifth century,[2] but it is

significant that the word *academicus* had become synonymous with
sceptic, a linguistic use that will remain unchanged until the seventeenth century. Although *scepticus* occurs in Aulus Gellius, the
technical word and its cognate terms will become common currency
only in the 1430s,[3] after the spread of Traversari's translation of
Diogenes Laertius.[4] This will undergo twelve editions before the
end of the sixteenth century, and will be very influential in establishing the conceptual, Latin vocabulary used by philosophers in the
following centuries. The sceptical terminology and arsenal of arguments will be initially based on Cicero's and Augustine's Latin
works. Pyrrhonism will reach the philosophical debate only in the
sixteenth and seventeenth centuries, through the Latinized technical
lexicon of Academic scepticism.[5]

In the early Middle Ages, there appears to have been no epistemological defence of scepticism as such, nor further attempts at refutation after Augustine's. If Christian religion was able to awaken the
saint from his sceptical nightmare, its robust sense of realism also
succeeded in preventing medieval philosophers from entertaining
logically possible questions on the nature of human knowledge, and
hence systematic sceptical doubts about its reliability. Or at least so
it seemed for a long time. In *De Anima*, Tertullian (160–240) had
already clarified the Christian attitude towards knowledge in rather
drastic tones: a Christian does not need to acquire much knowledge,
first because facts that are positively certain are few and, secondly,
because endless investigations are forbidden by Paul of Tarsus.
Curiosity is a vice and it is better to leave the fruits on the tree of
knowledge untouched. Man is not allowed to discover more than he
learns from God; and what he learns from God constitutes all he
needs to know.[6]

Superficially, such a hyper-realistic position could be considered
akin to that of the sceptical philosopher, whose *ataraxia* was compatible with a state of ignorance. However, the comparison would be
misleading, if taken seriously. The Christian thinker was not interested in denying the full intelligibility of reality to the human mind,
but keen on ranking the pursuit of mundane knowledge much lower
than the love and worship of God. The logical arguments intended to
humble human reason may be similar because the target of the
polemic is the same, namely human knowledge and its intellectual
pretensions. Indeed, Tertullian borrowed some of his dialectical

weapons from Aenesidemus, through the work of the physician and doxographer Soranus (98–138), who, in his turn, had probably read Aenesidemus' own work, which was still available during the early Middle Ages. Nevertheless, the difference between ancient scepticism and Christian anti-intellectualism remains substantial, in terms of their respective orientations: anti-dogmatism, tolerance, and mundane *ataraxia* in the former case, belief, dogmatism, and eternal salvation in the latter. Once systematic doubt has been instilled, ancient scepticism seeks to step back into suspension of judgement, whereas Christianized anti-intellectualism leaps forward into faith.

Together with the linguistic issue (even educated people no longer spoke or understood Greek, and medieval Latin had now moved far from its classic sources) religious "dogmatism" (in its usage by the Greek sceptics), theological interests, and the neglect of epistemological investigations contribute to explain why, in the eight centuries between Augustine and John of Salisbury, whose interest in sceptical issues also depends on Cicero, scant information about ancient scepticism was available, transmitted, and hence discussed. This does not mean that we should see the Middle Ages as "the Age of Faith," incapable of entertaining sceptical doubts because dogmatic, gullible, irrational, or merely acritical. As stressed by Reynolds [398], in those eight centuries we encounter, for example, a large variety of forms of unbelief, in many cultural contexts. The point is that the Middle Ages show no driving interest in sceptical arguments within the restricted philosophical and theological debates that may address issues concerning the nature and reliability of knowledge, when discussing ethical, religious, and epistemological questions at "a theoretical level." A methodological point seems in need of clarification here. Equating unbelief and scepticism, either during the Middle Ages or in the following epochs, without any further proviso, simply means muddling the history of scepticism and misinterpreting its importance. Scepticism has its own varieties but, on the whole, it is a technical and fairly distinct family of philosophical positions, not just a way of being a bit doubtful or questioning about the world. If anyone who raises a doubt, questions a religious assumption, or adopts a critical stance is to be called a sceptic, the very label ends up by covering too much and loses its meaning. "What does it take to *avoid* being a skeptic?" If the answer is "being absolutely dogmatic" then the reader knows that the label is misused, because every decent philosopher would probably qualify as being a bit of a sceptic.

Returning to our reconstruction, there may have been controversies over issues that may have a sceptical flavor for us, like the polemic contraposition of the patio of the Academy, representing the subtleties of Greek philosophy, and the temple of Solomon, representing the plain doctrine of Judaeo-Christian religion, which was common currency among Christian writers from Tertullian to Savonarola; or the interpretation of the book of *Ecclesiastes*, for a long time considered to be Solomon's work,[7] and the topos of *contemptus mundi*; or again the anti-intellectualist theses evident in the writings of Paul of Tarsus[8] and rooted in the Greek Apologists. But it should be noted that similar topics bore only a negative relation to the epistemological and ethical problems originally raised by ancient scepticism. They stressed the weakness of human knowledge in order to redirect the interest of the audience towards Christian faith, and hence to foster behavior consistent with it. The emphasis was not on the nature of knowledge, but on the attitude to be taken with respect to revelation, Christ's teachings, and the Old Testament. Witness the fact that, in this long interval, sources of information about ancient scepticism were largely forgotten rather than ostracized or exploited. Most texts in the Christian tradition contained few references to sceptical topics; and to the extent that this was not so, such references were largely disregarded. Important examples included:

- the *Stromata*[9] of Clement of Alexandria (150–211/215);
- Marcus Minucius Felix's *Octavius* (written sometime between 197–248). The *Octavius*, whose structure is modeled on Cicero's *De natura deorum*, contains an interesting, if brief, discussion between Caecilius (the pagan) and Octavius (the Christian) on the sceptical way of life. The work disappeared from view for Western scholars from the fifth until the sixteenth century and it is revealing that it was preserved as the last book of Arnobius' *Adversus Nationes*, another sceptical source (see below in this list). The *Octavius* seems to be among the first texts in which there starts to be confusion between Academics and Pyrrhonians;
- Tertullian's *De Anima*, and his *Apologeticum*, a work strictly connected with the *Octavius*;

- Hippolytus' *Refutatio Omnium Haeresium*;
- the *Praeparatio Evangelica* of Eusebius (ca. 256–339). This influential book contains several references to Pyrrhonian themes, but the second council of Nicaea (787) prohibited quoting Eusebius as a reliable source of correct belief because of his sympathetic position with respect to Arian doctrines;
- Arnobius' *Adversus Nationes*, written at the end of the third or at the beginning of the fourth century. Note that Arnobius had great influence on Huet and was well known to Bayle;[10]
- the *Divinae Institutiones* of Lactantius, who was Arnobius' pupil; and finally
- Augustine's works, not only the *Contra Academicos* but also *De Trinitate* and *De Civitate Dei*.

Other classical sources soon disappeared from the bookshelves of the medieval theologians. Examples include:

- Cicero, including his *De Natura Deorum*;
- the *Adversus Colotem* of Plutarch (between 50–120), which provides a wealth of information on the sceptical school;[11]
- the *Vitarum Auctio* and the *Hermotimus* by Lucian (b. 120).[12] Lucian's works disappeared from Western culture during the Middle Ages. As was often the case, Byzantine writers had more continuous access to them;
- *De optimo docendi genere* by Galen, a work in which the latter expounds the views of Academics and Pyrrhonians in the course of refuting them. Stephanus thought it worthwhile to publish it in Latin translation (the translation was by Erasmus), together with Diogenes Laertius' *Life of Pyrrho*, in his first Latin, printed edition of *PH* in 1562;[13]
- Aulus Gellius' *Attic Nights*, written in the latter half of the second century. Both Lactantius and Augustine knew the work. Later, it was even palimpsested and disappeared until the ninth century. Aulus Gellius provides a synthetic but valuable analysis of the similarities and differences between Pyrrhonians and Academics, which, though philosophically questionable, indicates that he still perceived the two sceptical schools as different;
- the *Life of Pyrrho* and the *Life of Timon*, written by Diogenes Laertius perhaps during the first half of the third century.

No text in either list succeeded in arousing widespread interest in the sceptical school.

At the end of the seventh century, Bede (672 or 673–735), certainly one of the greatest scholars of his time, provides an almost sympathetic reference to the Academics and the Pyrrhonians. In a passage from a sort of philosophical lexicon attributed to him,[14] which discusses passages from Aristotle and other philosophers and is organized alphabetically, under the letter D, we can read an entry on the value of the process of *Dubitare*. Bede suggests that a questioning attitude, not universal and unqualified, as is the case with the Academics and the Pyrrhonians, who mistakenly doubt everything (and here there is a reference to Aulus Gellius), but focused on specific cases, may turn out to be far from useless.

In the ninth century, we encounter some scattered and ill-informed remarks on the Pyrrhonians and the Academics in Rabanus Maurus. He compares the Academics to heretics, a deceptive interpretation not uncommon since the early Greek fathers, which had the most adverse effect possible on the transmission of the sceptical texts. A longer and more detailed description of the sceptical sect is provided by Photios in his *Bibliotheca*.[15] A comparison between the two writers is revealing.

On the Latin side of Europe, when the Middle Ages gave rise to an encyclopedic interest, Western scholars had to rely on secondary sources for their scarce information on the sceptical thinkers. Ignoring Greek, they had access only to texts transmitted in Latin, and hence almost exclusively concerning the Academic tradition, Tertullian being among the most important exceptions. In our case, Rabanus Maurus' sporadic observations were based on two sources. One was Jerome (ca. 340–420), who in turn was hinting at a fundamental question, vigorously debated during the fourth century, between Eunomius on one side and Basil and Gregory of Nyssa on the other, namely whether it is possible to have some knowledge of God (see Meredith [390]). The other was Isidore of Seville (ca. 560–630), who was relying in turn on Cicero, through the writings of Lactantius and perhaps again Jerome.[16] Now, Jerome was still able to distinguish between Plato's and the Sceptical Academy, and mentioned Cicero as a follower of the latter, but Isidore of Seville had already lost this distinction (Isidore of Seville [381], lib. 8, cap. 6 par. 11). By the time Rabanus was compiling his work, he had no clue about the difference between Plato's Academy and the new Academy or between different strands of scepticism (see *De Universo*, lib. XV, caput I, *De philosophis*). To him, it was all a big soup. The distinction between the two sceptical schools had been lost.

On the other side of Europe, Byzantine and Arabic scholars were in a better position than their Western colleagues, as they enjoyed knowledge of Greek and continuous access to at least some of the original works. Of course, this does not mean that scepticism enjoyed a good press. In the sixth century, Pyrrho was still sufficiently well known that the poet Julian the Egyptian could dedicate a sarcastic sepulchral epigram to him (Julian the Egyptian [383], p. 309). Equally dismissive is a reference to the Pyrrhonians to be found in a work attributed to David the Philosopher (fl. middle of sixth century). He thought that "the Pyrrhonians attempt to ruin everything" (see *Prolegomena Philosophiae* in TLG).

Sceptics were also called *ephektikoi*, i.e. suspensive, from the state of mind sought by the inquirer, *zêtêtikoi*, from the activity of investigation, *aporêtikoi*, i.e. dubitative (on the various names see *PH* I.7) or sometimes simply Academic, when the difference between the two brands of scepticism was missed, especially by Latin authors. Ammonios (died after 517) provides a brief explanation of the meaning of *ephektikoi* in his *In Aristotelis categorias commentarium* (TLG) and at least three of his most famous pupils, Olympiodoros of Alexandrian (ca. 500, died after 564/5), Simplikios (sixth century), and John Philoponos (ca. 490, died after 567/574), adopted the same terminology. Olympiodoros briefly mentions the "Ephectic" in his *Prolegomena* (TLG), and so does Simplikios in his *In Aristotelis categorias commentarium* (TLG). We do not know whether the latter discussed Pyrrhonism more at length elsewhere, but John Philoponos provides a slightly longer reference to Pyrrho and his sceptical way of living in his own *In Aristotelis categorias commentarium*, where he uses the term "ephectic" to refer to members of the sceptical school. Some years later, Elias of Alexandria (sixth century), who succeeded Olympiodoros as the head of the Alexandrian philosophical school, seems to have adopted the same terminology, if the work *In Aristotelis categorias commentarium* is to be attributed to him. Finally, Agathias (ca. 532–580) praised the "ephectic school" and both Pyrrho and Sextus Empiricus explicitly for their dismissive attitude to useless and endless debates over unresolvable questions.[17] Note that it is not clear whether Agathias was a sceptic himself.

In the seventh century, the Byzantine poet and liturgist Cosmas of Jerusalem[18] gave an explanation of Gregory of Nazianzus' negative comment on the Pyrrhonist position (with a significant, if brief, reference to the *tropi*, the problem of the criterion, and the distinction between Academic and Pyrrhonian scepticism) so that he must have had a decent acquaintance with the writings of the school, even if he does not mention Sextus explicitly. Two centuries later, we finally find Photios (born ca. 810, died after 893) including in his *Bibliotheca* some first-hand information about Aenesidemus' *Pyrrhonian Writings* that are now invaluable, since the original text is lost.[19] That he did not rely on Sextus may be just a matter of chance, or perhaps a sign that he considered the latter only a less interesting, secondary source, compared to Aenesidemus. We do not have a clue. A brief reference to Sextus and Pyrrho can also be found in the *Prolegomena in Hermogenis librum peri ideôn* (see TLG) by John Sikeliotes (fl. ca. 1000), and in the *Suda* (a lexicon compiled ca. 1000). The latter, which compiled other secondary literature, soon became a popular text and hence one of the primary sources of information on Pyrrho and Sextus.

To summarize, Western Europe was losing touch with the sceptical (and especially the Pyrrhonian) literature for want of linguistic skills, epistemological interests, and primary sources, and because of the increasing theologization of its philosophical investigations. Byzantine Europe was slightly better off, since at least some of these factors (especially the linguistic one) did not apply to the same extent.

A final remark must concern the coeval influence of Pyrrhonism on Arabic writers. The field is still to be fully explored but, in this case too, there seems to have been a wider availability of original texts than in Western countries.[20] A philosopher like Ghazzali (ca. 1058–1111), with his *The Incoherence of the Philosophers*, exercised a direct influence on the work of the Hebrew philosopher Judah Halevi (ca. 1085–1141), a key figure in twelfth-century Jewish thought, whose *Kusari* displays an interesting use of sceptical arguments against Aristotelian philosophy and in favor of religious faith – and some conjecture that he might have acted as a cultural bridge between Greek scepticism and the later critical philosophy of Nicholas of Autrecourt, especially as far as the analysis of the notion of causality is concerned.[21]

We have now reached the twelfth and thirteenth centuries. When medieval philosophers take some notice of sceptical themes, this is often connected with knowledge of Academic sources, thanks to Cicero and Augustine. Two authors are especially good examples: John of Salisbury (1125–1180) and Henry of Ghent (who taught in Paris, and died in 1293).

Some uses of scepticism have often represented a background condition for a fideistic defence of religious faith. *Mutatis mutandis*, this applies to sceptical trends in Arabic and Jewish culture as well as to some anti-intellectualist inclinations in European philosophy during the Middle Ages. John of Salisbury displays such a religious concern in his explicit attempt to revalue some moderate form of scepticism. According to him, the ambition of reason should be moderated by a reasonable distrust in the cognitive powers of man, unhelped by God.

John's sceptical sympathies have a Ciceronian root. He shares with Cicero an explicit aversion to any too radical form of scepticism. In his writings, there is no awareness of the epistemological challenge best represented by Pyrrhonism and Sextus' works.[22]

If scepticism is usually opposed to Aristotelianism, sometimes the metaphysical dualism and the distrust in perceptual knowledge embedded in Plato's philosophy have prompted radical forms of criticism of human cognition, and hence paved the way to forms of sceptical doubt. A century after John of Salisbury, Henry of Ghent, following Augustine, engaged in critical discussion of issues that to us have a sceptical ring.[23] And as in Augustine, "the refutation of these arguments rested upon the acceptance of a Platonic conception of human knowledge which granted to the Skeptics at least part of their own arguments" (Gilson [374], p. 447). Obviously, the major source of information was still the Latin and Academic tradition.

In the fourteenth century, there begins to develop an initial form of what one may consider nowadays a truly sceptical concern from an epistemological perspective. It is a graft from the sceptical tree probably unaware of its Greek roots[24] and, as far as we can tell from the meager evidence available, with no direct bearing on the sceptical debate that will flourish in the seventeenth century. The late medieval debate on proto-sceptical issues was connected rather with epistemological investigations resulting from factors such as a critical approach to Aristotle's texts, the spread of logical studies and hence the parallel debate upon the paradoxes and *insolubilia*, the coming to maturity of the controversy upon the nature of universals, and the discussion concerning the implications of the doctrine of the total contingency of the world. Ockhamism, for example, by developing to its final consequences the presupposition of God's boundless omnipotence, could raise doubts about the nature of reality and the power of reason that would find a conceptual echo in Descartes' *Meditations*. If God was really omnipotent, nothing was necessarily as it was; everything could have been otherwise. The possibility that things may in fact differ completely from the way they appear could be seriously and consistently entertained.[25] It is in this cultural context that we find Nicholas of Autrecourt (a fellow of the house of Sorbonne between 1320–1327) working on what can be correctly defined as sceptical themes.

Nicholas has attracted a significant amount of scholarly attention,[26] and quite rightly so, seeing that he is perhaps the only medieval philosopher to have advocated a sceptical approach to philosophy, although in the end his aim was certainly not Pyrrhonistic. Was Nicholas somehow exposed, perhaps only indirectly, to the doctrines presented by Sextus in his compendia?[27] Even though we know too little about his life and works to be able to do any more than entertain such a possibility, it should be noted that his first attempt to present scepticism as a respectable philosophical position was paralleled, on the literary side, by two significant events: a Byzantine revival of interest in Sextus' texts, and the production, in Western Europe, of three copies of the first Latin translation of the *Outlines* known so far. It seems that these manuscripts had no diffusion or influence within the intellectual community, but the fact that three copies of the same translation survive indicates that Sextus had finally begun to arouse at least some textual interest. As for the Byzantine context, Greek scholars in Eastern Europe had never completely lost sight of the sceptical literature, enjoying direct access to a wider selection of Pyrrhonian writings. To some extent, the same holds true for the twelfth century as well. However, possible continuity in the availability of Pyrrhonian texts is one thing; philosophical interest in them and discussion of their arguments is obviously quite another. Byzantine culture eventually showed a fascinating revival of the intellectual debate about scepticism, but not until the fourteenth century. Religious controversies, and a renewal of literary studies, are probably behind this recovery of sceptical issues, but always with the purpose of refutation rather than acceptance. Thus, Theodore Metochites (1270–1332) and his pupil Nicephorus Gregoras (ca. 1290/94–1358/61) study Sextus Empiricus' writings and discuss his arguments because they represent a disease that has already begun to corrupt the Church.[28] Gregory Palamas (ca. 1296–1359), who argued that knowledge of God can be obtained only by a mind enlightened by grace, shared a similar view and an equal dislike for Pyrrhonism, despite his profound disagreement with Nicephorus Gregoras. And in the same period, Nicolas Cabasilas (ca. 1290–1363), on other occasions a strong opponent of Gregoras, devotes an entire work (Cabasilas [364]) to the refutation of scepticism and Sextus Empiricus himself, although from the *Introduction*, which is the only part of the refutation still extant, it seems that he had only an indirect acquaintance with Sextus' writings.[29] Byzantine scholars and theologians, though divided by many internal controversies, could easily see Pyrrhonism as a common enemy. They felt the urge to refute the sceptical theses even though, as far as we know, no sceptical school was active at the time, nor were there individual philosophers advocating scepticism.

III THE RENAISSANCE

Perhaps the first major figure in the exchange of information about ancient scepticism is Gemistus Plethon (ca. 1360–1452). Plethon knew and was strongly averse to scepticism, and in his *Treatise upon the Laws* he attacked both Pyrrho's and Protagoras' doctrines in a single set of objections, although clearly distinguishing between them.[30] We know little about Plethon's sources, but when he visited Italy in 1438–1439, during the Council of Ferrara Florence, he was in contact with many scholars and might have spread information about Pyrrhonian doctrines, if not Sextus' works themselves. Both Francesco Filelfo (1398–1481) and Cardinal Bessarion (1403–1472), to mention only two humanists who owned Sextus manuscripts, were among his correspondents. Similar remarks apply to George of Trebizond (1395–1472/3) and Janus Lascaris (1445–1534). The former endorses Gregory's condemnation of Pyrrhonism as a Greek affliction, leading to heretical thought.[31] Janus Lascaris (1445–1534) provides us with information both on the presence of a manuscript containing Sextus Empiricus in the library of Lorenzo de' Medici before 1490, and on his own copy containing *M*. Three Sextus manuscripts are listed in the inventory of the Medici Library, made by Janus Lascaris some time before the death of Lorenzo de' Medici in 1492.

Lascaris' own copy, now Paris, Bibliotheque Nationale, gr. 2081, bears not only Lascaris' annotations, but also those of Matthaeus Devaris, his pupil and then secretary.[32]

Francesco Filelfo has usually been acknowledged as the first Italian scholar to have taken a significant interest in Sextus, at least as a literary source. It is well known that Filelfo mentioned Sextus Empiricus on different occasions in his works and in his correspondence. If one considers that the collection of Filelfo's letters was a sort of Renaissance "best seller," which circulated in at least nine different editions between 1454 and 1564, it becomes obvious that his remarks on Sextus Empiricus must have reached a much larger readership than the small group of scholars to whom his letters were originally addressed.

Humanists knew about many sceptical sources, including Sextus, but few took a philosophical interest in scepticism. The recovery and diffusion of manuscripts belonging to the sceptical tradition was followed, if not driven, by an initial reception informed by antiquarian, historical, and philological concerns. In particular, Sextus' writings were initially read as literary texts and erudite sources.

The documentary use of Sextus, based on the more general policy of attempting to recover the classical past, anticipated the philosophical impact that his work was going to have later on and it is well exemplified in Politian (1454–1494). Politian compiled a sort of abridged history of philosophy by collecting quotations and excerpts from the entire corpus of Sextus Empiricus' works, exploiting especially those initial paragraphs in which Sextus sketches the position of his adversaries.

Regarding the use of Sextus Empiricus as an historical source of information, it remains to be noted that this paved the way to a debate on the objective nature of historical knowledge in the middle of the sixteenth century.[33] Depending on the level of reading, Sextus' works could be considered a useful source of information about past philosophies or a critical warning against the ultimate unreliability of any claim to truth. Francesco Robortello (1516–1567), for example, defended the possibility of writing history against Sextus' arguments, in his De historica facultate disputatio (Robortello [400]).

The recovery and diffusion of Sextus' texts, although caused by literary, erudite, antiquarian, and philological interests, soon led to, and became intertwined with, the philosophical study of the sceptical doctrines, and gained further momentum from this theoretical interest. It was initially a matter of ethical and religious interpretation, and related to linguistic issues such as the interpretation of the Bible, the discussion of exegetical techniques, and the debate on free will and predestination. Scepticism's real essence is the defence of a constantly open, finely balanced, critical stance towards any dogmatic (in the common sense of the word) position. It is not an easy attitude, and the sceptic is usually a negative hero, a Samson who dies with all the Philistines when he makes the temple of certainties collapse. The discomfort of intelligence when confronted by a complex, multifarious, ever-changing world, elusive and scarcely intelligible because radically "other," is counterbalanced by the awareness of one's own moral detachment, intellectual integrity, and hence superiority with respect to the dogmatist (the believer), whom the sceptic considers to be philosophically naive. However, individual tolerance goes hand-in-hand with a lack of interest in the world and its destiny. Scepticism tends to be an individualistic philosophy, which needs some subjective responsibility and "social space" (the possibility of living a private life without necessarily interacting publicly with other people) to develop its non-dogmatic tranquility. Once the devastating critique of human reason began to spread, scepticism became, as we have seen, a double-edged sword. It could be used to challenge any ultimate, fixed system of universal truths, including religious ones, thus opening the way for agnosticism, free-thinking, and libertinism, as the Emperor Julian had already suspected, or it could be used to undermine confidence in any claim to knowledge in favor of faith and ethical conservatism. The "Christianization" of scepticism had medieval roots and Ciceronian influences in John of Salisbury. Scepticism was taken as an ally of Pauline anti-intellectualism, as later on in Pierre-Daniel Huet. A similar attitude was shared by the group of scholars and philosophers belonging to Savonarola's circle, especially Gianfrancesco Pico della Mirandola (1469–1533), who read Sextus in Greek and used his arguments extensively in his *Examen vanitatis*.[34] He helped to disseminate information about Sextus Empiricus among his contemporaries. According to Gianfrancesco, Savonarola had been suggesting to his followers that they read Sextus Empiricus as an introduction to Christian faith.

The interpretation of scepticism, in all its versions, as an anti-intellectualist tool and an introduction to religious faith, gained ground over the years, and acquired some prominence during the sixteenth century, motivating some of the efforts by translators and readers of Sextus. Gianfrancesco Pico della Mirandola, Paéz de Castro, Stephanus, Hervetus, and Montaigne all underlined, though in different ways and with various degrees of clarity, the ethical and religious aspect of their interest in the sceptical literature, looking at the suspension of epistemic commitment either from a counter-reformist perspective (De Castro and Hervet) or from a more human-istic and liberal point of view (Stephanus and Montaigne). The same alternatives can be found in the debate between Erasmus (d. 1536) and Luther (1483–1546) on scepticism.

The gradual growth in the number of Sextus manuscripts available in various libraries and circulating among scholars, and the initial development of Christian and ethical uses of the Pyrrhonian argu-ments, was paralleled by a geographical shift from Italy towards the North of Europe. During the first half of the sixteenth century, scep-tical doctrines found their most favorable reception in France, where a more epistemological interpretation began to develop. The spread of information about sceptical ideas beyond the Alps was such a large-scale phenomenon that in 1546, Rabelais could make Gargantua remark, in the *Tiers Livre*, that "now the most learned and most prudent philosophers are not ashamed to be seen entering in at the porches and facades of the schools of the Pyrrhonian, Aporrethic, Skeptic, and the Ephetic sects." Rabelais himself mocked a sceptical dialogue between Panurge and Trouillogan, using technical expres-sions close to the vocabulary of the sceptical and dialectical tradition. His parody is a clear sign that knowledge of the relevant literature was becoming more and more common at the beginning of the six-teenth century.

The epistemological debate on sceptical doubts, on the nature of empirical knowledge, and on scientific certainty would develop primarily at the beginning of the seventeenth century, once Sextus' writings and the recovery of scepticism had deeply affected French philosophy (Van Leeuwen [412]). Jacopo Sadoleto (1477–1547) attacked the sceptics (Sadoleto [401], p. 652), but Henricus Cornelius Agrippa von Nettesheim (1468–1535) defended them. Willibald Pirckheimer (1470–1530) translated some of Lucian's works and wrote an unpublished *Defence of Astrology* against Pico's *Disputationum adversus astrologos libri XII* and Gianfrancesco Pico della Mirandola's *De rerum praenotione libri XII*, in which he attacked Sextus Empiricus. Finally, Erasmus and Luther, to mention only two more important names, also showed a distinct awareness of sceptical doctrines.

In 1562, on the basis of a humanistic, tolerant, and "anti-dogmatic" interpretation of the sceptical theses, Henricus Stephanus (Henri Estienne, 1528–1598) published his Latin translation of the *Outlines*. By publishing the Latin translation of the *Outlines* without the Greek text, Stephanus was obviously addressing the educated public. And given the level of popularity already reached by Sextus, it is not surprising that his translation was an editorial success, though scholars disagreed on its value. The text was republished in 1569, this time together with Hervetus' Latin translation of *Adversus Mathematicos*. Gentianus Hervetus (Gentian Hervet, 1499–1584) was a scholar and a Catholic priest. He worked in Rome for Charles, Cardinal de Lorraine, with whom he went to the Council of Trent in 1562–1563. It is to him that the translation is dedicated (note that Guy de Brues had also dedicated his anti-Academic dialogues to him). Hervetus meant to carry on the process of "Christianization" of scepticism, where sceptical arguments are used to confound philosophers and heretical thinkers too critical of religious authority and dogmas. In his hands, scepticism became a powerful weapon for religious controversy, in defence of Catholic orthodoxy.

Both Latin translations of Sextus exercised a significant influence on the culture of the period almost immediately. Montaigne (1533–1592) is the most famous and indicative example.

Montaigne acquired his knowledge of Pyrrhonism through Diogenes Laertius, both in Latin and in Greek, Lucian, Aulus Gellius, Cicero, Politian, Galen, and above all from Stephanus' translation of *PH* (Villey [413]), which also contained a translation of Laertius' *Life of Pyrrho* and of Galen's *De optimo docendi genere*.[35] Besides, Montaigne also owned copies of Guy de Brues' *Dialogues* (Brues [361]) and of Agrippa's *De Incertitudine et Vanitate Scientiarum* (Agrippa [359]).

Montaigne probably never went back to Sextus' *Outlines*. Villey [413]) indicates that there are no references to Sextus and Pyrrhonian philosophy datable after 1580. And on the basis of a close analysis of Montaigne's quotations from Cicero's *Academica*, Limbrick [387]) has convincingly argued that, between 1580 and 1588, while writing the third book of the *Essays*, Montaigne's interest in scepticism acquired a more "Ciceronian" nature, inclining towards Academic scepticism, although Montaigne himself may not have drawn a sharp distinction between the two brands of scepticism.

Much has been written on Montaigne's scepticism, and this is not the place to re-analyze the topic. It is clear that Montaigne's debt to Stephanus' translation and interpretation of Sextus was notable.[36] The *Apology of Raimond Sebond* (1580) still interprets scepticism in a deeply ethical and Christian manner, as a means to moderate intellectual ambition, but this is not all. It should also be emphasized that the text already anticipates some of the epistemological possibilities implicit in the sceptical challenge, and hence can provide a nice and not too arbitrary threshold between the stage at which we can speak of the recovery of ancient scepticism, and the stage at which ancient scepticism is fully re-installed in the lively context of philosophical debate. It has been suggested that, by reading Sextus Empiricus, Montaigne moved from the logical and epistemological arguments of Pyrrhonism to his own ethical context (Brush [362]; see also Schiffman [402]). Yet this interpretation looks at Montaigne from a Cartesian perspective and may be slightly anachronistic, for it does not take into account the fundamental fact that, until that time, the feeble tradition of philosophical interpretations of the sceptical literature had been mainly one of ethical and religious readings. Montaigne was in line with his time. What should rather be said is that, in Montaigne, logical and epistemological themes already start to emerge, although they are still framed within a consistently pragmatic and religious picture. The fact that Montaigne reduced the case against reasoning or logic almost completely to Aenesidemus' "Ten Modes, which emphasize the diversity of opinion and the unreliability of the senses," is in keeping with the culture of the time.[37] The fact that he also discussed the problem of the criterion (*diallelus*) at length is a step forward into the purely epistemological debate to come. Interpreted on the basis of his quotations, Montaigne is a humanist; but it is sufficient to read one of the last sentences of the *Apology* – "We do not have any communication with Being" – to understand his position as the last of the great Renaissance philosophers. No scholastic or humanist philosopher could have felt such extraneousness. Modern philosophy was going to be based on such a feeling of being a foreigner to the world.

IV CONCLUSION

If, during the fifteenth and sixteenth centuries, the epistemological debate on scepticism, as we understand it now, was largely confined to the background, this was mainly because humanistic culture was not the right context within which such a radical attack on knowledge could flourish. As far as the principal interests of the humanists were concerned (i.e. literary and linguistic studies, Christian ethics, and the recovery of the past), sceptical works attracted limited but not insignificant attention. A scholarly culture like that of the humanists, interested in the history of thought and texts and still far from any idea of, let alone a faith in, the endless progress of scientific knowledge, was unlikely to be deeply and seriously affected by sceptical arguments at the epistemological level, as Descartes would be.

The correct way to understand the history of scepticism from Francesco Filelfo to Henricus Stephanus is to focus on the role played by humanists in recovering the knowledge of Sextus, rather than on the limited philosophical use of such writings in those years. In order to regain a dramatic role in the philosophical tradition, the contents of the *Outlines* and of *Adversus Mathematicos* had to wait until the epistemological developments at the end of the Renaissance, when Sextus began to gain some relevance in the discussion of astrological and historiographical topics. But it was only when philosophers were confronted by a vastly increased amount of scientific knowledge that they presented a fully epistemological interpretation of the cognitive enterprise. Only then did the sceptical attitude gain all its challenging power, acquiring those specifically epistemological features that we still attribute to it nowadays. After Montaigne, Pyrrhonism (rather than Academic scepticism) was less and less often interpreted as a way of life and an ethical philosophy, coming to play the role of a dialectical pole in the epistemological inquiry that would be fully exploited by Descartes.

In 1621, the first edition of the Greek text of both *PH* and *M* was finally published. Sextus' writings had become a classic, which no serious library could afford to lack. Exactly twenty years after the publication of Sextus in Greek, in 1641, there appeared in Paris the first edition of Descartes' *Meditations*. Descartes wrote that he had read some Scholastic authors and found them exceedingly boring.

He had then dipped into some sceptical treatises (Descartes [417], p. 76) and discovered in them a remarkably interesting procedure. In the *Meditations*, Descartes was presenting his thoughts about the foundation of human knowledge in terms of a reflection on the most systematic form of doubt, something that even Sextus Empiricus would have considered astonishingly radical.[38] He argued that only by defeating the very possibility of doubt could one be certain that science would be worthy of all the efforts already being made to advance it. He attempted to show that subjective reflection on the very activity of doubt could provide such a foundation. In this case, the originality of Descartes consisted in taking the sceptical arguments seriously from a purely epistemological perspective, without either becoming a sceptic himself, like Francisco Sanchez (1550–1623), or subjecting them to a theological, Christian, or ethical reading, like Pico della Mirandola, Guy de Brués (fl. 1554–1562), Montaigne, or Charron (1541–1603). The dualism required in order to entertain doubt seriously, the epistemological change brought about by the new scientific discoveries such as those of Copernicus and Galileo, the new geographical and astronomical explorations, the crisis of the Aristotelian-Scholastic paradigm in epistemology, the focus on the individual subject as the element on which a new theory of knowledge could hinge, the Reformation, the Counter-Reformation and the end of the Catholic monopoly in matters of religious faith and intellectual education, and the recovery of past philosophies with their irreconcilable disagreements, were among the factors that had opened a new era in the history of scepticism, an era in which we still find ourselves. During the seventeenth century, sceptical questioning became a valuable instrument of theoretical investigation in epistemology. The contents of Sextus' works overshadowed any other text in the sceptical tradition and became the target of endless refutations, which often missed the ethical value of the Pyrrhonian position and dealt with sceptical objections and arguments as if they were puzzles to solve, tricks to be unmasked, or traps to be avoided. It is possible that Descartes never read Sextus' work, but this is less crucial than it may seem because, by the time the *Meditations* were published, we should no longer speak of the influence of sceptical arguments on modern philosophy, but rather take them to be an integral part of it.

NOTES

1 The reader interested in pursuing further knowledge about the topic is invited to consult Schmitt [405], Floridi [357], and Popkin [355].

2 For example in a work against the Manicheans by Pope Leo I the Great (d. 461), *De Manichaeorum Haeresi et Historia Libri Duo*, Caput III, and in a brief entry in the famous *Anthologium* of John of Stobi (Stobaios, fl. fourth to fifth century).

3 Cf. Copenhaver and Schmitt [367], p. 241.

4 On Traversari's translation, see Stinger [408], pp. 71–77 and Gigante [373].

5 Ioli [380] has provided a philological analysis of how some key words in the Pyrrhonian tradition were translated into Latin.

6 Tertullian [410], pp. 4 and 97.

7 See Bultot [363]; Lazzari [385], and Hattaway [378].

8 For a discussion of the theme of Pauline fideism in relation to Stephanus' interest in Sextus, see Floridi [370]. For a moderately anti-intellectualist interpretation of Paul of Tarsus' *Letters to the Corinthians*, see Stowers [409].

9 On Clement of Alexandria's relation to Pyrrhonism, see Sepp [407], pp. 59–60.

10 On *Arnobiusdeutungen*, see Krafft [384], chs. 12–18.

11 Schroeter [216] provides a clear review of Plutarch's relation with both Pyrrhonism and Academic scepticism. See also Carlos Lévy, Chapter 4 "The Sceptical Academy: Decline and Afterlife."

12 On Lucian's philosophical sources, see Praechter [396], according to whom Sextus is not a source of Lucian, and Praechter [397].

13 On Galen's influence, likely in the case of Agrippa, cf. Nauert [392], pp. 142–43 and n. 84.

14 Venerabilis Bedae, *Sententiae, Sive Axiomata Philosophica ex Aristotele et Aliis Praestantibus Collecta, una cum brevibus quibusdam explicationibus ac limitationibus.* Sectio Prima. Sententiae Ex Aristotele Collectae, in *Patrologia Latina*.

15 Photios mentions Sextus explicitly only once in his *Library*, cf. 366a41–2 (vol. VI.94 in Photios [393]).

16 Faes de Mottoni has analyzed this early medieval tradition in Faes De Mottoni [368] and Faes De Mottoni [369].

17 Agathias, *Historiarum Libri II*, 129 in *Patrologia Graeca* (PG) 88, col. 1394 and Agathias [358], p. 79.

18 Cosmae Hierosolymitani, *Commentarii in Sancti Gregorii Nazianzeni Carmina*, Carmen CXIX, PG 38, cols. 555–556, which refers to PG 37, col. 684.

19 For detailed discussion of this text see R.J. Hankinson, Chapter 5 "Aenesidemus and the Rebirth of Pyrrhonism." Photios' summary of Aenesidemus' book (omitting a few criticisms, with which Photios concludes the chapter) is reproduced in LS (texts 71C, 72L). For the complete text see Photios [393], vol. III.119–23. Janáček [227] supports von Arnim's suggestion that Aenesidemus, who is Photios' source, was also the source of Clement of Alexandria's remarks on scepticism, and shows that Aenesidemus was also the source of Sextus Empiricus. The hypothesis is extended in Janáček [228], where Janáček maintains that Diogenes Laertius, Sextus Empiricus, and Hippolytus can all be shown to have relied on Aenesidemus' lost works.

20 Baffioni [360], vol. I, pp. 415–34, who corrects and improves on Horovitz' theses concerning the diffusion of Sextus' writings in Arabic philosophy, providing translations of several relevant passages from Ibn Hazm, Shahrastani, and Fakhr al-Din al-Razi, cf. Horovitz [379].

21 Wolfson [415], 234–38. On Ghazali's influence on Nicholas of Autrecourt, see the critical note in Van Den Bergh [411], vol. I, p. XXX. See also Weinberg [414], ch. V.

22 Liebeschütz [386], pp. 74–90.

23 On the sceptical problem of certainty in this context, see Schmitt [403], 231–58 and Schmitt [406], pp. 309–12.

24 On scepticism and medieval philosophy, cf. Jourdain [382]; Schmitt [404]; Porro [395]; Cavini [366]; Frede [371]; and Michalski [391].

25 On Ockham and the sceptical problem, see Floridi [357], and above all Richards [399]; McCord [389], 389–98, with further bibliography.

26 See Floridi [357].

27 Cf. Weinberg [414], pp. 83–84.

28 Gregoras [376], pp. XIX, 1, 5–10, 930; Guillard [377], pp. 79 and 206–7 provides relevant information on the Byzantine revival of interest in Sextus Empiricus during the fourteenth century.

29 Note that the entries in *The Oxford Dictionary of Byzantium*, in the *Enciclopedia Cattolica* and in the *Dictionnaire de Théologie Catholique* all warn the reader that sometimes Nicolas Cabasilas is confused with his uncle Nil Cabasilas. Since none of the three works altogether agrees with one another, the dates provided here are those given by the *Oxford Dictionary*, which is the most recent of the three.

30 Plethon [394], pp. 37–43: "Sur les doctrines opposées de Protagoras et de Pyrrho."

31 George of Trebizond [372], p. 489.

32 Müller [391a].

33 For a valuable analysis of the use of Sextus Empiricus in the early history of philosophical historiography, cf. Malusa [388].

34   On Gianfrancesco Pico's interest in scepticism, see Cao [365].
35   Montaigne probably studied the 1562 edition, since there are no refe-
     rences to M in his writings, cf. Villey [413], pp. 242–43 and 290.
36   See Gray [375].
37   On Aenesidemus' Ten Modes, see Paul Woodruff, Chapter 11 "The
     Pyrrhonist Modes."
38   For further discussion of Descartes' relation to the ancient sceptical tradi-
     tion, see Michael Williams, Chapter 15 "Descartes' Transformation of the
     Sceptical Tradition."

15 Descartes' transformation of the sceptical tradition

I SEXTUS AND DESCARTES

In a ground-breaking paper, Myles Burnyeat brings into focus what is surely, from a contemporary standpoint, the most striking difference between the scepticism found in Sextus Empiricus' *Outlines of Pyrrhonism*[1] and that which animates Descartes' *Meditations*[2]: Sextus' failure to pose in full generality the sceptical problem concerning our knowledge of the external world.[3] For while Sextus and Descartes both question our capacity for knowing the real natures of things, Descartes goes beyond this "essential" scepticism to pose an "existential" problem: how do we know that the external world even *exists*?

What accounts for this difference? A tempting answer, in part Burnyeat's own, contrasts the *practical* concerns of Sextus with the *theoretical* orientation of Descartes. Pyrrhonian scepticism is a way of life: the sceptic lives *adoxastos* (conventionally rendered "without belief"), letting his actions be guided by natural capacities and acquired habits rather than reasoned judgements. Conceiving scepticism as a way of living in the world, Sextus can hardly doubt the world's very existence. By contrast, Descartes treats scepticism as a mere methodological device, to be taken seriously only in the context of inquiries into "first philosophy," a context in which all practical concerns are temporarily set aside. Freed from practical constraint, Descartes can push scepticism to an unprecedented extreme.[4]

This explanation of Descartes' ability to pose a new and dramatic problem stresses competing conceptions of the *significance* of scepticism, a factor that must be of vital importance. However, as

Burnyeat points out, Descartes' radical doubt also involves decisive *theoretical* moves. Unlike almost all the ancients (sceptics or not),[5] Descartes thinks that truth can be obtained without going outside subjective experience, and that subjective states are objects of knowledge. Further, he comes to treat *his own body* as part of the external world. Are these moves made possible by transplanting ancient sceptical materials from a practical to a purely theoretical context? Or do the ancient materials undergo an additional and independent transformation? Burnyeat suggests the former, claiming that Descartes sees that "the traditional material supports a doubt more radical than the traditional skeptic had dared to suppose."[6] This underestimates Descartes' originality. Far from pushing traditional material farther, Descartes presents some wholly new sceptical arguments. Moreover, these arguments are embedded in a form of scepticism that differs from Pyrrhonism in structure as well as in intent. Descartes does not extend the ancient tradition: he reconfigures it.

Sextus' *Outlines* differs from that of Descartes' First *Meditation* not just in the absence of a particular problem but in *many* ways. Here are some of the most important.

(1) Pyrrhonian scepticism involves *suspension of judgement* (*epochê*), said to lead to peace of mind (*ataraxia*). Cartesian scepticism induces *doubt*, a state of uncomfortable indecision from which one would like to escape.

(2) For Sextus, scepticism is the antidote to doubt. Pyrrhonian sceptics begin as "men of talent" who are "troubled by the anomaly in things and puzzled as to which of them they should assent to" (*PH* 1.12). When they investigate matters systematically, they find that anomalies are even more pervasive than they had realized. This leads them to wide-ranging suspension of judgement and (to their surprise) to peace of mind. Accordingly, Pyrrhonian scepticism, as *epochê*, is *sustained*. For Descartes, the antidote to doubt is certainty. Thus, Cartesian scepticism, as doubt, is *temporary*, induced with a view to seeing how far it can be pushed before it breaks down. Where Pyrrhonian scepticism is final, Cartesian scepticism is only provisional or methodological.

(3) Pyrrhonian *epochê* is philosophically *neutral*. The Pyrrhonian sceptic suspends judgement on all philosophical (indeed all *theoretical*) views. Cartesian doubt is meant to be *selective*, bearing

unequally on competing metaphysical and epistemological views. In particular, the general doubt is supposed to make us particularly suspicious of the idea that knowledge comes primarily through the senses.

(4) Pyrrhonian *epochê* is at least partially sustained by arguments that involve detailed critical examinations of current theories in physics, ethics, grammar, etc. Cartesian doubt is entirely dependent on general sceptical arguments. So where Pyrrhonian scepticism is *discursive*, Cartesian scepticism is *compact*.

(5) Pyrrhonian *epochê* encompasses all theoretical temptations that the sceptic has encountered *so far*. Future temptations have to be met as they arise: the sceptic "goes on inquiring." Descartes dismisses *seriatim* examination of particular views as "an endless undertaking." Cartesian doubt takes in all Descartes' former beliefs, all at once. Indeed, it extends to any future beliefs that he might acquire by going on in his old way. Where Pyrrhonian *epochê* is *open-ended*, Cartesian doubt is *theoretically closed*.

(6) In its epistemological dimension, Pyrrhonism is *monotonous*. At bottom, the sceptical arguments that are most central to Pyrrhonism are all the same and lead to the same result: sustaining the sceptic in his state of *epochê*. Cartesian scepticism is *progressive*. Descartes presents a sequence of sceptical considerations, which expand and deepen his doubt. Where Pyrrhonian *epochê* is *flat*, Cartesian doubt is *stratified*.

(7) Sextus' most important sceptical arguments revolve around the relatively formal problem of avoiding a vicious *regress of justification* without falling into brute assumption or circular reasoning ("Agrippa's trilemma," as I have called it). Descartes depends on *indistinguishability arguments* invoking sceptical hypotheses (for example, that I am dreaming right now). In this respect, Descartes' arguments are closer to the Academic arguments recounted in Cicero's *Academica* than to anything in the *Outlines*.

(8) Sextus links scepticism with *actual disagreements*, thus with views that at least some people find plausible (or even evident). Descartes' sceptical arguments invoke *outrageous hypotheses* that no one believes.

(9) The point with which we began: Sextus never poses Descartes' fundamental problem: that concerning our knowledge of the external world.

Exploring these differences will bring into focus Descartes' transformation of the sceptical tradition.

II SCEPTICAL STANCES

Let me introduce the idea of a *sceptical stance*. The *components* of such a stance are one or more of three forms of scepticism: *doctrinal*, *suspensive*, and *prescriptive*.

Doctrinal scepticism is (acceptance of) a sceptical doctrine or thesis.[7] Sceptical theses can concern different levels of epistemic assessment. While one sceptic may hold that we have no knowledge, another may advance the more guarded meta-sceptical thesis that, so far as he can tell, we have no knowledge. Sceptical theses also differ in modal strength. A modally weak sceptical thesis will say, for example, that *in fact* we have no knowledge. Its modally strong counterpart will say that knowledge is *impossible*.

Where doctrinal scepticism involves accepting an epistemological thesis, suspensive scepticism involves a self-denying change in one's epistemic practices: for example, ceasing to claim knowledge, or even abandoning some significant portion of one's beliefs. A sceptical stance involves prescriptive scepticism when suspensive practice is guided by a *sceptical prescription,* such as "Don't claim knowledge" or "Suspend judgement."

All three components can vary in their *extent*: what a sceptic is sceptical *about*. We should notice three dimensions of variation.

Epistemic target. This may be knowledge (according to some demanding conception), justification (perhaps falling short of knowledge), or mere belief (justified or not).

Topical range. Scepticism can be *universal*, when no claim is exempt, or *restricted*, as in the case of external world scepticism. However, the well-known varieties of restricted scepticism (external world, other minds, induction, etc.) are still unusually general, for they encompass any and every claim in the category, including those that are by common sense standards certain or obvious.

Contextual scope. For example, some philosophers hold that scepticism can be taken seriously only in a special context, typically that of philosophical inquiry.

There is a rich variety of possible stances.

The *structure* of a sceptical stance is determined by the relation between its components. However, the possibility of structural variation is easy to miss, for there is a way of connecting the components so prevalent and appealing that it is easy to think of it as the *only* way. It is natural to think that to be rational rather than pathological, suspensive scepticism must be based on doctrinal scepticism via a practical-epistemic norm or *epistemic prescription*, stating the conditions in which knowledge may be claimed, judgement exercised, etc. In diagram form:

Doctrinal Scepticism + Epistemic Prescription
entail
Prescriptive Scepticism,
inducing (where possible)
Suspensive Scepticism

I call this the *Standard Model* of a sceptical stance.

Typically in a Standard Model stance, the doctrinal component is epistemic, targeting a high-value epistemic goal such as knowledge, while the suspensive component is doxastic, applying to belief. In this case, the epistemic prescription takes the form of a *doxastic norm*. Thus:

Doctrinal Epistemic Scepticism + Doxastic Norm
entail
Prescriptive Doxastic Scepticism,
inducing (where possible)
Suspensive Doxastic Scepticism

This is the Standard Model in its *typical form*.

To support an open-ended sceptical practice, doctrinal scepticism must be the conclusion of an argument for a wide-ranging and modally robust conclusion. To reach such a conclusion, the sceptic identifies an epistemic *goal*, a *method* by which this goal is supposedly attained, and an obstacle to our reaching the goal by way of the method. He concludes that our reach exceeds our grasp: that we cannot attain our goal with our available method. Diagramatically:

Epistemic Goal + Method + Obstacle
entail
Sceptical Thesis

This is the *Standard Sceptical Strategy* (Standard Strategy for short). In the modern period, it is the royal road to doctrinal scepticism.

In exploring the differences between Sextus and Descartes, the beginning of wisdom is to recognize that the Pyrrhonian stance does not conform to the Standard Model, whereas the stance adopted by Descartes at the end of the First *Meditation* is a paradigm of the Standard Model in its typical form.

The conformity of Descartes' stance to the Standard Model is readily shown. Descartes' path to his general doubt is guided by four commitments.

Epistemic Goal: Descartes aims to establish something "firm and lasting in the sciences." His epistemic goal is knowledge amounting to absolute certainty (at least for some fundamental truths). In the context of a purely theoretical inquiry, it is reasonable to investigate whether there are truths meeting this maximal standard.

Method: According to Descartes, all his former beliefs came to him "from the senses or through the senses" (CSM 12).

Obstacle: Everyday perceptual errors, involving objects that are hard to make out, show that the senses are not always completely reliable sources of information. But even in apparently ideal circumstances, sensory evidence cannot rule out sceptical hypotheses postulating systematic error (e.g. dreaming or demon-deception). So there is reason to doubt even the simplest and most obvious things.

Sceptical Thesis: The senses are nowhere a source of knowledge amounting to certainty. Certain knowledge is therefore impossible (unless an alternative source can be identified).

Doxastic Norm: Descartes announces that "Reason now leads me to think that I should hold back my assent from those opinions which are not completely certain and indubitable just as carefully as I do from those which are patently false" (CSM 12).

Descartes follows the Standard Strategy: his epistemic goal, proposed method, and surprising obstacles combine to establish a modally strong sceptical thesis. This doctrinal scepticism then combines with his doxastic norm to yield prescriptive scepticism: for "powerful and well-thought-out reasons ... I must withhold my assent from these former beliefs just as carefully as I would from obvious falsehoods" (CSM 15). As a rational being, he acts on this prescription, achieving suspensive scepticism.[8]

A Standard Model stance is *doctrinally based* and *prescriptively guided.* In consequence, such a stance is apt to carry a heavy load of philosophical commitments. Of course, the sceptic may argue that these commitments are not *his* but *ours*, or that the commitments belong to common sense rather than philosophical theory. However, norms and methods operating at the sceptic's level of generality cannot be read off the surface features of everyday epistemic practices. The sceptic may mean to invoke no more than "platitudes we would all accept" (to borrow a phrase from Barry Stroud). But what he must in fact invoke is *a theory of our everyday practices* (in effect, an epistemology) no matter how superficially "intuitive" his arguments may seem. The question of theoretical commitment is one over which Sextus and Descartes divide. As a result, Sextus' route to *epochê* is *nothing* like Descartes' route to his general doubt.

Sextus opens the *Outlines* with a tripartite classification of philosophers: there are Dogmatists, who believe they have discovered the truth; Academics, who treat truth as inapprehensible; and Sceptics, who are "still investigating" (*PH* 1.4). Sextus insists that Pyrrhonians are quite unlike Academics, whom he regards (fairly or not) as negative dogmatists (endorsers of modally strong doctrinal scepticism), thus not genuine sceptics at all. Thus, the *very first thing* that Sextus tells us is that he is not committed to doctrinal scepticism, at least not in any modally strong form.

The *second* thing Sextus tells is that his aim is only:

> to give an outline account [of the Sceptic way] stating in advance that with respect to none of the things that we will recount do we strongly maintain that they are just as we say; rather, according to our impression at the moment, we report like a chronicler on each one. (*PH* 1.4, my translation)

Sextus' task in the *Outlines* is to *present* sceptical procedures but neither to *rationalize* nor *recommend* them. It doesn't matter that disclaiming doctrinal scepticism leaves Sextus with no basis for sceptical prescriptions, since he doesn't issue any.

How is *epochê* sustained? Sextus' says that *epochê* comes from acquiring (usually inadvertently) a distinctive *ability*. Thus:

Skepticism is an ability to set out oppositions among things which appear and are thought of in any way at all, an ability by which, because of the equipollence in the opposed objects and accounts, we come first to suspension of judgment and afterwards to tranquility. (*PH* 1.8)

Scepticism is an ability "not in any fancy sense, but simply in the sense of 'being able to' " (*PH* 1.9). A sceptic is a virtuoso dialectician. He can take any claim or argument, commonsensical or theoretical, and find a countervailing claim or argument of roughly equal persuasive force. Faced with such offsetting claims, he suspends judgement. Sextus *defines* the sceptic as one who possesses this ability. He does not say that the sceptic *makes use* of this ability, for reasons yet to be explained. The sceptic *just is* someone who has acquired it (*PH* 1.11).

Although the spell of the Standard Model makes it difficult to do, we should take Sextus seriously here. Possessing the ability to orchestrate sceptical antitheses is the absolute bedrock of the Pyrrhonian stance. Sextus insists on this: "the chief constitutive principle" of scepticism is "every account's lying opposed to an equal account" (*PH* 1.12, my translation).[9] The sceptic is not one who *argues*, thus believes, that every proposition he might be tempted to accept can be offset by a countervailing proposition: he is one who can produce a suitable counterweight. Suspension of judgement has *nothing* to do with what a sceptic *believes*: it is wholly a matter of what he can *do*. The Pyrrhonian stance is *practical all the way down*.

Let us call the sceptic's procedure the *Method of Opposition* (being careful not to read too much into "Method"). We might be tempted to explain its workings as follows: we examine opposing views, judge them equally credible, and conclude that we ought not to assent to either. As rational creatures, we therefore suspend judgement. However, if the idea of scepticism as an ability is meant to provide an alternative to the Standard Model, this cannot be what Sextus has in mind. To *judge* that opposed views are equally credible would be to presuppose a criterion of belief-worthiness; and to base one's suspensive practice on an epistemic conclusion would entail guiding one's practice by a doxastic norm. To offer an escape from the Standard Model, the Method must be *criterion-independent* and *prescription-free*. Criterion-independence and prescription-freedom entail that

Pyrrhonian antitheses must be *psychologically effective*, rather than *epistemologically balanced*. Equipollence (*isostheneia*) is not judged but *experienced*, the experience leading *directly* to suspension of judgement. As Sextus explains:

> By "equipollence" we mean equality with regard to being convincing or unconvincing ... Suspension of judgment is a standstill of the intellect, owing to which we neither reject nor posit anything. (*PH* 1.10).

In an effective opposition, the poles *neutralize* each other, inducing *epochê* in the way that the bundles of hay paralyzed Buridan's ass. The connection between *isostheneia* and *epochê* is therefore conceptual. An antithesis involves equipollent poles if and only if it induces *epochê* (for me, here and now).

So understood, sceptical antitheses have to be orchestrated case by case, as theoretical temptations arise. Moreover, they are essentially topic-specific. Asked whether the sceptics deal with natural science, Sextus replies that:

> we touch on natural science in order to be able to oppose to every account an equal account ... This is also the spirit in which we approach the logical and ethical parts of what they call philosophy. (*PH* 1.18)

A claim from physics will be balanced by a countervailing claim from physics, an ethical claim by an ethical claim, and so on. But there is a problem. Sextus sets great store by the Modes of Suspension, which present straightforward sceptical arguments. If Pyrrhonian scepticism is practical all the way down, thus not based on general sceptical considerations, why are sceptical arguments so important?

Some critics think that the Modes underwrite the Method of Opposition, perhaps by guaranteeing the existence of oppositions. But this cannot be what Sextus intends. Consider the Five (Agrippan) Modes, given by Sextus as Dispute, Infinite Regress, Relativity, Hypothesis, and Circular Reasoning. Of the Five, only the first, Dispute, has any obvious connection with the Method. Further, insofar as the Five Modes work together, they are naturally read as building a case for doctrinal scepticism. This is how some contemporary readers take them. Dispute and Relativity, they claim, function as "Challenging" Modes, their point being to trigger a demand for justification. Once the need for justification is recognized, the sceptic deploys the remaining "Dialectical" Modes to show that an attempt to justify a claim – any claim – faces an insuperable obstacle in the form of a fatal trilemma.[10]

What about the Ten Modes? They are full of references to conflicting appearances and opinions, which may seem to give them a direct link to the Method. But matters are not so simple. To function as the poles of an effective antithesis, conflicting appearances must be *jointly cognitively available* (the sceptic must be able to bring them both vividly to mind) and *experientially equipollent*. The oppositions discussed in the Ten Modes do not meet these requirements. They are either altogether unavailable (the impressions of other animals, First Mode), available but not jointly (the impressions of youth and age, sickness and health, waking and dreaming, etc., Fourth Mode), or jointly available but not equipollent (conflicting moral judgements, Tenth Mode).

Someone may reply that this "problem" overlooks Sextus' point that the Method allows for setting up oppositions between appearances and/or judgements *in any way at all* (PH 1.31). So while conflicting ways of experiencing the world are not generally jointly available *as experiences* – being human, we cannot see the world as dogs do, nor when healthy can we see through the eyes of the sick – experiences can be *opposed by thoughts*. This is the kind of crosswise opposition we create when we argue that our current way of experiencing the world is only one among many.

This objection makes the problem more not less acute, for it highlights Sextus' interest in general sceptical arguments. According to Sextus, "we assent to what is present and affects us in the present." This is why, in practical life, immediate experience overrides arcane theoretical considerations. Accordingly, we can oppose an experience by a thought only when the experience is *recollected*, not while it is ongoing: that is, when we are thinking about our experiences (and those of others) and wondering whose experiences are the best guide to the nature of things. The conflicting appearances cited in the Modes become interesting when we ask how truth can be judged: by whom, by what faculty, in what circumstances, and so on. In effect, they raise the problem of the criterion: the question of whether our epistemic resources are adequate to our epistemic goal (of knowing the truth). But now we seem to be heading for doctrinal scepticism, and so back towards the Standard Model.[11]

This impression is reinforced by observing that the "oppositions" cited in the Modes do not lead directly to *epochê* anyway. In the most developed of the Ten Modes, Sextus argues for the existence of systematic disagreement in order to reach a *relativity lemma*. In the light of systematically conflicting appearances, all opinions and perceptions seem to be "relative" to something or other: the judge, the method or faculty employed, the condition in which it is used, the state of the object judged, and so on.

Relativity lemmas function as entering wedges for *undecidability arguments*. Knowledge aims at absolute truth, which is threatened by relativity. So can we escape relativity by giving reasons for preferring, say, our experiences over those of other animals? No. If we try to give such reasons, we embark on an infinite regress of reasons for reasons for reasons, or we make a brute assumption, or we find ourselves reasoning in a circle. The latter two options are the most likely: either we just assume that we (humans) are the judges of truth; or we appeal (at least implicitly) to our own cognitive powers in arguing for their superiority. The strategy on display in the most developed of the Ten Modes follows the template given abstractly in the Five.

There is no denying that Sextus presents sceptical arguments with the potential to establish modally strong conclusions. But whether this leads to a Standard Model stance depends on how he uses the arguments he presents.

Strategically, sceptical arguments can be deployed two ways: preemptively or reactively. (We might also say, offensively or defensively.) Deployed pre-emptively, they are the sceptic's first order of business, articulated to pose a challenge that anyone who thinks that knowledge is possible needs to overcome. This is how they are used in the Standard Model. But suppose that, for whatever reason, a philosopher is *already* sceptically inclined: he might then deploy sceptical arguments reactively to repel attacks on his sceptical orientation. Deployed this way, they would not be the basis of his sceptical practice, in the way that the Standard Model requires. Though I do not have space to argue the case in detail, I am certain that the second way is how Sextus means to deploy them.

In comparing him with Descartes, we noticed Sextus' tendency to link sceptical argumentation with actual disagreements. To contemporary epistemologists, this seems strange and unmotivated. When Charlotte Stough remarks that Sextus' emphasis on disagreement is "misleading because it suggests that the existence of such conflict is essential to the main arguments" she is voicing a natural contemporary reaction.[12] In current discussions of "Agrippan" scepticism, we go straight to the trilemma: "the regress problem," as we think of it. The suggestion that the Challenging Modes get the problem off the ground by triggering a demand for justification is no help. Contemporary epistemologists think that the demand is *already* triggered by a claimant's pretending to knowledge (or justified belief), which is why it is in place even for claims that no one disputes.

Suppose, however, that Sextus deploys sceptical arguments reactively. Then his linking them with actual disputes makes perfect sense. And there is an obvious need for them in such a role. It is no news to dogmatists that their claims can be disputed. However, dogmatic philosophies incorporate epistemologies: systematic accounts of how the truth can be known, hence how disputes can be resolved. Accordingly, the Pyrrhonian needs sceptical arguments: not to underwrite his own sceptical stance, but to counter the epistemological ideas of dogmatists.

The lure of epistemology, as offering an escape from dialectical scepticism, assures sceptical arguments a vital role in sustaining *epochê*. No sceptical doctrines need be endorsed. Quite the opposite. Deployed reactively, the sceptical considerations presented in the Modes do not ground, rationalize, explain, or give hints for the practice of the sceptic's Method: *they apply it in epistemology* ("logic"). And in fact, Sextus indicates early on that this is his intention. Recall his reply to the question "Does a sceptic deal with natural science?" Whether the subject is physics, ethics, or "logic" (epistemology), the sceptic proceeds in the same way: he sets up oppositions. Sextus is not so much an epistemological sceptic as a *sceptic about epistemology*.[13]

Of course, the sceptic can (and eventually Sextus does) oppose dogmatic epistemologies to each other. But sceptical arguments may be the only effective counter to the feeling that there *must be* a criterion of truth, even if it is hard to state in a fully satisfactory way. I would argue that this is what is going on in the Modes. They challenge something that lies deeper than technical epistemology and gives rise to it: our epistemic partiality for *ourselves* as judges of how things really are.[14]

Granted, in the Modes, Sextus only presents the sceptical side of the antithesis, so that his use of sceptical arguments is only *implicitly* oppositional. And when, in *Outlines* Book Two and *Against the Logicians* he does oppose particular epistemological theories, he seems to weight his arguments in the sceptic's favor. However, Sextus is alive to these features of his presentation and warns against being misled by them. The sceptic's presentation is unbalanced because it is not his business to make plausible epistemological ideas that are *already well known and well developed*. The sceptic's task is to make plausible something less well known and perhaps implausible to the uninitiated: the case for doctrinal scepticism. In other words, his task is to *create equipollence by redressing an existing imbalance with an imbalance of his own*. Sextus explains:

The skeptic's procedure is to refrain from making the case for things that are trusted, but, in their case, to be content with the common preconception as a sufficient basis – but to make the case for the things that seem *not* to be trustworthy, and to bring each of them into equal strength with the trust surrounding things deemed worthy of acceptance.[15]

The dialectical situation requires extra effort on the sceptical wing. The Pyrrhonian stance remains practical all the way down.

III   CERTAINTY AND STRATIFICATION

Let us recall the differences that we found between the Pyrrhonian and the Cartesian stances. We can summarize them in Table 15.1.

1–3 reflect the divergent understandings of the significance of scepticism: scepticism as a way of life versus scepticism as a tool of philosophical inquiry. However, the contrast is not captured precisely by saying that one stance is practical, while the other is merely theoretical. If "practical" means "having a suspensive component," both stances are practical. Nor would it be quite correct to say that, where Sextus suspends judgement in the course of common life, Descartes only doubts in the context of philosophical inquiry. It is arguable that Sextus only suspends judgement in the course of philosophical reflection. In everyday life, the Pyrrhonian sceptic (like everyone, most of the time) is guided by a practical criterion comprising four factors: natural cognitive capacities, passions and drives, culturally ingrained dispositions, and professional training. Since in everyday affairs the Pyrrhonian sceptic does not go in for "rational" belief-management, he does not so much *suspend* judgement as

Table 15.1. *Differences between the Pyrrhonian and Cartesian Stances*

Pyrrhonian Stance	Cartesian Stance
1. Suspension of judgement (*epochê*)	Doubt
2. Comfortable. Sustained. Final	Uneasy. Temporary. Methodological
3. Neutral	Selective. Casts particular suspicion on the senses
4. Involves topically specific arguments. Discursive	Exclusively epistemological. Compact
5. Serially developed. Open-ended	Once and for all. Closed
6. Monotonous/flat	Progressive/stratified
7. Agrippan Trilemma	Indistinguishability arguments
8. Sceptical arguments linked with real disagreements	Outrageous sceptical hypotheses
9. No external world scepticism	External world scepticism pre-eminent

dispense with it. Conversely, it would also be misleading to say that Cartesian scepticism has no effects outside the philosopher's study. For although the doubt of the First *Meditation* is itself temporary, it is meant to lead to a *permanent* reform of our epistemic practices, one that is by no means confined to first philosophy. Perhaps it is best to say Pyrrhonian scepticism is fundamentally *ethical*, whereas Cartesian doubt is of metaphysical and epistemological significance only.

Descartes' methodological intent explains his preference for the Standard Model, which is alone suitable for his methodological purposes. So does Sextus' ethical orientation explain his departure from the Model? No: there is no reason why an ethically directed sceptical stance should not have a doctrinal-prescriptive basis. (The Academic stance is a case in point, if Sextus is to be believed.) Sextus' preference for a non-standard structure is explained by his aim of avoiding *all* doctrinal commitments, which requires his stance to be practical all the way down.

The structural contrast accounts for 4 and 5: the topically specific, serial, and open-ended character of Pyrrhonian *epochê* versus the exclusively epistemological, once-and-for-all, and closed character of Cartesian doubt. But the structural contrast entails the strategic contrast between a pre emptive and a reactive deployment of sceptical arguments. So it also explains point 8: Sextus's linking of sceptical argumentation with real disagreement. However, while differences in significance and structure explain a good deal about the contrasts between the Pyrrhonian and Cartesian stances, they do not explain everything.

Descartes' methodological use of doubt explains why he *needs* the doubt to be selective, but not how it can be. Still less does it explain how it can be selective in the *specific way* that Descartes supposes. Further, while Sextus' reactive deployment of sceptical arguments explains why he connects them with real disagreement, we still lack an explanation of Descartes' entitlement to make use of outrageous sceptical hypotheses. Finally, the progressive character of Cartesian doubt, Descartes' preference for indistinguishability arguments, and the emergence of the external-world problem have not yet been addressed at all. We must look beyond generic features of the Standard Model to its specifically Cartesian articulation.

Why doesn't Descartes follow an Agrippan strategy, arguing that if our only reason for trusting in the reliability of the senses is itself dependent on sensory evidence, we have no non-circular way of validating our trust in them? Descartes is aware of this sceptical strategy, for he eventually defends his own rule of clear and distinct perception against a version of it (Arnauld's famous charge that Descartes' Divine guarantee theory, established with the aid of clear and distinct perception, is circular).

The key to Descartes' preferences with respect to sceptical arguments lies in their supposed selectivity. No strategy that threatens to bear equally on the sense and reason as sources of knowledge – and this obviously includes the Agrippan strategy – is suitable for inculcating the *original* doubt. Descartes' problem is to cast doubt on the reliability of the senses, not only in a way that does not require him to retain evidential commitments, but also in a way that does not invite extension to reason. Once his rule of clear and distinct perception is in place, it may need to be defended against Agrippan objections. But putting it in place requires a different approach.

To show that the senses do not yield certain knowledge, while leaving open the possibility that reason might, Descartes presents three obstacles, linked by two objections.

First Obstacle: The senses have often deceived me: round towers have appeared to me to be square, and so on. But if the senses are not completely reliable, they cannot yield certainty.

First Objection: This only shows that the senses do not always yield certainty, not that they never do. I am sitting in my dressing gown, in front of the fire, reading a book. I am not dealing with objects that are distant or otherwise hard to make out. In a case like this, there is no room for doubt.

Second Obstacle: I believe that I dream from time to time. But it is at least possible for a dream to replicate waking experience, down to the last detail. So going by sensory evidence alone, I cannot rule out the possibility that I am dreaming right now.

Second Objection: This only calls into question knowledge of particular complex objects. According to my conception of the role of the senses in thought, imagining (of which dreaming is a form) involves creatively recombining qualities that I have previously experienced. The certainty attaching to sciences such as physics and mathematics, which deal only with the most general characteristics of things and are indifferent to the existence of particular objects, remains intact.

Third Obstacle: My entire experience could be manipulated by God or (more piously) by an Evil Deceiver. It is possible that there is no external world, at least no world that is *anything like* the world as I understand it. (For example, it is possible that there is no *material* world.)

With the Third Obstacle, the external-world problem emerges in its most radical form, though the problem already takes an existential turn with the Second.

Now, while Descartes seeks an absolutely certain foundation for human knowledge, and while he thinks that some particular sciences, such as pure mathematics, are certain through and through, he does not suppose that everything we can rationally believe is absolutely certain. He is interested in degrees of certainty and the kinds of beliefs with which they are associated. Accordingly, the progress toward general doubt in the First *Meditation* is the mirror image of the reconstruction of human knowledge in *Meditations* Two to Six. Scepticism plays a *doubly* selective role, downgrading the senses in favor of reason and stratifying human beliefs according to the degree of certainty to which they are susceptible.

Descartes' first level errors (those involving round towers looking square, and so on) are entirely commonsensical. The case of dreaming is more complicated: while dreaming is a commonplace phenomenon, Descartes' conception of dreaming may be tendentious. But whatever we think of Cartesian dreaming, we can agree that deception by an Evil Deceiver is utterly unheard of. However, the Deceiver hypothesis (in its initial deceptive God version) only comes up at the level at which we are *already* accustomed to expect certainty: principally in mathematics. When our goal is certainty, even a logical possibility of error constitutes an obstacle: Descartes does not need reasons to think that he is actually the victim of demon deception. His epistemic target (and ultimate goal) legitimates the introduction of outrageous hypotheses.

Compare Descartes' progress towards general doubt with Sextus' procedure in the first four of the Ten Modes:

First Mode:	Who is the judge of truth: men or other animals?
Second Mode:	If men, which men in particular?
Third Mode:	If certain men, by what method, e.g. sense or faculty or combination thereof?
Fourth Mode:	If by a given method, in what circumstances or conditions (youth or age, sickness or health, awake or dreaming, etc.)?

The progression here is very different. Where Descartes confronts a vague and generic source of knowledge, "the senses," with a sequence of increasingly severe obstacles, Sextus considers a sequence of progressively narrower characterizations of the criterion of truth, each of which he confronts with the *same* obstacle. At each stage, Sextus argues that the different judges, faculties, or conditions generate systematically conflicting appearances, thereby seeming to establish that we cannot say how things are but only how they appear relative to something or other. He then deploys some variant of the Agrippan strategy to argue that we cannot escape relativity by privileging some particular set of appearances.[16] Because the obstacle is always the same, never more or less severe, Sextus' arguments are indifferent to degrees of certainty. The question on the table is always whether, in the face of conflicting appearances, we can rationally privilege some over others. And the answer is always "no."

The "flat" character of Pyrrhonian *epochê* goes hand-in-hand with Sextus' reactive deployment of sceptical arguments. Since Sextus has no interest in constructing a positive epistemology – indeed, he uses sceptical conclusions to oppose the very idea of epistemology – he has no use for arguments designed to distinguish degrees of certainty, or to sort beliefs according to them. Descartes favors indistinguishability arguments over Agrippan problems because the former are more readily adapted to the epistemic stratification he wants to reveal: the more outrageous the sceptical hypothesis, the more it takes in and the deeper it probes.

Descartes' relation to his goal of certainty is complex. Methodologically, the goal is vital, permitting the introduction of mere possibilities as reasonable grounds for doubt. On the other hand, the external world problem, once in place, is not tied to aspirations to certainty. The question is not whether I can be *certain* that I am not the victim of systematic deception but whether I have any reason whatsoever to think that I am not. Cartesian scepticism is *radical*. What makes this radicalization of the doubt possible? That such a question remains on the table shows that we have still not fully accounted for the emergence of external world scepticism.

IV DREAMERS, MADMEN, AND DOPPELGANGERS

Although the Deceiver hypothesis completes Descartes' general doubt, the dreaming argument introduces the ideas that make his radical conclusion possible. But dreaming is an ancient sceptical topic. We need to understand what is new in the way that Descartes handles it.

Sextus mentions dreaming *en passant* in the Fourth Mode. Thus:

Different appearances come about depending on sleeping or waking. When we are awake we view things differently from the way we do when we are asleep, and when asleep differently from the way we do when awake; so the existence or non-existence of the objects becomes not absolute but relative – relative to being asleep or awake. It is likely, then, that when asleep we will see things which are unreal in waking life, not unreal once and for all. For they exist in sleep, just as the contents of waking life exist even though they do not exist in sleep. (*PII* 1.104)

For Sextus, dreaming and waking belong with youth and age, or sickness and health, which also affect our experience in systematic ways. Sextus cites all these conflicting appearances in support of his accustomed relativity-lemma. Dreaming has no special significance.

Several features of Sextus's argument are worth noting.

(i)   *Occurrent persuasive equipollence.* While we are dreaming, dream-objects typically strike us as real. As Sextus says with reference to dreaming, "we assent to what is present in the present" (*PH* 1.113). Putatively epistemically "bad" states like dreaming can be as persuasive as putatively good states.

(ii)   *Cognitive lucidity.* Sextus does not suggest that dreaming involves mental confusion or any other kind of cognitive impairment. Youth and age, which are in the mix with dreaming and waking, are consistent with cognitive lucidity.

(iii)   *State-awareness symmetry.* Sextus does not pose Descartes' question, "How do I know that I am not dreaming now?" He seems content to concede that we know what state we are in: young or old, sick or well, awake or asleep. In this respect, the opposed states are epistemically on a par.

(iv)   *Content discrepancy.* Sextus takes it for granted that dreams differ in content from waking experiences.

(iv)   *Ontological neutrality.* Sextus does not distinguish dreaming from waking in terms of the existence and non-existence of the objects ostensibly presented in the two states. His suggestion seems to be that different conditions present different "worlds." The question of which is "real" is up for grabs.

Clearly, Sextus' "dreaming" argument is very different from Descartes'.

The sceptical considerations we encounter in the First *Meditation* are closer to those found in Cicero's *Academica*. And significantly, the topic of *Academica* II, in which Cicero defends Academic scepticism against the objections of Lucullus, is precisely that of *Meditation* I: whether the senses are a source of certain knowledge.

Cicero's use of dreaming differs from Sextus' in at least four ways. First, dreaming and allied phenomena loom much larger for Cicero than they do for Sextus. Secondly, Cicero distinguishes "non-perceiving" from "perceiving" states in ontological terms: in non-perceiving states, the objects that we ostensibly perceive do not exist. Thirdly, Cicero associates dreaming and waking with a very different range of state-pairs: not youth and age, but madness and sanity, drunkenness and sobriety. He also relates dreaming to the visions of the (supposedly) divinely inspired (of which dreams themselves may be an example). These associations link dreaming with cognitive impairment. It is not just that in dreams or visions we see things that aren't there: we are not fully lucid in our thinking. Fourthly, Cicero appears to concede that the lucid state involves greater cognitive powers. He writes:

As if anybody would deny that a man who has woken up thinks that he has been dreaming, or that one whose madness has subsided thinks that the things that he saw during his madness were not true. But that is not the point at issue; what we are asking is what these things looked like at the time when they were seen. (Acad. 2.88)[17]

On this commonsense view, when we are in a good state, we typically (though perhaps not absolutely invariably) have a strong and correct conviction that we are. In bad states, this is not so. This *state-awareness asymmetry* is plausible with respect to the states with which Cicero associates dreaming. When I am sane or sober, I generally firmly and correctly believe that I am. But the madman often thinks he is sane and drunks commonly entertain delusions of sobriety. Equally, when dreaming, I may think that I am really seeing things. But when I wake up, I will normally have no serious doubt that I have been dreaming. All that Cicero insists on is that, in a bad state, I can be *occurrently* misled, which is compatible with my errors being *reliably retrospectively identifiable*.

While only weakly sceptical, Cicero's arguments are sufficient for his purpose, which is to defend Carneades' doctrine that "probability" is sufficient for the needs of life. In Carneades' view, while no single impression yields certainty, impressions become more (or less) credible according to how they fit in (or fail to fit in) with subsequent impressions. By contrast, Cicero's anti-sceptics think that rational belief and action require a basis in certain knowledge conveyed by *individual impressions* (*kataleptic* impressions, as the Stoics call them). If the source of such certain knowledge is sense-perception, there must be particular perceptual episodes that are world-revealing and error-proof. Such episodes must exclude my being *occurrently* misled by a dream. It is not enough that I may *reasonably decide on the basis of further experience* that I was only dreaming. Such a retrospective decision exemplifies the kind of "probabilistic" reasoning that is the Academic *alternative* to intrinsically certain impressions.

Anticipating Descartes, Cicero attacks sense-certainty with indistinguishability arguments. However, Cicero offers two distinct kinds of argument, each exploiting its own kind of "indistinguishability." One kind is phenomenological and epistemic, the other content-related. With respect to epistemic indistinguishability, Cicero's point is that impressions carry no infallible hallmark of veridicality. It is often suggested that genuine perceptions have a superior vividness, or feeling of reality, that dreams lack. Cicero replies that, for as long as they last, non-veridical modes of experience may be just as persuasive as veridical modes.

This argument does *not* require Cicero to hold that dreams might be *identical in content* to waking perceptions. So far as I can judge, the possibility of a dream's fully replicating waking experience never crosses his mind. Rather, when he appeals to the possibility of content-identical experiences, he associates such experiences not with dreams, where we "see" things that don't exist, but with perceptions of *objects that cannot be told apart*: eggs, identical twins, and such. This is his *second* type of indistinguishability argument. Call it his *doppelganger* argument.

Dreams and doppelgangers involve different kinds of error. Dreams involve existential error. In my cups, I am not wrong about what I think I see (pink rats): my error is to suppose that the rats exist. If I cannot (at the time) detect my error, this is because (in my impaired state) my experience is *just like seeing*. Cases of content-indistinguishability involve errors of *identification*. I see someone who may *be* Gaius, though I can't be sure since I can't tell him from his twin Titus. Seeing Gaius is just like seeing Titus. Since any object *might* have a doppelganger, I can never be certain, on the basis of a single perception, which particular object I am seeing. In one case, then, I can't distinguish *seeing* from *seeming to see*. In the other, I can't distinguish *what I see* from something *just like it*.[18]

Now like Cicero, Descartes distinguishes waking from dreaming in terms of the existence or non-existence of the objects we think we see. But there the similarity ends. Descartes does not initially associate the dreaming/waking contrast with *anything* else. Indeed, Descartes explicitly *distances* dreaming from madness. He mentions the possibility of madness as an obstacle to sense-based certainty even in ideal conditions of perception, but only to dismiss it. He would, he says, be mad to take this possibility seriously (CSM 13). This dismissal of the madness is mandated by his intention to use scepticism selectively, stacking the deck in favor of "reason" while stratifying the doubt. Secondly, detaching dreaming from madness lets Descartes treat dreaming as a cognitively lucid state: we can think in our dreams, not just dream that we think. If our thoughts do not concern the existence of particular objects, ostensibly seen, they can amount to knowledge, for all the dreaming argument has shown.

How is even a limited existential doubt made possible? For Descartes, in contrast to Cicero, dreaming and waking are epistemically on a par, phenomenologically and epistemically. But Descartes makes a further move. Not only can dreams be as vivid and persuasive as waking experiences, they can *reproduce their content*. Descartes' dreaming argument is thus a novel hybrid, involving elements from Cicero's two kinds of indistinguishability argument. Cartesian dreaming *detaches the possibility of content-identical experiences from causation by indistinguishable objects*. Dreaming becomes a lucid state in which no real objects correspond to those ostensibly perceived, a state that is *comprehensively* indistinguishable from veridical perception.

There is a dramatic change between the first and second levels of Cartesian doubt. At the first level, we make errors about how objects are: not because they are utterly indistinguishable but because they are indistinguishable in the circumstances. This argument is weaker than Cicero's doppelganger argument. But at the second level we face the possibility of existential error, arising not from *experiences of doppelgangers* but from *doppelganger experiences*.

We can summarize the similarities and differences between dreaming arguments in Table 15.2.

Although a source of existential error, Cartesian dreaming is a cognitively lucid state not intrinsically incompatible with the knowledge of general facts (not implying the existence of the

Table 15.2. *Similarities and differences between dreaming arguments*

	Sextus: dreaming	Cicero: dreaming	Cicero: doppelgangers	Descartes: dreaming	Descartes: demon deception
Allied states	Dreaming/waking associated with youth/age, sickness/health	Madness, intoxication, visions	None	None (initially)	Dreaming
Existential error in bad state?	?	Yes (limited)	No	Yes (limited)	Yes (total)
Bad state lucidity?	Yes	No	Yes	Yes	Yes
Good/bad symmetry?	Yes	No	N/A	Yes	Yes
Occurrent equipollence?	Yes	Yes	N/A	Yes	Yes
Content identity?	No	No	Yes	Yes	Yes

particular objects ostensibly seen). But are there *particular* facts that we know, whether we are awake or dreaming? Yes: we know how things appear; or better, we have *knowledge of facts about sensory appearances*. Descartes' transformed dreaming argument is the pivot of his First *Meditation* scepticism because it serves to introduce the conception of "experience" that is the essential foil for knowledge of external things.[19] Dreaming shows that *the senses alone* are incapable of providing knowledge of external reality.[20]

The stage is set for the final extension and radicalization of the doubt. Descartes' dismissal of madness notwithstanding, dreams and the visions of madmen have something in common: both arise from the spontaneous activities of the brain and animal spirits, without the aid of distal objects. But while on this commonsense conception dreams remain *causally* anchored in the external (material) world, the dreaming argument suggests a notion of experience that can be *conceptually* disconnected from any idea of material existence. Experience in a demon world is *dreaming without a body*, or even a brain. This is how Descartes' own body becomes one more external object or thing "without the mind," a conception of the human person that neither Sextus nor Cicero ever contemplates. The dreaming argument opens the way for the Evil Deceiver, thus a possibility of total existential error that no amount of merely experiential knowledge can exclude.

V CONCLUSION

Everyone knows that Pyrrhonian and Cartesian scepticism differ in significance. Whereas the Pyrrhonian stance is part of a way of life – life without philosophy or theoretical convictions of any kind – the Cartesian stance is provisionally inculcated for methodological purposes, within the context of inquiry into first philosophy. Less widely recognized is their difference in structure. The Pyrrhonian stance does not conform to the Standard Model, whereas the Cartesian stance is exemplary of it. Less appreciated still is the way in which, within the structure of the Standard Model, Descartes transforms ancient sceptical topics concerning perceptual error. The vehicle of this transformation is Descartes' new dreaming argument. This argument points towards a notion of perceptual experience that is conceptually unconnected with commitments to the existence of material things. This conception of experience permits the construction of a sceptical problem not to be found in Sextus or Cicero: that concerning our knowledge of the existence, and not just the nature, of the external world.

The historical story is therefore an important philosophical lesson. Many contemporary epistemologists continue to think of external world scepticism as an "intuitive" problem, emerging from reflection on apparent platitudes concerning our knowledge of our surroundings. As our comparison of Descartes with the ancient sceptics has revealed, this is dubious. The Cartesian problem is an invention, not a discovery.

NOTES

1   I follow the translation of Annas and Barnes [40] except where noted. Annas and Barnes change the title of the work from *Outlines of Pyrrhonism* to *Outlines of Scepticism* on the grounds that the original title may not be understood by modern readers. I am grateful to Richard Bett for very helpful discussion of matters of translation.

2   I follow the translation of Cottingham, Stoothoff, and Murdoch [416], vol. 2. References given in the text by "CSM" and page number.

3   Burnyeat [425]. Burnyeat's paper, which is extraordinarily rich and touches on every essential point concerning the preconditions for the emergence of the Cartesian problem, has influenced me greatly.

4   Descartes' problem just might be anticipated by St. Augustine. See *Against the Academics*, 3.11.24. At the opening of this chapter Augustine's sceptical interlocutor asks, "How do you know that the world exists ... if the senses are deceptive" (tr. from King [58]). However, Augustine attaches no special importance to this question and the discussion goes nowhere. Nor is it clear that he understands the problem in precisely Descartes' way. Augustine's anticipation of Descartes' problem, if that is what it is, is not fully Cartesian. It would be an interesting exercise to add Augustine's version of the dream argument to those analyzed in section IV.

5   The Cyrenaics may be an exception.

6   Burnyeat [425], 37.

7   I will use "doctrinal scepticism" to refer both to sceptical theses and to the outlook of philosophers who accept them. This ambiguity, typical of "isms," should be harmless.

8   Descartes' account of error shows that he has a strongly voluntaristic view of belief. Errors "depend on both the intellect and the will

simultaneously ... [A]ll that the intellect does is to enable me to perceive the ideas which are subjects for possible judgments" (CSM 39).

9 *To panti logoi logon ison antikeisthai.* Annas and Barnes give: "The chief constitutive principle of scepticism is *the claim* that to every account an equal account is opposed; for it is from this, we think, that we come to hold no beliefs" (*PH* 1.12, my emphasis).

"Claim" suggests commitment to a thesis. I suspect the influence of the Standard Model. Thanks to Richard Bett for discussion of this important passage.

10 Fogelin [433], p. 116. See also Hankinson [68]. The terminology of "Challenging" and "Dialectical" Modes is Fogelin's. Hankinson [68], p. 182 marks the same division with "Material" and "Formal."

11 See Paul Woodruff, Chapter 11 "The Pyrrhonian Modes," which also speaks of an apparent mismatch between the character of the Modes and the purpose for which Sextus seems to intend them.

12 Stough [73], p. 77.

13 In this, he is the precursor of Hume and Wittgenstein.

14 Hence their starting point: humans versus other animals. Also noteworthy is Sextus' choice for his first Agrippan argument: the "biased judge" version of the circularity problem: "[W]e shall not be able ourselves to decide between our own appearances and those of other animals, being ourselves part of the dispute" (*PH* 1.59).

15 *Against the Logicians* Book 1 (=*M* 7), section 443. I follow the translation of Bett [42].

16 Sextus sometimes emphasizes the threat of brute assumption, sometimes that of circular reasoning, and sometimes that of infinite regress.

17 I follow the translation of Rackham [25].

18 In the doppelganger argument, the question of persuasive equipollence doesn't come up in a straightforward way, unless we postulate a feeling of recognition.

19 Not fully explicit until the Third *Meditation*.

20 On the importance for Descartes of the idea that knowledge might come from "the senses alone," I have profited from an as yet unpublished paper by Barry Stroud, presented at a conference on scepticism at the University of Edinburgh, May 2008.

BIBLIOGRAPHY

This bibliography has two aims: to provide details of all scholarly works referred to in the essays in this volume, and to offer a comprehensive (though not exhaustive) survey of scholarship in the area. With respect to the latter goal, given the likely readership of this volume, there is a bias towards scholarship in English. For a number of reasons, there is also a bias towards works published in roughly the last thirty years.

The bibliography is organized into sections, as shown in the Table of Contents below. Some works might naturally belong in more than one section. In some cases this is explicitly indicated: at the end of some sections, a short list of relevant works listed in other sections is appended. But it would be impossible to do this in every case, and so it should be borne in mind that the divisions are not foolproof. Nonetheless, this layout is intended, and may be expected, to be more useful than a single long list with no thematic divisions.

CONTENTS

I SOURCE MATERIALS IN THE ORIGINAL LANGUAGES

1.1 Editions of Greek and Latin texts, collections of fragments

1.1.1 Texts of Sextus Empiricus

The standard text of Sextus Empiricus is the four-volume Teubner edition, *Sexti Empirici Opera*, which consists of:

[1] Vol. I, *Purrhôneiôn Hupotupôseis (Outlines of Pyrrhonism)* in 3 books, ed. H. Mutschmann, rev. J. Mau (Leipzig: Teubner, 1958)

[2] Vol. II, *Adversus Dogmaticos* in 5 books (=*M* 7–11: *Against the Logicians, Against the Physicists, Against the Ethicists*), ed. H. Mutschmann (Leipzig: Teubner, 1914, reprinted 1984)

[3] Vol. III, *Adversus Mathematicos* in 6 books (=*M* 1–6: *Against the Grammarians, Rhetoricians, Geometers, Arithmeticians, Astrologers, Musicians*), ed. J. Mau (Leipzig: Teubner, 1961)

[4] Vol. IV, *Indices*, collected by K. Janáček (Leipzig: Teubner, 1962)

An expanded edition of vol. IV was published as:

[5] Janáček, K. 2000 *Sexti Empirici Indices* (Florence: Leo S. Olschki)

Vols. I–III are out of print; Mutschmann's original 1912 version of vol. I (*PH*) can be found online at www.archive.org/details/rsoperarecensuito1sextuoft

A more recent edition of *Against the Musicians* is:

[6] Davidson Greaves, D. 1986 *Sextus Empiricus. Against the Musicians (Adversus Musicos)* (Lincoln/London: University of Nebraska Press). With translation, introduction and notes.

A Greek text of Sextus can also be found in the four volume Loeb translation by R. G. Bury, see below [39]; however, with rare exceptions Bury follows the earlier

[7] *Sexti Empirici Opera*, ed. I. Bekker (Berlin: Reimer, 1842), which the Teubner edition generally supersedes. Also of interest is:

[8] Fabricius, J. A. *Sexti Empirici Opera Graece et Latine*, originally published in 1718 and reissued in a two volume revised version in 1840–1842 (Leipzig: Kuehniana); besides the text itself, this includes Latin translations by Stephanus and Hervetus as well as explanatory notes (also in Latin) that are occasionally very helpful.

1.1.2 Editions of the fragments of other Pyrrhonian and Academic sceptics

[9] Barigazzi, A. 1966 *Favorino di Arelate. Opere* (Florence: F. Le Monnier). With Italian commentary

[10] Decleva Caizzi, F. 1981 *Pirrone: Testimonianze* (Naples: Bibliopolis). With Italian translation and commentary.

[11] Di Marco, M. 1989 *Timone di Fliunte: Silli* (Rome: Edizioni dell' Ateneo). With Italian translation and commentary.

[12] Mette, H. J. 1984 "Zwei Akademiker heute: Krantor von Soloi und Arkesilaos von Pitane" *Lustrum* 26: 7–94.

[13] Mette, H. J. 1985 "Weitere Akademiker heute: Von Lakydes bis zu Kleitomachos" *Lustrum* 27: 39–148.

[14] Mette, H. J. 1986–87 "Philon von Larissa und Antiochus von Ascalon" *Lustrum* 28: 9–63. The section on Philo is, however, superseded by the Appendix to Brittain [195].

1.1.3 Editions of texts or fragments of other authors or schools, or of multiple authors or schools including sceptics

[15] Bastianini G. and Sedley D. N. 1995 Anonymous Commentary on Plato's *Theaetetus*, in *Corpus dei Papiri Filosofici Greci e Latini Parte III: Commentari* (Florence: Olschki), pp. 227–562. With Italian translation and commentary.

[16] Casevitz, M. and Babut, D. 2002 Plutarque. *Œuvres morales. Traité 72. Sur les notions communes, contre les Stoïciens* (*On Common Conceptions*) (Paris: Belles Lettres). With French translation and commentary.

Reviewed by:

[17] Boys-Stones, G. R. 2004 *Classical Review* 54: 338–40.

[18] Casevitz, M. and Babut, D. 2004 Plutarque. *Œuvres morales. Traité 70. Sur les contradictions des Stoïciens* (*On Stoic Contradictions*) (Paris: Belles Lettres). With French translation and commentary.

[19] Chiesara, M. L. 2001 *Aristocles of Messene: Testimonia and Fragments* (Oxford: Oxford University Press). With translation and commentary.

[20] Deichgräber, K. 1965 *Die Griechische Empirikerschule: Sammlung der Fragmente und Darstellung der Lehre*, 2nd edn. (Berlin/Zürich: Weidmann). Fragments of the Empirical school of medicine plus explanatory essay in German.

[21] Diels, H. 1901 *Poetarum Philosophorum Fragmenta* (Berlin: Weidmann). Includes fragments of Timon.

[22] Dorandi, T. 1991 *Filodemo: Storia dei Filosofi: Platone e l'Accademia* (*P. Herc. 1021 e 164*) (Naples: Bibliopolis). With Italian translation and commentary.

[23] Lloyd-Jones, H. and Parsons, P. 1983 *Supplementum Hellenisticum* (Berlin and New York: de Gruyter). Includes fragments of Timon.

[24] Long, A. A. and Sedley, D. N. 1987 *The Hellenistic Philosophers* (Cambridge: Cambridge University Press), 2 vols. Texts organized by schools and themes: translations and philosophical commentary in vol. 1, Greek and Latin texts and philological commentary in vol. 2.

[25] Rackham, H. 1933 *Cicero, De Natura Deorum and Academica* (Cambridge, MA: Harvard University Press, Loeb Classical Library). With translation (however, the recent translation of Brittain [56] is much better).

[26] Spencer, W. G. 1935–38 *Celsus, De Medicina* (Cambridge, MA: Harvard University Press, Loeb Classical Library), 3 vols. With translation.

[27] Taylor, C. C. W. 1999 *The Atomists, Leucippus and Democritus: Fragments*. With translation and commentary (Toronto: University of Toronto Press).

[28] Tecusan, M. 2004 *The Fragmens of the Methodists I: Methodism Outside Soranus* (Leiden/Boston: Brill). Fragments with English translation and introduction.

[29] Westerink, L. G. 1990 ed. *Prolégomènes à la philosophie de Platon* (Paris: Belles Lettres).

For texts of Galen, see 4.5.1.

For texts of Christian and post-ancient authors, see 4.6.2.

1.2 *Linguistic and other philological studies*

1.2.1 Karel Janáček

A key figure in this area is Karel Janáček. Janáček's major works are:

[30] Janáček, K. 1948 *Prolegomena to Sextus Empiricus* (Olomouc: Nákladem Palackého University).

[31] Janáček, K. 1972 *Sextus Empiricus' Sceptical Methods* (Prague: Universita Karlova).

He also wrote a great number of short essays, mostly in English or German, which have recently been collected and reprinted (and, for the few originally in Czech or Russian, translated into German) in:

[32] Janáček, K., 2008 *Studien zu Sextus Empiricus, Diogenes Laertius und zur pyrrhonischen Skepsis*, J. Janda and F. Karfik eds. (Berlin/New York: de Gruyter).

Perhaps the most significant of these, which is cited separately in this volume, is:

[33] Janáček, K., 1963 "Die Hauptscrift des Sextus Empiricus als Torso erhalten?" *Philologus* 107: 271–77.

For a retrospective on Janáček's work, see:

[34] Janda, J. 2006 "Karel Janáček, Sextus Empiricus und der neupyrrhonische Skeptizismus" *Acta Universitatis Carolinae Philologica* 1 (Graecolatina Pragensia XXI), pp. 29–49. This piece includes a complete bibliography of Janáček's works on Sextus and Pyrrhonism. On Janáček's methods see also Barnes [219], sec. X; Bett [41], Appendix C.

1.2.2 Other wide-ranging studies

Other significant and wide-ranging philological studies are:

[35] Blomqvist, J., 1968 "Textkritisches zu Sextus Empiricus" *Eranos* 66: 73–100.
[36] Heintz, W. ed. Harder, R. 1932 *Studien zu Sextus Empiricus* (Halle: Max Niemeyer Verlag).

1.2.3 Specific topics

On specific topics see also:

[37] Blomqvist, J. 1974 "Die Skeptika des Sextus Empiricus" *Grazer Beiträge* 2: 7–14.
[38] Perilli, L. 2005 "'Quantum Coniectare (non) Licet.' Menodotus between Sextus Empiricus (P. 1.222) and Diogenes Laertius (9.116)" *Mnemosyne* 58: 286–93

2 TRANSLATIONS AND COMMENTARIES

2.1 Sextus Empiricus

The only complete English translation of Sextus is that of:

[39] Bury, R. G. 1933–49 (Cambridge, MA: Harvard University Press, Loeb Classical Library), 4 vols. (On the facing Greek text see under 1.1 above.) Vol. 1 contains *PH*, vol. 2 *M* 7–8, vol. 3 *M* 9–11, vol. 4 *M* 1–6. But this translation is outmoded and philosophically unreliable, and should be avoided whenever a more recent substitute is available. Currently available are:
[40] Annas, J. and Barnes, J. 2000 Sextus Empiricus, *Outlines of Scepticism*, 2nd edn. (Cambridge: Cambridge University Press).
[41] Bett, R. 1997 Sextus Empiricus, *Against the Ethicists (Adversus Mathematicos XI)* (Oxford: Clarendon Press). With commentary.

[42] Bett, R. 2005 Sextus Empiricus, *Against the Logicians* (Cambridge: Cambridge University Press).

Reviewed by:

[43] Machuca, D. 2008 *Bryn Mawr Classical Review* 2008.01.11 (online).
[44] Blank, D. L. 1998 Sextus Empiricus, *Against the Grammarians (Adversus Mathematicos I)* (Oxford: Clarendon Press). With commentary.
[45] Mates, B. 1996 *The Skeptic Way:* Sextus Empiricus' *Outlines of Pyrrhonism* (New York: Oxford University Press). With commentary.

See also Davidson Greaves [6].
   Translations of Sextus into other languages include:

[46] Bergua Cavero, J. 1997 Sexto Empírico, *Contra los profesores libros I–VI* (Madrid: Editorial Gredos).
[47] Flückiger, H. 1998 *Gegen die Dogmatiker (M 7–11)* (St. Augustine: Academia).
[48] Hossenfelder, M. 1999 *Grundriss der pyrrhonischen Skepsis (PH)*, 3rd edn. (Frankfurt: Suhrkamp).
[49] Jürss, F. 2001 Sextus Empiricus, *Gegen die Wissenschaftler, Buch 1–6 (M 1–6)* (Würzburg: Königshausen & Neumann).
[50] Pellegrin, P. 2002 Sextus Empiricus, *Contre les professeurs* (Paris: Éditions du Seuil). Includes Mau's text [3] with occasional deviations.

Reviewed by:

[51] Machuca, D. 2004 *Ancient Philosophy* 24: 503–10.
[52] Russo, A. 1972 *Contro i matematici. Libri I-VI* (Rome: Laterza).
[53] Spinelli, E. 1995 Sesto Empirico, *Contro gli etici* (Naples: Bibliopolis). With commentary; includes Mutschmann's text [2].
[54] Spinelli, E. 2000 Sesto Empirico, *Contro gli astrologi* (Naples: Bibliopolis). With commentary; includes Mau's text [3] with very occasional deviations.

2.2 Other authors

[55] Barnes, J. 1975 Aristotle: *Posterior Analytics* (Oxford: Clarendon Press) (2nd edn. 2002). With commentary.
[56] Brittain, C. 2006 Cicero, *On Academic Scepticism* (Indianapolis/ Cambridge: Hackett). With introduction and notes.
[57] Goulet-Cazé, M.-O. 1999 Diogène Laërce: *vies et doctrines des philosophes illustres* (Paris: LGF, Livres de poche).

[58] King, P. 1995 Augustine, *Against the Academicians and The Teacher* (Indianapolis/Cambridge: Hackett). Includes excerpts from other texts relevant to Augustine's attitude to scepticism.

[59] Marcus, R. 1953 Philo, *Questions and Answers on Genesis*, translated from the ancient Armenian version of the original Greek (Cambridge, MA: Harvard University Press, Loeb Classical Library, Philo Supplement I).

For translations of: (a) Galen, see 4.5.1; (b) post-ancient and other Christian authors, see 4.6.2; except for Descartes, who is under 4.7.1.

See also under 1.1, some of which texts include translations and commentaries.

3 SECONDARY LITERATURE: GENERAL

3.1 General studies of ancient scepticism

[60] Bailey, A. 2002 *Sextus Empiricus and Pyrrhonean Scepticism* (Oxford: Clarendon Press). (Includes discussion of Academics, despite its title. This is also true of Dumont [64] and Robin [70] below.)

[61] Brochard, V. 1923 *Les Sceptiques grecs* (Paris: Vrin). Originally published 1887; reissued 2002 (Paris: LGF, Livre de Poche).

[62] Chiesara, M. L. 2003 *Storia dello scetticismo greco* (Turin: Einaudi).

[63] Dal Pra, M. 1975 *Lo scetticismo greco*, 2nd edn. (Rome: Laterza).

[64] Dumont, J. P. 1972 *Le Scepticisme et le Phénomène. Essai sur la signification et les origines du pyrrhonisme* (Paris: Vrin).

[65] Frede, M. 1997 "The Sceptics" in D. Furley ed., *Routledge History of Philosophy*, vol. II, *From Aristotle to Augustine* (London: Routledge), pp. 253–86.

[66] Gigante, M. 1981 *Scetticismo e epicureismo* (Naples: Bibliopolis).

[67] Goedeckemeyer, A. 1905 *Die Geschichte des griechischen Skeptizismus* (Leipzig: Dieterich'sche).

[68] Hankinson, R. J. 1995. *The Sceptics* (London/New York: Routledge).

[69] Ricken, F. 1994 *Antike Skeptiker* (Munich: Beck).

[70] Robin, L. 1944 *Pyrrhon et le Scepticisme grec* (Paris: Presses Universitaires de France). Reissued 1980 (New York/London: Garland Publishing).

[71] Sedley, D. N. 1983 "The Motivation of Greek Skepticism" in Burnyeat [78], pp. 9–29.

[72] Spinelli, E. 2005 *Questioni scettiche. Letture introduttive al pirronismo antico* (Rome: Lithos).

[73] Stough, C. 1969 *Greek Skepticism* (Berkeley/Los Angeles: University of California Press).

Reviewed by:

[74] Frede, M. 1973 *Journal of Philosophy* 70: 805–10.

3.2 Collections of articles on multiple topics, or multi-author studies, in which ancient scepticism is a main or the main focus

[75] Algra, K., Barnes, J., Mansfeld, J., and Schofield, M. eds. 1999 *The Cambridge History of Hellenistic Philosophy* (Cambridge: Cambridge University Press).
[76] Barnes, J., Brunschwig, J., Burnyeat, M., and Schofield, M. eds. 1982 *Science and Speculation: Studies in Hellenistic Theory and Practice* (Cambridge: Cambridge University Press).
[77] Brunschwig, J. 1994 *Papers in Hellenistic Philosophy* (Cambridge: Cambridge University Press).
[78] Burnyeat, M. F. ed. 1983 *The Skeptical Tradition* (Berkeley/Los Angeles/ London: University of California Press).
[79] Burnyeat, M. and Frede, M. eds. 1997 *The Original Sceptics* (Indianapolis/Cambridge: Hackett).
[80] Everson, S. ed. 1990 *Epistemology: Companions to Ancient Thought 1* (Cambridge: Cambridge University Press).
[81] Giannantoni, G. ed. 1981 *Lo scetticismo antico* (Naples: Bibliopolis), 2 vols.

Review essay by:

[82] Stopper, M. R. 1983 "Schizzi Pirroniani" *Phronesis* 28: 265–97.
[83] Görler, W. 1994 "Ältere Pyrrhonismus, Jüngere Akademie, Antiochos aus Askalon" in H. Flashar ed., *Grundriss der Geschichte der Philosophie, Die Philosophie der Antike*, Bd. 4, *Die hellenistische Philosphie* (Basel: Schwabe), pp. 719–989.
[84] Long, A. A. 2006 *From Epicurus to Epictetus: Studies in Hellenistic and Roman Philosophy* (Oxford: Clarendon Press).
[85] Schofield, M., Burnyeat, M., and Barnes, J. eds. 1980 *Doubt and Dogmatism: Studies in Hellenistic Epistemology* (Oxford: Oxford University Press).
[86] Sihvola, J. ed. 2000 *Ancient Scepticism and the Sceptical Tradition*, Acta Philosophica Fennica (Helsinki: Philosophical Society of Finland), vol. 66.
[87] Striker, G. 1996 *Essays on Hellenistic Epistemology and Ethics* (Cambridge: Cambridge University Press).
[88] Voelke, A. J. ed. 1990 *Le scepticisme antique: perspectives historiques et systématiques*, Cahiers de la Revue de théologie et de philosophie 15 (Genève).

3.3 Other studies partly or wholly about topics other than ancient scepticism, but of relevance

[89] Allen, J. 2001 *Inference from Signs: Ancient Debates About the Nature of Evidence* (Oxford: Clarendon Press).

[90] Annas, J. 1990 "Stoic Epistemology" in Everson [80], pp. 184–203.

[91] Annas, J. 1992 "Plato the Sceptic" in *Oxford Studies in Ancient Philosophy*, suppl. vol. 3, pp. 43–72. Revised version in P. Vander Waerdt 1994 *The Socratic Movement* (Ithaca/London: Cornell University Press), pp. 309–40.

[92] Annas, J. 1993 *The Morality of Happiness* (New York: Oxford University Press).

[93] Bett, R. 1999 "Reactions to Aristotle in the Greek Sceptical Traditions" *Méthexis* 12: 17–34.

[94] Bett, R. 2006 "Socrates and the Sceptics" in S. Ahbel-Rappe and R. Kamtekar eds., *A Companion to Socrates* (Oxford: Blackwell), pp. 298–311.

[95] Bonazzi, M. 2003 *Academici e Platonici* (Milano: LED).

[96] Bonazzi, M. 2003 "Un dibattito tra academici e platonici sull'eredità di Platone. La testimonianza del *Commentario anonimo* al Teeteto" in *Papiri filosofici. Miscellanea di studi* IV (Florence: Olschki), pp. 41–74.

[97] Brennan, T. 1996 "Reasonable Impressions in Stoicism" *Phronesis* 41: 318–34.

[98] Brennan, T. 2005 *The Stoic Life* (Oxford: Clarendon Press).

[99] Dillon, J. 1977 *The Middle Platonists* (London: Duckworth).

[100] Dillon, J. 2003 *The Heirs of Plato: A Study of the Old Academy 347–274 BC* (Oxford: Clarendon Press).

[101] Dorandi, T. 1991 *Ricerche sulla cronologia dei filosofi ellenistici* (Stuttgart: Teubner).

[102] Ferrary, J.-L. 1988 *Philhellénisme et impérialisme* (Rome: École française de Rome).

[103] Frede, M. 1983 "Stoics and Sceptics on Clear and Distinct Impressions" in Burnyeat [78], pp. 65–94.

[104] Frede, M. 1999 "Stoic Epistemology" in Algra *et al.* [75], pp. 295–322.

[105] Hadot, I. 2005 *Arts libéraux et philosophie dans la pensée antique*, 2nd edn. (Paris: Vrin).

[106] Hadot, P. 2002 *What is Ancient Philosophy?* (Cambridge, MA: Harvard University Press), trans. M. Chase. Original French publication 1995.

[107] Inwood, B. 1985 *Ethics and Human Action in Early Stoicism* (Oxford: Clarendon Press).

[108] Ioppolo, A.-M. 1986 *Opinione e Scienza* (Naples: Bibliopolis).

Review essays by:

[109] Annas, J. 1988 "The Heirs of Socrates" *Phronesis* 23.1: 100–12 and
[110] Maconi, H. 1988 "Nova Non Philosophandi Philosophia" *Oxford Studies in Ancient Philosophy* 6: 231–53.
[111] Lévy, C. 1993 "Le concept de *doxa* des Stoïciens à Philon d'Alexandrie" in J. Brunschwig and M. Nussbaum eds., *Passions and Perceptions* (Cambridge: Cambridge University Press), pp. 250–84.
[112] Long, A. 1974 *Hellenistic Philosophy: Stoics, Epicureans, Sceptics* (London: Duckworth). Reprinted with updated bibliography by University of California Press, 1986.
[113] Long, A. A. 1988 "Socrates in Hellenistic Philosophy" *Classical Quarterly* 38.1: 150–71.
[114] Nussbaum, M. 1994 *The Therapy of Desire: Theory and Practice in Hellenistic Ethics* (Princeton: Princeton University Press).
[115] Perin, C. 2005 "Stoic Epistemology and the Limits of Externalism" *Ancient Philosophy* 25: 383–401.
[116] Reed, B. 2002 "The Stoics' Account of the Cognitive Impression" *Oxford Studies in Ancient Philosophy* 23: 147–80.
[117] Sharples, R. 1996 *Stoics, Epicureans and Sceptics: An Introduction to Hellenistic Philosophy* (London/New York: Routledge).
[118] Striker, G. 1990 "The Problem of the Criterion" in Everson [80], pp. 143–60.
[119] Striker, G. 1996 "*Kritêrion tês alêtheias*" in Striker [87], pp. 22–76. Originally published in German 1974.
[120] Striker, G. 1996 "*Ataraxia*: Happiness as Tranquillity" in Striker [87], pp. 183–95. Originally published 1990.
[121] Warren, J. 2002 *Epicurus and Democritean Ethics: An Archaeology of Ataraxia* (Cambridge: Cambridge University Press).
[122] Woodruff, P. 1986 "The Sceptical Side of Plato's Method" *Revue Internationale de Philosophie* 40: 22–37.
[123] Zeller, E. 1909 *Die Philosophie der Griechen in ihrer geschichtlichen Entwicklung*, Pt. 3, vol. II, 4th edn. (Leipzig: Reisland).

4 SECONDARY LITERATURE: PARTICULAR PHILOSOPHERS AND TOPICS

4.1 Antecedents to Greek scepticism

[124] Barnes, J. 1976 "Aristotle, Menaechmus, and Circular Proof" *Classical Quarterly* 70: 278–92.
[125] Barnes, J. 1987 "An Aristotelian Way with Scepticism" in Mohan Matthen ed., *Aristotle Today* (Edmonton: Academic), pp. 51–76.

[126] Brunschwig, J. 1996 "Le fragment DK 70B 1 de Métrodore de Chio" in K. A. Algra, P. W. van der Horst, and D. T. Runia eds., *Polyhistory: Studies in the History and Historiography of Greek Philosophy Presented to Jaap Mansfeld on his 60th Birthday* (New York/Leiden: Brill), pp. 21–40.

[127] Brunschwig, J. 2002 "Democritus and Xeniades" in V. Caston and Daniel W. Graham eds., *Presocratic Philosophy: Essays in Honor of Alexander Mourelatos* (Aldershot: Ashgate), pp 159–67.

[128] Burnyeat, M. F. 1976 "Protagoras and Self-Refutation in Plato's *Theaetetus*" *Philosophical Review* 85: 172–95. Reprinted in Everson [80], pp. 39–59.

[129] Burnyeat, M. F. (unpublished) "All the World's a Stage Painting: Scenery, Optics and Greek Epistemology."

[130] DeLacy, P. 1958 "*Ou mallon* and the Antecedents of Ancient Scepticism" *Phronesis* 3: 59–71.

[131] Fine, G. 1998 "Plato's Refutation of Protagoras in the *Theaetetus*" *Apeiron* 31.3: 201–34.

[132] Fine, G. 1998 "Relativism and Self-Refutation: Plato, Protagoras, and Burnyeat" in Jyl Gentzler ed., *Method in Ancient Philosophy* (Oxford: Clarendon Press), pp. 138–63.

[133] Irwin, T. 1988 *Aristotle's First Principles* (Oxford: Clarendon Press).

[134] Lee, M. 2005 *Epistemology after Protagoras: Responses to Relativism in Plato, Aristotle, and Democritus* (Oxford: Clarendon Press).

[135] Long, A. A. 1981 "Aristotle and the History of Greek Scepticism" in Dominic O'Meara ed., *Studies in Aristotle* (Washington, DC: Catholic University Press), pp. 79–106. Revised version in Long [84], pp. 43–69.

[136] Sedley, D. 2004 *The Midwife of Platonism: Text and Subtext in Plato's Theaetetus* (Oxford: Clarendon Press).

[137] Svavarsson, S. H. 2009 "Plato on Forms and Conflicting Appearances: The Argument of *Phaedo* 74a9-c6" *Classical Quarterly* 59.1: 60–74.

[138] Taylor, C. C. W. 1980 "All perceptions are true" in Schofield *et al.* [85], pp. 105–24.

[139] Tsouna, V. 1998 *The Epistemology of the Cyrenaic School* (Cambridge/New York: Cambridge University Press).

Also relevant is Brunschwig [152].

4.2 Pyrrho and early Pyrrhonism

[140] Ausland, H. 1989 "On the Moral Origin of the Pyrrhonian Philosophy" *Elenchos* 10: 359–434.

[141] Bett, R. 1994 "What Did Pyrrho Think about 'The Nature of the Divine and the Good'?" *Phronesis* 39: 303–37.

[142] Bett, R. 1994 "Aristocles on Timon on Pyrrho: The Text, its Logic and its Credibility" *Oxford Studies in Ancient Philosophy* 12: 137–81.

[143] Bett, R. 2000 *Pyrrho, his Antecedents, and his Legacy* (Oxford: Oxford University Press).

Reviewed by:

[144] Castagnoli, L. 2002, *Ancient Philosophy* 22: 443–57.

[145] Bett, R. 2002 "Pyrrho" in E. Zalta ed., *Stanford Encyclopedia of Philosophy*, online: http://plato.stanford.edu/archives/fall2002/entries/pyrrho/, revised version 2006, http://plato.stanford.edu/archives/sum2006/entries/pyrrho/

[146] Bett, R. 2002 "Timon of Phlius" in E. Zalta ed., *Stanford Encyclopedia of Philosophy*, online: http://plato.stanford.edu/archives/fall2002/entries/timon-phlius/, revised version 2006, http://plato.stanford.edu/archives/sum2006/entries/timon-phlius/

[147] Brennan, T. 1998 "Pyrrho and the Criterion" *Ancient Philosophy* 18: 417–34.

[148] Brunschwig, J. 1992 "Pyrrhon et Philista" in M.O. Goulet-Cazé, G. Madec, and D. O'Brien eds., *Sophiês Maiêtores, "Chercheurs de sagesse" – Hommage à Jean Pépin* (Paris: Institut d'études augustiniennes 1992), pp. 133–46

[149] Brunschwig, J. 1994 "Once Again on Eusebius on Aristocles on Timon on Pyrrho" in Brunschwig [77], pp. 190–211.

[150] Brunschwig, J. 1994 "The Title of Timon's *Indalmoi*: From Odysseus to Pyrrho" in Brunschwig [77], pp. 212–23. Original French publication 1990.

[151] Brunschwig, J. 1997 "L'Aphasie pyrrhonienne" in C. Lévy and L. Permot eds., *Dire l'évidence (Philosophie et rhétorique antiques)* (Paris: L'Harmattan), pp. 297–320.

[152] Brunschwig, J. 1999 "Introduction: the Beginnings of Hellenistic Epistemology" in Algra *et al.* [75], pp. 229–60.

[153] Burnyeat, M. 1980 "Tranquillity Without a Stop: Timon, Frag. 68" *Classical Quarterly* 30: 86–93.

[154] Conche, M. 1994 *Pyrrhon ou l'apparence*, 2nd edn. (Paris: Presses universitaires de France).

[155] Ferrari, G.A. 1968 "Due fonti sullo scetticismo antico (Diog. Lae. IX, 66–108; Eus., Praep. Ev., XIV, 18, 1–20)" *Studi Italiani di Filologia Classica* 40: 200–24.

[156] Ferrari, G.A. 1981 "L'immagine dell' equilibrio" in Giannantoni [81], pp. 339–70.

[157] Flintoff, E. 1980 "Pyrrho and India" *Phronesis* 25: 88–108.

[158] Long, A.A. 2006 "Timon of Phlius: Pyrrhonist and Satirist" in Long [84], pp. 70–95. Original version 1978.

[159] Reale, G. 1981 "Ipotesi per una rilettura della filosofia di Pirrone di Elide" in Giannantoni [81], pp. 245–336.

[160] Sakezles, P. 1993 "Pyrrhonian Indeterminacy: A Pragmatic Interpretation" *Apeiron* 26: 77–95.

[161] Svavarsson, S. H. 2002 "Pyrrho's Dogmatic Nature" *Classical Quarterly* 52.1: 248–56.

[162] Svavarsson, S. H. 2004 "Pyrrho's Undecidable Nature" *Oxford Studies in Ancient Philosophy* 27: 249–95.

[163] von Fritz, K. 1963 "Pyrrhon" in *Paulys Realencyclopädie der class-ischen Altertumswissenschaft* 24 (Stuttgart: Druckenmüller), pp. 89–106.

[164] Warren, J. 2000 "Aristocles' Refutations of Pyrrhonism (Eus. *PE* 14.18.1–10)" *Proceedings of the Cambridge Philological Society* 46: 140–64.

[165] Wilamowitz-Moellendorff U. von 1881 *Antigonos von Karystos* (Berlin: Weidmann).

4.3 The Sceptical Academy

4.3.1 Covering multiple periods

[166] Inwood, B. and Mansfeld, J. eds. 1997 *Assent and Argument. Studies in Cicero's Academic Books, Proceedings of the Seventh Symposium Hellenisticum* (Leiden: Brill).

[167] Lévy, C. 2005 "Les petits Académiciens: Lacyde, Charmadas, Métrodore de Stratonice" in M. Bonazzi and V. Celluprica eds., *L'eredità platonica: studi sur platonismo da Arcesilao a Proclo* (Naples: Bibliopolis), pp. 53–77.

4.3.2 Arcesilaus and Carneades

[168] Algra, K. 1997 "Chrysippus, Carneades, Cicero: the Ethical *Divisions* in Cicero's *Lucullus*" in Inwood and Mansfeld [166], pp. 107–39.

[169] Allen, J. 1994 "Academic Probabilism and Stoic epistemology" *Classical Quarterly* 44: 85–113.

[170] Allen, J. 1997 "Carneadean Argument in Cicero's *Academic* Books" in Inwood and Mansfeld [166], pp. 217–56.

[171] Allen, J. 2004 "Carneades" in *Stanford Encyclopedia of Philosophy*, http://plato.stanford.edu/entries/carneades/

[172] Annas, J. 2007 "Carneades' Classification of Ethical Theories" in A. M. Ioppolo and D. N. Sedley eds., *Pyrrhonists, Patricians, Platonizers: Hellenistic Philosophy in the Period 155–86 BC* (Naples: Bibliopolis).

[173] Arnim, H. von 1895 "Arkesilaos" in *Pauly-Wissowa, Realenzy-klopädie* II 1 (Stuttgart: Metzler), pp. 1164–68.

[174] Bett, R. 1989 "Carneades' *Pithanon*: A reappraisal of its Role and Status" *Oxford Studies in Ancient Philosophy* 7: 59–94.

[175] Bett, R. 1990 "Carneades' Distinction Between Assent and Approval" *Monist* 73: 3–20.

[176] Brittain, C. 2005 "Arcesilaus" in *Stanford Encyclopedia of Philosophy*, http://plato.stanford.edu/entries/arcesilaus/

[177] Brittain, C. and Palmer, J. 2001 "The New Academy's Appeals to the Presocratics" *Phronesis* 46.1: 38–72.

[178] Cooper, J. 2004 "Arcesilaus: Socratic and Sceptic" in J. Cooper, *Knowledge, Nature, and the Good, Essays on Ancient Philosophy* (Princeton: Princeton University Press), pp. 81–103.

[179] Couissin, P. 1983 "The Stoicism of the New Academy" in Burnyeat [78], pp. 31–63. Translation of "Le stoicisme de la nouvelle Academie" *Revue d'historie de la philosophie* 3 (1929): 241–76.

[180] Frede, D. 1996 "How Sceptical were the Academic Sceptics?" in R. Popkin ed., *Scepticism in the History of Philosophy* (Dordrecht: Kluwer), pp. 1–25

[181] Ioppolo, A. M. 2000 "Su alcune recenti interpretationi dello scetticismo dell Accademia. Plutarch. *Adv. Col.* 26, 1121f–1122f: una testimonia su Arcesilao" *Elenchos* 21: 333–60.

[182] Ioppolo, A. M. 2008 "Arcésilas dans le *Lucullus* de Cicéron" in *Cicéron, Revue de Métaphysique et de Morale* 1: 21–44.

[183] Lévy, C. 1978 "Scepticisme et dogmatisme dans l'Académie: 'l'ésotérisme' d'Arcésilas" *Revue des Etudes Latines* 56: 335–48.

[184] Long, A. A. 1986 "Diogenes Laertius, the Life of Arcesilaus" *Elenchos* 7: 429–49. Revised version ("Arcesilaus in his Time and Place") in Long [84], pp. 96–113.

[185] Long, A. A. "Scepticism about Gods" in Long [84], pp. 114–27. Originally published 1990.

[186] Obdrzalek, S. 2006 "Living in Doubt: Carneades' *Pithanon* Reconsidered" *Oxford Studies in Ancient Philosophy* 31: 243–80.

[187] Perin, C. 2006 "Academic Arguments for the Indiscernibility Thesis" *Pacific Philosophical Quarterly* 86.4: 493–517.

[188] Schofield, M. 1999 "Academic Epistemology" in Algra *et al.* [75], pp. 295–354.

[189] Shields, C. 1994 "Socrates Among the Skeptics" in P. Vander Waerdt ed., *The Socratic Movement* (Ithaca/London: Cornell University Press), pp. 341–66.

[190] Striker, G. 1980 "Sceptical Strategies" in Schofield *et al.* [85], pp. 54–83.

[191] Striker, G. 1981 "Über den Unterschied zwischen den Pyrrhoneern und den Akademikern" *Phronesis* 26: 353–69. English translation in Striker [87], pp. 135–49.

[192] Thorsrud, H. 2002 "Cicero on his Academic Predecessors: The Fallibilism of Arcesilaus and Carneades" *Journal of the History of Philosophy* 40: 1–18.

[193] Thorsrud, H. (forthcoming) "Radical and Mitigated Skepticism in Cicero's *Academica*" in W. Nicgorski ed., *Cicero's Practical Philosophy* (Notre Dame: Notre Dame University Press).

Also relevant are Bett [220] (section I), Bett [221], Frede [278], Striker [264].

4.3.3 Late Academy

[194] Barnes, J. 1989 "Antiochus of Ascalon" in M. Griffin and J. Barnes eds., *Philosophia Togata* (Oxford: Clarendon Press), pp. 51–96.

[195] Brittain, C. 2001 *Philo of Larissa: The Last of the Academic Sceptics* (Oxford: Oxford University Press).

[196] Burnyeat. M. 1997 "Antipater and Self-Refutation: Elusive Arguments in Cicero's *Academica*" in Inwood and Mansfeld [166], pp. 277–310.

[197] Glidden, D. 1996 "Philo of Larissa and Platonism" in R. Popkin ed., *Scepticism in the History of Philosophy* (Dordrecht: Kluwer), pp. 219–34.

[198] Glucker, J. 1978 *Antiochus and the Late Academy* (Göttingen: Vandenhoek & Ruprecht).

Review essay by:

[199] Sedley, D. N. 1981 "The End of the Academy" *Phronesis* 26: 67–75.

[200] Glucker, J. 1995 "*Probabile, Verisimile*, and Related Terms" in J. Powell ed., *Cicero the Philosopher* (Oxford: Clarendon Press), pp. 115–44.

[201] Görler, W. 1997. "Cicero's Philosophical Stance in the *Lucullus*" in Inwood and Mansfeld [166], pp. 36–57.

[202] Görler, W. 2008 "*Perturbatio uitae, si ita sit, atque officiorum omnium consequatur*. A propos d'un mode d'argumentation cicéronien", *Cicéron, Revue de Métaphysique et de Morale* 1: 45–60.

[203] Hankinson, R. J. 1997 "Natural Criteria and the Transparency of Judgment: Antiochus, Philo and Galen on Epistemological Justification" in Inwood and Mansfeld [166], pp. 161–216.

[204] Lévy, C. 1992 *Cicero Academicus, Recherches sur les Académiques et sur la philosophie cicéronienne* (Rome: École Française de Rome).

[205] Lévy, C. 1992 "Cicéron créateur du vocabulaire latin de la connaissance" in P. Grimal ed., *La langue latine langue de la philosophie* (Rome: École Française de Rome), pp. 91–106.

[206] Tarrant, H. 1985 *Scepticism or Platonism* (Cambridge: Cambridge University Press).

4.3.4 Aftermath of the Academy

[207] Babut, D. 1969 *Plutarque et le stoïcisme* (Paris: Presses universitaires de France).

[208] De Lacy, Ph. H. 1953 "Plutarch and the Academic Sceptics" *Classical Journal* 49: 79–85.

[209] Donini P. L. 1986 "Plutarco, Ammonio e l'Accademia" in F. E. Brenk-I Gallo eds., *Miscellanea plutarchea. Atti del I Convegno di studi su Plutarco (Roma, 23 novembre 1985), Quaderni del Giornale Filologico Ferrarese* 8, pp. 203–26.

[210] Holford-Strevens, L. 1997 "Favorinus: The Man of Paradoxes" in M. Griffin and J. Barnes eds., *Philosophia Togata II* (Oxford: Clarendon Press), pp. 188–217.

[211] Ioppolo, A. M. 1993 "The Academic Position of Favorinus of Arelate" *Phronesis* 38: 183–213.

[212] Ioppolo, A. M. 2002 "Gli Accademici *neôteroi* nel secondo secolo d.C." *Methexis* 15: 45–70.

[213] Lévy, C. 1986 "Le 'scepticisme' de Philon d'Alexandrie: une influence de la Nouvelle Académie?" in A. Caquot, M. Hadas-Lebel and J. Riaud, eds., *Hellenica et Judaica. Hommage à V. Nikiprowetzky* (Louvain/Paris: Peeters), pp. 29–41.

[214] Lévy, C. 1991 "Pierre de Valence, historien de l'Académie ou académicien?" in P.-F. Moreau ed., *Le scepticisme au XVIe et au XVIIe siècle* (Paris: Albin Michel), pp. 174–87.

[215] Opsomer, J. 1998 *In Search of the Truth: Academic Tendencies in Middle Platonism* (Brussels: Koninklijke Academie voor Wetenschappen, Letteren en Schone Kunsten van Belgie). Available from Brepols.

[216] Schroeter, J. 1911, *Plutarchs Stellung Zur Skepsis, Inaugural Dissertation Königsberg* (Greifswald: Druck J. Abel).

[217] Warren, J. 2002 "Socratic Scepticism in Plutarch's *Adversus Colotem*" *Elenchos* 23: 333–56.

4.4 Pyrrhonism

For Pyrrho and his immediate successors, see 4.2. With the exception of 4.4.1, this part of the bibliography includes only works relating to Aenesidemus and his successors.

4.4.1 Covering multiple periods (including early Pyrrhonism and its relation to the Pyrrhonism initiated by Aenesidemus).

[218] Bächli, A. 1990 *Untersuchungen zur pyrrhonischen Skepsis* (Bern/Stuttgart: Haupt).

[219] Barnes, J. 1992 "Diogenes Laertius IX 61–116: The Philosophy of Pyrrhonism" in H. Haase ed., *Aufstieg und Niedergang der Römischen Welt* II.36.6 (Berlin: de Gruyter), pp. 4241–301.

[220] Bett, R. 1998 "The Sceptics on Emotions" in T. Engberg-Pedersen and J. Sihvola eds., *The Emotions in Hellenistic Philosophy* (Dordrecht: Kluwer), pp. 197–218.

[221] Bett, R. 2003 "Rationality and Happiness in the Greek Skeptical Traditions" in Jiyuan Yu and Jorge J. E. Gracia eds., *Rationality and Happiness: From the Ancients to the Early Medievals* (Rochester, NY: University of Rochester Press), pp. 109–34.

[222] Brunschwig, J. 2006 "Pyrrhonism" in M.-L. Gill and P. Pellegrin eds., *A Companion to Ancient Philosophy* (Oxford: Blackwell), pp. 465–85.

[223] Decleva Caizzi, F. 1995 "Aenesidemus vs. Pyrrho: il fuoco scalda 'per natura' (Sextus *M* VII 215 e XI 69" in L. Ayres ed., *The Passionate Intellect* (New Brunswick/London: Transaction Publishers), pp. 145–59. Reprinted in *Elenchos* 17 (1996): 37–54.

[224] Lévy, C. 2001 "Pyrrhon, Enésidème et Sextus Empiricus: la question de la légitimation historique dans le scepticisme" in A. Brancacci ed., *Antichi e moderni nella filosofia di eta imperiale* (Naples: Bibliopolis), pp. 299–326.

4.4.2 Aenesidemus

[225] Bett, R. 2005 "Le signe dans la tradition pyrrhonienne" in J. Kany-Turpin ed., *Signe et prédiction dans l'antiquité* (Saint-Étienne: Publications de l'Université de Saint-Étienne), pp. 29–48.

[226] Decleva Caizzi, F. 1992 "Aenesidemus and the Academy" *Classical Quarterly* 42: 176–89.

[227] Janáček, K. 1976, "Zur Interpretation des Photios-Abschnittes über Ainesidemos" *Eirene* 14: 93–100. Reprinted in Janáček [32].

[228] Janáček, K. 1980 "Ainesidemos Und Sextos Empeirikos" *Eirene* 17: 5–16. Reprinted in Janáček [32].

[229] Mansfeld, J. 1995 "Aenesidemus and the Academics" in L. Ayres ed., *The Passionate Intellect* (New Brunswick/London: Transaction Publishers), pp. 236–48.

[230] Pérez-Jean, B. 2005 *Dogmatisme et scepticisme: L'héraclitisme d'Énésidème* (Villeneuve d'Ascq: Septentrion).

[231] Polito, R. 2004 *The Sceptical Road: Aenesidemus' Appropriation of Heraclitus* (Leiden/Boston: Brill).

[232] Schofield, M. 2007 "Aenesidemus: Pyrrhonist and 'Heraclitean'" in A.M. Ioppolo and D.N. Sedley eds., *Pyrrhonists, Patricians, Platonizers: Hellenistic Philosophy in the Period 155–86 BC* (Naples: Bibliopolis), pp. 271–338.

[233] Viano, C. 2002 "'Énésidème selon Héraclite': la substance corporelle du temps" *Revue philosophique* 192: pp. 141–58.

[234] Woodruff, P. 1988 "Aporetic Pyrrhonism" *Oxford Studies in Ancient Philosophy* 6: pp. 139–68.

See also Bett [143], ch. 4.

4.4.3 Sextus Empiricus

(a) On our almost complete ignorance of Sextus' life, see:

[235] House, D. K. 1980 "The Life of Sextus Empiricus" *Classical Quarterly* 30: 227–38.

(b) The following works deal with aspects of Sextus' general outlook and approach:

[236] Allen, J. 1990 "The Skepticism of Sextus Empiricus" in *Aufstieg und Niedergang der Römischen Welt* II.36.4 (Berlin: de Gruyter), pp. 2582–607.

[237] Barnes, J. 1983 "Ancient Skepticism and Causation" in Burnyeat [78], pp. 149–203.

[238] Barnes, J. 1990 "Pyrrhonism, Belief and Causation: Observations on the Scepticism of Sextus Empiricus" in *Ausfstieg und Niedergang der Römischen Welt* II.36.4 (Berlin: de Gruyter), pp. 2608–95.

[239] Barnes, J. 1994 "Scepticism and Relativity" in A. Alberti ed., *Realtà e ragione: studi di filosofia antica* (Florence: Olschki), pp. 51–83.

[240] Barnes, J. 2007 "Sextan Scepticism" in D. Scott ed., *Maieusis: Essays in Ancient Philosophy in Honour of Myles Burnyeat* (Oxford: Oxford University Press), pp. 322–34.

[241] Barney, R. 1992 "Appearances and Impressions" *Phronesis* 37: 283–313.

[242] Brunschwig, J. 1980 "Proof Defined" in Schofield *et al.* [85], pp. 125–60.

[243] Brunschwig, J. 1988 "Sextus Empiricus on the *kritêrion*: the Sceptic as Conceptual Legatee" in J. Dillon and A. Long eds., *The Question of "Eclecticism": Studies in Later Greek Philosophy* (Berkeley/Los Angeles: University of California Press), pp. 145–75.

[244] Brunschwig, J. 1990 "La formule *hoson epi tôi logôi* chez Sextus Empiricus" in Voelke [88], pp. 107–21. English translation in Brunschwig [77], pp. 244–58.

[245] Burnyeat, M. 1982 "The Origins of Non-Deductive Inference" in Barnes *et al.* [76], pp. 193–238.

[246] Castagnoli, L. 2000 "Self-Bracketing Pyrrhonism" *Oxford Studies in Ancient Philosophy* 18: 263–328.

[247] Couissin, P. 1929 "L'origine et l'évolution de l'*epochê*" *Revue des Études Grecques* 42: 373–97.

[248] Ebert, T. 1987 "The Origin of the Stoic Theory of Signs in Sextus Empiricus" *Oxford Studies in Ancient Philosophy* 5: 83–126.

[249] Everson, S. 1991 "The Objective Appearance of Pyrrhonism" in S. Everson ed., *Psychology: Companions to Ancient Thought* 2 (Cambridge: Cambridge University Press), pp. 121–47.

[250] Fine, G. 2000 "Sceptical Dogmata: Outlines of Pyrrhonism I 13" *Methexis* 12: 81–105.

[251] Glidden, D. K. 1983 "Skeptic Semiotics" *Phronesis* 28: 213–55.

[252] Glidden, D. K. 1994 "Parrots, Pyrrhonists and Native Speakers" in S. Everson ed., *Language: Companions to Ancient Thought* 3 (Cambridge: Cambridge University Press), pp. 129–48.

[253] Ioli, R. 2003 "*Agôgê* and related concepts in Sextus Empiricus" *Siculorum Gymnasium* N.S. 56: 401–28.

[254] Long, A. A. 1978 "Sextus Empiricus on the Criterion of Truth" *Bulletin of the Institute of Classical Studies* 25: 35–49.

[255] Machuca, D. 2008 "Sextus Empiricus: His Outlook, Works, and Legacy" *Freiburger Zeitschrift für Philosophie und Theologie* 55: 28–63.

[256] McPherran, M. 1987 "Sceptical Homeopathy and Self-Refutation" *Phronesis* 32: 290–328.

[257] Palmer, J. 2000 "Skeptical Investigation", *Ancient Philosophy* 20: 351–75.

[258] Pappenheim, E. 1874 *De Sexti Empirici librorum numero et ordine* (Berlin: Nauck).

[259] Perin, C. (forthcoming) *The Demands of Reason: An Essay on Pyrrhonian Scepticism* (Oxford: Oxford University Press).

[260] Perin, C. 2006 "Pyrrhonian Scepticism and the Search for Truth" *Oxford Studies in Ancient Philosophy* 30: 337–60.

[261] Spinelli, E. 1991 "Sceptics and Language: *phonaí* and *lógoi* in Sextus Empiricus" *Histoire Épistémologie Langage* 13.2: 57–70.

[262] Spinelli, E. 2004 "L'esperienza scettica: Sesto Empirico fra metodologia scientifica e scelte etiche" *Quaestio* 4: 25–43.

[263] Stough., C. 1984 "Sextus Empiricus on Non-Assertion" *Phronesis* 29: 137–64.

[264] Striker, G. 2001 "Scepticism as a Kind of Philosophy" *Archiv für Geschichte der Philosophie* 83: 113–29.

[265] Vogt, K. 2006 "Skeptische Suche und das Verstehen von Begriffen" in Ch. Rapp and T. Wagner eds., *Wissen und Bildung in der antiken Philosophie* (Stuttgart: Metzler), pp. 325–39.

[266] Warren, J. 2003 "Sextus Empiricus on the Tripartition of Time" *Phronesis* 48: 313–43.

[267] Williams, M. 1988 "Scepticism Without Theory" *Review of Metaphysics* 41: 547–88.

[268] Wlodarczyk, M. 2000 "Pyrrhonian Inquiry" Cambridge Philological Society Supplementary vol. 25.

Also relevant is Striker [191].

(c) On the Modes, especially (but not exclusively) in Sextus, see:

[269] Annas, J. and Barnes, J. 1985 *The Modes of Scepticism: Ancient Texts and Modern Interpretations* (Cambridge: Cambridge University Press).
[270] Barnes, J. 1990 *The Toils of Scepticism* (Cambridge: Cambridge University Press).
[271] Barnes, J. 1990 "Some Ways of Scepticism" in Everson [80], pp. 204–24.
[272] Striker, G. 1983 "The Ten Tropes of Aenesidemus" in Burnyeat [78], pp. 95–115.

(d) On what kinds of belief, if any, are open to a Pyrrhonist of Sextus' variety, and what action will be like for such a Pyrrhonist, see:

[273] Barnes, J. 1982 "The Beliefs of a Pyrrhonist" *Proceedings of the Cambridge Philological Society* n.s. 28, pp. 1–29.
[274] Bett, R. 2008 "What Kind of Self Can a Greek Sceptic Have?" in Pauliina Remes and Juha Sihvola eds. *Ancient Philosophy of the Self*, (Springer Science/Business Media B.V., New Synthese Historical Library 64), pp. 139–54.
[275] Brennan, T. 2000 "Criterion and Appearance in Sextus Empiricus" in Sihvola [86], pp. 63–92. Original version 1994.
[276] Burnyeat, M. 1980 "Can the Sceptic Live his Scepticism?" in Schofield *et al.* [85], pp. 20–53. Reprinted in Burnyeat [78], pp. 117–48.
[277] Burnyeat, M. 1984 "The Sceptic in his Place and Time" in R. Rorty, J.B. Schneewind, and Q. Skinner eds., *Philosophy in History* (Cambridge: Cambridge University Press), pp. 225–54.
[278] Frede, M. 1984 "The Sceptic's Two Kinds of Assent and the Question of the Possibility of Knowledge" in R. Rorty, J.B. Schneewind, and Q. Skinner eds., *Philosophy in History* (Cambridge: Cambridge University Press), pp. 255–78.
[279] Frede, M. 1997 "The Sceptic's Beliefs" in Burnyeat and Frede [79], pp. 1–24. Originally published in German 1979.
[280] La Sala, R. 2005 *Die Züge des Skeptikers: Der dialektiker Charakter von Sextus Empiricus' Werk* (Göttingen: Vandenhoek & Ruprecht).

For a brief summary and assessment in English, see the review by:

[281] Castagnoli, L. 2007 *Classical Review* 57: 370–72.
[282] Morrison, D. 1990 "The Ancient Sceptic's Way of Life" *Metaphilosophy* 21: 204–22.

[283] Ribeiro, B. 2002 "Is Pyrrhonism Psychologically Possible?" *Ancient Philosophy* 22: 319–33.
[284] Vogt, K. 1998 *Skepsis und Lebenspraxis: Das pyrrhonische Leben ohne Meinungen* (München: Alber Verlag).

Of these works, the articles by Barnes, Burnyeat, and Frede are collected in Burnyeat and Frede [79].

(e) On Sextus' practical attitudes, and his treatment of issues in ethics, see:

[285] Bett, R. 1994 "Sextus's *Against the Ethicists*: Scepticism, Relativism, or Both?" *Apeiron* 27: 123–61.
[286] Grgic, F. 2006 "Sextus Empiricus on the Goal of Skepticism" *Ancient Philosophy* 26: 141–60.
[287] Hankinson, R.J. 1994 "Values, Objectivity and Dialectic: the Sceptical Attack on Ethics; its Methods, Aims and Success" *Phronesis* 49: 45–68.
[288] Hankinson, R.J. 1997 "The End of Scepticism" *Kriterion* 38: 7–32.
[289] Machuca, D. 2006 "The Pyrrhonist's *ataraxia* and *philanthrôpia*" *Ancient Philosophy* 26: 111–39.
[290] McPherran, M. 1989 "*Ataraxia* and *Eudaimonia*: Is the Sceptic Really Happy?" *Proceedings of the Boston Area Colloquium in Ancient Philosophy* 5: 135–71.
[291] McPherran, M. 1990 "Pyrrhonism's Arguments Against Value" *Philosophical Studies* 60: 127–42.
[292] Moller, D. 2004 "The Pyrrhonian Skeptic's *Telos*" *Ancient Philosophy* 24: 425–41.
[293] Thorsrud, H. 2003 "Is the Examined Life Worth Living? A Pyrrhonian Alternative" *Apeiron* 36: 229–49.
[294] Tsouna-McKirahan, V. 1996 "Conservatism and Pyrrhonian Skepticism" *Syllecta Classica* 6: 69–86.

See also the introduction and commentary to Bett [41].

(f) Sextus' attitude to religion is discussed in:

[295] Bett, R. 2009 "Sextus Empiricus" in N. Trakakis and G. Oppy eds. *History of Western Philosophy and Religion*, vol. 1, *Ancient Philosophy and Religion* (Stocksfield: Acumen Publishing).
[296] Bett, R. 2007 "*Against the Physicists* on Gods (*M* IX.13–194)" in K. Algra and K. Ierodiakonou eds. 2007 Symposium Hellenisticum Proceedings.

On this topic see also Annas [422], Knuuttila and Sihvola [431], Long [185].

(g) On Sextus' treatment of the specialized sciences (*M* 1–6), see:

[296a] Barnes, J. 1986 "Is Rhetoric an Art?," *Darg Newsletter* 2, pp. 2–22.

[297] Barnes, J. 1988 "Scepticism and the Arts" in Hankinson [343], pp. 53–77

[298] Bett, R. 2006 "La double 'schizophrénie' de *M* 1–6 et ses origines historiques" in Delattre [302], pp. 17–34.

[299] Brisson, L. 2006 "*Contre les Arithméticiens (Pros Arithmêtikous)* ou contre ceux qui enseignent que les nombres sont des principes" in Delattre [302], pp. 67–77.

[300] Cortassa, G. 1981 "Sesto Empirico e gli 'Egkuklia Mathemata'" in Giannantoni [81], vol. II, pp. 713–24.

[301] Dalimier, C. 2006 "Sextus Empiricus et les débordements ontologiques de 'la grammaire prophète'", in Delattre [302], pp. 89–103.

[302] Delattre, J. ed. 2006 *Sur le* Contre les professeurs *de Sextus Empiricus* (Villeneuve d'Ascq: L'Université Charles-de-Gaulle, Lille 3).

[303] Delattre, D. 2006 "Présence de l'èpicurisme dans le *Contre les Grammairiens* et le *Contre les Musiciens* de Sextus Empiricus" in Delattre [302], pp. 47–65.

[304] Delattre, J. 2006 "La critique de l'enseignement dans le *Contre les Géomètres* et le *Contre les Astrologues* de Sextus Empiricus" in Delattre [302], pp. 119–33.

[305] Desbordes, F. 1982 "Le langage sceptique. Notes sur le *Contre les grammairiens* de Sextus Empiricus" *Langages* 65: 47–74.

[306] Desbordes, F. 1990 "Le scepticisme et les 'arts libéraux': une étude de Sextus Empiricus *Adv. Math.* I-VI" in Voelke [88], pp. 167–79.

[306a] Dye, G. and Vitrac, B. 2009 "*Le* Contre les géométres *de Sextus Empiricus: sources, Cible, Structure" *Phronesis* 54: 155–203.

[307] Fortuna, S. 1986 "Sesto Empirico: *egkyklia mathemata* e arti utili alla vita", *Studi Classici e Orientali* 36: 123–37.

[308] Freytag, W. 1995 *Mathematische Grundbegriffe bei Sextus Empiricus* (Hildesheim/New York: Olms).

[309] Krentz, E. M. 1962 "Philosophic Concerns in Sextus Empiricus, Adv. Math. I" *Phronesis* 7: 152–60.

[310] Longo Auricchio, F. 1984 "Epicureismo e scetticismo sulla retorica" in *Atti del XVII Congresso Internazionale di Papirologia* (Naples: Centro Internazionale per lo Studio dei Papiri Ercolanesi), pp. 453–72.

[311] Mueller, I. 1982 "Geometry and Scepticism" in Barnes *et al.* [76], pp. 69–95.

[312] Pellegrin, P. 2006 "De l'unité du scepticisme sextien" in Delattre [302], pp. 35–45.

[313] Pérez-Jean, B. 2006 "La problematique du tout et des parties dans le *Contre les Grammairiens* et le *Contre les Rhéteurs*" in Delattre [302], pp. 79–87.

[314] Rispoli, G. M. 1992 "Sesto Empirico e Filodemo contro i musici" in A. H. S. El-Mosalamy ed., *Proceedings of the XIXth International Congress of Papyrology (Cairo, 2–9 September 1989)* (Cairo: Ain Shams University, Center of Papyrological Studies), vol. I, pp. 213–48.

[315] Sluiter, I. 2000 "The Rhetoric of Scepticism: Sextus Against the Language Specialists" in Sihvola [86], pp. 93–123.

(h) Sextus' relations to earlier Greek philosophers are discussed in the following set of essays:

[316] "Sesto Empirico e il pensiero antico" *Elenchos* 13 (1992).

Of these, essays cited in this volume are:

[317] Decleva Caizzi, F. "Sesto e gli scettici," pp. 279–327.

[318] Isnardi Parente, M. "Sesto, Platone, l'Accademia antica e I Pitagorici," pp. 119–67.

Essays in English are:

[319] Sedley, D. "Sextus Empiricus and the Atomist Criteria of Truth," pp. 19–56.

[320] Annas, J. "Sextus Empiricus and the Peripatetics", pp. 201–31.

4.5 Scepticism and medical theory

4.5.1 Galen, texts and translations

Aside from the sceptics themselves, the most important ancient author for this topic is Galen. A useful and accessible collection of relevant works in translation is:

[321] Walzer, R. and Frede, M. 1985 *Galen, Three Treatises on the Nature of Science*, translated with an introduction (Indianapolis: Hackett).

However, many of Galen's texts are still difficult or impossible to find (even in Greek) in accessible modern editions. The standard edition of his collected works is still:

[322] Kühn, C. G. 1821–33 *Galeni Opera Omnia* (Leipzig), 19 vols. Reprinted Hildesheim, 1965, usually abbreviated K.

A helpful "Guide to the Editions and Abbreviations of the Galenic Corpus" forms Appendix A of:

[323] Hankinson, R. J. 1998 *Galen: On Antecedent Causes*, edited with an introduction, translation and commentary (Cambridge: Cambridge University Press).

The works by Galen (or attributed to him in antiquity) that are cited in "Pyrrhonism and Medicine" (ch. 12) in this volume are as follows (listed in order of appearance):

[324] *Outline of Empiricism (Subfiguratio empirica, Subfig. emp.)*: text in Deichgräber [20], translation in Walzer and Frede [321].

[325] *On the Therapeutic Method (De methodo medendi, MM): text* in K vol. X, translation of books 1 and 2, with commentary, by R. J. Hankinson (Oxford: Oxford University Press, 1991).

[326] *On Medical Experience*: survives only in Arabic translation, English version in Walzer, R., *On Medical Experience: First Edition of the Arabic Version with English Translation and Notes* (Oxford: Oxford University Press, 1944), translation reprinted in Walzer and Frede [321].

[327] *Medical Definitions (Definitiones Medicae, Def. med.)*: a spurious work, text in K vol. XIX.

[328] *On the Sects for Beginners (De sectis ingredientibus, Sect. ingred.)*: text in vol. 3 of I. Marquardt, I. Mueller, and G. Helmreich eds., *Galeni Scripta Minora (SM)* (Leipzig: Teubner, 1884–91), 3 vols, translation in Walzer and Frede [321].

[329] *On the Best Sect (De optima secta)*: a spurious work, text in K vol. I.

[330] *Introduction or the Doctor (Introductio seu medicus, Introductio)*: a spurious work, text in K vol. XIV.

[331] *On diagnosing pulses (De dignoscendibus pulsibus)*: text in K vol. VIII.

4.5.2 Overviews

Good overviews of the topic can be found in the following standard histories of scepticism:

Brochard [61], Livre IV ch. 1, "Les médicins sceptiques: Ménodote et Sextus Empiricus".

Hankinson [68], ch. XIII, "Scepticism in the Medical Schools."

Robin [70], Part IV, ch. 1, "Scepticism et médicine: la médicine empirique en général."

4.5.3 Other studies

[332] Allen, J. 2004 "Experience as Source and Ground of Theory in Epicureanism" in P. Lang ed. *Re-inventions: Essays on Hellenistic and Early Roman Science, Apeiron* XXXVII no. 4.

[333] De Lacy, P. 1991 "Galen's Response to Skepticism" *Illinois Classical Studies* 16: 283–306.

[334] Edelstein, L. 1967 *Ancient Medicine: Selected Papers of Ludwig Edelstein*, O. Temkin and C.L. Temkin eds. (Baltimore: Johns Hopkins University Press).

[335] L. Edelstein, "The Methodists" in Edelstein [334], pp. 173–91.

[336] L. Edelstein, "Empiricism and Skepticism in the teaching of the Greek Empiricist School" in Edelstein [334],pp. 195–203.

[337] Eijk, P.J. van der 2005 "The Methodism of Caelius Aurelianus: Some Epistemological Issues" in P.J. van der Eijk, *Medicine and Philosophy in Classical Antiquity: Doctors and Philosophers on Nature, Soul, Health and Disease* (Cambridge: Cambridge University Press), pp. 299–327. Originally published 1999.

[338] Frede, M. 1983 "The Method of the So-called Methodical School of Medicine" in Barnes *et al.* [76], pp. 1–23.

[339] Frede, M. 1988 "The Empiricist Attitude Towards Reason and Theory" in Hankinson [343], pp. 79–97.

[340] Frede, M. 1990 "An Empiricist View of Knowledge: Memorism" in Everson [80], pp. 225–50.

[341] Gourevitch, D. 1991 "La pratique méthodique: Définition de la maladie, indication et traitement" in P. Mudry and J. Pigeaud eds., *Les Écoles Médicales a Rome Actes du 2ème Colloque international sur les textes médicaux latines antiques* (Geneva: Droz), pp. 51–81.

[342] Hankinson, R.J. 1987 "Causes and Empiricism: A Problem in the Interpretation of Later Greek Medical Method" *Phronesis* 32: 329–48.

[343] Hankinson, R.J. ed. 1988 *Method, Medicine and Metaphysics: Studies in the Philosophy of Ancient Science, Apeiron* XXI no. 2.

[344] Lloyd, G.E.R. 1983 *Science, Folklore and Ideology* (Cambridge: Cambridge University Press).

[345] Matthen, M. 1988 "Empiricism and Ontology in Ancient Medicine" in Hankinson [343], pp. 99–121.

[346] Mudry, P. 1990 "Le scepticisme des médecins empiriques dans le traité *De la Médecine* de Celse: modeles et modalités" in Voelke [88], pp. 85–96.

[347] Pellegrin, P. 2004 "Scepticisme et sémiologie médicale" in R. Morelaon and A. Hasnawi eds., *De Zénon d'Élée à Poincaré. Receuil d'études en hommage à Roshdi Rashed* (Louvain/Paris: Peeters), pp. 645–64.

[348] Philippson, R. 1881 *De Philodemi libro, qui est Peri sêmeiôn kai sêmeiôseôn et Epicureorum doctrina logica* (Berlin: Berliner Buchdruckerei Actien-Gesellschaft).

[349] Pigeaud, J. 1991 "Les Fondements du Méthodisme" in P. Mudry and J. Pigeaud eds., *Les écoles médicales à Rome* (Geneva: Droz), pp. 7–50.

[350] Staden, H. von 1975 "Experiment and Experience in Hellenistic Medicine" *Bulletin of the Institute of Classical Studies* 22: 178–99.

[351] Staden, H. von 1983 "Hairesis and heresy: the case of the *haireseis iatrikai*" in B. F. Meyer and E. P. Sanders eds., *Jewish and Christian Self-Definition*, (Philadelphia: Fortress Press), vol. 3, pp. 76–100. Published 1982 London: SCM Press.

[352] Vallance, J. T. 1990 *The Lost Theory of Asclepiades of Bithynia* (Oxford: Clarendon Press)

4.6 Rediscovery and influence

4.6.1 General accounts

A leading figure on the Renaissance and early modern rediscovery of Pyrrhonism was R. H. Popkin. Popkin's main work on the subject, appearing in a succession of ever-expanding editions, is:

[353] Popkin, R. 1960 *The History of Scepticism from Erasmus to Descartes* (Assen: van Gorcum). Revised version in 1964 (Assen:van Gorcum) and 1968 (New York: Harper and Row). Followed by:

[354] Popkin, R. 1979 *The History of Skepticism from Erasmus to Spinoza* (Berkeley/Los Angeles: University of California Press). And finally:

[355] Popkin, R. 2003 *The History of Scepticism from Savonarola to Bayle* (New York: Oxford University Press).

Also of interest is the following collection of essays:

[356] Popkin, R. ed. Watson, R. and Force, J. 1980 *The High Road to Pyrrhonism* (San Diego: Austin Hill Press).

A valuable recent study, more philologically rigorous (and more philosophically sober) than Popkin is:

[357] Floridi, L. 2002 *Sextus Empiricus: The Transmission and Recovery of Pyrrhonism* (New York: Oxford University Press).

4.6.2 Specific texts and studies

The following list, including almost all the texts and studies cited by Luciano Floridi, Chapter 14 "The Rediscovery and Posthumous Influence of Skepticism," covers a wide range of periods and traditions from late antiquity up to (but not including) Descartes.

[358] Agathias 1967 *Historiarum Libri Quinque* (Berlin: W. de Gruyter).

[359] Agrippa, H. C. 1974 *On the Vanitie and Uncertaintie of Artes and Sciences* (Northridge, CA: California State University Press).

[360] Baffioni, C. 1981 "Per L'ipotesi di un Influsso della Scepsi sulla Filosofia Islamica" in Giannantoni [81], pp. 415–34.

[361] Brues, G. d. 1953 *The Dialogues of Guy de Brues: A Critical Edition; with a Study in Renaissance Scepticism and Relativism by Panos Paul Morphos* (Baltimore: Johns Hopkins University Press).

[362] Brush, C. 1966 *Montaigne and Bayle: Variations on the Theme of Skepticism* (The Hague: M. Nijhoff).

[363] Bultot, R. 1980 "Cosmologie Et Contemptus Mundi" in *Sapientiae Doctrina, Mélanges de Théologie et de Littérature Médiévales Offerts À Dom Hildebrand Bascour O.S.B.* (Leuven: Abbaye du mont César), pp. 1–23.

[364] Cabasilas, N. 1899 *Introduction to a Refutation of Skepticism* (Bonnae: ex G. Georgi Tipographeo Academico).

[365] Cao, G. M. 1994 "L'eredità Pichiana: Gianfrancesco Pico Tra Sesto Empirico e Savonarola" in P. Viti ed., *Pico Poliziano e L'umanesimo di Fine Quattrocento* (Firenze: Olschki), pp. 231–45.

[366] Cavini, W. 1977 "Appunti Sulla Prima Diffusione in Occidente Delle Opere Di Sesto Empirico" *Medioevo* 3: 1–20.

[367] Copenhaver, B. P. and Schmitt, C. B. 1992 *Renaissance Philosophy* (Oxford: Oxford University Press).

[368] Faes de Mottoni, B. 1981 "Isidoro di Siviglia e gli Accademici" in Giannantoni [81], pp. 393–414.

[369] Faes de Mottoni, B. 1982 "Lattanzio e gli Accademici" *Mélanges de l'École Française de Rome Antiquité* 94.1: pp. 335–77.

[370] Floridi, L. 1992 "The Grafted Branches of the Sceptical Tree: Noli Altum Sapere and Henri Estienne's Latin Edition of Sexti Empirici Pyrrhoniarum Hypotyposeon Libri III" *Nouvelles de la République des Lettres* 11: 127–66.

[371] Frede, M. 1988 "A Medieval Source of Modern Scepticism" in R. Claussen and R. Daube-Schackat eds., *Gedankenzeichen, Festschrift Fur K. Oehler* (Tubingen: Stauffenburg).

[372] George of Trebizond 1984 *Collectanea Trapezuntiana, Texts, Documents and Bibliographies of George of Trebizond* (Binghamton, NY: Medieval and Renaissance Texts and Studies in conjunction with the Renaissance Society of America).

[373] Gigante, M. 1988 "Ambrogio Traversari Interprete di Diogene Laerzio" in G. C. Garfagnini ed., *Ambrogio Traversari nel Vi Centenario Della Nascita* (Firenze: Olschki), pp. 367–459.

[374] Gilson, E. 1955 *History of Christian Philosophy in the Middle Ages* (London: Sheed and Ward).

[375] Gray, F. 1977 "Montaigne's Pyrrhonism" in R. C. La Charité ed., *O un Amy! Essays on Montaigne in Honor of Donald M. Frame* (Lexington, KT: French Forum), pp. 118–36.

[376] Gregoras, N. 1830 *Byzantinae Historia* (Bonnae: Impensis Ed. Weberi).

[377] Guillard, R. 1926 *Essai Sur Nicéphore Grégoras* (Paris: Geuthner).

[378] Hattaway, M. 1968 "Paradoxes of Solomon: Learning in the English Renaissance" *Journal of the History of Ideas* 29.4: 499–530.

[379] Horovitz, S. 1915 *Der Einfluss der Griechischen Skepsis auf die Entwicklung der Philosophie bei den Arabern, Jahres-Bericht des Jüdisch-Theologischen Seminars Fraenckel'scher Stiftung für das Jahr 1909* (Breslau: Schatzky).

[380] Ioli, R. 1999 "Sesto Empirico Nelle Traduzione Moderne" *Dianoia* 4: 57–97.

[381] Isidore of Seville 1982 *Etimologías: Edicion Bilingüe* (Madrid: Editorial Católica).

[382] Jourdain, C. 1888 "Sextus Empiricus et la Philosophie Scolastique" in C. Jourdain, *Excursions historiques et philosophiques à travers le moyen age* (Paris: Firmin Didot), pp. 199–217. Originally published 1858.

[383] Julian the Egyptian 1917 *Greek Anthology VII. 576* (London: Heinemann).

[384] Krafft, P. 1966 *Beiträge zur Wirkungsgeschichte des Älteren Arnobius* (Wiesbaden: Harrasowitz).

[385] Lazzari, F. 1965 *Il Contemptus Mundi Nella Scuola di S. Vittore* (Napoli: Istituto Italiano per gli Studi Storici).

[386] Liebeschütz, H. 1950 *Mediaeval Humanism in the Life and Writings of John of Salisbury* (London: The Warburg Institute).

[387] Limbrick, E. 1977 "Was Montaigne Really a Pyrrhonian?" *Bibliothèque d'Humanisme et Renaissance* 39: 67–80.

[388] Malusa, L. 1981 "L'uso Storiografico' di Sesto Empirico, da Gianfrancesco Pico a Montaigne" in G. Santinello ed., *Storia delle Storie Generali della Filosofia* (Brescia: La Scuola), pp. 37–51.

[389] McCord, A. M. 1970 "Intuitive Cognition, Certainty and Scepticism in William Ockham" *Traditio* 26: 389–98.

[390] Meredith, A. 1975 "Orthodoxy, Heresy and Philosophy in the Latter Half of the Fourth Century" *Heythrop Journal* 16: 5–21.

[391] Michalski, K. 1969 *La Philosophie au Xive Siècle: Six Études* (Frankfurt: Minerva GmbH).

[391a] Müller, K. 1884 "Neue Mittheilungen über Janos Lascaris und die Mediceische Bibliothek" *Zentralblatt für Bibliothekswesen* 1: 334–412.

[392] Nauert, C. G. J. 1965 *Agrippa and the Crisis of Renaissance Thought* (Urbana, IL: University of Illinois Press).

[393] Photios 1962 *Bibliothèque* (Paris: Les Belles Lettres). Greek text with French translation.

[394] Plethon, G. G. 1966 *Traité des Lois* (Amsterdam: A. M. Hakkert).

[395] Porro, P. 1994 "Il Sextus Latinus e l'immagine dello Scetticismo Antico nel Medioevo" *Elenchos* 14: 229–53.

[396] Praechter, K. 1892 "Skeptisches bei Lukian" *Philologus* 51(N. F. 5):
       284–93.

[397] Praechter, K. 1898 "Zur Frage Nach Lukians Philosophischen Quellen"
       Archiv für Geschichte der Philosophie 11.4: 505–16.

[398] Reynolds, S. 1991 "Social Mentalities and the Case of Medieval
       Scepticism" *Transactions of the Royal Historical Society* 6.1: 21–41.

[399] Richards, R.C. 1968 "Ockham and Skepticism" *The New
       Scholasticism* 42: 345–63.

[400] Robortello, F. 1548 *De Historica Facultate Disputatio* (Florentiae).

[401] Sadoleto, J. 1538 *Iacobi Sadoleti de Laudibus Philosophiae Libri Duo*
       (Lugduni: Apud Seb. Gryphium).

[402] Schiffman, Z.S. 1984 "Montaigne and the Rise of Scepticism in Early
       Modern Europe: A Reappraisal" *Journal of the History of Ideas* 45:
       499–516.

[403] Schmitt, C.B. 1963 "Henry of Ghent, Duns Scotus and Gianfrancesco
       Pico Della Mirandola" *Mediaeval Studies* 25: 231–58.

[404] Schmitt, C.B. 1972 "The Recovery and Assimilation of Ancient
       Scepticism in the Renaissance" *Rivista Critica di Storia della
       Filosofia* 27: 363–84.

[405] Schmitt, C.B. 1972 *Cicero Scepticus, A Study of the Influence of the
       Academica in the Renaissance* (The Hague: Nijhoff).

[406] Schmitt, C.B. 1976 "Filippo Fabri and Scepticism: A Forgotten Defence
       of Scotus" in A. Poppi ed., *Storia e Cultura del Santo* (Vicenza: Neri
       Pozza), pp. 309–12.

[407] Sepp, S. 1893 *Pyrrhonëische Studien, I. Teil: Die Philosophische
       Richtung des Cornelius Celsus; II. Teil: Untersuchungen auf dem
       Gebiete der Skepsis* (Freising: Inaugural Dissertation).

[408] Stinger, C.L. 1977 *Humanism and the Church Fathers: Ambrogio
       Traversari and Christian Antiquity in the Italian Renaissance*
       (Albany, NY: State University of New York Press).

[409] Stowers, S.K. 1990 "Paul on the Use and Abuse of Reason" in D. Balch,
       E. Ferguson and W. Meeks eds., *Greeks, Romans, and Christians,
       Essays in Honor of Abraham J. Malherbe* (Minneapolis: Fortress
       Press), pp. 253–86.

[410] Tertullian 1947, *De Anima*, J.H. Waszink ed. (Amsterdam:
       Meulenhoff). Latin text with English commentary.

[411] Van den Bergh, S. 1954 *Averroes Tahafut Al-Tahafut (the Incoherence
       of the Incoherence)* (London: Luzac), 2 vols. translated from the Arabic
       with introduction and notes.

[412] Van Leeuwen, H.G. 1963 *The Problem of Certainty in English
       Thought, 1630–1690* (The Hague: Nijhoff).

[413] Villey, P. 1933 *Les sources et l'évolution des essais de Montaigne* 2nd edn. (Paris: Hachette), 2 vols.

[414] Weinberg, J. R. 1969 *Nicolaus of Autrecourt: A Study in 14th Century Thought*, 2nd edn. (New York: Greenwood Press).

[415] Wolfson, H. A. 1969 "Nicolaus of Autrecourt and Ghazali's Argument against Causality" *Speculum* 44: 234–38.

4.7 *Comparisons between ancient and modern periods*

4.7.1 Descartes

The standard collection of central works of Descartes in English is:

[416] Cottingham, J., Stoothoff, R. and Murdoch, D. 1985 *The Philosophical Writings of Descartes*, translated and edited (Cambridge: Cambridge University Press) 3 vols.

The most recent and accessible English-language edition of the *Meditations* is:

[417] Descartes, R. 2006 *Meditations, Objections, and Replies*, R. Ariew and D. Cress eds. and trans. (Indianapolis/Cambridge: Hackett).

4.7.2 Comparative studies of ancient Greek/Roman scepticism and scepticism in other times and places

[418] Annas, J. 1996 "Scepticism, Old and New" in M. Frede and G. Striker eds., *Rationality in Greek Thought* (Oxford: Clarendon Press), pp. 239–54.

[419] Annas, J. 1996 "Scepticism about Value" in R. Popkin ed., *Scepticism in the History of Philosophy* (Dordrecht: Kluwer), pp. 205–18.

[420] Annas, J. 1998 "Doing Without Objective Values: Ancient and Modern Strategies" in S Everson ed., *Ethics: Companions to Ancient Thought 4* (Cambridge: Cambridge University Press), pp. 193–220. Original version 1986.

[421] Annas, J. 2000 "Hume and Scepticism" in Sihvola [86], pp. 271–85.

[422] Annas, J. (forthcoming) "Ancient and Modern Scepticism about Religion".

[423] Bett, R. 1993 "Scepticism and Everyday Attitudes in Ancient and Modern Philosophy" *Metaphilosophy* 24: 363–81.

[424] Bett, R. 2000 "Nietzsche on the Skeptics and Nietzsche as Skeptic", *Archiv für Geschichte der Philosophie* 82: 62–86.

[425] Burnyeat, M. 1982 "Idealism and Greek Philosophy: What Descartes Saw and Berkeley Missed" *Philosophical Review* 91: 3–40.

[426] Fine, G. 2000 "Descartes and Ancient Skepticism: Reheated Cabbage?" *Philosophical Review* 109: 195–234.

[427] Fine, G. 2003 "Subjectivity, Ancient and Modern: The Cyrenaics, Sextus, and Descartes" in J. Miller and B. Inwood eds., *Hellenistic and Early Modern Philosophy* (Cambridge: Cambridge University Press), pp. 192–231.

[428] Fine, G. 2003 "Sextus and External World Scepticism" *Oxford Studies in Ancient Philosophy* 23: 341–85.

[429] Garfield, J. 1990 "Epoche and Sunyata: Skepticism East and West" *Philosophy East and West* 40: 287–307.

[430] Hiley, D. 1987 "The Deep Challenge of Pyrrhonian Skepticism" *Journal of the History of Philosophy* 25: 185–213.

[431] Knuuttila, S. and Sihvola, J. 2000 "Ancient Scepticism and Philosophy of Religion" in Sihvola [86], pp. 125–44.

[432] Penelhum, T. 1983 "Skepticism and Fideism" in Burnyeat [78], pp. 287–319.

On this topic, see more generally the essays in the second half of Burnyeat [78]. Also relevant is Everson [249].

5 OTHER MODERN WORKS CITED

[433] Fogelin, R. 1994 *Pyrrhonian Reflections on Knowledge and Justification* (Oxford/New York: Oxford University Press).

[434] Mackie, J. L. 1977 *Ethics: Inventing Right and Wrong* (Harmondsworth: Penguin).

[435] Sartre, J. -P. 1973 *Existentialism and Humanism*, translation and introduction by P. Mairet (London: Eyre Methuen Ltd.).

INDEX

INDEX LOCORUM